Learning That Lasts
Integrating Learning, Development, and
Performance in College and Beyond

Marcia Mentkowski & Associates

Learning That Lasts

Author Associates

Marcia Mentkowski

Glen Rogers

Austin Doherty

Georgine Loacker

Judith Reisetter Hart

William Rickards

Kathleen O'Brien

Tim Riordan

Stephen Sharkey

Lucy Cromwell

Mary Diez

Jean Bartels

James Roth

Learning That Lasts

Integrating Learning, Development, and Performance in College and Beyond

Marcia Mentkowski and Associates

Jossey-Bass Publishers • San Francisco

Jossey-Bass books and products are available through most bookstores. To contact Jossey-Bass directly, call (888) 378–2537, fax to (800) 605–2665, or visit our website at www.josseybass.com.

Substantial discounts on bulk quantities of Jossey-Bass books are available to corporations, professional associations, and other organizations. For details and discount information, contact the special sales department at Jossey-Bass.

TCF Manufactured in the United States of America on Lyons Falls Turin Book. This paper is acid-free and 100 percent totally chlorine-free.

Library of Congress Cataloging-in-Publication Data

Mentkowski, Marcia.
    Learning that lasts: integrating learning, development, and performance in college and beyond / Marcia Mentkowski and associates.—1st ed.
        p. cm.—(The Jossey-Bass higher and adult education series)
    Includes bibliographical references and indexes.
    ISBN 0-7879-4482-3 (hard: acid-free paper)
    1. Learning. 2. College teaching—United States. 3. Education, Higher—United States—Curricula. 4. Critical thinking—Study and teaching (Higher)—United States. I. Title. II. Series.
    LB1060.M464 2000
    370.15'23—dc21

                                                                        99-050759

FIRST EDITION
HB Printing 10 9 8 7 6 5 4 3 2 1

The Jossey-Bass
Higher and Adult Education Series

Contents

List of Tables, Figures, and Exhibits

Tables

Figures

Exhibits

For learners and their teachers

Preface

In this book, *learning that lasts* refers to an integration of learning, development, and performance. It connotes change in behavior and flexibility in perspective, enduring commitments, and transformative elements that carry the individual forward through unexpected experiences, roles, and life events. We show how this kind of learning during college connects to performance up to five years postcollege and leads to continuous and confident learning. The assumption that learning during college, personal growth, and competent performance after college are inexorably linked is fundamental to higher education. But how individuals and organizations develop these connections is not well understood. Bringing about deep and durable learning for each learner while dealing with disparities in access, opportunities, and achievement often seems beyond our grasp.

This book on learning that lasts and its relationship to teaching provides compelling evidence, gathered over twenty-four years, of the connections joining education, work, citizenship, and personal and family life. It offers support in the growing debate among policymakers, employers, foundations, and educators for the position that educators can and should take professional responsibility for student learning and for the performance of graduates and that colleges can know about and improve institutional effectiveness. For students, faculty, and academic staff, it identifies what elements of a curriculum—an entire educational program—have challenged and supported students in their learning. For a college as a learning community, the book articulates how a college learns about, organizes for, and contributes to deep and durable student learning.

History and Purposes of Our Studies

Learning That Lasts is one outgrowth of a long-term inquiry into student learning at Alverno College in Milwaukee, Wisconsin, a four-year, independent liberal arts college for women that prepares students for careers in the professions. The story of Alverno's creation of an innovative curriculum and consequent institutional transformation dates back twenty-seven years and has been described in many other publications (Alverno College Faculty, 1976/1992; Diez, 1990; Truchan & Gurria, 1997; Loacker & Mentkowski, 1993; Read & Sharkey, 1985).

This book tells a different yet parallel story of ongoing inquiry into how students experience their education in this curriculum and college culture, how they learn and develop in college, and how they perform and contribute in postcollege settings. Because faculty designed this curriculum as centered on each student's learning across time, this inquiry is primarily longitudinal. Faculty and staff have studied student and alumna learning systematically, infused what they have learned from their colleagues in higher education consortia and from the literature, and reflected on their own and their students' learning in a community centered on learning. We have chosen this time to synthesize and present these sustained inquiries because of our commitments to colleagues who are transforming teaching and learning across higher education and because of increasing societal interest in institutional transformation and what can be learned about it from consortia of colleges and universities organized and funded for that purpose.

Twenty-four years ago, our purpose for systematically studying student and alumna learning was focused on illuminating what in our educational approach was especially successful or weak, in order to concentrate efforts toward improvement. Over the years a dynamic interplay has developed among several purposes and has continually renewed our interest in studying learning processes and learning outcomes. From initial explorations of what works, we moved to include a testing of our educational assumptions and learning principles. This led us to expand our modes of inquiry and interpretation for establishing how a curriculum and college culture as a total experience contribute to student achievement of broad learning outcomes. With this book, we enter the next phase of interpretation and dialogue centered on the nature of learning that lasts. Our purposes have expanded from relatively particularistic or local interests in how to continually develop a curriculum and college culture that optimizes learning for each student, to more general interests in the college experience and higher learning as a process. Gradually we became involved in investigating the influences of college learning on personal, intellectual, and social development when the graduate as performer and contributor enters other areas of involvement, including a profession, family life, and civic responsibilities.

This book explores what we have learned over more than two decades of systematic and rigorous study of dynamic student learning processes and outcomes in a changing context. It is a step toward grounding a theory and practice of education centered on the learner and learning. It also provides evidence-based analyses of collaborative work by faculty and other academic personnel at our own college and by colleagues in consortia of other institutions. Thus, it connects theory, research, and practice and so can encourage others who are pursuing curriculum development and institutional transformation toward learning that endures.

A Scholarship of Connection and Engagement

As a college, we have come to view ourselves as a community of professionals who are committed to teaching and scholarship to enhance student learning and to benefit communities and the individuals our students ultimately serve. This book reflects our efforts to bridge some commonly perceived divides: between the liberal arts and the professions, theory and practice, research and teaching, course content and metacognitive processes, educational mission and societal mandate. It reflects a definition of scholarship that connects these elements by integrating multiple commitments and responsibilities. This kind of integrated scholarship entails dynamic interaction among the participants: faculty, students, academic staff, researchers, administrators, and others directly connected to the college, such as volunteer assessors and internship mentors, trustees, alumnae, professionals who are not our graduates, and members of local and national advisory councils. It also includes faculty, staff, and administrators who represent colleges and universities that join Alverno in consortia of institutions. Each involvement provides for an interplay of critique and contribution.

Over the years, we have extended our inquiry to include many others from across higher education whose critique we seek and consider, for mutual benefit. Understanding who our colleagues are—their interests, commitments, contexts for interpretation, purposes for inquiry, and uses for information—becomes an essential part of the work itself. Our scholarship thus becomes more broadly contributing because it is not only integrative and participative, but also because it engages enduring challenges and is responsive to widely felt needs.

This book, as a test of learning principles, can serve other faculty and staff groups during the deliberative process of shaping learning experiences and curricula in other settings. Of course, what occurs in one local context can be *adapted, not adopted*. Educators as scholars must deal with the limits of carrying out studies with particular students in a particular context, while abstracting more general understandings about learning that can be useful to future students. They must also deal with the limits of using methods in any one discipline in a cross-disciplinary search for evidence of learning.

In this context, the search for external comparisons is essential though controversial. The studies here include comparisons within and between students and alumnae over time; comparisons of alumnae performance to that of outstanding professionals who are not Alverno alumnae; and comparisons to external criteria and norms, where that information is available. Similarly, although each consortium in which this college has participated is made up of unique and individual institutions, we have searched for differences and commonalities that contribute to a broader perspective than just our own institution.

The student and alumna participants who contributed to our longitudinal studies across ten years described in Parts Two and Three represent much of the diversity of an urban campus that offers liberal arts and professional programs. These learners are from a wide range of economic and educational backgrounds. Most are the first generation in their families to attend college. They are students from late adolescence to middle age. About half came to Alverno direct from high school, and half are working adults. They are drawn from the local metropolitan area, where they are likely to remain after graduation. They are employed before, during, and after their college education, and all are women. The studies discussed in Part Four with more recent student and alumna groups represent an even more culturally diverse population. Almost one-third currently are African American or Hispanic American from local communities. Three-fourths remain first-generation college students. Most live off campus. If prospective students choose to attend an institution other than this college, they will likely choose the large, public, state university in the city. Thus, participants reflect national trends in college enrollment toward a more even mix of younger and older adult learners, more women, and more ethnically diverse groups. Their experiences increase our insights into an understudied sector of the American college student population. Information about graduates from this college therefore has significance outside the specific context in which Alverno's educational program was created and studied, even though our college, like every other, has its own particular institutional identity.

Although Alverno's undergraduate degree population is exclusively women, our work within consortial settings lends credence to the view that findings from *Learning That Lasts* also have meaning for coeducational programs. This is not a book about gender differences, however. We have not conducted studies of samples of women in relation to samples of men. We have made observations about these learners as women, because faculty and staff consider them as women when developing curriculum and other support services. This book's findings encourage the exploration of overlaps in experiences and possibilities in coeducation. Further, this book is not a study of women's lives and does not report findings on these women in relation to studies about women more generally. It is worth noting, however, that our longitudinal cohorts of women entered as first-generation students during what Kathleen Hulbert and Diane Schuster (1993) call "the era of liberation." None of the fifteen longitudinal studies summarized in their book included a sample of working, first-generation college students. Thus, the reader will note this subtext in quotations from participants and will appreciate that the goal of these women has been to take their place in society as capable and contributing learners, professionals, and citizens.

The evidence from consortia of institutions has also compelled us to learn to look beyond a particular institution's more visible characteristics, such as size and scale (Alverno has around 100 full-time faculty, 2,000 students, and classes averaging around 20 to 25), or particular structures (faculty rely on performance assessment and criteria to validate learning of abilities integrated in the disciplines rather than testing and grades). Much larger institutions have also created strategies for interactive learning at the school or department level. There, a campus of 20,000 can feel like a college of 2,000 to any one student or instructor. Departments face the same issues that are significant in smaller institutions. Although other faculty submit grades rather than validations as those at this college do, for example, their students learn to judge process in relation to explicit learning outcomes in the major field and high expectations for individual achievement rather than aggregate norms alone. Nevertheless, each reader will make judgments about the meaning, value, and evidence for the kind of education practiced at any undergraduate college and how it connects or does not connect to the reader's own campus.

The integration of theory, research, and practice is a gradually emerging paradigm in higher education today, one that we illustrate throughout the book. This paradigm contrasts with one where researchers do research and then educators apply it. But too often the research goes without application, we have learned. Further, educators also do educational research and educational researchers also educate. Our goal is to demonstrate that operation under this newer, integrated paradigm is a more interactive and effective research design and implementation model that is possible at various levels of practice (course, program, college, institution, consortia) and yields new discoveries about integrated learning, development, and performance—the main substance of *Learning That Lasts.*

Overview

Learning That Lasts is divided into four parts. Part One, the introduction to the book, sets out the conceptual, contextual, and method background for the book as a whole. Chapter One explores the general topic and common tasks and fundamental issues that drive inquiry about learning in higher education. Chapter

Two introduces four ways of knowing about learning. It sketches multiple methods from diverse paradigms for inquiry that arise naturally from the broad multidisciplinary backgrounds of college faculty and staff, discusses the strengths and limitations of each approach, and examines how each capitalizes on the diversity of perspectives within a college and outside it.

Part Two uses the dual channels of research at Alverno and the published literature to search for the characteristics of durable learning. It presents discoveries about learning that emerge from long-term studies of students and alumnae, with comparisons across time and ultimately with standards drawn from a large set of studies of effective professionals outside the Alverno community. These findings shed a distinct light on educational practices that foster learning that lasts because these studies were conducted in the context of a curriculum and an institution that transformed itself. Enough detail is offered about the college, its students, and findings from the published literature for readers to confirm and question possible generalizations to their own college situation.

Part Three presents Alverno's educational theory of learning that lasts, derived from different voices, sources of ideas and evidence, and contexts of practice. We present this theory in parallel forms. One form is a picture of domains of growth (reasoning, performance, self-reflection, development) that are integrated through three transformative learning cycles (using metacognitive strategies, self assessing role performance, and engaging diverse approaches, views, and activities). Another form is a set of principles for understanding learning that lasts with examples of action principles that illustrate how the individual instructor or advisor connects new ideas about learning with teaching, advising, and curricular practices.

Part Four reflects on the meaning and implications of learning that lasts at each level of educational practice, from the individual and collaborative work of faculty and staff to the level of collegiate culture as a whole. It shows how groups of faculty and academic staff might take up collaborative inquiry for reflecting on practice in their own setting, using principles for discourse. It presents a generalized set of curricular elements from a wide range of sources that support learning that lasts, in the context of useful strategies for assisting readers in identifying educational assumptions and learning principles in their own curriculum. The empirical efforts in this part enable a redefinition of inquiry and faculty and staff scholarship in teaching and learning. A picture of learning that lasts at the organizational level emerges through studies by consortia that have been braving the current press of institutional transformation. Guidelines and action principles reflect the organizational acts and mid- and long-range strategies that foster transformation in support of learning. The final chapter posits new challenges and reflects on how various groups can initiate and continue conversations about learning that lasts in their own settings.

We have designed this book so different readers, depending on their role as faculty member, professional staff member, administrator, policymaker, or graduate student, can enter each part in a different order. We occasionally cycle back to key, grounding ideas that may appear to be the same, but take different forms as the level and context of practice change across each part of the book. Such is the nature of practice—difficult to discuss sequentially—because ideas are complex and multidimensional, yet overlapping. Our goal is to provide enough signposts so individuals with different responsibilities can read for their particular role and also read across the book. As a further aid to diverse readers, we set out our specific intentions and purposes before each part.

Throughout this book, we present substantive evidence for our inferences about learning that lasts, how our own approach to higher education contributes to it, and what educational assumptions and learning principles are transferable. In our experience, almost all readers are also interested in the method and context when interpreting findings. Chapter Two provides a broad overview; we trust that our other decisions about where to include methods and contexts, in chapters and appendixes, meet with readers' needs to critique them and to consider them in their own interpretations. We do not expect that others will attempt to replicate these methods precisely because some features are shaped to our particular context.

Educational Value Frameworks

This book is intended to be explicit about educational frameworks and values insofar as it describes the development of a set of educational assumptions and learning principles that both ground and emerge from this inquiry. We think this adds clarity to a search for common ground because educational value frameworks at Alverno not only involve its history and identity as an institution, but also intertwine with the ongoing studies of curriculum development and curricular outcomes across higher education. Alverno students say that their college education becomes part of their identity, and that they expect their learning experiences to open doors to further achievement, opportunity, and contribution. Our inspiration to sustain systematic study of teaching for learning has grown from our commitment as educators to these students and from their willingness to take on this task with us.

This book is, in part, both a test of and an argument for our value frameworks and assumptions about education. We intend it as a scholarly argument, based on study, evidence, analysis, and consideration of alternative interpretations. As such, it is more likely to transcend a particularistic stance and to provide information that makes critical judgments possible and more probable. At the same time, it presents and argues for the conclusions we have drawn from our experience of inquiry, curriculum development, and in consortia of institutions. Further, we acknowledge that when responsibilities of educators to teaching, scholarship, and service to the larger society are simultaneous considerations, commitments to education as a profession and to scholarship may at times be competing frames of reference.

Often values and rhetorical themes remain implicit in scholarly work. Discussing these explicitly enhances clarity. So readers can more easily make connections to, and see the differences in, their own interests, commitments, and settings and those of the authors, we introduce each chapter by making our educational commitments explicit. Setting context for what one knows and respecting what others know is a common strategy for engaging in a mutually framed dialogue in a college.

Audiences

Potential audiences for this book span higher education. They include college educators from a range of disciplines and professions, some with interdisciplinary and interprofessional experience. We define *educators* broadly throughout this book to include faculty, professional academic staff, student services personnel, administrators, researchers, and policymakers in all types of colleges and universities. Some are interested in and committed to transforming higher education: determining and articulating learning outcomes, building curricula, assessment, advising, and resident life systems. Some are studying higher education, researching adult learning and development, conducting studies of college outcomes and curricula, or developing a philosophy of education. Some are working to enhance the quality of higher education as members of accrediting groups, state and national agencies, professional associations, or funding agencies.

Other readers span the education continuum and are invested in educational transformation: classroom teachers, instructional and curriculum developers, academic and student affairs administrators and staff, career counselors, program evaluators, and professional school faculty. They serve leadership functions in school, college, and professional school transformation. They head institutes in graduate schools where faculty have come together to study and improve teaching and learning, and education and development departments in business and industry. They include the new cadre of professionals who are developing learning and assessment processes for distributed and distance learning. Many of these groups interact regularly with various publics who are becoming more informed about educational issues: employers who expect to be able to judge the quality of education as they hire and train employees, public representatives who advocate for the wider public interests of prospective students and their families, or others generally invested in undergraduate education.

We trust that readers join our interest in exploring learning that makes a difference across a lifetime. Such understanding can enable more effective participation in the continual redesign of undergraduate education by reformulating the meaning of a degree, holding to the standards and ideals it engenders, and learning from the contributions of graduates what new goals educators and learners might jointly set for higher education.

Milwaukee, Wisconsin   MARCIA MENTKOWSKI
January 2000   AND ASSOCIATES

Acknowledgments

We acknowledge the students, alumnae, and professionals outside the Alverno community who have contributed to this work so generously. We are also indebted to many individuals, institutions, friends, and funding agencies that have stood by us and stimulated us with their critique and own contributions. They are legion. We are particularly grateful to colleagues at those institutions that participated with us in externally funded, formal consortia (Appendix K lists these agencies and institutions). By participating in a consortium over time, few can remain provincial, avoid contributing, or ignore a colleague's critique. The clarification of evidence about learners and their learning (rather than recognition of the institution, its faculty, and its staff) that is required by one's colleagues leaves no institution unchallenged.

Many other colleagues have been a shining light in our collective lives. You know who you are. Together, you range from the individual faculty member to the institutional team, from the professional staff advisor to the college president, from the learning and development theorist to the educational researcher, from the elementary school teacher to the medical school professor, from the trustee to the education journalist. Each of you had reasons for visiting our campus, joining us in our workshops, or inviting us to your campus or organization. You continue to critique our sessions at national conferences, challenge us through consortia, and review our publications. We often find a commonality of expression that tempers our diversity of experiences and mission when discussing educational questions with you.

We acknowledge all past and present members of the research team and external consultants who guided this work in many ways, in particular: Karen Wagner Adair, Zita Allen, Mary Lou Arnold, Tamar Ben-Ur, Lynn Chabot-Long, Deborah Deemer, Milton

Hakel, Lyle Spencer and associates of Hay/McBer & Company, Inc., Mark Hein, Lynne Kleinman, George Klemp, Jane Loevinger, John McAdams, William McEachern, Sally Mertens, Nancy Miller, N. C. M. Ross (formerly Nancy Much), Pam Sandoval, Kathleen Schwan Minik, Mary Talbott, and Beverly Weeden. We thank many external reviewers, including Mary Brabeck, Sheryl Hruska, Wilbert McKeachie, Arthur Chickering, Stephen Thoma, and Mary Ellen Weimer for their insights and persistence. Jossey-Bass senior editor Gale Erlandson provided challenge and sustenance along the way.

We acknowledge funds from several government agencies and foundations: the U.S. Department of Education's National Institute for Education funded the formal research from 1977 to 1981; the Fund for the Improvement of Postsecondary Education (FIPSE) supported consortia of institutions to pursue various collaborative inquiries on teaching, learning, and assessment. We thank the W.K. Kellogg Foundation and The Pew Charitable Trusts for funding other consortia of institutions. We acknowledge the president of Alverno College, Sister Joel Read, and the Alverno Board of Trustees for the wisdom, confidence, and institutional support that sustains long-term inquiries about learning and education as part of the values and responsibilities of a college.

We have been deeply affected by the loss of many who inspired us during the long course of this work. They include Ernest Boyer, Kenneth Burke, John Flanagan, John Fredrickson, Paulo Freire, Robert Greenleaf, Marcia Guttentag, Margaret Keane Harlow, Lawrence Kohlberg, Robert Menges, David McClelland, Samuel Messick, Henry Murray, William Perry, Jr., James Rest, Donald Schön, and Ralph Tyler. You, their colleagues, have continued their interests and commitments. Continue to challenge us, and to help us build bridges from your work to ours. We thank you, and acknowledge your contributions throughout this book.

MARCIA MENTKOWSKI
AND ASSOCIATES

The Authors

Throughout the writing of this book, a principal challenge was to clarify and articulate what we mean by collaborative authorship, a process that honors individual perspectives and rigorous critique but is, at its heart, interactive. For ease of citation, the cover of this book names Marcia Mentkowski and Associates; the frontispiece lists each author associate of *Learning That Lasts*. However, the broader collaborative authorship used to produce this book contrasts with the more traditional joint authorship designated by a list of individual authors. Such a list would run too long. For clarity in this book, "we" means the author associates or, for brevity, the "authors," although many of the ideas in this book represent the collective wisdom and experiences of Alverno educators across the college.

In this sense, Alverno educators have jointly authored this book because they have jointly determined the questions to be studied, discussed the methods, debated interpretations, generated the connections to curriculum and to student learning that make findings useful, and cycled through these processes continually. This interactive inquiry, however, does not mean that everyone has had to do everything. For practical reasons, they have entrusted a process of formal inquiry to particular individuals and groups of colleagues, principally Alverno's educational research and evaluation team and the faculty and administrator team in the committee on research and evaluation who are listed as author associates. These two teams have involved other groups of colleagues across the college and beyond in consortia, as well as students, alumnae, and other professionals. This kind of collaboration makes possible an integrated work (in contrast to a series of discrete, separately authored chapters) that communicates an integrated substance and knowledge base, without subsuming individual contributions and perspectives.

The current faculty and academic staff and administrators of this college are included in the list of contributors to collaborative authorship. The listing assumes that these individuals will continue to critique the ideas in this book and that some have contributed most through their critical appraisal of these ideas. Nonetheless, we emphasize that the broadly based authorship of this book conveys the nature of the collaborative inquiry that produced and is responsible for this work. Thus, we join a host of faculty, staff, educational researchers, evaluators, and institutions wrestling with new and emerging definitions and meanings of scholarship.

Author Associates

Marcia Mentkowski is professor of psychology and director of the Office of Educational Research and Evaluation. She chairs the Research and Evaluation Committee. She holds a Ph.D. in educational psychology from the University of Wisconsin, Madison.

Jean Bartels is professor of nursing and chaired the Nursing Division until 1999. She holds a Ph.D. in nursing from the University of Wisconsin-Milwaukee.

Lucy Cromwell is professor of English. She holds a Ph.D. in English from the University of Wisconsin-Milwaukee.

Mary Diez is professor of education and dean of the Graduate Program. She holds a Ph.D. in communication from Michigan State University.

Austin Doherty is professor of psychology and director of the Alverno College Institute. She holds a Ph.D. in psychology from Loyola University.

Georgine Loacker is professor of English and chairs the Council for Student Assessment. She holds a Ph.D. in English language and literature from the University of Chicago.

Kathleen O'Brien is professor of business and management and vice president for academic affairs. She holds a Ph.D. in management from the University of Wisconsin, Madison.

Judith Reisetter Hart is senior research analyst in the Office of Educational Research and Evaluation. She holds an M.S. from Iowa State University and is a doctoral candidate in educational psychology at the University of Wisconsin, Madison.

William Rickards is senior research associate in the Office of Educational Research and Evaluation. He holds a Ph.D. in leisure studies from the University of Illinois at Urbana-Champaign.

Tim Riordan is professor of philosophy and associate dean for academic affairs. He holds a Ph.D. in philosophy of education from Marquette University.

Glen Rogers is senior research associate in the Office of Educational Research and Evaluation. He holds a Ph.D. in social psychology from the University of Kentucky.

James Roth is professor of history. He holds a Ph.D. in history from the University of California–Berkeley.

Stephen Sharkey is professor of social sciences and chairs the Behavioral Sciences Division. He holds a Ph.D. in sociology from the University of Connecticut.

Contributors to Collaborative Authorship

Throughout this book we emphasize the need to take collective responsibility for learning that lasts. In that spirit, we consider it essential to recognize the faculty and academic staff who, through their efforts as educators, have contributed significantly to the creation of this work: Jeana Abromeit, Zita Allen, Gidget Asonwha, Dawn Balistreri, Jody Balzer, Smita Baman, Jane Baranowski, Sandra Barkow, Colleen Barnett, Carole Barrowman, Jean Bartels, Kathleen Beaver, Robert Birney, Nancy Bornstein, Patricia Bowne, Joyce Tang Boyland, Laurel Bragstad, Russell Brooker, J. Dolores Brunner, Kathleen Bultman, Katherine Bundalo, Patricia Burke, Rebecca Burton, Richard Butler, Cathy Carey, Kevin Casey, Richard Cato, Karron Caulker, Lynn Chabot-Long, James Chenevert, Geralyn Chesner, Debra Chomicka, Anthony Collins, Suzann Collins, Glennys Compton, Lucy Cromwell, Marian Czarnik, David Dathe,

Kathleen Davis, Cate Deicher, Bernardin Deutsch, Mary Diez, Austin Doherty, Margaret Earley, Linda Ehley, Anita Eikens, Marjorie Ann Eisenmenger, Charles Elftmann, Zohreh Emami, Elizabeth Engel, Donna Hogans Engelmann, Joyce Fey, Harry Fleddermann, Kim Folstein, Jane Frederick, Carla Freeman, Marla Freuden, Angela Frey, Benedicta Fritz, Annette Garcia, Suzann Gardner, Dianne Gardner-Gletty, Patricia Geenen, Abera Gelan, Sandra Graham, Lori Gramling, Regina Grantz, Cynthia Gray, Jean Groshek, Lauralee Guilbault, George Gurria, Constance Haas, Eric Hagedorn, Bonnie Halwas, Susan Hansen, Patricia Hartman, Patricia Hartmann, Jacqueline Hass, Myriam Hegemann, Kathryn Henn-Reinke, Melissa Holland, Andrew Hopkins, Thomas Hovorka, Mary Hueller, Carolyn Ilion, Patricia Jensen, Sandra Johansen, Andrea Johnson, Bonnie Joseph-Coonan, Lois Kailhofer, Sheila Kershek, Beth Kilday, Brenda Kilpatrick, Eunjung Kim, Mary Kitten, Judith Klein, Lynne Kleinman, Martha Kliebenstein, Diane Knight, Catherine Knuteson, Carol Krause, Wendell Kringen, Kathy Lake, Nancy Lamers, Joyce Lange, Dara Larson, Dimitri Lazo, Daniel Leister, Susan Leister, Dena Lieberman, Jonathan Little, Georgine Loacker, Mary Georgia Matlock, William McEachern, Paula McGinnis, Susan McKeown, James McNamara, Tina McNamara, Suzanne Mente, Marcia Mentkowski, Agnes Meysenburg, Julie Millenbruch, Victoria Thorpe Miller, Kenneth Moe, Rita Nawrocki-Chabin, Marlene Neises, Barbara Nevers, James Norden, Jennifer Northern, Virginia Oberholzer, Kathleen O'Brien, Robert O'Brien Hokanson, Debbie Olguin, Lorraine O'Malley, Elizabeth Palmer, Amy Parenteau, Joanna Patterson, Maria Terese Patterson, Kathryn Perkins, Marie Elizabeth Pink, Meg Pledl, Muriel Plichta, Kathy Pommering, Susan Pustejovsky, Jill Raab, Margaret Rauschenberger, Joel Read, Marilyn Reedy, Judith Reisetter Hart, Karen Renner, Jacqueline Rice, William Rickards, Tim Riordan, Glen Rogers, Peter Roller, Linda Romm, Nancy Ross, James Roth, Richard Runkel, Robert Saemann, Sharon Safar, Gail Safranski, Greta Salem, Geraldine Sarver, John Savagian, Celestine Schall, Linda Scheible, Ann Schlaefer, Jennifer Schmidt, Mary Ann Schmidt, Jo Ann Schmitz, Virginia Schuldenberg, Judeen Schulte, Janet Schurr, Kathleen Schwan Minik, Margaret Sebern, Amy Shapiro, Stephen Sharkey, Sheryl Slocum, Paul Smith, Marguerite Sneed, Mary Ellen Spicuzza, Judith Stanley, Vallimae Sternig, Lola

Stuller, Kelly Talley, Kathleen Thompson, Kate Tisch, Christine Trimberger, Leona Truchan, Ann van Heerden, Virginia Wagner, Patricia Walsh, Kate Weishaar, Luanne Wielichowski, Susan Witkowski, Eileen Witten, Karen Wuethrich, Sherry Wulff, Mary Yanny, Lisa Youretz, and Sol Nazari Zetley. Although they are not listed here, we also recognize the important contribution of all former faculty and academic staff.

Learning That Lasts

Part One

Introduction

This book is about learning that lasts—an integration of learning, development, and performance—and what kind of education contributes to it during and after college. We clarify how this kind of learning is understood by the learner, how it contributes to the development of the person, and how this learning is realized through effective performance in work, personal, and civic life. This understanding means clarifying not only learning as an ongoing process but also the learning outcomes that become part of an individual. Learning that is lasting—that is, mindful and emotional, intellectual and committed—characterizes the lifelong learner who becomes a seeker, a pilgrim, a pathfinder to integrity.

The kind of education that most contributes to lasting learning is likely to be found in a blend of the ideals and practices of three traditions in higher education: the residential liberal arts college, the college with service and value traditions, and the larger land grant university system with its professional schools and community colleges. Learning that lasts forms an emerging center for consolidating these traditions, provided educators can make connections among them.

Chapter One introduces broad themes and purposes that undergird a quest for learning that lasts. We reflect on the challenges that have emerged across the many institutions that make up higher or postsecondary education. Almost immediately, we turn to the common tasks that flow from these themes and are grounded in the deeper meanings that bind educators together: the fundamental issues about learning that readers can likely trace to the early beginnings of their own college or university. These tasks and issues lead to questions about learning that lasts that call for the study of student learning by educators at the same time that they are effecting it through an educational program.

Chapter Two introduces educators' ways of knowing about learning in the context of educational practice. Four ways of knowing are particularly relevant to addressing questions about learning that lasts: formal research, collaborative inquiry, literature and practice review in higher education, and learning by educating. Studies of learning that are conducted inside diverse and dynamic educational settings have educational significance for students, provided they are connected to educational assumptions as well as to ideas about learning. Thus, learning by educating in a particular setting is a fourth way of knowing about learning. Although this book is not primarily about Alverno College, we describe its assumptions about education and how learning works for students in enough detail so the reader can use it as a resource in traversing those parts of the book that rely on a deeper understanding of the context in which it was written.

Chapter One

Themes and Purposes

Few other themes have penetrated the public consciousness at the turn of the millennium more than learning. Our future as a democratic society seems intimately related to our capacity to learn and to foster learning. Children begin life as learners; learning postpones aging. A person who cannot keep learning, and learning particular things in particular ways, is left aside, despite our awareness of multiple intelligences, cultural and individual differences, and global connections.

Higher Education: Goals and Responsibilities

Our society increasingly turns to educators in higher education to take leadership in realizing its educational goals. How those goals are clarified and how they might be best met are debated continually. The following themes are particularly prevalent now.

Maximizing Individual Potential in a Pluralistic Democracy

An important societal concern is the magnitude of unrealized human potential. Clearly, neither students nor society can afford learning that is lost through immediate forgetting, overwhelming information, dashed dreams, or incoherent educational programs. Younger and older learners, part-time and full-time, students with needs for more and less effort and resources, those who reside on campus, or who drop in and out of various programs—each must be able to count on developing integrated learning. Students often experience the ramifications of lost learning well before they do, or do not, graduate from their colleges. So far, the terms *liberal learning, higher learning, learning to learn,* and *lifelong learning* have served as a stopgap measure. The challenge in the years ahead is to provide an increasingly varied population with access to this kind of higher education. Meeting it implies clear expectations for learning outcomes, diverse opportunities for developing and assessing unique student learning patterns, and a variety of settings for applying achievements. One purpose here is to clarify the essential aspects of what is generally understood as lifelong learning and what it means for current and future learners.

Integrating Learning, Development, and Performance

To understand what is possible for learners to realize across a lifetime, we have defined *learning that lasts* as an integration of learning, development, and performance. A college education can and does make a difference for most students (Pascarella & Terenzini, 1991); the conviction that learning, development, and performance can and should be explicitly integrated during college by each student is a relatively new emphasis. One of the purposes of this book is to explore how students combine these elements and why these are essential to learning that lasts. The challenge is to foster student development and performance as well as learning. Our purpose is to explore how students integrate learning, development, and performance, and how such integrated learning is shaped, so that it will endure.

Connecting Education, Work, Personal Life, and Citizenship

Traditionally most colleges and universities have focused on assisting their students to realize their personal goals and become effective, contributing members of society. Yet many roles for which colleges now prepare students are no longer traditional. The settings where graduates work are increasingly complex. The workplace now calls for both belt tightening and high performance. Graduates fill low-paying and part-time jobs as well as long-term professional positions, where they are expected to create their own roles. Others are self-employed. In each case, graduates must be able to sustain their personal integrity and construct their own ideas about situations and roles as they look for creative solutions to problems. There are new challenges as well in raising children and contributing to one's community. Meeting these demands takes a new kind of thinker, leader, parent, and citizen, personally responsible and capable of asserting individuality through community action. This challenge implies linking knowledge, reflection, judgment, and action so that education is a precursor to enriched work, family life, and citizenship. Our purpose here is to contribute to a discussion about redefining the meaning of the undergraduate degree so that three traditions in higher education—liberal arts, education in the professions, and moral character—are joined.

Transforming Undergraduate Education

The meaning and impact of college learning are embedded in social, historical, and political contexts. Despite higher education's past and current success in teaching for integrated learning and effective transition to life after college, the increased frustration with the way we as a society are carrying out our responsibilities here at home and abroad has generated a new urgency for changing the ways that professionals educate people. A growing number of educators (Boyer, 1987; *Daedalus,* 1999; Edgerton, 1997; Zemsky & Massy, 1995) argue that rethinking the meaning of the degree cannot be realized without a major rethinking of the college and its role in all kinds of learning. Some wonder if degrees are obsolete (Langenberg, 1997), and others whether college as a physical place for learning can survive a move toward incorporating distance and distributed learning. Others wonder if the faculty as a group can survive as a distinct group of professionals, when "the faculty" may be replaced by an ever growing number of culturally diverse adult learners who, aided by the new technologies, primarily teach each other. Thus, faculty, administrators, and professional staff in many colleges and universities are finding themselves returning to primary questions: What is learning, and who is it for? What is our responsibility for it? and Who best learns with us? The answers can lead to transforming ideas, actions, and institutional structures for learning-centered educational programs. The challenge is to continually transform higher education and its institutions (Green, 1997) to better respond to such questions. We believe that colleges can meet this challenge and that universities can meet it within their colleges. Because the outcomes that accrue are so valuable, it is also practical to move in this direction.

Taking Professional Responsibility for Student Learning

Education is in principle a joint responsibility for individual learners, educators, citizens, and their institutions. Yet many educators believe they have a professional responsibility to define and take up each of these challenges rather than responding to cycles of public dissatisfaction. They value independence in thought and action but increasingly find it valuable to take up these responsibilities by working together within and across institutions of higher education. Through collaborative learning, educators hope to better integrate insights from theory, research, and practice to form educational policy and to shape their own institution's performance. We advance the multiple, diverse ways of knowing about learning that undergird learning that lasts, primarily because these modes of inquiry support the trend toward multidisciplinary and collaborative work across the liberal arts and professions and across the roles that make up various levels of practice. This emphasis on diverse means and methods is connected to our concerns for a viably transformed higher education that focuses on student learning and learning-centered educational programs.

Our goal here is to aid that resolve by clarifying how contemporary educational themes and their implied challenges grow out of responsibilities that educators have been grappling with in the last century and will continue to face in the next. For educators to work on these responsibilities together means identifying tasks that they have in common. This is difficult when disciplinary interests and commitments to improving teaching and learning diverge. However, if enough of these tasks reflect both the scholarly interests and professional commitments of many educators who work across roles, departments, academic and student services positions, and the diversity in perspectives, settings, and experiences across higher education, it becomes more feasible for educators to work on such tasks collaboratively. In the abstract, the educator and policymaker, the education critic and disciplinary specialist, the practitioner and researcher, the employer and legislator, who each occupies multiple roles with overlapping pursuits and responsibilities, can also work together when they share concerns in common.

Common Tasks and Fundamental Issues

Educators who take up responsibilities for lasting learning share these common tasks: (1) understanding learning; (2) understanding the learner; (3) envisioning learners as educated, mature, and effective over time; (4) preparing students in college to enact their learning as graduates; (5) fostering learning outcomes through educational programs; (6) organizing colleges for learning; and (7) redefining inquiry on learning and teaching and its uses and consequences. Underneath each of these tasks are fundamental issues that educators confront as they carry out these tasks. For example, to understand learning, they ask, "What is *learning?*" and "*What* is learned?"

Understanding Learning

Learning is both process and outcome, often interwoven. Many educators and researchers are engaged in the study of learning in order to define it in ways that make it more accessible to learners and their teachers. We join that work to ground learning that lasts, recognizing that any observations of what is being learned are often inseparable from how one understands knowledge, its epistemology, and their connection to meaning systems. These are often contradictory (Minnich, 1990).

What Is Learning?

Erik De Corte synthesizes effective learning as constructive, cumulative, self-regulated, goal oriented, situated, and collaborative (1995). Jack Mezirow argues for a missing dimension of many psychological theories: "*Meaning*—how it is construed, validated, and reformulated—and the social conditions that influence the ways adults make meaning of their experience" (1991, p. xii). He refers to "reflective discourse" as a way to make meaning—to learn. Peter Jarvis (1992) believes that learning "is the essence of everyday living and of conscious experience; it is the process of transforming

that experience into knowledge, skills, attitudes, values, and beliefs . . . the continuing process of making sense of everyday
experience—and experience happens at the intersection of a conscious human life with time, space, society, and relationship" (p.
11). Student meaning making is a central dimension of student
learning. For us, enduring learning is a process that involves the
whole person: learning is integrative.

Learning from experience—that is, experiential learning—is
another way of defining learning. Students can analyze their own
experience as learners in a variety of formal and informal contexts.
They can apply the cyclical model that David Kolb (1984) presents:
experiencing concretely, reflectively observing, forming abstract
concepts, and actively experimenting. Learners can analyze their
preferences through Kolb's Learning Style Inventory (1976). Educators often assist students to gain an understanding of learning
styles and to identify their own preferences. We found early on that
with practice and self-reflection, students gain the ability to mod-
ify their learning preferences to deal most appropriately with a particular situation. They understand their own cognitive-emotional
processes during college (Doherty, Mentkowski, & Conrad, 1978;
Mentkowski, 1988). Understanding learning styles is only one part;
learning by doing is another. Experience of all kinds is central
to learning. Faculty and students, through classroom experiences,
internships, practica, and other kinds of fieldwork, learn to reflect
on their own experiences as valid data for understanding and action, provided they are guided to do so (Cromwell, 1993; Grantz &
Thanos, 1996; Hutchings & Wutzdorff, 1988).

In an effort to connect the theory and practice of experiential
learning in higher education, Pat Hutchings and Allen Wutzdorff
(1988) identified some central shared assumptions that they and
their colleagues used when designing and evaluating learning experiences across a curriculum: learning involves the whole student;
knowing and doing work together in a dialectic whereby each is
constantly redefining the other; self-reflection, or reflection on
oneself as a learner, brings together knowing and doing; and experiential learning is a concept and practice that must permeate a
college curriculum in a systematic and developmental manner. The
authors explained curriculum-wide applications: The tension set
up by continuously confronting knowledge and action must be

carefully fostered and developed in multiple settings. In this way, each can inform and transform the other as student learning progresses in a cyclical fashion toward integration of knowledge and ability.

What Is Learned?

What can be learned encompasses developed abilities (Anastasi, 1983) and domain knowledge (Alexander, 1992). De Corte's recent review (1995) sets forth aptitudes involved in skilled learning and thinking:

1. Flexible application of a well-organized, domain-specific knowledge base, involving facts, symbols, conventions, definitions, formulas, algorithms, concepts, and rules which constitute the substance of a subject-matter field (see e.g., Glaser, 1991).
2. Heuristic methods, i.e., systematic search strategies for problem analysis and transformation, such as carefully analyzing a problem specifying the knowns and the unknowns, decomposing a problem into subgoals, finding an easier related or analogous problem, working backward from the intended goal or solution (see e.g., Schoenfeld, 1992). . . .
3. Metacognitive knowledge and skills involving knowledge concerning one's own cognitive functioning, on the one hand, and activities relating to the self-monitoring and regulation of one's cognitive processes, on the other. The latter include such skills as planning a solution process; monitoring an ongoing solution process; evaluating and, if necessary, debugging an answer or solution; and reflecting on one's learning and problem-solving activities (Brown, Bransford, Ferrara, & Campione, 1983).
4. Affective components, involving beliefs, attitudes, and emotions which reflect the whole range of affective reactions to learning, and vary in the degree of affect involved, namely from rather cold for beliefs to hot for emotions (McLeod, 1990; De Corte, 1995, pp. 97–98).

De Corte concludes from his literature review that expert performance is characterized by the integration and interaction of these aptitudes. In addition, he acknowledges that this categorization may underrepresent the role of dispositions and emotions that sensitize learners to contextual possibilities and incline them to act toward particular ends.

This is a useful list, but the term *aptitudes* seems burdened by its association with decontextualized testing. We prefer Anne Anastasi's (1980, 1983) *developed abilities,* in part because we have found that the language of abilities communicates broadly across educators, employers, and professionals (Mentkowski & Doherty, 1983, 1984a, 1984b; Mentkowski & Rogers, 1993). Moreover, *developing abilities* is a broader term than *acquisition of skill, competence,* or *expertise.* Other terms than *ability,* such as *skill,* can serve if there is no dichotomy between knowledge and skill, and skills are defined and discussed in the context of learning in the disciplines (Doherty, Chenevert, Miller, Roth, & Truchan, 1997).

Abilities are complex combinations of motivations, dispositions, attitudes, values, strategies, behaviors, self-perceptions, and knowledge of concepts and of procedures: "These combinations are dynamic and interactive, and they can be acquired and developed both through education and experience. Abilities become a cause of effective performance when these components are integrated. A complex ability cannot be observed directly; it must be inferred from performance. . . . 'Ability' is a *concept* that communicates, because it is also *experienced.* One can conceptualize abilities and also experience having or using one's abilities in situations" (Mentkowski, Loacker, & O'Brien, 1998, pp. 13, 15). Abilities are connected to multiple intelligences that, to some degree, may be both inherent in the person and strong dispositions by the time students reach college. Situated learning perspectives further emphasize how context is inseparable from the person and developed abilities (Lave & Wenger, 1991). Educators focus primarily on those aspects of abilities that are teachable and, in some fashion, transferable. That means assisting learners in integrating their abilities with their unique qualities—an often untapped reservoir of human potential—and to integrate their developing abilities with the domains of knowledge in their field of study.

The focus on performance as part of what is learned has become widespread. In *Competence at Work: Models for Superior Performance,* Lyle Spencer and Signe Spencer (1993) articulated a range of competencies necessary for effective performance. In *What Work Requires of Schools,* the U.S. Department of Labor (Secretary's Commission on Achieving Necessary Skills, 1991) calls for the creation of curricula that develop the competencies needed in a talent-driven workplace. Calls for integrating learning and performance come from outside the workplace too. Lynn Curry, Jon Wergin, and Associates (1993) have explored the need to transform professional education in the light of new theories of learning and competence. David McClelland and his colleagues pioneered ideas about competence as an outgrowth of diverse liberal arts colleges in *A New Case for the Liberal Arts* (Winter, McClelland, & Stewart, 1981). Further articulating the integration of liberal arts abilities with dimensions of workplace competence is a next step. That means assisting students to make relationships across disciplines and perceive learning less as a set of discrete experiences and courses and more as an integrated and lifelong process that enables them to perform effectively during and after college. In the U.K., the concept of *capability* is meant to promote this confluence of integrated competence and lifelong learning (Stephenson & Yorke, 1998).

In a similar sense, fulfilling the need for integrated learning requires a continuous and concerted faculty and staff effort to develop students' awareness of their own developing abilities and how they are integrated in their performance:

> Beginning students, for example, engaged in the process of identifying their own values, benefit from an instructor's conscious use of the vocabulary and theoretical frameworks of an analytical process in the discipline. It may seem obvious to educators that the valuing process is also an analytical process, but it is not obvious to students who are initially unselfconscious of their own cognitive activity. . . . In our efforts to assist students to integrate their learning it is important that we focus their attention on the actual cognitive and affective processes involved so that students expand and deepen their understanding of these intellectual activities. [Alverno College Educators, 1977/1998, sec. 1-c, p. 5]

What is learned moves beyond learning processes and complex multidimensional abilities to encompass the integration of learning with the development of the whole person. William Perry's (1970, 1998) concept of learning processes interwoven with outcomes over time has influenced the Alverno faculty's work and that of many others in higher education. His constructs for understanding what is learned in the areas of intellectual and ethical development are instructive in describing the movement of a student from a dualistic perspective on truth as fact versus error to someone with a reasoned ability to see many perspectives while developing commitment to personal values and convictions. Perry's scheme and its remarkable iterations (Baxter Magolda, 1992; Belenky, Clinchy, Goldberger, & Tarule, 1986; King & Kitchener, 1994), along with other research on human development, reinforces the notion that some learning has transformative results. Learning outcomes so conceived include attributes of the person and cumulative learning effects, and result in college students' ultimately taking responsibility for their own learning. Jane Loevinger's (1976) early work on ego development confirmed what many faculty had also discovered: that many personality characteristics are developmental and that life experiences can come together to stimulate extraordinary change in the person.

Thus, a broader integration of learning, development, and performance is necessary, especially as conceptions of performance move beyond discrete descriptions of behaviors and behavioral outcomes. In graduate education in management and organizational behavior, Richard Boyatzis, Scott Cowen, David Kolb, and Associates (1995) also have moved toward an emerging integration of learning, development, and performance. In this regard, the teaming of Boyatzis, whose earlier work focused on performance (1982), and Kolb, whose earlier work focused on experiential learning theory and development (1984), represents a coming together of each of the prior integrations to describe a theory of self-directed learning.

For educators, understanding learning means clarifying both processes and outcomes. However, definitions of learning processes become inseparable from what is learned, especially when educators consider who the learner is as a person. William Perry (1970), Arthur Chickering (1972), and David Kolb (1984) have all illuminated the connections between learning as process and learning as outcome. Practitioners as theorists have yet to develop such a picture of lasting learning. What is learned that is enduring, we believe, needs to include the capacity to construct one's self over time: as a learner in college, as a learner in a field of study, as a learner across several roles and contexts, and as an integrated person with a distinctive stance. The educator asks: "How does the student develop an identity as a learner? Can the learner build a history of the self as learner, a kind of autobiography that captures the ebb and flow of learning and its outcomes for the individual?"

Understanding the Learner

Educators converge in their interest and commitment to understanding the student as a learner and as an individual. Diversity in student population, in terms of age, race, gender, cultural background, and academic preparation, has been rapidly increasing in many institutions of higher education. Policymakers, employers, faculty, and scholars of higher education now seem to share a more intense interest in how these student populations learn, what they achieve in college, and what they will take with them after graduation. This diversity has prompted a challenge to primary assumptions about prerequisites for college-level learning: that there will be, and that students will seek, opportunity for college learning; that students will be motivated to learn and capable of learning at entrance; that their "educability" (Dave, 1973) in a particular college has been developed during previous schooling; and that acquisition of a degree guarantees employability. Thus, educators "select" students for college learning; employers "select" the college where a prospective employee was educated. Those primary assumptions no longer hold to the extent they once did. The increasing diversity of those who come to college has shattered the assumption that only some students can learn in college, but an open door that does not include graduation is indefensible. Prerequisites for learning—opportunity, motivation, and educability—developed in one culture obviously make one a beginner in another. Thus, college educators must more consciously develop opportunities to ensure students' successful transitions before, during, and after college.

Who Is Learning?

Because the origins of learning are in the learner's experience, educators start with who the learner is. What each learner understands depends on what each already knows, believes, and values. It also involves the interaction of the learner's prior learning with the educator's prior learning. It is conditioned by the contexts in which each learner has experienced his or her own learning process and that of others. This means acknowledging who learners are without categorizing each (for example, as "privileged," "young," "elite," "disadvantaged," or "adult"). Stereotypes can lead to unfounded expectations for students' learning. More recent terms—"the new student," "adult learner," and "lifelong learner"—can also miscommunicate and lead to unwarranted assumptions. For example, John Richardson and Estelle King (1998) found that older learners as a group are not at a disadvantage compared with younger students. We concur.

Like many other institutions, Alverno has an increasingly diverse student population. A rich mix of students comes from a variety of economic, ethnic, and cultural backgrounds and a wide range of age and experience. This kind of diversity can make for exciting and productive learning, but it also poses increasing challenges for faculty and staff. Students for whom English is a second language or students who have been employed in a work environment with mostly routine tasks, for example, often need special assistance from their classroom teachers and tutors. Furthermore, the differences among students can be a source of conflict as well as enrichment, even as they enhance the diversity of student perspectives across the campus.

The faculty are also finding increasing diversity in the kind of academic preparation students bring to this college. A growing number of students dropped out of high school and recently completed equivalency programs. Many of them are bright and motivated but have been out of a formal learning environment for a while and need to learn what is necessary to be successful in such an environment. The same is true for many students who come directly from high school. Faculty and staff are giving increased attention to matters like personal responsibility and appropriate study habits as part of their teaching. These students expect and demand that learning be useful as well as more deeply meaningful and so challenge faculty to make college learning applied as well as abstract.

The lives of students are increasingly complicated. For example, many Alverno students are parents, frequently single parents.

In addition, the student who does not work or have a family, or both, is now the exception rather than the rule. This means that students have more to manage and sometimes lack the skills to do so. It is a challenge to recognize the complexity of their lives, support them in the process, and yet hold them to the kind of learning that faculty know will serve them best when they graduate. This challenge is compounded by the fact that an increasing number of students today seem to be experiencing severe personal crises in their lives that inevitably affect their ability to maintain a focus on their studies. Nevertheless, faculty are struck by what many students manage given the nature of their lives. Instructors are called to be much more aware of changes in the broader society. They are also becoming more cognizant of the learning needs of students with learning differences. Recognizing the different learning needs and goals of students becomes part of helping them develop the abilities faculty believe should characterize graduates and for ensuring that different learning histories enrich the breadth of learning processes for other students as well.

Faculty members who are committed to understanding the learner find this increasing diversity a welcome challenge. Employers and policymakers support educators' taking up this challenge because working students, especially women across age groups, have recently entered higher education in large numbers and have become an increasingly important social, economic, and political influence. Information about working students' learning is important for refining programs that are based on assumptions that all students can learn and that educators have a good deal of the professional responsibility for this learning as students enter an unfamiliar environment or area of study (Cross, 1981). Both causal mechanisms of growth within the context of student experience and patterns of learning outcomes in understudied populations can contribute to the understanding of diversity that faculty seek when they ask, "Who is learning?"

Who Is Learning For?

In a learner-centered context, a dynamic tension can arise between the questions, "*Who* is learning?" and "Who is learning *for?*" The tension resides in the relationship between teacher and learner, which is both equal and fiduciary, but also in the moral relationship between the learner and other intended beneficiaries of his or her learning. Educators seek to ensure access and achievement for each learner and support the individual to pursue "learning for its own sake." However, most educators are also prompted by their own expectation that graduates will ensure benefits for others (clients, patients, students, colleagues, consumers, family members). They are reinforced in this goal by students who expect to do something with their education, that is, to pursue as well "learning for others' sake."

In a learner-centered context, there is tension between the goals of "learning for its own sake" and "learning for others' sake." Thus, discussion among educators about the meaning of the degree can quickly digress into dichotomies between the goals of a classical liberal arts degree and a vocational degree and whose goals and values should predominate—those of the faculty, students, or society. The task for higher education is to resolve these dichotomies by integrating a liberal arts education, that of the professions, and the service and value traditions that undergird the moral atmosphere of a college. Martha Nussbaum (1997) supports this kind of argument in *Cultivating Humanity: A Classical Defense of Reform in Liberal Education*. She argues that reform of curriculum in higher education should yield "citizens of the world" as well as critical self-examination. John Seely Brown and colleagues argue that "the breach between learning and its use . . . may well be a product . . . of our education system" (Brown, Collins, & Duguid, 1989, p. 33). It is no longer conscionable that an integrated education be offered primarily to college students in residential liberal arts colleges, professional schools of medicine, law, and ministry, or institutions with strong faith or service traditions.

"Who is learning for?" builds on the relationships between faculty and their educational institutions and the multiple publics that higher learning serves. It links the development of educational programs with those who are most affected by the performance of graduates. These relationships are clearest in professions education (for example, nursing, teacher education, management, and art therapy), but the concept applies to all disciplines when the focus is on the performance and contribution of graduates. The dynamic of these concerns—whom faculty teach, what learners' goals are, and who will be affected by their performance—can become a defining debate for educators.

Envisioning Learners as Educated, Mature, and Effective over Time

Educators and policymakers are jointly engaged in shaping a vision of student achievement that informs the public debate about education and what educational goals should be. Creation of this vision is of broad interest because it speaks to higher education's responsibility to engage public policy in education and to expand the role for citizens in deciding what quality education is and how to secure it for themselves and their children. Establishing the links between the preparation of both students who attend college direct from high school and that of experienced adults, and their performance after schooling, is tied to a fundamental question: "What *can* be learned in relation to what *is* actually being learned?" Following that comparison, the educator asks, "What *ought* to be learned?"

What Ought to Be Learned?

Educators, policymakers, and the public have all initiated discussion about what should be taught, what students should be learning, and what the effective graduate should be able to do. This set of interests and commitments crosses the educational spectrum from preschool to college to graduate or professional school—and to continuing education across one's professional lifetime.

To take up this challenge, educators need a more complete picture of what it means to develop a valuing process, self-directed learning, and goals for service toward "composing a life" with spirit and improvisation (Bateson, 1989). Such a life is punctuated by "common fire" (Daloz, Keen, Keen, & Parks, 1996) in a life of "moral commitment" (Colby & Damon, 1992). Each of these authors has studied individuals who are exemplars of such a picture of adult maturity. Many educators have long ago given up the notion that faculty judgment in college predicts which students reach such ineffable goals in adulthood. Rather, educators want to concentrate on fostering such capacities and qualities in each of their students. These educators need a more illuminative picture of human growth and integrated learning while students are still in school, with a corresponding view of what "educated," "mature," and "effective" mean.

Public Debate on Goals and Standards

Public policymakers continually advise that educational goals must reflect rapid changes in economic and global conditions. Many educators across the educational spectrum share a commitment to clarify public expectations of what students will require for success. What should students learn and be able to do? Out of this conversation on goals, questions on standards arise: Are faculty satisfied that students are achieving at the level that faculty expect them to achieve? How do faculty define those levels of learning and performance? How do they know these levels will be appropriate for future performance? What should the standards and performance criteria for student achievement be? Are employers and students satisfied that graduates meet expected performance standards or criteria to the level that makes them effective now and for the future? For us, such questions are embodied in our students' performance. Alumna outcomes cannot be taken for granted if educators hope to refine the meaning of a degree over time. There is some indication that this series of questions is gaining ground over prior pressures to compare graduates from one institution with those of another, particularly when answers to these questions are necessary for rethinking what to teach and what students should learn, setting performance standards, and identifying benchmarks for program effectiveness.

Educational goals, when defined through criteria or performance standards, can communicate how students should be performing when the goals are met. Of equal concern is describing the level of proficiency that students should reach by graduation, a discussion complicated by diversity in student preparation and unequal access to quality instruction. The complexity of this conversation is compounded by issues around who should create content standards and decide the level of performance required. This debate often occurs in the context of how the professions and the public negotiate their relationship. What values are central to the professions as a provider of service? What kind of dispositions should students develop? How do faculty define and foster student formation of moral character and the sense of purpose needed for becoming professionally responsible for the public welfare?

Preparing Students in College to Enact Their Learning as Graduates

Understanding what learners can learn and how to characterize educated, mature, and effective learners over time moves front and center when public representatives in state governments ask institutions to show the "value-added" of a college experience. At the same time, technology and globalization have created demands for performance in workforce and civic arenas that challenge existing definitions of broad preparation in college. The result is that educators in the liberal arts and the professions increasingly find that their rationales for commitment to student learning intersect. The common task has always been to prepare students in college to enact their learning as graduates. But the idea of preparation has come to mean connecting learning throughout the educational process to what one does and how and why one does it, so that each learner envisions a personal future of contributing through his or her competence and capacity to realize shared values.

How and Why Does Learning Happen?

For the educator, how this kind of learning happens in the classroom and outside it and why it happens appear to be two distinct questions. These questions, when asked scientifically, often take this form: "Why do humans learn the way they do?" Research on brain function and artificial intelligence or basic studies in perception and attention are only a small part of the answer because educators must coalesce around the common task of fostering learning. However, joining the two is a fundamental issue. As educators learn about deep and enduring learning, they aim to facilitate it in college and beyond. The challenge for educators is to articulate to each other what they know about lasting learning, and how and why students develop and do it. For example, faculty may believe that learning involves a change in behavior; includes development of abilities that incorporate, apply, and extend knowledge; and is enhanced when the learner sets out to achieve explicit goals. They may intuit that learners benefit when educators make learning explicit—make it available as an object of study. They may appreciate what it means for a faculty to make learning outcomes explicit as abilities that are integrated with the content of a discipline. They may acknowledge the ways in which students learn content—incorporating it into cognitive, emotional, and self schemas and using it to enact performance and reflecting on it so that content becomes part of deep, enduring learning. *Learning to learn, mindful learning,* and *thinking about thinking* are all phrases that educators use to refer to how learners engage when they make their own mental models and learning processes explicit. How do such learning processes, when made explicit and developed as part of what ought to be learned in liberal learning, enable graduates to develop learning that is lasting?

Many faculty can articulate the conditions or contexts that encourage these learning processes and the kinds of powerful pedagogies they might use. They may design learning so that the learner experiences intellectual, emotional, and moral conflicts or disequilibrium. Faculty understand that learner satisfaction can be detrimental to learning, encouraging complacency rather than searching, passivity rather than action, a belief that "teachers teach me" rather than "I learn and develop myself as a learner." Thus, faculty resist the label "student as customer." Yet how might they describe the "student as learner"?

Faculty Expectations for Transfer of Learning

Educators may assume that learners who develop and demonstrate learning outcomes that meaningfully define a liberal education integrate those outcomes into personal and professional responsibility for active contribution to society. But this expectation builds on a concept of learning as transferring a certain knowledge base integrated in a set of abilities. What metacognitive strategies might effect this transfer across contexts and over time during college? How do learners make it part of who they are? How do learners construct how they understand transfer, and what ways of learning do they use to connect learning in one area with another?

Faculty may assume that internalized and individualized learning strategies enable a learner to perform effectively in college and when changing careers, anticipating challenges in the workplace, and integrating career and family roles. But how do learners continue to make learning work for themselves? Can they describe how they learn, discuss their personal growth, and identify and give examples of their unique capabilities? Can they analyze their experience for how they combined their unique qualities and describe their transitions and pathways to effective learning? Can they provide a window on what it means to become an expert, mature, and effective learner in college and afterward?

Fostering Learning Outcomes Through Educational Programs

Those with broad interests in the improvement of undergraduate education expect to make independent judgments about the value, worth, and effectiveness of educational programs. Judgments imply multiple lines of evidence about learning outcomes. Educators and the public alike want to know what graduates can do and how effectively they can do it as a result of an educational program.

Public Debate on Educators' Responsibilities

Higher education increasingly has found itself in the limelight. Critics wonder whether graduates are sufficiently prepared to perform and ask whether higher education is adequately meeting its responsibilities to assess student performance and make well-considered judgments about student achievement. Many campus practitioners share these concerns and are engaged in inquiry about their own students' learning. They are using information about learning to improve curricula and to demonstrate student achievement in their own settings. However, educators need to make greater strides in linking college learning processes and effective performance as a graduate learning outcome.

Public Debate on Learning-Centered Education

A number of educators promote a paradigm shift from teaching to learning (Barr & Tagg, 1995; Boyatzis et al., 1995) as a remedy for discrepancies between what ought to be learned and what learners are actually learning. This shift is an outgrowth of the focus on student learning outcomes; such a shift is learning centered. One impetus is the recent focus on continuous quality improvement in higher education, where programs are student centered because the adult student is a "customer" around whom the "business" of education revolves. Another is the need to develop a framework for distance learning or satellite campuses, where a teacher is on video a city away (Laurillard, 1993). Still another is a push toward efficiency and productivity in higher education, where "time to degree" is compressed under the assumption that learning should be the constant and time the variable (Johnstone, 1993). Among those trends is a need to understand what kind of teaching leads to what kind of learning and what the basis is for the teacher-student relationship that Astin (1977) and Chickering (1972) have long promoted as a central factor emerging from research on learning in college. Clarifying what *student centered* or *learning centered* means for creating educational programs leads to reflection on team learning and organizational learning (Senge, 1990), participatory cultures that strengthen program quality (Haworth & Conrad, 1997), and learning communities (Hill, 1982; Matthews, Smith, MacGregor, & Gabelnick, 1996; Smith, 1991) and also raises issues of faculty scholarship and tenure (Boyer, 1990; Rice, 1996).

What Are Learners Learning, and What Ought to Be Learned?

As noble as the goal may be, creating learning-centered educational programs that "yield" educated, mature, and effective graduates is fraught with problems. Younger students may not share these goals; older adults may believe they cannot afford them. Large institutions with thousands of students who stop in or out of college often may have few, if any, ways of tracking accomplishments of such broad learning outcomes. How might educators know whether and how these accomplishments accrue and whether it is worth the effort to find out? Answering this question is difficult unless faculty challenge the assumptions and learning principles that underlie an entire curriculum. What that means for any institution is undeniably context specific, and it is particularly challenging for faculty to make changes in an educational program that is longstanding and perceived to be relatively effective (Elbow, 1986). However, more educators across higher education are asking what ought to happen and how to organize for it (Schneider & Shoenberg, 1998).

Organizing Colleges for Learning

To heed the call to place greater emphasis on noticing the teaching-learning connection means rethinking the aims of education in relation to a renewed understanding of student learning in the context of a curriculum. Educators are interested in how educational assumptions, values, and learning principles shape an educational program in times of rapid change. During their search for common questions to shape educational transformation, their implicit conceptual frameworks surface, and shifts lead to reflection. The discussion about organizing for learning has meaning in part when it illuminates the broader educational assumptions on which a faculty at an institution has formulated its curriculum. Faculty often begin looking for colleagues to analyze how assumptions and the visible curriculum compare. Thus, another intersection arises from an increasing trend of educators' joining together in identifying questions and strategies for organizing for learning and for guiding educational transformation.

Public Debate on Educational Transformation

With such a set of challenges before us, it seems wise and useful to consider what higher education institutions can learn from each other about the kinds of programs that best foster learning. Rethinking higher education's structures and strategies, as well as its primary assumptions, is likely to be a luxury on campuses where immediate problems absorb all resources. Nevertheless, some educators are collaborating in looking for ways to deal with common issues, despite diversity in settings and the need to resolve localized problems, in the hope that changes can be cost-effective. Higher education associations and foundations (for example, American Association for Higher Education, American Council on Education, The Pew Charitable Trusts, and the W.K. Kellogg Foundation) have been supporting consortia of institutions that are taking up institutional transformation and restructuring to discover and then promote learning environments that work for undergraduates. Such efforts frame a more common ground and guide for ongoing transformation. For example, questions concerning what teachers should teach encompass questions about what students should learn. Queries about educational inputs entail questions about outcomes. Although common questions do not necessarily inspire change, they can focus energy and priorities. We sense a greater urgency among educators, policymakers, and funding agencies for translating ideas into action principles.

When and Where Does Learning Happen?

It seems clear that strategies and structures for organizing learning are a priority. We find that many colleagues in higher education, K–12, and professional schools have an action-oriented interest in educational transformation and are committed to creating curricular innovations that incorporate new assumptions about learning. These colleagues—both individual faculty and also departments, colleges, and consortia of institutions—are eager for opportunities to observe other learning processes and understand their outcomes. They have heightened interests in creating curricula that are student and learning centered, developmental, and coherent. Some are invested in ability-based learning and curricula, and student assessment connected to teaching and learning. Significantly, among those interested are other persons from all walks of life, who view lifelong learning as essential to ongoing professional and civic contribution. This is an increasingly salient view within business and professional organizations that are also questioning the educational assumptions and learning principles that drive reform and are addressing common tasks that can guide educational transformation over the long term. Web-based technology opens up new possibilities for when and where learning happens and has contributed to an unprecedented blurring of the boundaries between education and work.

Redefining Inquiry, Its Uses, and Its Consequences

One resource in higher education that too often goes untapped is the ability of faculty to study the learning of their students. Generating new knowledge is the bread and butter of research universities, and it is used to outstanding effect in focusing policy on troubling issues (such as economic policy, biomedical research funding, and race relations). However, another intersection of interests and commitments joins educators, researchers, and policymakers in the search for better understanding of faculty roles and for faculty to use their talents to connect theory and practice, teaching and research, and program improvement and accountability. Higher education seems to be viewing these elements as neither directional (for example, from theory to practice) nor a set of parallel but uncoordinated activities. Rather, faculty regularly debate how to realize the multiple responsibilities associated with research and teaching, and discuss the scholarship of teaching (Hutchings & Shulman, 1999). Policymakers question whether universities commit adequate time to teaching, given their research responsibilities. Associations and agencies are bringing together multiple groups to collaborate on shared interests, such as annually generating guiding research questions within cohering interests and tasks in higher education (for example, American Association for Higher Education Research Forum, 1999). Educational researchers equally probe directions for research on the most ineffable goals, such as moral development (Bebeau, Rest, & Narvaez, 1999; Kuhmerker, Mentkowski, & Erickson, 1980).

Public Debate on Use and Consequences of Inquiry

In these hopeful but still too few contexts, the nature of inquiry itself is being redefined to give as much emphasis to the usefulness and consequences of findings as to the groundbreaking nature of the questions studied. The setting in which questions are generated and findings are interpreted is front and center in this new equation. Practitioners are often leading this rethinking because of their problem-based focus (Gibbs, 1996). Developing inquiry in the service of student learning pushes a redefinition in particular ways. Practitioners think more about the enduring constructions of learning, development, and performance that emerge from and inform effective educational practice. Funding agencies give more priority to applied research on critical social issues, including educational reform. Educational researchers more often ask how information is used, and they question findings not tested in practice.

How Do Educators Study Learning in a Dynamic Context of Practice?

Scholarship—its means and ends—is no longer a closed, disciplinary discussion, or the prerogative of a single scholar isolated from the setting and consequences of application (Boyer, 1990; Davis & Chandler, 1998; Glassick, Huber, & Maeroff, 1997). We have learned that persons across higher education are searching for methods that are as meaningful to information users as they are to those who generate the information. Faculty from one discipline question and borrow from the methods used by another discipline. Policymakers question not only how evidence was generated, but where and how it might be used. Use becomes another scale for weighing evidence in decision making. Thus, policymakers share an interest in method with educational researchers, who challenge approaches to inquiry that are inappropriate for contextualized problems. In the information age, the search for new ways to conduct inquiry becomes a joint enterprise.

Framing Inquiry About Learning That Lasts

Common tasks in this chapter represent crossroads where the interests and commitments of educators intersect and cohere (see Table 1.1). In practice, these tasks can initiate practical conversations on campus and trigger discussion of fundamental issues about learning that have traditionally shaped higher education expertise and resolve. Initiating and then sustaining those conversations through inquiry is an evolving, long-term effort. On many campuses, faculty and staff often initiate discussions about what ought to be learned in relation to what learners are actually learning. They then compare what is possible for humans to achieve with what ought to be learned. In the case of Alverno, intense, ongoing conversations about relationships between the real (is), the ideal (ought to be), and the possible (can achieve) led faculty to explore and clarify their responsibilities for current and future learning outcomes, including learning after college. These comparisons brought them back to definitional questions from an empirical, cross-disciplinary, and practice perspective. Their current theory of learning that lasts emerged from evolving studies of what learners have been actually learning. Each of the common tasks and fundamental issues became linked to the practical, contextual questions about learning that lasts and related questions about undergraduate learning that we take up across this book.

Although there is a substantial intersection of interests and commitments among various groups across higher education, common, practical tasks represent divergent yet overlapping concerns. Each group will use its own personal and professional experience as a

Table 1.1. Framing Inquiry About Learning That Lasts.

Common Tasks	Fundamental Issues	Questions About Learning That Lasts	Related Questions
About Learning:			
a. Understanding learning	a. What is *learning*? *What* is learned?	a. Does learning last, and if so, what kind of learning lasts? How are domains of human growth related to learning? to performance?	a. What is the ebb ard flow of learning for an individual? for a whole class?
b. Understanding the learner	b. *Who* is learning? Who is learning *for*?	b. For whom does learning last?	b. How do students develop responsibility for learning to learn—and to unlearn?
c. Envisioning learners as educated, mature, and effective over time	c. What can be learned? What is actually being learned?	c. Do learners who acquire complex, multidimensional learning outcomes benefit themselves and also contribute to others?	c. How do students develop skills and dispositions for working together? What is "experience," and how does it relate to particular kinds of liberal learning in the disciplines?
d. Preparing students in college to enact their learning as graduates	d. How and why does learning happen?	d. What do educators know about learning that bears on teaching? Does teaching lead to learning? Does student assessment lead to learning?	d. What is the role of practice, performance, insight, assessment, and reflection in learning? How does learning differ in specific contexts? What is the nature of transfer of knowledge and skills to internships and service?

Table 1.1. Framing Inquiry About Learning That Lasts, cont'd.

Common Tasks	Fundamental Issues	Questions About Learning That Lasts	Related Questions
About Education:			
e. Fostering learning through educational programs	e. What ought to be learned? What can be learned? What are learners learning?	e. What elements of a learning-centered curriculum challenge and support students in achieving learning goals?	e. What do educators know about the learning-to-teaching connection? What do they recommend and do?
f. Organizing colleges for learning	f. When and where does learning happen?	f. How does a focus on learning that lasts translate into educator learning at the organizational level?	f. What role does education have in fostering learning? What do consortia of institutions believe and do?
g. Redefining inquiry on learning and teaching and its uses and consequences	g. How do educators study learning in a dynamic context of practice?	g. How does inquiry about learning integrate theory, research, and practice?	g. What are the important questions about learning and what kinds of methods for studying learning also make inquiry useful?

backdrop against which to formulate questions about learning on their own campus. The study of learning that lasts in the context of educational practice is essential to advancing these common tasks and understanding these fundamental issues. But it also takes place at several different levels of action: what it means to be an educated, mature, and effective learner; what the individual faculty or staff member might do; what a department might do; what a dean might do; what an educational researcher might do; and what part higher education as a profession might play.

The framework for *Learning That Lasts*, illustrated through various roles and levels of practice, provides principles for action and something more: it facilitates seeing a full-fledged process of inquiry as potentially integrated into each undergraduate institution. Such inquiry, based on diverse voices, sources of ideas and evidence, and contexts of practice across higher education, is also a campuswide conversation. We mean this book to contribute to the discourse about how students integrate learning, development, and performance and how integrated learning is shaped over time. As such, the concept of learning that lasts provides a strategy to rethink the enduring and fundamental challenges learners and educators are facing at the beginning of this millennium.

Chapter Two

Educators' Ways of Knowing About Learning

When educators address learning that lasts to advance their own knowledge about it, they construct what they know in ways that make it useful, that make the connections between learning and education in their own settings. Knowledge about learning and what kinds of education foster it can be built in several distinct yet overlapping ways: formal research, collaborative inquiry, and review of literature and practice in higher education. A fourth way is learning by educating—knowing that emerges from the continually changing context of educators' experience and their constantly modified practice. Each of the four is a complementary way of knowing, a mode of inquiry, an integral and broadening approach to studying learning that lasts. Each chapter draws on all four. Each way of knowing also forms the basis of more particular study methods.

Use of multiple ways of knowing has the practical value of producing or exposing one to multiple perspectives. Using these ways of knowing simultaneously generates knowledge about learning from different levels of practice and disciplinary perspectives. The continuing challenge is to make connections among this diversity of viewpoints to discern integrating ideas about learning. Taking up this challenge is less daunting than it first appears, because it is consistent with core value frameworks that ground higher education. Perspective taking, or facility with multiple discourses, is a fundamental feature of inquiry in liberal arts education, just as perspective taking in interpersonal relationships is a fundamental feature of professions education. Each position values diversity in perspective among individuals, societies, and cultures, yet respects common learning.

To study learning that lasts for maximum educational significance for students, educators need to frame their questions about
what to study and decide how to study it. In this chapter, we lay the
groundwork for understanding ways of knowing about learning.
To do so, we assume that educators want to use their studies of
learning that lasts to understand how learning outcomes relate to
each other and to link outcomes to elements of educational programs that are learning centered. Such studies must connect directly to what educators know about education as it drives their
practice. Studies that are useful to others explain patterns of learning outcomes in relation to potentially transferable elements within
a curriculum that is designed to foster learning that lasts.

In any educational context or culture, a faculty's assumptions
about education provide a grounded source of ideas linked to a
particular setting. While studies of learning should be coherent
with the educational assumptions of a faculty, those assumptions
should also be continually challenged by the diversity in professional or disciplinary frameworks (Cole, 1996; Much, 1995) and
the assumptions and experiences of educators at diverse campuses.
Studies seldom meet these standards.

Such limitations are not a surprise. Those who seek to provide
in-depth explanations for the interconnections among learning
outcomes must bring together competing sources of ideas and evidence to integrate multiple domains of student growth. To relate
curricular elements to learning outcomes, they must clarify program elements at a time when the more prominent trend has been
to maximize curricular diversity through ever-increasing course of-
ferings at the expense of coherence among curricular elements
that enable students to integrate their learning within and across
disciplines and contexts. And they must also document evidence
and interpretations for curricular causes of growth during college.
Even after all of this work, it is difficult to demonstrate a strong longitudinal research link between elements of a particular undergraduate curriculum and substantive learning outcomes, and still
account for other sources of influence (Pascarella, Edison, Nora,
Serra Hagedorn, & Terenzini, 1996). Moreover, the study of long-
term effects is still in its infancy. Pascarella and Terenzini (1991)
observe that "in attempting to synthesize the evidence for the long-
term effects of college on the development of general cognitive
skills, we must rely almost totally on surveys that ask alumni about

their retrospective perception of the influence or benefits of college" (p. 153). In spite of the difficulties, educators nevertheless remain committed to using research to investigate how alumna performance, continual learning, and developmental outcomes are linked to an educational program designed for these connections. This goal is at the center of educational reform in a number of countries including Australia (Candy, 1991), the United Kingdom (Otter, 1999), and the United States.

A practical necessity for any educational improvement effort that builds on evolving frameworks or pedagogies is to put core educational assumptions to a systematic test, as Boyatzis and his colleagues (1995) did in their nationally recognized M.B.A. program at Case Western Reserve University; they tested the learning and development principles that faculty have been using to strengthen some of the features of their program. Janet Loxley and John Whiteley (1986) tested the principles of student development underlying their innovative character development program at the University of California–Irvine by documenting changes in student development outcomes in resident life. Both of these groundbreaking works studied broad learning outcomes in context; each demonstrated the potential value of linking interventions with outcomes. Faculty who expect that explicit educational frameworks drive inquiry might feel stymied unless educational communities rearticulate their aims and philosophies (Gibbs, 1996).

Framing Studies of Learning That Lasts in Context

One breakthrough in carrying out such studies was to situate programmatic research investigating learning, development, and performance within a collaborative community of inquiry. Benefiting from systematic research within a community of inquiry requires additional levels of work. For example, Marcia Baxter Magolda (1992) describes how she came to better understand knowing and reasoning in college by listening to her students at Miami University as they articulated their reasoning. Out of this, she provided her interpretations of reasoning patterns for higher education faculty. Boyatzis and others (1995) have discussed how Case Western faculty began forming consensus for an innovative curriculum initiative, stimulated in part by exploring how findings from their studies of student learning were linked to evolving corporate faculty perspectives on curriculum. In this way, these faculty have placed their own findings in sharper relief for faculty at other institutions who want to examine their own stances on learning. This goal, of integrating curriculum theory building and programmatic research on learning in context, can reveal much about how a corporate faculty's ongoing inquiry becomes a set of diverse yet coherent ways of knowing about learning.

Despite these successes, studying learning that lasts in context presents some unique challenges. One is that faculty, administrators, advisors, student services personnel, and researchers, each with different voices, need to remain co-investigators in a shared concern. Another is that sources of ideas and evidence need to be diverse yet provide for coherence. Still another arises from the need for diverse contexts of practice within and across settings. Limiting the context to one institution adds depth of perspective because there is enormous variability across disciplines and time in a single college. However, ideas in one setting can also become so embedded in a college as one context of practice that educators from other campuses cannot easily identify or benefit. It is all the more critical, then, that educators both articulate their internal, or contextual, perspectives on learning and education (for example, Case Western's management faculty ideas and evidence on learning and development) and also open up their own experience through credible, substantive findings drawn from external perspectives (for example, Baxter Magolda's ideas and evidence on knowing and reasoning in college). Thus, such approaches to inquiry must allow for colleagues on and off campus to make comparisons. For example, a range of externally derived theoretical frameworks enable external comparisons to educational frameworks of the Alverno faculty.

We rely on four complementary yet multifaceted ways of knowing. Cognitive-developmental theory, social constructionist and constructivist theory, and performance theory have grounded the first way, *formal research*. Critical theory, social constructionist theory, and theories of the scholarship of connection and engagement have grounded the second, *collaborative inquiry*. Discipline-based theories of learning, development, and performance and educational theories that account for long-term student learning outcomes have guided the third, *review of literature and practice*. Integrating findings from these distinct but overlapping ways of knowing about learning is feasible in part because these modes of inquiry have become part of a particular educational setting over a significant period of time.

It is the fourth way of knowing, *learning by educating*, that often best serves a particular group of educators in making the kinds of comparisons of ideas and evidence that lead to shifts in their thinking, so that they can directly affect practice with their new insights. The advantage of this mode of inquiry is realized when a faculty and staff have articulated their deeply held internal perspectives with enough clarity to make external comparisons possible for themselves and others. Such inquiry can become a crucible for comparing ideas and evidence across disciplines. Collaborative inquiry within consortia of institutions can allow for comparisons across contexts of practice.

Each of the four ways of knowing that undergird *Learning That Lasts* is grounded in ideas about learning, inquiry, and educational practice. We have often used contrasting methods to study broad questions about learning that lasts in part because methodologists in cognitive science who expand the study of learning call for diverse methods within a single context. Of course, particular concrete methods must further ground the evidence for each way of knowing.

Formal Research as a Way of Knowing

Three substantive themes have organized the formal research: (1) student as learner, (2) learner as developing person, and (3) graduate as performer and contributor. Each theme calls forth a distinctive approach to describing the outcomes of education, and so we have studied each through particular and distinct grounding methods, disciplinary connections, and paradigmatic stances. Each, however, remains informed by the overall inquiry. For each, we have followed the same students and an aspect of their learning over a ten-year time span, from entry to five years postcollege, and we have also studied the potential causal relationships with the curriculum and the college environment for twenty-four years.

Studying Learning Outcomes

Student as learner, the first source of ideas and evidence from formal research, has focused on how students understand their learning in the context of the Alverno curriculum and how they continued to learn after college. We have listened carefully to each learner's perspective through open-ended, confidential interviews at the end of each year in college and five years later, and in the process have discerned patterns in student perspectives on the Alverno culture and curriculum. The theme of student as learner is drawn from a recent meta-analysis of a series of studies completed on student and alumna perspectives interviews over twenty-two years. The analyses were predominantly grounded in the theoretical paradigm of social constructionism, taking as their point of departure the role of social context and the ways that shared language and practices shape the individual's frameworks for understanding and acting. This theoretical frame for looking at the student and alumna constructions also benefits from the hindsight apparent from the alumna interviews. It provides unique insight into how students have co-constructed the curriculum in relation to faculty, staff, and setting.

Learner as developing person is the second source of ideas and evidence. Broad developmental patterns over the life span have emerged from the same students' responses to paper-and-pencil measurements to provide a window on individual development, so educators can broaden their understanding of the potential goals for education. The instruments reflect descriptions of human potential by psychologists of intellectual, moral, and ego development across the life span and the kinds of motivational dispositions that may influence learning and performance across time. This theme has been grounded in multiple theoretical frameworks, many of which share in the broad discourse of the discipline of developmental psychology. In their multiplicity, they focus on the development of the individual's frameworks for interacting with others, affectively responding to situations, and intellectively grasping the world. The predominant paradigmatic stance is constructivism, which emphasizes the active role of the individual in constructing understandings. We have probed how these patterns develop with statistical strategies that integrate the findings and address the challenge of demonstrating statistically the link between college learning and later performance.

The combined methodology for the two themes allows for the practice of both the "first and second psychology" (Cole, 1996) represented by Piagetian and Vygotskian traditions—that is, the intrapsychological and interpsychological developments of the person in relation to his or her environment. Theoretically we can practice the first psychology across contexts, as in "student as developing person"; we practice the second only by understanding the meaning students give to learning in a college environment, where the symbols and signs of learning have been changed as in "student as learner." This allows us to study more carefully how learning happens when the relationships of the symbols, signs, and activities of learning (abilities in disciplines, ability levels, assessment) are made explicit. Often these signs and symbols of learning are in sharp contrast to those represented in the kinds of learning environments and practices that students have experienced before coming to this college (subject matter, course sequence, testing, grading). Further, the methodology—employing judgment, measurement, and a longitudinal design—allows us to understand student learning, development, and performance not only through a system of categories, but through understanding students as holistic persons (White, 1994).

Graduate as performer and contributor is the third source of ideas and evidence from formal research. We have taken up the societal question of how these same learners contribute as graduates five years after college in work, family, and civic life, focusing on actual performance as the individual has related it to us. Performance allows for an intense study of the connections between human dispositions and performance in everyday contexts after college and for tracing their long-term relationships. Here graduates bring their own constructions of situations to bear through performance interviews that probed what actually happened and why. Researchers conducted deep, independent analysis of that performance, based on what outstanding performers do in other roles and contexts. Out of this source, we have created a picture of performance described through key abilities that make a difference in the graduate's career development and faculty judgments of their day-to-day effectiveness. This source of ideas and evidence is relatively ecumenical in its stance, but its paradigmatic viewpoint can be traced to John Dewey's pragmatic theory of action in context. It draws extensively on methods and theories that industrial and organizational psychologists use to study workplace performance. Thus, this third theme serves to triangulate the findings from the other two themes by disentangling conclusions from the limitations of particular disciplinary methods or theories (Cook & Campbell, 1979; Kuhn, 1962).

This third theme illustrates a larger point about the connection between formal research and what we call the scholarship of connection and engagement. As a connecting theme, "graduate as performer and contributor" uses a language of abilities that resonates to employers, the general public, and educators from a range of disciplinary perspectives. It also has engaged many external communities by exploring a diversity of work, family, and civic settings.

Design, Participants, and Data Sources

To study these multiple themes, we employed a multimethod, triangulated, and longitudinal design that simultaneously emphasized in-depth and integrative analyses and involved the intensive participation of a large number of students and alumnae across ten years. This design required considerable investment in research staff (Mertens & Rogers, 1986), participant involvement (Reisetter & Sandoval, 1987), data management (Ben-Ur, 1986), and progressive analysis and reporting over twenty-four years (Mentkowski & Doherty, 1983, 1984a, 1984b; Mentkowski et al., 1991). College research, ours included, has often used cross-sectional approaches, for example, comparing freshman to seniors, but cross-sectional comparisons are generally understood to be difficult to interpret because population differences and attrition are usually a likely cause of any observed differences. In contrast, a longitudinal approach enables a clearer picture of individual and aggregate change. (Figure 2.1 provides a summary of the overall design.)

We began the longitudinal research by inviting all of the 706 students to participate who entered the college in 1976 and 1977 as undergraduate degree-seeking students in the time frame that

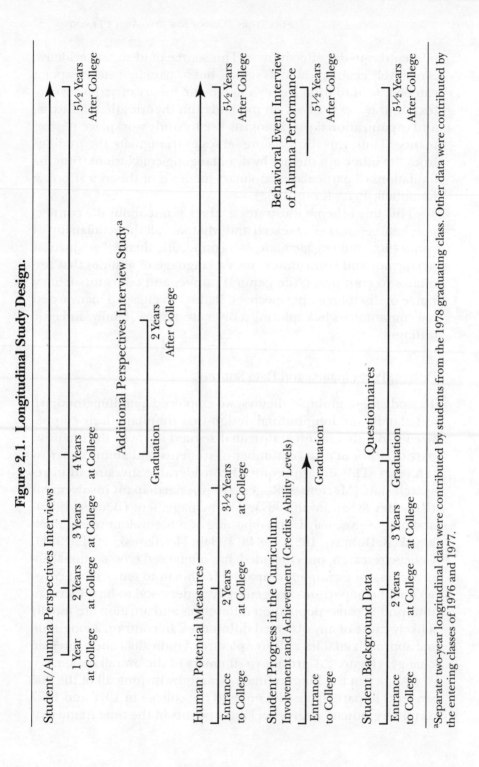

Figure 2.1. Longitudinal Study Design.

Student/Alumna Perspectives Interviews

| 1 Year at College | 2 Years at College | 3 Years at College | 4 Years at College | 5½ Years After College |

Additional Perspectives Interview Study[a]

| Graduation | 2 Years After College |

Human Potential Measures

| Entrance to College | 2 Years at College | 3½ Years at College | 5½ Years After College |

Behavioral Event Interview of Alumna Performance

| 5½ Years After College |

Student Progress in the Curriculum
Involvement and Achievement (Credits, Ability Levels)

| Entrance to College | Graduation |

Questionnaires

Student Background Data

| Entrance to College | 2 Years at College | 3 Years at College | Graduation | 5½ Years After College |

[a]Separate two-year longitudinal data were contributed by students from the 1978 graduating class. Other data were contributed by the entering classes of 1976 and 1977.

the curriculum was offered (weekday or weekend). They ranged in age from seventeen to fifty-five. Half were entering college directly from high school, and half were returning adults; 80 percent were first-generation college students. In contrast to the current student body, study participants were more likely to be Caucasian. (In 1980 minority enrollment was 7 percent, in 1989 it was 17 percent, and in 1999 it was 38 percent.)

Across a ten-year time span, participating students in the two cohorts completed a battery of external measures at four key points (1976/1977, 1978/1979, 1980/1981, and 1985/1986): entry to college, one and one-half years after entry, three and one-half years after entry, and five and one-half years after most participants had graduated. A random sample of participants, with replacements (n = 99), also completed interviews exploring their perspectives on learning at the end of each year in college and as five-year alumnae at five key points. Throughout the student years of assessment, eligibility for participation in the longitudinal research was determined by initial participation in the first assessment (97 percent) and enrollment in the college at the time of assessment. Alumnae became eligible for completing the fourth time of assessment in the five-year alumna follow-up by having participated as students in at least two of the three prior assessments, yielding an alumna sample frame of 358.

The longitudinal study strategy uses a range of theoretical frameworks, approaches, and instruments drawn from inside and outside the college. We used seventeen research instruments to collect data. Students and alumnae completed more than twenty thousand questionnaires, tests, essays, and interviews in order to assist us in determining how they learn, develop, and perform during and after college. Typically each student invested three to five hours in the research effort at each time of assessment; each alumna invested another five to ten hours. At the level of the individual measures, student participation rates ranged from 84 to 99 percent; alumna participation rates ranged from 59 to 88 percent. Overall, between 89 and 93 percent of the students participated, and 87 percent of the alumnae participated. For the 13 percent of alumnae who were nonparticipants, 5 percent refused to participate, and 8 percent expressed interest in the study but did not complete their participation for a variety of reasons. Parallel to the two main cohorts of students entering in 1976 or 1977, a separate cohort of students, the graduating class of 1978, participated ($n = 63$). Of these, thirty-seven completed a Perspectives Interview at graduation and again as two-year alumnae ($n = 32$).

Data collection and analysis for the two main cohorts were accomplished through multiple strategies. First, trained interviewers listened carefully to students and alumnae in individual, in-depth, confidential interviews to discern their perspectives on their learning experiences. Through an iterative, thematic analysis of these transcribed Perspectives Interviews (including ethnographic techniques), researchers developed a textured picture of how students and alumnae changed their perspectives on learning, performance, and growth across the years and, most significant, how they viewed these changes in relation to the curriculum and milieu of the college.

Second, we fielded a battery of human potential measures to chronicle longitudinal development. These external measures were grounded in strong theoretical frameworks. They include those articulated by Lawrence Kohlberg (moral development), David Kolb (experiential learning), Jane Loevinger (ego development), David McClelland (motives and competence), William Perry (intellectual and ethical development), Jean Piaget (cognitive development), and James Rest (moral reasoning). Trained coders scored the data. We developed multi-indicator measurement models in order to link back to these theoretical foundations and used statistical analyses to explore patterns and trends in aggregate longitudinal growth on each human potential measure.

Third, we studied student progress in the performance-based curriculum as a potential cause of change. We measured progress in the curriculum through already existing faculty judgments that validated students for demonstrating specified levels of abilities on over one hundred performance assessments in the curriculum. (Faculty make these judgments in relation to explicit developmental performance criteria that integrate content in the disciplines and professions and are built into curriculum ability definitions at the level of general education and the majors.) We used statistical analyses to explore the potential causal relationships between progress in the curriculum and changes in the individual's growth and development as measured by the external human potential measures. Questionnaires and background information provided data on other potential sources of change.

Fourth, trained interviewers used a confidential, two-hour Behavioral Event Interview originated by McClelland to probe alumna performance in family, work, and civic roles. Researchers coded five-year alumna performance against criteria for forty-two specific abilities synthesized from over eight hundred studies of professionals and illuminated by curriculum abilities defined by Alverno faculty. Through statistical and qualitative analyses of alumna performance, we examined patterns in alumna abilities, performance effectiveness, and potential relationships to curriculum preparation. Fifth, we used questionnaires to collect background information and additional information on curriculum perspectives, continued learning, career plans and achievement, family life, and civic involvement.

Limitations of Generalizability and Specificity

Alongside the strengths of the longitudinal study are potential issues in interpreting the generality or specificity of the findings. First, the participants attended college in the late seventies and most graduated in 1980 and 1981. They were contacted again in 1985 and 1986. Therefore, we take care in generalizing the findings to the population of students entering college or graduating today (Ben-Ur, Rogers, Deemer, & Mentkowski, 1989). Nevertheless, the study does inform us about a population category that has not usually been included in earlier studies of students and alumnae: first-generation women college students who are of both traditional and nontraditional age, work before, during, and after college, and generally do not reside on campus.

Second, the study was conducted not only in a specific period of time, but also in the context of a particular college. Indeed, one purpose of the study was to explore whether and how broad patterns of learning, development, and performance might be linked to specific and distinctive aspects of the Alverno curriculum. Where we could, we have compared our findings to other studies, to provide a context for limiting both overgeneralizing and undergeneralizing beyond this college's context. At times, we have more or less firmly interpreted findings in relation to particular contextual features in the curriculum. Thus, we provide some purchase on questions of generalizability of both Alverno educational assumptions and findings. However, we did not control for selection—who did or did not attend college—because the effects of college are well established (Pascarella & Terenzini, 1991). Neither was our question of interest a comparison of students at this college to those who chose or graduated from other colleges. In a concurrent effort, however, external researchers have compared Alverno student gains on some of the same external measures to gains by students at seven other institutions in relation to each institution's educational goals. These cross-sectional findings were reported in *A New Case for the Liberal Arts,* where "Clare College" is the pseudonym for Alverno (Winter, McClelland, & Stewart, 1981).

Third, a comprehensive ten-year longitudinal study that is broad in focus does not routinely provide direct, specific information for even local improvement, except at its beginning. Such a use became less sustainable over time, as the curriculum changed, in part because faculty use direct, specific information from the student performance assessment system to shape it (see Mentkowski & Loacker, 1985). However, departments in this college that are now working to evaluate general education or major field outcomes for current students continue to use the long-term results as a broad backdrop against which they can interpret more focused and specific research that they are pursuing. Both nursing and business and management majors were well represented in the study, as were, though to a lesser degree, education, professional communications, and broad categories of other majors in the arts, sciences, and humanities.

Fourth, it is worth reiterating that this study is limited to women participants. We have made comparisons on some external measures that have norms from male and female samples, and studies of the performance of males are integrated into the codes for analyzing alumnae performance. Where we have comparisons, our findings have supported cross-gender generalizations. Nonetheless, the degree to which these findings would generalize to men is largely an open question, one that colleagues in our institutional consortia often consider. We engaged students in these studies as part of their participation in the curriculum, with assurances of strict confidentiality, and it was with that understanding that they agreed to participate over the ten years. To maximize participation and the diversity of the sample, we focused our studies on learning and deliberately did not administer personality measures or conduct interviews to elicit intimate self-disclosures about their lives as women—even though almost all of these women volunteered such information. Interview excerpts were edited for confidentiality and clarity, and all student and alumna names are pseudonyms.

Collaborative Inquiry as a Way of Knowing

Collaborative inquiry is an interactive, participative, and critical process of professional collaboration, of mutual exploration of ideas and evidence. It is mutually beneficial, responsive to educational concerns, and enhances learning by educators. It redefines faculty work as including multidisciplinary scholarship wherein faculty formulation of theory, along with research and practice, leads to new insights. As such, collaborative inquiry is another way of knowing about learning, and it has its own themes, paradigmatic stances, concrete methods, and limitations. While educators often experience responsibilities to teaching, research, and service as conflicting and overwhelming, collaborative inquiry on learning that lasts has the potential to integrate these traditional components of the educators' role. Still, collaborative inquiry about student learning is probably more likely to take place in a teaching institution that takes primary and collective responsibility for the education of each student.

Studying Learning and How to Foster It

Educators gain shared insights not only by exploring learning in college and beyond, but also by working together to interpret and envision enduring learning as a prelude to fostering it in a broadly diverse student body. When their formal research is embedded in a community of collaborative learning and inquiry, faculty and staff can more easily use findings to inform cross-disciplinary and interdisciplinary conversations about their practice. Practice-based insight that emerges in the context of a collaborative community of inquirers is qualitatively different from insights that may occur when formal research is not embedded in practice, for example, where researchers do research and practitioners apply findings later.

Through collaborative inquiry, educators surface and articulate their educational theories. Such educators therefore integrate theory, research, and practice from diverse voices, sources of ideas and evidence, and contexts of practice. They use learning principles to inform patterns of action in curriculum development or institutional restructuring. They discern how principles and patterns might resonate across diverse campuses.

Designs

Collaborative inquiry usually calls for designs complete with stimulus materials that bring diverse voices, sources of ideas and evidence, and contexts of practice to the discourse. A smaller group of teachers and researchers may create, pilot, and revise these designs. Designs are gradually made explicit through processes that may function somewhat like "instruments" that evoke faculty and staff perspectives and performances. These processes are generally interactive and anticipate the need for effective analysis, communication, and social interaction, along with the time and other resources that a group needs to generate products in a public forum. Anticipating who might be involved in any activity, along with their interests, commitments, expertise, and experiences, is part of ensuring an appropriate mix of voices from individuals and groups inside and outside a particular context of practice. The teaching faculty who are developing and implementing curriculum, as well as other academic professionals, steadily become participant researchers, along with others who bring a breadth and depth to the work as educational researchers. Designs that are inclusive broaden involvement, investment, and perspectives.

Internal Collaborative Inquiry in a Context of Practice

Educators at Alverno have had to create collaborative processes and institutional structures that can make such studies inclusive and practical, while sustaining broad-based involvement and investment, deepening critique through diverse perspectives, using new discoveries about learning, and fostering conflict resolution. This has meant working toward a culture of inquiry in which studies of student learning can be pursued from a variety of perspectives: the work of individual faculty members in their courses, departmental work in general education and the major fields, collaborative faculty and staff work in college-wide studies, and collaboration with campus representatives from consortia of institutions. It also meant involving Alverno's academic educational research and evaluation office and the academic affairs office extensively. The redefinition of faculty work—rather than an add-on—makes the study of learning and teaching in one's program central to disciplinary scholarship.

Another implication is that collaboration develops as a complex engagement of multiple groups of inquirers. This has meant finding ways to engage in rigorous self-questioning amid articulated common goals, while often breaking up the tasks of generating questions, interpreting findings, drawing implications, and integrating other sources of information and experience. In writing *Learning That Lasts,* for example, the authors drew on these multiple investments:

- Faculty and staff ask questions about improving learning.
- Administrators consider the common tasks that the institution must address and find the resources for college-wide inquiry and participation in consortia.
- Students and alumnae sustain participation in demanding research protocols over a ten-year time span to make meaning of their own learning and growth.
- A team of educational researchers turn broad questions into researchable ones, rigorously carrying out a breadth and depth of studies.
- Departments and committees engage in critique and debate about questions, methods, findings, interpretations, and related policy-making.
- A standing committee of faculty, administrators, and educational researchers conceptualize systems of inquiry and their support, evaluation, and use.
- Colleagues from across higher education critique and contribute to each of these investments.

Engaging multiple investments is an approach to inquiry that integrates multiple perspectives. It means *standing in* educational practice in terms of enacting the most direct procedures, tasks, and strategies, as well as *standing beside* it in a parallel process to explore different applications of practice. It also means *standing aside* to study larger effects and theoretical constructions. This perspective taking increases the feasibility of inquiry as it interacts with other college-wide systems with overlapping or divergent purposes and competing demands for resources. (Other publications further explore the meaning of Alverno scholarship: Alverno College Research and Evaluation Committee, Office of Research and Evaluation, & Additional Faculty and Staff, 1993; Mentkowski, 1996; Riordan, 1993.)

External Collaborative Inquiry Across Contexts of Practice

To maximize the diversity of voices, sources of ideas and evidence, and, especially, contexts of practice, *Learning That Lasts* is implicitly shaped by long-term conversations and peer review with long-standing colleagues in various communities across a range of institutions—those who do and do not share Alverno's educational commitments and scholarly interests. In this sense, they are partners in collaborative inquiry. These dialogues, we have learned, contribute another level of understanding about learning. They have convinced us that the higher education community deeply cares—as do we—about how students learn and how they develop personally and professionally after college, although undergraduate student learning is a second priority for some educators.

Members of consortia of institutions have created designs for collaborative inquiry that enable goal setting and consequent data gathering of sources, such as in-house institutional goal statements, learning outcomes, assessment techniques, progress reports on ability-based learning, and presentations of data from student outcomes studies. Other designs have focused on improving the flow of a conversation, with consequent analysis of transcripts of consortium meetings for questions and insights. Interactive activities have enabled campus representatives to develop a kind of oral history of their progress for consortium colleagues. These histories lend further context and credibility to descriptions of practice that, for reasons of confidentiality and rapid change on a campus, are not included in a published work by a particular institution or by a consortium. Designs also support comparisons by campus representatives as they discern integrating ideas about learning. In one consortium that included Alverno, eleven institutions—from secondary schools to postsecondary to professional schools—met as a consortium over a three-year period not only to examine their own practices but also to define educational assumptions that would be broadly applicable in support of teaching and learning. Members created several designs to gather data about institutional change. For comparison, we then analyzed the experiences of still other consortia that did not include Alverno in order to posit broad guidelines for institutional renewal that could support a coherent effort to implement the principles of learning that lasts.

In the consortium meetings, the dynamics of collaborative inquiry were similar to our campus experience. We noticed how each campus representative in a consortium was standing inside his or her own particular educational setting, standing beside it, and standing aside from it as well. Members continually noted the challenges that arise from bringing together diverse institutions to yield benefits for both individual and common purposes. Often it was a challenge to experience another setting only by listening to another set of faculty and staff voices as they discussed creating curriculum or to see videos of students as they learned or performed. Still, campus representatives found they could build bridges to their own students, experiences, and campus. We and our colleagues have noticed that when taking up this bridge building, it remains essential to form one's own interpretations and simultaneously examine one's own experiences as a backdrop in order to participate in generating ideas and evidence across contexts of practice.

Limitations

One limitation of collaborative inquiry is that it often requires some initial point of commonality of purpose and experience to join in deliberation. Common tasks and practical questions can serve this purpose, but these can easily lose ground in the different ways that campuses experience them. Designs can help, but these are often less likely to be transportable than are those of either formal research on one campus or review of the theory, research, and practice literature. Thus, collaborative inquiry often requires discovering the different conventions and criteria for inquiry in a particular context and making these explicit, so that participants can design strategies for discovering diverse and coherent purposes and strategies. Further, deliberation about complex ideas about teaching and learning can easily become challenges to an individual's professional identity. The very act of collaborative inquiry around a new set of questions, common tasks, or fundamental issues about learning challenges faculty and staff identity in all areas at once: as disciplinary experts, as educators, and as persons. Collaborative inquiry also challenges institutional identity, for example, when institutions had more or less in common than they had expected. Without agreed-on strategies for deliberation, such conversations may exacerbate rather than resolve problems.

Further, the conversations required by collaborative inquiry may have a good deal of emotional weight that can distance participants fairly quickly. For example, diversity in disciplinary perspectives and their underlying value frameworks elicit intellectual passions, especially when participants discuss the validity of evidence. However, these feelings are often more readily identifiable and parsed by faculty and staff, who are practiced at discovering these. In contrast, when emotional weight in a conversation derives from implicit conflicts in scholarly interests or larger educational commitments, as occurs when making meaning from diverse perceptions of what being an educator means, it is more difficult for participants to develop emotional distance.

As participants move toward shifts in thinking that affect current practice, strategies for sustaining emotional distance are doubly needed. Meeting minutes can help when much of the emotional weight of conversation is not made public in minutes. Sometimes audiotaping interactions for transcription and analysis can make meaning more observable so that it can be more easily acted on—provided there is the trust necessary for turning on a recorder. In such cases, separating the emotional content through analysis of text and listening to the audiotape for emotional content later can uncover unique ideas or infer meaning in common. However, when collaborative inquiry begins to overlap with formal research methods, it can often require more resources than initially planned. For example, transcript analysis may stop short of establishing interjudge agreement because validity can be established through participant review of interpretations. Such collaborative inquiry goes much beyond listening to the reporting out of activities and reflections, although it might start there. If coherence in assumptions within the diversity of campuses, students, administrators, and faculty is to emerge, collaborative activity continues over time. We have not, however, studied how well ideas and evidence from consortia hold beyond the time funded for consortium activity.

Literature and Practice Review as a Way of Knowing

The integration of learning and education emphasizes the importance of studying student learning and teaching practices in a complex framework. By convention, literature review—analyses of diverse voices, ideas, and evidence from books and journal articles—provides a critical third leg. It is reflected by citations in a text or references in conversation. Integrating theory and research with practice puts some additional demands on literature review as a way of knowing. Thus, we distinguish review of the literature of practice—analyses that describe, illustrate, or demonstrate professional practices. The needs of practice generally move much faster than the research publication process. On the one hand, journals and books are likely to address the enduring aspects of learning and practice. Educators may need to search for, select, and analyze research in topic areas (adult learning, for example) before research in broader areas (like college curricula) can advance theoretically. On the other hand, the questions of a given faculty can be far in advance of resources on the cutting edge, and review of practice such as monitoring demonstration projects is an important step toward new discoveries and theory development. Actively engaging colleagues through their project reports, occasional papers, conference presentations, and participation in consortia serves to surface crucial knowledge that is emerging and often still primarily tacit within and across various contexts of practice. Analysis of in-house literature across institutions (for example, analyses of mission statements across campuses or enrollment statistics is a common strategy. When the topic is lasting learning, and studying it calls for framing studies in context, there are additional challenges.

Data Sources for Review of Practice

Review of the literature of practice has become a critical and essential means to inquiry about learning. As a source of testing ideas and evidence, it often goes hand in hand with collaborative inquiry into observed practice. Different conventions apply than to a review of the published literature of books and journals; sources are harder to find because they are more proprietary, and because practitioners "do" more than they often describe in writing. Review of practice carried out by practitioners is more easily attempted with documented data sources (for example, articulated educational assumptions, student performance patterns, edited videos of faculty interactions, faculty descriptions of programs).

We have conducted internal reviews of the Alverno literature of practice by analyzing faculty, staff, and administrative publications on the curriculum and college. We have generally confined our review of the external literature of practice to our collaborative, published work with consortia of institutions in which we have been members, where two- or three-day meetings or week-long workshops with campus representatives from the same institutions over a number of years are part of the activity. Reports are available because funding agencies require them. Because consortia are also fertile ground for consortium members to design and participate in collaborative inquiry, reports often contain syntheses of analyses of practice by individual members. These reports are the basis for integrating ideas about learning across diverse institutions. We provide observations and implications from findings and experiences in these consortia that we think are evidence based and justifiably transferable. We have analyzed published reports of the practices of five consortia of institutions (including Alverno) that have tested assumptions related to learning-centered education and have reported on those experiences. We have extended these ideas from consortia in which this college was not involved to broaden the guidelines for how transformation happens; these ideas are also based on public reports.

Limitations

Because this book focuses on integrating theory, research, and practice, it does not present an exhaustive review of the literature from the study of higher education. Further, extensive, observation-based implications from more on-site, systematic research at individual institutions by scholars of higher education are an essential part of review of practice. However, we cite only works that are directly applicable or are guides to a particular topic. Further, institutions often invite discipline-based researchers in to study educational cultures as "cases." Yet these studies should be balanced by the institutions themselves, where members mount analyses of their own culture. Although our experience with being studied as a case has been valuable (Darling-Hammond, 1997; Grant & Associates, 1979; Winter, McClelland, & Stewart, 1981), it nevertheless confirmed for us that such studies cannot substitute for self-directed inquiry by a college.

We did not review the literature of practice from the many individual colleges that are educating for learning that lasts and are also engaged in studies of student learning outcomes within their own institutions (see Banta & Associates, 1993; Banta, Lund, Black, & Oblander, 1996). Instead, we relied on consortia of institutions, which have become more common in higher education since the impact of assessment and restructuring movements. Limiting review of practice to literature by consortia rather than by individual institutions does not allow for naming the specific practices of individual institutions. If we do name an institution's specific practice, we cite publications that ground it. Visiting other institutions to learn or consult, or for benchmarking, is often a necessary part of review of practice. We do not report on our own such visits, however, because site-based observation or study of another campus was not our purpose. We rely only on reports authored by the consortia themselves.

Integrating Three Ways of Knowing About Learning

Given the limitations of each way of knowing, using multiple strategies from a range of paradigms is one means to enhance meaning because each strategy serves to increase rigor and confidence in conclusions. However, usability of inquiry and its consequences in practice remains a major criterion for judging validity and benefits. Thus, reporting findings and stimulating reflections on current theory, practice, and relevant literature in higher education are part of the knowledge base. And so formal research, collaborative inquiry, and review of literature and practice are joined in this book, integrating its parts. The fourth way of knowing, learning by educating, is a necessary condition for integrating the first three ways in order to foster learning that lasts. It provides the context for integrating theory, research, and practice toward that goal.

Learning by Educating as a Way of Knowing

Despite our continuing efforts to know about learning through formal research, collaborative inquiry, and review of literature and practice, educators know about learning primarily through educating day to day. Educators live with learning by educating in a college—a learning ecology. As educators reflect on and refine their particular practices, they have to figure out the relationship of their own ideas about education to their ideas about learning, while acknowledging that learning goes on all the time in settings other than formal education. We agree with Jarvis (1992) that learning and education are not the same and that education is narrower than learning.

In this sense, achieving coherence within the diversity of practice in each educational setting and mission requires a dynamic educational philosophy that undergirds an approach to learning. Clarifying this philosophy in an equally dynamic context of practice involves bringing to collective awareness the educational assumptions and learning principles that shape teaching, curriculum, and learning across a program and an institution. Making sense of practice interactively draws out the deepest and most useful understandings about learning. *Learning by educating* evokes and shapes formal research, review of literature and practice, and collaborative inquiry for the shared purposes of learning-centered education.

These ideas serve as an overarching premise for this book and suggest how and why educators benefit from the description of the educational assumptions and learning principles embedded in situated practice at another institution. But we have additional reasons for now turning some attention to our own practice. First, we intend to begin where educators begin: with what we know first-hand from learning by educating. Second, by beginning here, we can illustrate what we distinctly mean by this way of knowing—a way that calls for concrete as well as abstract understanding. Third, we are impressed by the epistemological reasons for doing this.

In higher education today, more and more educators are working out of the "second psychology" (Cole, 1996), which argues that meaning cannot be developed outside of context (Mishler, 1979). In a postpositivist tradition as well, learning "effects" are ambiguous without understanding the "treatment" or "intervention" (Campbell & Stanley, 1963). From a critical theory perspective, historical and social contexts heavily influence what can be known (Popkewitz, 1998). In the light of all three traditions, readers cannot hope to make individual, evidence-based judgments without some understanding of the culture in which this work was created, who created it, and the nature of the intervening learning experiences. These traditions extend to describing—at least in outline form—Alverno College as a culture and as an educational program.

The distinction between a focus on learning and one on education may be overlooked, impeding understanding of different practices. Alverno's faculty gradually distinguished education from learning by clarifying their educational philosophy and articulating their knowing about education as assumptions. By continually making educational assumptions explicit, they expected to refine their educational program. In the process, they became committed to the idea that their educational assumptions required them to engage in a sustained study of learning: what it is, what it means in terms of student learning outcomes, and how it is to be effected by practice. For them, the fourth way of knowing links educational assumptions with an educational program and shapes what to study.

Table 2.1 illustrates how assumptions about education (column 2), when made explicit and compared to prior assumptions that need to be rethought or unlearned (column 1), can organize both a learning-centered educational program (column 3) and ideas for what to study (column 4). Both the questions about learning that lasts and assumptions about education ground how to study learning. Each of these critical connections can also serve as a context for interpreting learning that lasts and for thinking through learning principles that can frame teaching and curriculum.

Table 2.1. Mapping Relationships of Educational Assumptions, Educational Program Elements, and Studies of Learning.

Prior Assumptions to Be Unlearned/Expanded	Educational Assumptions[a]	Educational Program Organized as Frameworks for Learning[b]	What to Study About Learning
Education is primarily a matter of understanding information or constructing new knowledge: Students learn to know first and then to do.	Education goes beyond knowing to being able to do what one knows.	Learning experiences are organized as frameworks for learning.	Study learning, development, and performance during and after college; study forms of integration in personal, professional, and civic life with integrated inquiry methods.
Educators are responsible mostly for exposing students to new ideas and for delivery of instruction.	Educators are responsible for making learning more available to the learner by articulating expected learning outcomes and making them public.	Ability-based learning is focused on student learning outcomes.	Study learning outcomes in relation to progress in the curriculum, learner's experience, and prior learning.
Learning about the specialized content and practicing the expertise of the discipline or profession ensures developed abilities.	Abilities and disciplines are an integrated framework for learning.	Individual abilities are frameworks for learning. Learning is integrated in a liberal arts approach to the professions. Abilities integrated with disciplines, interdisciplinary areas of study, and professions are a framework for learning.	Study student learning outcomes in the context of general education and the major.
Faculty test and grade student work in order to credential students in subject-matter standards and to predict their later effectiveness; faculty judgments are sufficient for student improvement.	Assessment is integral to learning.	Student assessment is a framework for learning by the individual student.	Study self-reflection and self assessment.

Education should primarily develop intellectual abilities.	Education should develop the whole person: mind, heart, and spirit.	Educating for learning-to-learn, maturity, and service is a framework for learning that integrates the college experience.	Study growth within a learning community.
Students learn in the ways that faculty teach and assess. Students are similar in motivation, ways they learn, and personal development.	Educators are responsible for providing multiple opportunities for students to develop and assess their learning in varied ways and contexts. Individuals differ widely in motivation, learning styles, personal development, and ways of performing.	Multiple and diverse learning and assessment strategies and environments expand ways of student learning and respect and respond to individual differences.	Study what makes for independent, self-sustained, purposeful learning. Study socially constructed/collaborative learning. Study interactions among individual differences, educational experiences, and learning outcomes.
Students should learn what faculty have learned.	Abilities must be carefully identified in relation to what contemporary life requires.	Abilities defined through developmental performance criteria reflect performance standards.	Study the continuing development of abilities inferred from performance. Study "ineffable" learning outcomes across time in relation to curriculum and college culture.
Students have developed their value frameworks by the time they reach college. Students' study in the liberal arts or professions leads to personal and professional responsibility.	Educators are responsible for providing opportunities for students to integrate their own value frameworks with those of the liberal arts, the professions, and education.		Study changing perspectives on educator roles.
The goal of teaching is exposing students to what they ought to learn.	The goal of teaching is student learning.		

Table 2.1. Mapping Relationships of Educational Assumptions, Educational Program Elements, and Studies of Learning, cont'd.

Prior Assumptions to Be Unlearned/Expanded	Educational Assumptions[a]	Educational Program Organized as Frameworks for Learning[b]	What to Study About Learning
The goal of inquiry on teaching, learning, and assessment is educator learning.	The goal of inquiry on teaching, learning, and assessment is educator and student learning.		Study educators' learning in relation to that of students.
A curriculum is a collection of courses that maximize diversity of perspective where students achieve credits and grades that reflect progressive levels of achievement of subject matter standards.	A curriculum maximizes coherence within diversity. It maximizes each student's development and requires each student to meet standards. Developing a curriculum calls for educator investment in a community of learning and judgment.		Study elements of a curriculum in relation to diverse and integrative learning outcomes, those required for graduation and expected but not required. Study individual and aggregate patterns.
The goals of an institution of higher education are teaching, research, and service: when faculty independently carry out these activities, they have met their responsibilities to the institution.	One goal of a learning community is constantly learning, continuously improving, and transforming. Individuals act in independent and interdependent ways.		Study institutional connections and decisions for transformative acts.

[a]Adapted from Alverno College Faculty (1979/1994); Consortium for the Improvement of Teaching, Learning and Assessment (1992); Loacker (1991); Mentkowski (1998); Riordan (1993).

[b]Alverno College Faculty (1973/1996). See Appendix A.

Knowing About Education: Assumptions

Among all the Alverno faculty's assumptions that undergird the educational program at this college, the following have been instrumental in shaping how they define a college degree, refining the idea that learning that lasts is a desired outcome of education, shaping a curriculum, and deciding what and how to study learning. Articulating these assumptions meant rethinking prior ones. (These are compared in Table 2.1, columns 1 and 2.)

• *Education goes beyond knowing to being able to do what one knows.* Students should be able to link knowing and doing in ways that enable effective performance and contribution. A student's learning outcomes, situated in college, should transfer, that is, enable effective performance and valued contribution in novel settings and emerging roles in a range of potential contexts. Inherent in this assumption is the concept that learning outcomes are abilities that students develop in order to use the knowledge they have constructed.

• *Educators are responsible for making learning more available to the learner by articulating expected learning outcomes and making them public.* Establishing clearly identified learning outcomes at the institutional, program or department, and course level is essential for students' learning. Expected learning outcomes should be determined and continually refined for coherence within diversity, breadth and depth across areas of study, and within a developmental curriculum that holds students to standards. Clarifying outcomes creates multiple points of entry into the learning process for varied learners at varied levels. Because these outcomes serve as a profile of the liberally educated person, faculty see the abilities as multidimensional, cumulative, and integrated; as having affective or emotional as well as cognitive or intellectual components; as open to further development; and as transferable to new experiences.

• *Abilities and disciplines are an integrated framework for learning.* Abilities as learning outcomes aid learning in the disciplines and professions and from experience. A learner benefits from the development of abilities integrated with subject matter and experience when those abilities inform and connect teaching, learning, and assessment and are supported by a coherent educational system that reinforces the integration of abilities and disciplines across a curriculum.

• *Assessment is integral to learning.* The assumption that assessment is integral to learning contributes significantly to each student's continued learning. Faculty define student assessment as a multidimensional process that is integral to learning, which involves observing performances of an individual learner in action and judging them on the basis of public criteria that are developmental, with resulting feedback to that learner—in effect, performance assessment. Faculty define the ability to judge one's own work—self assessment—as integral to the student assessment process.

• *Education should develop the whole person: mind, heart, and spirit.* Identity as a learner, performer, and person is integral to learning. Liberal arts, professions education, and values education should be integrated.

• *Educators are responsible for providing multiple opportunities for students to develop and assess their learning in varied ways and contexts.* Individuals differ in prior learning, motivation, learning styles, personal development, and ways of performing. Multiple and diverse learning and assessment strategies expand ways of student learning.

• *Abilities must be carefully identified in relation to what contemporary life requires.* Because abilities are complex and multidimensional, curriculum-defined abilities are integrated in performance in multiple modes and various contexts.

• *Educators are responsible for providing opportunities for students to integrate value frameworks from the liberal arts, the professions, and education.* Learning strategies that are focused on integration of value frameworks provide ways for learners to understand the mutual influence of each on the others.

Knowing About Teaching: Assumptions

The assumptions about education have analogous implications for how teachers see their work and how teaching is defined. Teachers' expertise has often been defined by special, advanced knowledge in a discipline and its applications in courses and curriculum. A more elaborated and explicit concern for learning means particular shifts in that construction. Teaching becomes a matter of multidisciplinary expertise, including the analytic ability to relate course and program content to the individual differences among learners, collaborate with others across departments in developing teaching and learning experiences in a coherent, developmental curriculum, and sustain ongoing inquiry into the entire educational program. Teaching itself becomes an integration of theoretical frameworks across disciplines and of pedagogical practices specific to and general across fields. The scholarship of teaching and learning blends demonstration, evaluation, illumination, and discovery. When such an integrated practice is carried out in a collaborative and interactive context within a department or campus, teaching, like learning, can become a topic of public discussion and a source of questions.

These questions do not lend themselves to easy and final answers, for example, "What have we learned about the meaning of teaching and our identity as educators?" Nevertheless, Alverno and other faculty agree on some convictions about partial answers, and these inform their practice as educators (Riordan, 1993; Consortium for the Improvement of Teaching, Learning and Assessment, 1992). This reflection has led, in turn, to four additional assumptions with comparisons to prior ones (see Table 2.1, columns 1 and 2):

• *The goal of teaching is student learning.* The process of teaching involves organizing one's courses, the curriculum, and the broader institution to foster active and interactive student learning. Teaching is a scholarly activity that requires rigorous and dynamic discourse about its nature and practice. Disciplines are frameworks for student learning.

• *The goal of inquiry on teaching, learning, and assessment is educator and student learning.* Educator learning is evident in student learning. Contextually useful results have general implications for current and future learners and educators in various settings.

• *A curriculum maximizes coherence within diversity. It maximizes each student's development and requires each student to meet standards. Developing a curriculum calls for educator investment in a community of learning and judgment.* The process of implementation and institutionalization of a curriculum is as important as the curriculum itself. The process is dynamic, iterative, evaluative, and continuous.

• *One goal of a learning community and institution is constantly learning, continuously improving and transforming.* Educators pursue a collaborative and interactive practice that values the freedom to inquire and advance learning. When educators claim that a college

connects education with work, parenting and family responsibilities, and citizenship in a demonstrable way, then institutional effectiveness is grounded in the performance of graduates and its
link to excellent teaching.

Knowing About Learning: Learning and Action Principles

For educators, a faculty's educational assumptions are tied up with
assumptions about learning. The connection between education
and learning led Alverno faculty to identify their educational program as learning centered. Shared assumptions about learning include the conviction that learning is a student-centered, active
process and that learning is experience based. The outcomes of
the learning process are lifelong abilities that are teachable and
transferable.

The more that faculty dealt with their assumptions by implementing an entire educational program, the more they worked together to refine assumptions as more focused principles. Thus,
over a decades-long inquiry, learning principles became a conceptual framework for understanding the relationships between
student learning and educator action. Faculty drew on models of
learning from a range of sources and arrived at a set of definitions
of learning that could serve justifiably as principles and would have
implications for program design. For example, faculty worked together to construct the following learning and action principles
for assessment design:

1. If learning is to be integrative and experiential, assessment
   must judge performance. . . .
2. If learning is to be characterized by self-awareness, assessment
   must include expected outcomes, explicit public criteria, and
   student self assessment. . . .
3. If learning is to be active and interactive, assessment must
   include feedback and external perspectives as well as
   performance. . . .
4. If learning is to be developmental, assessment must be cumulative and expansive. . . .
5. If learning is to be transferable, assessment must be multiple
   in mode and context. [Alverno College Faculty, 1979/1994,
   pp. 17–19]

These principles were developed early in the program, based on educators' experience with learning. They have been a sustaining and dynamic framework.

Refining learning principles is a constant task in learning-centered programs at many campuses (American Association for Higher Education, American College Personnel Association, & National Association of Student Personnel Administrators, 1998). For example, Alverno faculty early on determined that learning is integrative and experiential, characterized by self-awareness, active and interactive, developmental, and transferable, and they built curricular learning processes around these terms. However, in implementation and through extended review, they challenged their own understanding of learning (Cromwell, 1993; Doherty, Mentkowski, & Conrad, 1978; Grantz & Thanos, 1996; Hutchings & Wutzdorff, 1988). For example, they found learning as integrative to be puzzling because there were so many aspects to integration (Doherty et al., 1997; Mentkowski, 1988); and so they had to probe each aspect in more depth. From the start, faculty had defined learning as developmental with an emphasis on the student as an individual learner. Over the years, faculty probed the kinds of transitions that enable progress in the curriculum by analyzing patterns of student achievement. This led to a greater understanding of how to build curriculum around progressive outcomes for different abilities and how to integrate these with various and changing developmental needs, stages, and styles of different learners. These integrations led to more carefully honed performance standards or criteria for beginning, intermediate, and advanced students and ways to assist students to develop their own criteria. Faculty and staff studies suggested additional concerns as well. For example, they saw that the theoretical tension between learning as situated that has emerged from cognitive science and has confronted the long-held notion of learning as transferable had to be better understood. As part of rethinking the learning-to-teaching connection, faculty and staff extended these learning principles to integrate different voices, sources of ideas and evidence, and contexts of practice. Thus, we include emerging ideas in the revised— and somewhat overlapping—principles that have become one form of Alverno's educational theory of learning that lasts (see Chapter Seven).

Learning-Centered Educational Program Elements at Alverno College

Assumptions and principles are realized in an educational program. Undergirding both assumptions and program elements are educational value frameworks that fundamentally affect how transportable these assumptions and principles might be to another learning culture or institutional mission. Several educational value frameworks are a foundation for education and learning at Alverno: "all students can learn and each deserves an education," "educators and students are partners in learning," and "colleges lead and serve students and society." A key implication is that an educational program should be learning centered—for example, that learning experiences should be organized as frameworks for learning. Another is that education should be affordable, so that access is not limited by the learner's ability either to study or to earn an education by themselves alone. In Table 2.1, educational program elements (column 3) rest beside educational assumptions (column 2).

Mission and Aims

The broadest program element is the mission and aims of a college. Alverno College has existed for this purpose: "to assist women of all ages and a variety of backgrounds to learn and develop personally and professionally so that they will be productive in a continually changing work environment and be prepared to assume responsibilities supportive of a more beneficent society. To assure that this purpose is fulfilled, the college has continued to transform itself . . . continually reconceptualizing and reorganizing itself to enhance the learning of its students" (Alverno College Office of Academic Affairs, 1997a, p. 2).

One implication of this mission and aims is that an entire educational program should be designed to foster learning. Another is that the term *educators* includes faculty, administrators, and professional academic and student services staff who see themselves as partners in learning, including the view that all personnel across the college are partners in the effort (Alverno College Office of Academic Affairs, 1997b). (Appendix A contains program specifics.)

Learning as Ability Based and Focused on Student Learning Outcomes

The educational program designed by Alverno faculty is ability based and is focused on rigorously assessed student outcomes, integrated into a liberal arts approach to the professions. To earn an Alverno degree a student demonstrates eight broad abilities, at increasingly complex levels, in general education and in the student's areas of specialty:

- Communication (reading, writing, speaking, listening; visual, quantitative, and technological literacy)
- Analysis
- Problem Solving
- Valuing in Decision-Making
- Social Interaction
- Global Perspectives
- Effective Citizenship
- Aesthetic Responsiveness

Realizing that disciplines provide distinctive contexts for the development and demonstration of abilities, the faculty designed a general framework of six developmental levels (see Appendix A). The framework provides a guide to ensure levels of comparability across discipline and interdisciplinary areas—the settings in which students develop and demonstrate their abilities. The framework is used by faculty to design courses and other learning experiences and to create criteria for assessing and evaluating student performance. (The framework is more fully described in Alverno College Educators, 1977/1998; Alverno College Faculty, 1976/1992, 1979/1994.)

Learning as Integrated in a Liberal Arts Approach to the Professions

The eight abilities at the center of Alverno's educational program have been the classic expectations of a sound liberal arts education, and Alverno has organized its curriculum to ensure that students acquire them. Every course—humanities, fine arts, natural sciences, mathematics, behavioral sciences—has been structured to help students practice and advance in one or more of these abilities as a framework for their mastering of the required subject matter. For students and faculty, the development of these abilities is the backbone of learning at Alverno. They form Alverno's general education curriculum, a structural framework that helps students integrate their learning and faculty integrate their teaching. When students make the transition to their major field, they expect to find frameworks in that discipline that will help to organize and make sense of the data and experiences they encounter. They hear their major described in terms of these abilities in language more specific to the field. When students begin advanced studies, this strong liberal arts base is designed to enable them to move beyond the immediacies of their studies. Within each major, students continue to develop the required broad abilities redefined by faculty in the disciplines and professions (Alverno College Education Faculty, 1996; Alverno College History Faculty, 1994; Alverno College Mathematics Faculty, 1999; Alverno College Nursing Faculty, 1999; Alverno College Professional Communication Faculty, 1999; Alverno College Psychology Faculty, 1995; Alverno College Religious Studies Faculty, 1997; Alverno College Social Science Faculty, 1998).

Learning as a Framework for Student Assessment

Alverno's assessment program is an integral part of this curriculum—as much a part of the learning process as it is a part of the evaluation process. To help students and faculty judge progress in student development of the eight abilities and comprehension of subject matter, faculty designed an assessment approach that differs from traditional testing and grading: it determines not just what a student knows but also how well she can evoke and use that knowledge in a variety of situations. It also requires evaluation of strengths and weaknesses by both faculty and student through observation, judgment, and feedback in relation to explicit criteria. Students receive evaluative statements of achievement rather than traditional letter grades. Periodically throughout their educational program, students are also assessed by professionals from the Milwaukee community who have been trained by Alverno faculty to assess students in several key abilities or to provide co-assessment in their major area of study (Alverno College Faculty 1979/1994). This approach to assessment became key to continually transforming the way faculty defined student learning, created effective teaching approaches, and designed program and institutional assessment (Loacker & Mentkowski, 1993). It also became key to studying learning.

Learning as a Framework for Educating Toward Maturity and Service

Alverno educators' ultimate goal is the development of each student as an educated, mature adult with such personal characteristics as a sense of responsibility for her own learning and the ability and desire to continue learning independently; self-knowledge and the ability to assess her own performance critically and with balance; and an understanding of how to apply her knowledge and abilities in many different contexts. In addition to the eight abilities required for graduation, there are others that faculty expect all students will develop to varied degrees. These include the faculty-identified performance characteristics of integration, independence, creativity, awareness of capability, commitment, and habituality. Other abilities include those expected of a liberally educated person prepared for lifelong development that is professional and civic as well as personal: learning how to learn, self assessment, cooperation and collaboration in community activity (academic, civic, professional), understanding oneself in relation to the world of work and civic duty, and understanding oneself in a multicultural context (Alverno College Faculty, 1979/1994, p. 87).

Limitations

Articulating educational assumptions, faculty-defined learning outcomes, and sketching program elements are only a part of knowing about education in any setting. They do offer an opportunity to see differences in perspective and thus another basis for comparison. Here, we communicate the context of this work by describing its more transportable aspects. However, these broad statements cannot substitute for either diversity and nuances in faculty and staff perspectives or the narrative form that teachers and students use to describe their learning by educating. Assumptions cannot substitute for observing or experiencing a program in action.

Learning by educating must include how and why a curriculum and learning culture evolved.

Integrating Four Ways of Knowing About Learning

The evidence base for *Learning That Lasts* is grounded in a scholarship of connection and engagement with communities of scholars devoted to inquiry about teaching and learning. This commitment as inquirers intersects with a commitment as educators, evidenced by the fact that these studies have taken place in a specific setting but also across contexts of practice in consortia. A faculty needs to articulate their assumptions about education as they emerge in their own educational culture. By connecting assumptions to what and how to study learning, they test these assumptions themselves and allow for comparisons to sources of ideas and evidence that are external to a particular college. In this way, ideas and evidence emerge from various contexts of practice, of which each can serve as an applied laboratory or ethnographic field situation.

Finally, we think a book that is most useful for educators who are transforming teaching and learning is likely to be both informative about new knowledge and reflective of educational assumptions and commitments. The challenge is to give explicit recognition to each of these functions. So *Learning That Lasts* is also intended as an informative, descriptive study of the processes of student learning, development, and performance within a particular college culture and learning context and of the causal relationships among these elements and their postcollege expression. It extends participation beyond Alverno students in some instances, and beyond the Alverno campus to various settings that graduates experience after graduation. The integration of the four ways of knowing requires that each draws on multiple theoretical frameworks and external comparisons of broad interest to the higher education community. Such an integrated inquiry also factors in critique from long-standing colleagues external to an institution, and analyses of practice from consortia of institutions. The processes revealed inform and broaden understanding of how to approach common tasks and fundamental issues in learning and learning-centered education.

Part Two

Exploring Learning in College and Beyond

Part Two answers the question, "What is learning that lasts?" by elaborating our explorations of student as learner (Chapter Three), learner as developing person (Chapter Four), and graduate as performer and contributor (Chapter Five). In doing so, we develop a picture of the learner over time that educators can use to open up what learners can achieve. In each chapter, we seek to communicate broad and new understandings and to ground our inquiry in stances and methods rooted in traditions of scholarship. Each chapter is a substantive and in-depth program of study, distinct and contrasting. Yet each is connected as well to the others through the longitudinal sample of learners who participated over a ten-year time span. For example, the social constructionist and qualitative perspective of Chapter Three contrasts with the developmental and measurement perspective of Chapter Four, and yet each is informed by the other because the same participants contributed. The picture of effective performance and its antecedents in Chapter Five rests on theory and measurement of competence of the same students at work as alumnae.

Part Two provides a comprehensive look at the meaning of student learning and opens up our understanding of the magnitude of unrealized human potential. We begin by probing how students construct meaning out of their education, listening to their voices, and end by questioning how graduates sustain college learning, enacting it in their lives. Throughout, these concerns are joined with an analysis of the individual's integration and the supportive features of curriculum and college culture. Learning so constructed is a basis for reconsidering the meaning of the undergraduate degree.

Chapter Three

Student as Learner

The cultural ethos and formal curricula of educational institutions shape the ways that students think, feel, and relate to others; students, for their part, exert a reciprocal influence. Educators are engaging increasingly diverse student populations, changing the nature of education itself. Students possess unique knowledge of their learning environments and learning experiences. We begin with students' voices—some younger, some older, many first-generation college students—because we believe education should center on student learning. We have used in-depth, confidential, longitudinal interviews for studying students' perspectives on their learning to see what meaning it has for them and how they experience an ability-based curriculum and learning-centered education.

This chapter shows how a college curriculum can have a lasting influence on how students construct their learning, development, and performance during and after college. We have inquired into whether and how students and graduates use curricular concepts, values, and practices in their everyday life, interviewing them at the end of each year in the curriculum and then later as alumnae. To what extent do these take on personal meaning for the students and become part of their conceptual resources for interpreting and acting across a range of events and contexts? Do they become an intrinsic part of a student's social and intellectual growth, and persist after college in personal and professional development? We found that many students began college with expectations that faculty would tell them what they needed to learn and memorize for examinations. In the beginning, they often struggled, but the majority later sensed a transformation in themselves, in how they now owned their unique ways of learning and had forged a deeper understanding of themselves and others.

Social Learning and Complex Abilities

Emerging theories of learning are providing new ways of understanding how students develop. In this chapter, we take a contextualist and social constructionist perspective, viewing development as a progressive patterning that occurs across time in a particular context. Cognitive organization, personal experience, values, and action skills have their most crucial origin and development in group patterns, which the person learns through interaction with others. Even interoceptive, or self-reflective, skills can be conceptualized as socially taught and learned practices (Harré, 1995; Bloor, 1983). Constructionist perspectives propose that learning and experience are the outcome of patterns constituted or constructed by interaction communities (Cole, 1977; D'Andrade, 1981). The social context of learning involves interaction with other persons and the sharing of a common language, a system of terms or categories, and a context of social practices in which those terms are understood.

Social constructionist and contextualist views emphasize learning and cognition as action embedded in social systems, where shared language and practices shape development. These perspectives are congruent with what Jerome Bruner (1990) and others call the "second cognitive revolution," with its emphasis on individuals as purposive agents who—in organizing meaning, experience, and actions—"trade" in conceptions of experience and performance formed by their culture. The theoretical perspective of this chapter contrasts sharply with approaches that suggest universal stagelike sequences of development. Nonetheless, we have used our awareness of some of the descriptions of contextually sensitive developmental theorists, such as Perry (1970), to gain insight into culturally normative expressions of "mature" behavior.

An individual's intellectual and personal functioning can be seen as complex, integrated patterns of abilities that include knowledge, capabilities, cognitive and social processes, perceptions and attitudes, and values. In this chapter, we examine these developmental patterns at Alverno College and ask if and how they might be traced back to influences of the college's curriculum and culture. Does students' progressive engagement with the conceptual structures and language of the educational social system reveal itself in their continuing symbolic construction of themselves and their learning?

Samples and Methods for the Perspectives Studies

This chapter synthesizes findings from a series of longitudinal studies into student perspectives on their learning, drawing in particular on an extensive meta-analysis (Mentkowski, Much, Kleinman, & Reisetter Hart, 1998). These studies thematically analyzed 308 of 479 Perspectives Interviews from one hundred students and alumnae. The studies were completed between 1982 and 1998 by various researchers, although there has been considerable continuity in the research team (see Appendix B). The meta-analysis focused on the themes that emerged with strongest emphasis and that were substantiated across the studies. This meta-analysis operated at both the level of identifying themes replicated across studies and a secondary analysis of the excerpts from the one hundred students and alumnae. The secondary analysis was an iterative process of validating themes, developing new ones, and consolidating what could be learned from the full range of interviews.

Perspective Interviews

Trained interviewers, who were not teaching faculty, asked students, in open-ended confidential interviews of one to three hours, to narrate their experiences of learning and development in college (Mentkowski & Much, 1980). The interview included relatively generic questions, such as, "What do you think the ideal Alverno student should be like in order to get the most out of her learning experience?" with follow-up questions: "Are students here really like that?" [If yes] "Why are they like that?" Other questions were more direct, such as, "How would you describe the rationale for the Alverno learning process?" The alumna Perspectives Interview (Mentkowski & Much, 1980/1985) paralleled the student interview, with questions redesigned to reflect later experiences in the community, workforce, and family. The purpose of the interviews was to follow the course of learning and development through college from the point of view of the student's own descriptions. Alumnae, either two or five years after college, were asked to speak about their continued learning and development and to draw relationships between their recent learning experiences and antecedents in college education. As researchers, we established relationships with participants that account, to a degree, for their participation (83 percent to 99 percent across assessments) over a ten-year period and for the quality of the interviews (Reisetter & Sandoval, 1987).

One major framework for these qualitative analyses was iterative reading and thematic analysis of the transcribed interviews, taking chunks of texts—typically a paragraph or more—and identifying emerging themes about learning, abilities, and growth, gradually building and verifying interpretations. In addition, the analyses examined how the eight curriculum abilities were understood and used. We cannot report frequencies for most of the patterns, but we often do, more impressionistically, report estimates, such as "some" or "many." Even here, we have to be delicate in our reporting because "a little" can mean "a lot" when some topic was not directly elicited by the interview, and "a lot" can mean "a little" when it was.

Samples

Sample sizes vary according to particular analyses. (Appendix B displays the sample composition of the individual studies consolidated into this meta-analysis.) Our focus in this chapter is on patterns of development across years rather than longitudinal case studies. Among students, there were also some demographic factors that may have affected patterns of learning and development, though we have not systematically analyzed the influence of these factors for the interview sample. Many of the students in the sample came from family backgrounds that could be described as socially conservative with respect to gender roles and family roles. For example, sometimes participants noted that in their families, children (especially daughters) were not supposed to contradict, question, or argue with fathers. In such environments, there would often have been little or no family interest in discussing a girl's career beyond a job that was understood to be secondary to marriage and family life. At the time of the study, over 90 percent of the women in this college were Caucasian, which contrasts with Alverno's current minority enrollment of over one-third.

When the interview studies began, Alverno College had just created a parallel time frame for completing a bachelor's degree in four years. It differed from the established weekday time frame primarily in that the curriculum was offered in classes that met every other weekend. The purpose was to accommodate the increasing numbers of older women who wanted to return to school and needed to continue full-time jobs or coordinate their education with combined responsibilities for jobs and family life. Women in the weekend time frame represented a somewhat different population from those who entered directly from high school. The older women had a greater variety of life experiences and more responsibilities than younger students; these may have been the more likely influences on some of the different patterns we observed.

The majority of the studies focused on women who attended this college in the weekday time frame, which was more likely to attract recently graduated high school students. Much and Mentkowski (1984) report on one of the most comprehensive analyses of the student years ($n = 47$), which focused exclusively on women who entered directly from high school, at age seventeen or eighteen. Mentkowski, Much, et al. (1998) included older students and alumnae who attended college in the weekend time frame ($n = 13$), and Deemer (1993) studied alumnae from both the weekday and weekend time frame who entered college either directly from high school ($n = 17$) or as adult learners ($n = 8$). Several studies (see Appendix B) focused on a weekday sample of graduating seniors and two-year alumnae ($n = 32$), some of whom entered as older adult students ($n = 7$). Rather than continuing to refer to weekday versus weekend time frames, we describe students by their age—as *younger adults, direct from high school* or as *older, more experienced, adult learners* (ages twenty-three to fifty-five)—but it should be kept in mind that age overlaps with program time frame.

The Learning Environment: Organizational Culture and Learning

The social context of learning might be described as a local culture. D'Andrade (1981, 1984, 1990) suggests that culture can be thought of as learned and shared systems of meaning, communicated primarily by natural language. Such meanings not only include representations of what is in the world, but also concurring ways of acting and feeling. A college may be considered a social organization in the same way that a corporation or any other goal-directed group might be. Every organization has its own (local) culture, which is a subculture existing within and drawing from the broader fields of the encompassing culture. Each will emphasize certain elements of the broader culture and subdue others (Much, 1995).

One aspect of an organizational culture is its historical identity as an ongoing yet changing social entity. Another is the purposeful features of the culture, which come from the social goals and practices that members of the organization hold consciously, discuss, and cultivate. This is the social, intellectual, and communicative order that the organization strives to be. In most colleges, these purposeful features include curriculum design, instructional methods, and related conceptualizations of mission. Another aspect is the set of incidental features of an organizational culture—that is, those that are unplanned and perhaps unforeseen. Dorothy Holland and Margaret Eisenhart (1990) found, for example, that many students focus more on relations with the opposite sex than on the educational goals promoted by an institution. This chapter primarily focuses on how students and alumnae represent the curriculum and other purposeful features of the organizational culture rather than the historical or incidental aspects of that culture.

Emergent Themes in Student and Alumna Learning

We identified six major themes in the student and alumna perspectives: (1) developing conceptual abilities, (2) developing interpersonal abilities, (3) experiential validation of curriculum and experiential learning, (4) developing skills for independent and social learning, (5) identity development as a learner and professional, and (6) perspectives on the college as a social environment. A general finding was that alumnae continued to use conceptual models of learning and performance learned in the curriculum. Students and alumnae identified several key features of the curriculum that supported their learning, including the student assessment process (with its focus on performance, self assessment, and feedback), experiential learning, classroom discussion, work in groups, and the curriculum's conceptualization of abilities. From the curriculum and the culture of the college, students developed interpersonal abilities and an interpersonal orientation toward learning that became central to how they learned as alumnae. The skills of analysis, systematic problem solving, and communication were just as important from the student or alumna point of view. We also found that the abilities in the curriculum often became integrated (for example, Problem Solving and Social Interaction) as metacognitive strategies for performing.

Developing Conceptual Abilities

Alverno's curriculum abilities can be viewed in many ways; students and alumnae may view them quite differently from the way faculty and program designers do, and observers may view them differently still. In broad perspective, these curriculum abilities can be viewed as embodying a condensed theory of knowledge and learning—an applied epistemology. They are prescriptive rather than merely descriptive; that is, they concern both what higher learning is and what it should be.

Abilities as Theory of Knowledge and Performance

Among the student's first challenges is to establish a working knowledge of the ability-based program: mastering its specialized language of learning, identifying its elements and categories, and seeing the relationships among them. In effect, students face the task of beginning to grasp the reasoning and action schemas represented by the curriculum abilities and understanding how each is related to the others. This ultimately means grasping them as an overarching integrated conceptual system, encompassing assumptions about how people learn, what they learn, and what the outcomes of learning should be.

We found that some students progressed from a relatively strong conceptual or philosophical grasp of the program to putting this knowledge into practice. Other students seemed to proceed from accumulating experiences of success and insight and later grasping the overall meaning and rationale of ability-based learning. This latter kind of progression appeared to be more common for both students who had entered directly from high school and those who were adult learners (Mentkowski, Much, et al., 1998; Much & Mentkowski, 1984). Although the differing approaches were not mutually exclusive, individual students seemed to emphasize one or another when they described the processes by which they had reached higher levels of understanding. A third pathway to understanding, social communication, should not be overlooked or underestimated. It was apparent throughout the texts that students were systematically coached in the terminology of the curriculum ability models and their language of learning. They appeared to have been explicitly taught the Alverno theory of learning and the rationales for the Alverno learning process. As a result, some students developed the beginnings of a holistic view of the curriculum early on. For example, Jennifer, only a year out of high school, says:

> I think it's an attempt to help the student to recognize all phases of learning and all concepts of learning, not just to learn psychology for what it is, but to learn psychology and how it's related to analysis and problem solving and stuff like that. It kind of gives you more of a well-rounded education rather than just straightforward like many of the other schools offer. It was difficult to adjust to at first, but once I started realizing what the whole system meant and how you could apply a lot of the stuff, it made a lot of sense to me and I found it to be a very effective way of learning.

Nevertheless, many students initially struggled to understand the curriculum, and some found it problematic. In her first year, Lucile, an eighteen-year-old student, remembers "coming to orientation and just going, 'Someone tell me what's going on.' And it's just having to readapt into a different kind of environment, . . . thinking, 'Is this really for me? Am I going to be able to understand this ever? It's so complicated.'" Some entering students did not realize at first that they would be expected to analyze and draw relationships between concepts; instead, they thought that they would just be reading and memorizing content. Advanced students, looking back, recalled the challenges of learning the curriculum, saying that their understanding evolved.

For many younger students, the third year seemed to be a major turning point for beginning to integrate the curriculum abilities conceptually and understand how they were all used together. Students usually attributed this insight to characteristics of the curriculum, saying that the advanced-level abilities were more integrated than the beginning levels had been. They began to talk about these abilities as internalized resources. For example, Bernadine, at age twenty, says, "In a way a lot of what I've learned in the area of communicating with people and problem solving, interpersonal relationships, knowing myself and my values, all has become a part of me and helps in communicating with my friends and people in the community. I find these capabilities helpful."

Analysis, Problem Solving, and Valuing in Decision-Making as Conceptual Abilities

Students often associated their thinking, reasoning, and reflecting with Analysis, Problem Solving, and Valuing in Decision-Making, three of the eight abilities taught in the curriculum. For some time, however, students generally focused more on Social Interaction, Communication, and Valuing in Decision-Making than they did on Analysis or Problem Solving (Mentkowski, Much, et al., 1998). Another data source confirmed that these students came to this college initially preferring to learn through concrete experience relative to abstract conceptualization as measured by Kolb's Learning Style Inventory (1976). They then moved, in effect, toward greater balance as they gained appreciation for abstract learning. Longitudinal statistical analysis of the inventory by the population types (described in Chapter Four) suggested that students who came directly from high school showed relatively less gain in their appreciation for abstract conceptualization than did those who had delayed college or transferred to this college (see Appendix C).

Younger adults often consolidated their learning in the third year, commenting that they had begun to notice changes in their reasoning processes. In comparison to their more experienced peers, however, younger undergraduates seemed generally less articulate in describing the curriculum abilities, perhaps because they had more limited opportunities to experience their usefulness. Nonetheless, by their third year, they had opportunities to work in off-campus settings related to their field of study, using their learned abilities at work and observing the results. Some transferred this process to other settings in their lives. Three years after high school, at age twenty, Tanya says, "Talking to patients is different because of what we've learned here. Targeting what I say to people at work . . . taking situations that come up and being able to pull them apart analytically, carefully, objectively. I don't get into arguments or misunderstandings. [Before,] I was too subjective."

Alumnae also often highly valued and frequently used Analysis and Problem Solving skills in the work setting, as well as in personal decision making. For example, Megan says:

> I tend to be more analytical, and I don't take a lot of situations at face value. I try to dig a little deeper, and if something is happening in my department that I don't understand, I won't take the first solution that comes across my desk because I find that may not be the only solution or the best solution. I really go through that Problem Solving process of defining what the problem is, what information can I add to it, how can I analyze this, what kinds of solutions can I come up with and, then, make a decision based on the short- and long-term outcome of it.

We found examples outside the work setting too. Significant personal life decisions, along with those about career direction, particularly seemed to bring out reflection on values as an intellectual complement to thinking about issues and solving problems. Students and alumnae noticed how appreciation of the values and perspectives of others helped them solve problems; thinking about their values sometimes became a personal focus for integrating intellectual skills in the earlier years of college, for both the younger and older groups (Mentkowski, Much, et al., 1998).

Blending Conceptual and Interpersonal Abilities

Valuing in Decision-Making and Social Interaction abilities in the first two years seemed to support students in learning how to approach alternative perspectives—learning tolerance first and then beginning to appreciate the differing values of others. Students were sometimes reluctant to enter this kind of inquiry and dialogue or to expose their own values to the group. They seemed to learn better ways to engage the diverse views of their peers through classroom discussions, experiences, and group work, but sometimes contrasting beliefs resulted in discordant feelings for first- and second-year students. Students sometimes also described confronting alternative perspectives in the content of their liberal arts coursework, for example, in studying diverse ways of life.

As alumnae, many of these women seemed to have established a firm sense of their own values, bringing this self-understanding to their reflective analyses of new situations. Still, alumnae, especially recent graduates, sometimes had experiences of discordance all over again as they confronted different value systems in the workplace or the community after college. Even when they struggled with these emotionally charged challenges, they continued to use what they had learned in the curriculum about valuing and analytical processes as conceptual reference points for being sensitive to the presence of diverse value systems and feeling comfortable in their company.

It was notable that alumnae seemed to take for granted the unity and integration of the curriculum abilities (Deemer, 1993; Deemer & Mentkowski, 1990; Mentkowski, Much, & Giencke-Holl, 1983; Mentkowski, Much, et al., 1998). This was something that a sizable proportion of the younger adult students had struggled to understand (Much & Mentkowski, 1982, 1984). The postcollege experience apparently enhanced the chances for alumnae to realize how the models fit together in a unified approach. Perhaps it was that once they were on their own, they were compelled to use the models for self-guided learning and solving problems. This might also explain why older, more experienced students, who came to college with responsible positions in employment and other settings, seemed to have a head start over younger students.

Developing Interpersonal Abilities

Students and alumnae also often commented that they had gained greater mastery and control over their interpersonal communications as a result of their curricular learning. Near graduation, Connie says, "I would value Communication most, because I think an idea does no good unless you can communicate it to other people. I think the Communication ability is the root of all the other abilities." As an alumna, Wanda recollects, "We were taught in our more advanced communications classes . . . the awareness of how other people respond to your words and checking with them—perception checking." Others commented on other specific skills in oral or written communication. Students and alumnae also highly valued the skills in Social Interaction that they learned in the curriculum. Darlene expresses a common sentiment found in the interviews: "Social Interaction is very important. In order to get along in this world, you have got to be able to interact with other people, and you may be forced into a situation where you must interact with someone that you normally wouldn't cross the street to say hello to. And you have to learn how to interact with these people, and learn how to interact with them successfully. And that's important in the business world and in your own private life. It's extremely important."

Both students and alumnae provided insights about the development of their social skills. A few observed that critique in Social Interaction was adjusted to individual needs and facilitated the growth of self-confidence and social competence, as well as reflective thought. More generally, students felt they were brought into close contact with the ideas and opinions of their peers. They often talked about how they became aware of differing perspectives as a result of classroom activities or discussions. The student interviews suggested there was also an ongoing critique of interaction skills and strategies, but students also said there was a group atmosphere where they felt safe exposing their views and their questions. A safe atmosphere for exposing views needs to be contrasted with what in some settings may be a more typical kind of tacit agreement not to discuss or explore divergent views. For example, at another college, Carol Trosset (1998) found that students avoided discussions that might bring them into contact with perspectives with which they disagreed and tended to persevere in the belief that they had a right not to have their views challenged.

Collaborative Discussion and Work

Students and alumnae alike attributed the development of their interpersonal abilities to a range of curricular influences (Deemer, 1993; Mentkowski & Doherty, 1984b). They frequently recalled the high level of group interaction and collaborative work. They felt that they were expected to cooperate with, listen to, and respect others in their everyday classroom work. As an alumna, Arleen recollects that assignments were designed so that it was more efficient to form a group and work together: "There was no way in the world we could do it all, so we had to share it. We had to, 'You do this, and I'll do that and you do that,' to manage to get through, and the ones that didn't learn that real quick were the ones we lost along the way." Connie observes that not letting the group down was a powerful motivator for her studies, but some disliked group work because not all peers "pulled their own weight."

As students were educated in a model for interpersonal processes in group work, they practiced these skills in classroom discussions that were structured to encourage both participation and listening. Jennifer says, "There were quite a few classes where you would get in a circle and all be participating. You were part of the class, asking questions. Especially when you sit in a circle, you can see the others. I like to look at people when they're talking and see other people asking questions or making comments. You're part of it. It makes it more alive. I guess mostly it was like having a conversation with another person."

First- and second-year students were often impressed by their first exposures to group discussion of discrepant beliefs, feelings, and values. Important assumptions and beliefs, learned in the family and community environments, might be rethought in the context of alternatives presented by peers and instructors. Both the students and alumnae reported increased awareness and sensitivity to others as a result of education in values awareness and communication skills. Tina says, "It's been easier for me to have patience with people because at Alverno I learned that people have other ideas. Those things color their value system. Their value system colors their decisions. Their value system colors the way they react to other people too."

Students learned to commit to group as well as individualistic goals. Lea, as an alumna, says, "You have to be committed; otherwise the group doesn't go." As an alumna, Connie articulates how she thinks interpersonal abilities she learned are crucial for the workplace:

> Getting all these people together and trying to accomplish a goal together, we had to learn to solve problems within the group. We had to learn how to get along with the diverse personalities—how

to incorporate everyone's skills and how to include everyone and use our abilities to the maximum. And the group work stands out in my mind as being of the most benefit to me, because in any situation, in the working world especially, there are very few jobs where you're isolated. Even the computer programmer that sits and does specific programs has to take those programs out and has to give them to people and explain how they work and has to listen to people in order to find out what kind of program to write for the application. And so working with people in a group is essential to any activity in life.

Feedback as a Social Learning Process

The college culture appeared to affect the way feedback was given, received, and used. Students observed that feedback was given in such a way that they did not feel it was rejecting or discouraging or placing an unbalanced focus on negative aspects of performance. Instead, they experienced it as supportive criticism that reinforced the principles of effective interaction that they were learning. Students commented on feedback from instructors, outside assessors, and peers; indeed, students at every level mentioned the feedback process as an important support for learning and motivation.

In the first and second years, many students found that feedback was a major support to their understanding of the curriculum abilities. Advanced students sometimes mentioned that faculty feedback led to the confirmation of both their abilities and their self assessment capacities. Students observed that feedback procedures assisted them in forming accurate perceptions of their abilities and establishing internal standards with which to evaluate their own work. For some students, positive interactions with faculty or peers appeared to have been an important factor motivating achievement in the absence of grades. Students responded, as they told us, to their teachers' expectations and personal recognition.

Experiential Validation of Curriculum Abilities and Experiential Learning

The ability-based curriculum is predicated on the idea that learning takes place within action contexts. Students and alumnae identified what might be called experiential validation as one of the major supports to learning in the Alverno environment (Deemer, 1993; Much & Mentkowski, 1982, 1984). Experiential validation of the curriculum is essentially a student's observation that she has grown in some valued ability (or abilities) through her learning experiences.

Experiential Validation During College

Work situations often seemed to test and validate the curriculum's ability models, as well as the student's capacity to use them. The most common outcome of internships, field experiences, or concurrent employment was confirmation of both the models and the skills. As a result, students developed confidence in their own ability to make judgments and take action in a work setting. Most students grasped the curriculum learning process by pursuing what might be called an inductive or empiricist approach. Especially for less experienced students, the observation that "it works" preceded the conclusion that "it makes sense." Relationships that were not appreciated deductively—as a set of premises that should lead to given outcomes—were discovered as facts of experience in hindsight; this process sometimes continued well after graduation.

Communication and Social Interaction were prominent in initial experiential validation. The first change in themselves that both younger and older adult students often noticed was an increase in their social or public speaking skills (Mentkowski, Much, et al., 1998; Much & Mentkowski, 1982, 1984). For example, a number of students noticed an increased ability to interact with others—based on subjective feelings of social comfort, conversational ease, and comments from others—and took this as strong evidence for the value of the ability-based program. In the context of her concurrent experience in the workplace, Faye at age thirty-three talks about how her first year in college is changing the way she communicates: "I am more careful of what people are saying. I try to understand what they mean. That came from taking communication courses. I'm more careful of what I say—the words I use or the connotations. That is something I learned from going to school."

Experiential validation was ongoing through the college years and after (Deemer, 1993; Deemer & Mentkowski, 1990; Mentkowski, Much, & Giencke-Holl, 1983; Mentkowski, Much, et al., 1998; Much & Mentkowski, 1982, 1984). Students who entered

Alverno directly from high school sometimes seemed to have doubted the value of their work on the curriculum abilities, until they saw that these curricular models functioned well in off-campus preprofessional situations.

Reasoning skills and conceptual abilities were also noticed and mentioned, though somewhat less frequently, as sources of validation. Angela, a forty-year-old freshman, was aware of positive changes in her reading and comprehension. She felt these were a result of applying her skills in Analysis: "We would be working on something, and my whole perception would change as I was researching it. When you start looking at something and analyzing it, it often comes out much different." Near graduation, Sylvia compares her current experience with how she felt at age eighteen: "I was scared as a freshman . . . but now I can see why you had to do certain things, and I can see where I've improved in Problem Solving or Analysis or whatever. I realize that those skills are important in the real world. I was participating in a company trainee program, and we were given an assignment, a case analysis, which is exactly what we had been doing here." Even some of the younger students in their first two years thought they had benefited from Analysis and Problem Solving. In social situations, they might notice that they were thinking and reasoning well by comparison with peers, family members, and others. Sometimes family members or friends might comment on their developing abilities.

Conceptual Barriers to Experiential Validation During College

It was important for students to make a connection between the curriculum and real-world demands in some satisfactory way (Much & Mentkowski, 1982, 1984). Otherwise they might go through college feeling dissatisfied with assignments in the ability-based curriculum, wishing that they had been doing something more directly preparatory to their envisioned careers. Students sometimes discounted the importance of various kinds of skills and abilities to entry-level jobs in their fields. For example, a few nurses seemed to underestimate the importance of interpersonal interaction or problem-solving skills in their profession.

Heather, a young nursing student near graduation, directly questions the content of the curriculum in relation to what she thought she needed: "This year we haven't had more than two lectures worth our time. You get frustrated 'cause you're thinking you should be studying content for nursing boards this summer. They omit a lot of physiological parts and stress the psychosocial part. Yet in a clinical setting, the demands are knowing lab values and the physiological process going on in a person—knowing what interventions to make. What they teach you and what you're supposed to do are two different things."

In other cases, barriers appeared to be the result of noticing that their college education had not perfectly reflected everything about actual practice. Wilma comments, "All the instructors are teaching you one theory of how children learn. Once you go into that experience and you see that children don't learn that way, you start to question. 'Why isn't this instructor teaching me another model of learning; why does she think this model of learning is best for every student, when it's not?'" Whether these kinds of perceptions had some validity or not, they seemed for a noticeable minority of students to reflect a conceptual barrier to experiential validation of the curriculum.

Alumnae who did not make a firm connection between curriculum abilities and their work might be partially disillusioned with their education or disillusioned with the world outside college by comparison. For some advanced students, on-site preprofessional experience reassured them of the value of their learned skills. For a distinct minority, it resulted in a focus (at least temporarily) on the discrepancies between their education and what they thought they needed.

Experiential Learning as Support
for Experiential Validation

Experiential learning in action contexts supported validation of the curriculum abilities. As students progressed, their experiential learning became increasingly focused on opportunities to test out their curriculum abilities in meaningful work-related contexts (Much & Mentkowski, 1984). For a student who came directly from high school, opportunities to apply learning in an off-campus internship—clinical work, practice teaching, business internships, or fieldwork—enabled her to test the efficacy of the curriculum framework in a way that an older, more experienced student was able to do earlier because of the professional responsibilities she may have held. This is consistent with what we found on Kolb's Learning Style Inventory (1976). Students who came directly from high school were, compared to older adults, less likely to prefer to learn through active experimentation relative to reflective observation (cf. Kolb, 1984; Mentkowski & Giencke-Holl, 1982). This was statistically confirmed for two of three older adult groups: those who began college as a new life task or who transferred from another institution (cf. Ben-Ur, Rogers, Reisetter, & Mentkowski, 1987). Younger students may have tended to initially prefer reflective learning simply because they lacked experience with more active learning approaches in school.

Many of the twenty- or twenty-one-year-old students in their third year internships were continuously challenged, perhaps for the first time, to put things together on the spot and to think and act in ways that were situationally appropriate. This was perhaps the most strenuous test of the student's ability to think and act as a competent member of a work community. As a result of feedback and self assessment in this practice environment, she often assured herself that she would be able to fulfill postcollege work roles (Much & Mentkowski, 1982, 1984). Students nearly unanimously appreciated internship or field experiences. Longitudinal analysis (see Chapter Four) of Kolb's Learning Style Inventory confirmed that students generally increased in their preference for learning through active experimentation relative to reflective observation across the ten years of the study (see Appendix C).

Third-year students generally preferred experiential methods in the classroom as well. They had come to prefer practical and interpersonally oriented learning to traditional reading, writing, and paper-and-pencil testing methods if they considered them isolated from application. Julie Lynn, even as a second-year student at age nineteen, illustrates how one student came to appreciate peers as a support to learning:

> So I think I've learned a great deal through the other people—teachers, when they are helping me specifically, or other students, when you sit down and talk to them. Because you can learn a lot more. You can get a lot more perspective rather than just reading from a book. Because there are a million ways to look at some-

thing . . . so it's like you've got a nurse who is a teacher—she can give you experiential advice or views—and then you also have a lot of students who are mothers themselves, and you also have students who are sharing the common experiences. You can share them together and you're getting a lot more points of view rather than just sitting and not talking about what you are learning.

Darlene, an older student near graduation, expresses well the comparative advantage of entering college with real-world experience that could enable her to challenge the theory she found in books: "In our classes, we have experiences of a give-and-take type, where we can say, 'Now this management model that we're studying sounds terrific; however, as a student and working woman, I have seen that applied, and it doesn't always work that way.'" Faye, a freshman, says, "Before, college learning was more purely academic and not practical. This Alverno approach to learning is more of a practical approach, so that you can apply whatever you learn to the job or profession you choose." Alumnae extended this understanding of experiential learning as a continuous process—with the application, testing, and integration of abilities and theory in action—to include what we saw as an implicit expectation that they would, *of course,* be thinking and performing in context, adapting their stances and strategies as needed by the particular situation (cf. Mentkowski & Doherty, 1984a).

Experiential Validation After College

A particularly interesting observation was that experiential validation of the curriculum abilities appeared to have continued after college in family, community life, and, especially, the workplace, where sometimes it became stronger than it had been during college. Alumnae seemed to achieve insights that they had not grasped (by their own reports) during college. In particular, learned abilities to think through problems and effectively interact with others were even more appreciated after graduation. Alumnae talked about how what they learned about valuing, communication, and social interaction processes had given them an advantage over others in the workplace. This sometimes was true even for alumnae who began as older adult learners. For example, Sabrina observes, "We really didn't comprehend until later what they had really taught us. . . . We graduated with the personal tools that you need to go into any line of work, any occupation, any further schooling. And I see the difference between working with a group of people who have never had training in group process and with the women at Alverno. I see the difference in how smoothly it works."

Most often, alumnae appeared to try, within the limits of what they saw as possible, to hold to the ideals of interpersonal performance learned in the curriculum. A few said they had acceded to what they saw as the brute reality of the workplace; they might look back nostalgically at the social milieu they had enjoyed at the college and wish that the society of the workplace could be more like it. But even where the abilities did not give full or immediate interpersonal efficacy, alumnae seemed to view their interpersonal models as superior, continuing to use them as their own conceptual reference points, as a basis for improving interactions. In this way, their learned models for performance contributed to successful appraisal and resolutions of workplace (or other) situations.

Developing Skills for Independent and Social Learning

The development of independent learning means that the student has become able and more willing to take on personal responsibility for learning, that is, searches out, recognizes, and develops the means for his or her learning. Students who reported some trouble in the area of conceptualization of abstract relationships tended also to have some difficulty with increasing demands for independent learning. In the context of an ability-based curriculum, independent learning means that the abilities themselves become progressively internalized as resources that can be used to acquire knowledge and skill across many kinds of situations, as well as becoming standards that can be used to evaluate one's own performance (self assessment). Students highly valued self assessment and described it as a way to identify their strengths and weaknesses in relation to specific performances (cf. Marienau, 1999). The most important function of feedback was to help students learn to evaluate their own level of performance and focus their efforts to improve their skills.

Barriers to Conceptualizing
Independent Learning

A number of first- and second-year students who had entered college directly from high school expressed resentment, frustration, or ambivalence toward the expectation that they learn how to learn on their own. A first-year student had wanted to be told what to do; she seemed to have had intellectual difficulty taking initiative in her assignments. Jamie says, "I like situations where I am told exactly what to do. That's another thing I had a hard time getting used to here—that I'd say, 'How long should this be?' and they'd go, 'Well, as long as you feel is necessary.' 'Well, what's that: a paragraph or a page?' They give you criteria for what you have to do, but you're never sure if you are meeting them all. I live in fear of leaving one out." Some students initially seemed to misunderstand the curriculum abilities as rote recipes rather than as conceptual models for guiding performance, becoming especially confused when their take on the abilities was challenged by advanced-level work.

Although faculty designed the ability-based curriculum to encourage independent learning, students who came directly from high school often found the curriculum itself to be a source of initial confusion, and they appreciated getting a great deal of support and guidance in learning about how the curriculum worked. When students were not able to discern the process models represented by the curriculum, they were more likely to perceive the abilities as unauthentic, purposeless, and extra work. These students sometimes did not seem to understand how the ability requirements could organize their study of content (see Much & Mentkowski, 1984). Students who did not understand independent learning continued to feel bound by specific faculty directives and close supervision, not knowing how to use these models as fixed reference points from one assignment to the next, feeling they needed to be told what to do each time.

Use of Assessment Criteria and Feedback

Some students early on found assessment and feedback more personal and meaningful than grades, but many students at first found these learning processes problematical. In one study, seven of thirty-eight young college students in their first year out of high school acknowledged some difficulty in making sense of the criteria for assessment or whether their performance had met the criteria (Much & Mentkowski, 1982). The criteria could seem senseless, or the assessor's interpretation would seem unreasonable in some way. Some students indicated that this had been a repeated problem, suggesting that they had some general confusion about how to understand criteria or standards. A few went through three or four years of college wishing they had grades, which they believed would have told them more about how they met standards for performance and achievement than did feedback based on specific criteria.

Other students had gotten a sense of satisfaction and achievement from meeting the criteria for assessment. The criteria and the feedback process seemed to have given them a ground for evaluating their own abilities and achievements (Much & Mentkowski, 1982). Young adults in their first year in college mentioned feedback as helpful in this way (fourteen of thirty-eight). Younger and older adults initially differed in the extent to which they valued the assessment process over a traditional grading system. Older adult learners more quickly saw that the assessment system, with its feedback and criteria, gave them a good way to evaluate their own abilities. For all students this was key. Wanda, an older student, observes:

> I think for some people, the ability-based situation is frustrating because there is not a visibly communicable way of measuring progress. My mother would still ask me, 'Did you get your report card? What was your grade point?' My boss says the same thing. But the whole ability-based thing has been good for me, partially because I feel the competition is with self, and I also don't feel the need to strive for an A. If I'm giving it my best, then, for me, that's enough. . . . I think I get sufficient feedback to know what I'm doing well and what I'm not doing well. I'm more my own measure.

In general, the students acquired a broader perspective on their abilities through repeated experiences of the assessment and feedback process, and they began to be able to evaluate their work with reference to internalized standards transmitted through the feedback process.

Independent Learning After College

A substantial proportion of graduates consciously continued to use the curriculum ability models and self assessment processes, especially in the workplace, drawing on independent learning skills they had developed in college. Mae says, "There were many different things that we were taught, suggestions that were given you from your supervising teachers. When you're in a situation and faced with it, all of a sudden you start bringing these things out. I went back to many of my classes and tried to think, 'How can I apply this to this?' trying to take every bit of education that I had and put it together in a workable process." Several of the younger two-year alumnae remembered their anxiety when they first realized they were truly responsible for professional performance that would affect others. Some felt that they were more motivated to learn in their work settings than they had been in college.

Alumnae often called on interpersonal and reflective thinking skills to help them learn in the workplace. We noted a large variety of ways in which Social Interaction skills could be important for on-the-job learning. For example, Marjorie, a young graduate in business, used her interpersonal skills to learn how to establish rapport and "pick up on the signals" that tell her when she can accomplish something with her supervisor and when she should wait. Beverly highlighted her experiences of adapting Social Interaction and Problem Solving skills to new environments: "You are in a totally new environment, so you have to think more in terms of how do I do this in this situation, how is it different from what I have been doing, and what priorities are important here as compared to where I was." She was mindfully transferring the abilities she had learned to a different setting and task structure.

Independent Learning and Learning from Others

Both students and alumnae were especially articulate about how they developed independent learning skills. Ironically, their development of independent learning in this college sometimes seemed to mean taking responsibility for learning from and with peers as well; some said that their skills in learning from others had increased. Emmy, an alumna who began as an older adult learner, recollects how students often struggle and then progress in how they understand the curriculum as a framework for this kind of independent and interdependent learning:

> I had no faith in the curriculum. I just didn't. But . . . by the end of the four years, you saw how it worked. You didn't know how to learn in the first place. You just didn't know that. You didn't even know you didn't know how to learn. Why are we taking this stupid liberal arts? I don't want to read about—whatever it was we read about—and I don't want to write a newspaper article, and I don't want to do this. . . . You started out by meeting people who thought it was as stupid as you did, but who had skills that helped you to get it done. It only became clear as you went along why they put the curriculum together the way they did.

Identity Development as a Learner and Professional

Certain themes for identity development began in the early years of college and seemed to pick up momentum through college and on into the alumna years. We searched for identity themes by observing what personal attributes the interviewee consciously identified with and predicated as belonging to herself, including characteristics, behaviors, and preferences, both positive and negative. A person's identity attributes can be positively or negatively charged for the person. In its social construction, identity can also refer to the attributes other people ascribe to a person. These other-ascribed attributes will usually agree in part and disagree in part with the person's self-ascribed attributes. Such an identity is a complex concept or system. The process of coming to know oneself—one's strengths and weaknesses, one's values and needs—reflects the self-differentiating or self-defining character of identity development. We identified six highly interrelated identity themes: education and confidence, self-knowledge and broadened awareness, developing a professional identity, exploration of values, developing a collaborative identity, and changing identity and interpersonal relationships.

Education and Confidence

The student's development of a general sense of confidence that she is capable of performing or learning how to perform in most situations was one of the most robust findings across all of the interview analyses (Deemer, 1993; Deemer & Mentkowski, 1990; Giencke-Holl, Mentkowski, Much, Mertens, & Rogers, 1985; Mentkowski, 1983; Mentkowski, Much, & Giencke-Holl, 1983; Mentkowski, Much, et al., 1998; Much & Mentkowski, 1982, 1984). Both students and alumnae mentioned the importance of feedback during college as a support to their learning and confidence. Students usually noted that feedback clarified criteria, helped them to improve performance, or showed them that they had done something well. As students garnered self-knowledge and confidence, they became capable of questioning expert criticism of their performance. As an alumna, Zoe recollects her student experience: "When I first came, we had to tape our speeches and then go discuss them. I probably would have accepted anything anybody said. Later, I found that I could disagree with my assessor. I would have never been able to do that before. I know what my strengths and weaknesses are, what I'm capable of doing well."

Alumnae and older adult learners as seniors seemed to have an especially broad view of the role of feedback. The experience had taught them to accept and use criticism and to be more objective about themselves. They had become better able to separate their overall worth from a specific performance and to put momentary "failures" into realistic perspective. This capacity supported and was supported by their personal confidence. They had developed a more robust sense of capability, a self-image that did not depend on succeeding in every instance or succeeding at everything. Some had learned how to manage their initial responses to setbacks. The alumna's developing perceptions of capability or competence often involved specifically knowing what she already could do and what she did well. She usually perceived that she had improved her ability to evaluate her performance against internal and external standards and attributed this increased capacity to her college learning.

Alumnae generally described themselves as becoming more confident and convinced of their ability to make valuable contributions, more willing to take constructive risks, and more able to voice their point of view in work-related or other social interactions. They said they had come to feel more comfortable, self-assured, and able to manage all types of social situations—workplace, family, and community. Their confidence seemed linked to skills

in interacting with others, communicating ideas, thinking analytically, solving problems, and pursuing intrapersonal insight. This
process of developing abilities and identifying them with the self
sometimes began as early as the first year of college.

Self-Knowledge and Broadened Awareness

Alumnae in particular experienced identity growth in workplace
contexts, as well as in family and community life. (The interview explored most extensively their sense of career development.) This
process often began early in college; students often noted a relationship between their broad learning in the liberal arts and personal growth (Much & Mentkowski, 1982, 1984). Students regarded
further learning about their own abilities as contributing to "finding out what kind of person I am." Nineteen-year-old Julie Lynn,
in her second year, says, "I took a really good course. The teacher
got you to think about yourself. I found myself reflecting, thinking
about myself. I never used to think much about things that were
important to me. Now I worry more about how I feel, not always
pleasing others; I make my own judgment, instead of taking others'."

Self-knowledge of this type appeared to be a valued asset, used
for planning and decision making, for knowing one's own position
on issues, and maintaining a balanced perspective and good judgment when confronted with social pressures and the influences of
others. Students often said they were discovering their values, skills,
learning styles, or other personal attributes. They spoke of expanded awareness or an enriched field of knowledge and experience on which they could draw. This included awareness of social
and intellectual processes and relationships, as well as a greater
store of knowledge to bring to their experiences. Darlene says,

> I'd like to get out and get involved with the local historical society
> . . . get out and work with the community more. I'm really excited
> about that kind of thing. Through a lot of my work here, I discov-
> ered there is such a need for that kind of thing. Wasn't it sad when
> they tore down that beautiful old mansion downtown? They wanted
> the space for a parking lot. Because of being here and some of the
> architecture we studied, I became more aware of the need for cul-
> tural things to take place—the need for people to stand up for
> some of the things that are important.

Alumnae described themselves as being much more aware of the world around them than they had been before college, more aware of social issues and more capable of seeing issues and events from multiple perspectives. For some, this meant expanded interests—the enjoyment and discovery of art, music, or literature—and a sense of being well rounded. Some students appreciated the role of the liberal arts earlier than others. At the end of her first year and now nineteen years old, Tanya says, "If you are well rounded, at least a little bit, you can talk to other people who are interested in other things, and you are receptive to learning. . . . If you don't have a well-rounded education, you don't have a foundation. . . . It's just the fact that our world is made up of so many different people. If you are going to get along in it, you've got to be able to talk to them and, especially in nursing, listen to them. It's helpful to have a little store of knowledge about everything—the environment and everything." For others, like Darlene, it sometimes meant social activism that would not have occurred to them before, because they had not been as aware of certain problems or had not considered the contributions they might make. The alumna's new range of awareness influenced the way she made decisions and choices and the kinds of action that she would take.

Developing a Professional Identity

For some students who came directly from high school, their second year in the curriculum often heralded a developing sense of professionalism that began to organize their learning experiences. The process of defining a future professional role, forming career goals, and making long-range plans for a satisfying career unfolded in a recognizable pattern. Professional identity often became primary around the second year for nursing students; for others, it more often happened in their third or fourth year (Much & Mentkowski, 1982). Sometimes this awareness took the form of their beginning to imagine how the curriculum abilities might relate to specific kinds of situations in the job environment. This preprofessional socialization was facilitated by internships that provided students a chance to translate theory into strategy and action. They might acquire "different insight in how I would treat people in a nursing home" or what it is like "to take what was in the book and adapt it" when "there's no looking it up and it's not how it was in the book." In short, such experiences gave students a better definition of their chosen professional role.

These students simultaneously began to form ideals about their profession, based on certain beliefs, conveyed to them by their teachers, about what constituted ideal professional performance. Mariah, then nineteen years old, says in her second year, "The program realizes that a nurse today can be more than she ever could be, and in that sense that's reaching a little bit of a different goal, but I didn't really specify my goal of being a nurse. But now that I'm here, it alters my goal a little bit, changes it." Nursing for her was no longer just a matter of becoming a nurse, or even a capable nurse, but a matter of "the kind of nurse I want to be. I want to see myself as the ideal nurse, able to show that professionalism." By their third or fourth year, students across the professions more generally began to explore with increasing complexity the nature of their future job roles and professional ideals. They connected their vision of the integration of the curriculum abilities with their vision of professional roles, becoming increasingly aware of discrepancies between textbook portraits of work responsibilities and actual practice. They generally came to appreciate the liberal arts aspect of their education for the contributions it made to professional identity. The idea of being "well rounded" (which, for Alverno students, often refers to general abilities, including knowledge) became linked to the concepts of professionalism. Emmy, an older alumna, expresses this well: "You just do it every day: the problem solving especially, the networking, the people skills, having the broad base in the humanities, having the ability to see a bigger perspective, the fact that you're committed to something and you follow it through. The fact that you do learn to trust others in a group situation—that you learn you have to—because you can't do it all, and especially in my business. It's the same things that I see that we learned here every day."

The first two years after college, as these women entered careers and adapted to professional roles and work environments, appeared to be either a critical transition or a crossroad for changing directions. Alumnae were coordinating their learned abilities, self-concepts, and personal values with professional demands, values, opportunities, and limitations (Mentkowski, Much, & Giencke-Holl,

1983). They were testing their capacities and trying to prove themselves in the workplace. Hulbert and Schuster (1993) have suggested that women tend to be fairly flexible in midlife, valuing
whatever roles they have chosen. We found that when alumnae
confronted major disappointments at work, they often seemed to
have actively and flexibly considered how they might change their
circumstances and then moved on to other career roles that afforded
more support for positive professional identity. Growth in aspects of
identity appeared to continue to take place in the five years after
graduation, sometimes nourished by positive career experiences.

Exploration of Values

Students associated their exploration of their values with finding
new ways of understanding who they were or might become. Many
students, older and younger, appeared never to have been asked
to think about their values analytically and reflectively before, and
at first found it unfamiliar and sometimes intimidating. Later, Valuing in Decision-Making usually became a source of identity definition and personal satisfaction. Leanne, in her first year, describes
her first experiences at age nineteen with making her values explicit: "I had to think about which values came first and what was
more important to me. I don't think I had done that before. My
values turned out a little differently than I thought. That was interesting. I've been thinking about it a lot since." Angela, a forty-year-
old freshman, describes her struggle with Valuing but nevertheless
found herself "analyzing myself more and starting to realize why I
am doing certain things. I'm glad that Alverno is bringing this out."
In her third year, she says, "Valuing is something that I never gave
any thought to before I came here. At the beginning, I thought I
didn't have any values. But it was really the fact that I had never
taken the time to think about how I feel and why." By the second
or third year, it became more common for students to mention
their increased self-reflective skills.

   Understanding and appreciating divergent values formed a special learning domain in the workplace for some alumnae. Gabrielle,
looking back as a five-year alumna, says, "In my experiences with
working with people, the one thing that I've noticed is if a college
education gives you anything, it gives you a broader perspective—
there are lots of different ways to do things, different ways to live,

different values, morals, whatever—and perhaps more of an acceptance of that in other people." Sometimes workplace situations would take them back to the challenges they encountered early in college: confronting, appreciating, and eventually existing with divergent value systems and ways of life. This happened when the alumna's job brought her into close contact with persons or groups who had value structures that differed markedly from her own. Often it occurred while moving into closer contact with a multicultural workforce or clientele; sometimes it occurred in confronting supervisors and colleagues with different interpersonal and organizational values. In particular, some found that the interpersonal values that they identified with in college, such as open communication, trust, and cooperation, were not the group standards of other corporate cultures.

Developing a Collaborative Identity

Some of the older students early on noted that they were changing in how they related to others, and they could link this to the curriculum. Wanda says in her first year, then age thirty-one, "I think that through the small group discussions, we are encouraged to consider the viewpoint that other students bring in and the variety of their experiences." Younger students tended to make this kind of observation later. Both younger and older students oriented increasingly toward listening to and even drawing out the opinions of others in relation to common purposes. Students who entered college with more experience more readily seemed to reflect explicitly on how they were changing in their attitudes toward cooperation and personal achievement. In her second year, Wanda says, "There's a competition, but it is a team sort of spirit. I enjoy the group experiences a lot. . . . I've never been much of a risk taker, but I'm probably more inclined to take risks now than I was before when I don't know something. But I feel it is not necessary for me to achieve at the loss of someone else."

As these students progressed, they talked more about a deeper capacity for relating to others and appreciating what others had to contribute. For example, they described themselves as individuals who valued, and regarded as part of their own identity, being able to "work as a group," do "teamwork," "resolve conflicts," and "reach a consensus." Betsy, age thirty and a junior, says, "The behaviors and the process that's used in working in a group has sort of become second nature to me. So when I'm at work now, I can see what behaviors are being exhibited and what behaviors need to be exhibited in order to move the group forward toward its goal. That's something I learned here and something I would have been totally unaware of if I hadn't been here. . . . If I see something happening, I am in a position where I can take some action and correct the situation."

Experiences in working collaboratively in groups also seemed to provide older students with a crucial stimulus for reflecting on what kind of a person they wanted to be. Connie says in her second year:

> It was a new situation for me to reach a consensus and to try and relate to each and every member of your group. It's kind of a hard thing to learn how to do. I was surprised: the group consensus was always better than I could do singly because of the input of the five or six of us that were in the group, coming from such different educational situations. My experiences in this college have influenced my attitudes about other people, about small groups, and how you can work together so much better than you can work apart. How necessary it is to be able to communicate, so I now have a goal to become a better communicator. Small group behavior—it was really an experience for me to see people trying to relate and play roles and work out aggressions and things like that. . . . Not only have my educational goals changed, but also my goals toward relating to people. I want to relate to people so much better that I make a conscious effort to relate to people now.

Working collaboratively with others did not mean that students or alumnae forsook their own stance as professionals with independent views (cf. Deemer, 1993). In her third year, Angela observes,

> In this college you are learning to communicate with people; you are learning to talk with people and trying to think of ways of getting your ideas across—to clearly state what your objective is, or your thesis, or what your main points are, and then go on to explain it. We find a lot of people who can do the work, but they can't explain it to somebody. I think what they are doing here is really good. . . . You are learning that, while group work sometimes takes a little longer to complete a task, sometimes you gain so much from

different perspectives that people are coming from that in the long run what we do may end up being a little bit better. Plus, you have other people that are part of it, and they are willing, normally, to work with you, and to work hard on it.

The development of collaborative identity might be postulated as a series of steps in which the individual first acquires the ability to express personal opinions and then recognizes the value of collaboration with others who hold different views. The steps following the development of individual voice seem to include the development of abilities that specifically facilitate working in groups; an orientation toward listening to others and taking their views into account; and, ultimately, a recognition that working with others to resolve differences and achieve group goals is a valued part of the individual's identity.

Changing Identity and Interpersonal Relationships

Some alumnae described college as their first experience of a different viewpoint on women in society. In their college years, they noted that they were encouraged to take themselves and their education seriously; to think about themselves, their identities, their values and aspirations; and to take control of their own lives, believe in their worth, and not be reticent about expressing themselves in public. The older, more experienced women seemed more likely than others to comment on these self-defining stances while still undergraduates (Mentkowski, Much, et al., 1998). For some students it was also significant that they were now seeing many women who held positions of substantive authority and expertise. Some said that their female instructors had been their first female role models for achievement in contexts other than domestic ones. The college environment, including its approaches to both learning and interpersonal relationships, thus supported change in students' identity as women.

Some researchers have suggested that women, in particular, have a more connected or collaborative approach to learning and relating to others (Bakan, 1966; Baxter Magolda, 1992; Chodorow, 1978; Gilligan, 1982; Goldberger, Tarule, Clinchy, & Belenky, 1996; Noddings, 1984). We observed that a number of women made a point of explicitly identifying themselves with this perspective. Sabrina, looking back as an alumna, says,

What they do here, it's a people-oriented approach to learning, which I think, by the way, will be shown later to be a woman's approach. It's that woman energy, and I'm so proud to be a part of it, and I think that's what Alverno is. It's that woman energy that we called a new curriculum and we called a new way of learning, which in effect just said, respect people, nurture each other, which is a woman's thing, right? . . . The fact that it was all women didn't mean that we withdrew from life. It meant that we simply had a very supportive environment in which to learn about ourselves.

As an outcome of their educational experience, alumnae developed a stronger and more well-defined sense of self and of boundaries; although they remained concerned about the welfare of others, they had also come to view it as right and good that they be concerned about themselves (cf. Gilligan, 1982). They believed that they could make worthwhile contributions in the workplace and the community. They gained what Gilligan (1982) describes as voice: becoming able and willing to express their perspectives to others and to stand up for their views in the face of disagreement and criticism (Deemer, 1993). They also often seemed to attain a certain effectiveness in getting themselves heard by others.

Close personal relationships are generally considered an important aspect of a person's identity. When changes in identity occur, changes in these relationships also occur, and vice versa. The Perspectives Interviews addressed personal life and family issues only briefly, but comments on education, work, and family life concerns, including those involving parents, spouses, and children of participants, sometimes arose spontaneously. Sometimes changes were welcomed by all concerned, but even then they did require adjustments. In the best of cases, personal changes enriched family relationships. Angela says, "Maybe it was the fact that I was learning to interact more with people and express my feelings. By talking to my daughter, telling her what I thought and drawing out her feelings, we ended up coming to a better understanding, and things started to ease off."

Sometimes changes disrupted relationships that had been based too inflexibly on outgrown identities (cf. Josselson, 1987, 1996). A woman's personal and intellectual growth was not always well received by family members or by a partner who did not grow or learn with her. Older adult students seemed more likely than younger students to encounter friction in the family or with friends as a result of their growth, perhaps because these women began college with established identities and commitments in career and family. In her third year, Lottie says,

> I am sure I have to be a different person for coming here. I know I am. Relating to my friends and my family is so hard. Now, some of my friends that I talk to, I just feel sometimes I really can't relate to them any more. Then I get together with some of my friends who went to college right out of high school. I can really relate to them. . . . Alverno is a big part of my life, so you want to be able to discuss things. When I come home from work or school, I also want to tell my husband all this stuff. We had a big blow-up once. He said, 'Well, you come home and tell me all this stuff, and I don't know what you are talking about.' So you don't really have that much to say to each other anymore.

The implied caveat here is that developmental education should acknowledge its potential costs and risks and, where possible and appropriate, seek to limit or balance them.

Perspectives on the College as a Social Environment

The majority of students and alumnae suggested that Alverno's social atmosphere—a warm and personal small-campus environment—was a distinctive support to their learning. They mentioned that they experienced support, individual attention, pervasive group work, and intense classroom discussions. A number of students and alumnae commented on the importance of closely knit networks of friendships. They noted that the college's social milieu and its support system complemented the formal curricular specifications for social interaction abilities. Instructors, they said, created an environment in which students could feel safe discussing their ideas. Jennifer says, "It wasn't like everyone was trying to get the top rank in the class. Everyone helped everyone else." In the context of their being challenged by the curriculum, students and alumnae said that they formed supportive peer groups in this environment, building on experiences in participatory classroom discussion and group work. Some women developed remarkably strong peer support systems. As an alumna, Darlene recollects, "You support each other. If you're having a tough time, it's a chance to sit down with somebody that's going through the same thing, and you really pull each other through." In one instance, however, a student expressed some anguish over not being fully accepted by a closely knit group of friends.

Students said they felt encouraged to voice their individual observations and points of view in class. They did not feel intimidated by instructors and were not afraid to ask questions in class or approach teachers after class for individual help. Students often said that faculty dispelled much of their anxiety about failure. Emmy observes, "You're going to get some help if you're doing badly. You don't have to be so afraid." Much and Mentkowski (1984) found that twenty-five of thirty-eight first-year students (ages eighteen and nineteen) specifically identified the attention and interest of the faculty as an important support to their learning. Tina, a forty-one-year-old alumna, recollects, "They gradually built up a person's self-image by never putting anybody down. As you go through four years, your self-esteem goes up." Reassurance came when the instructor not only recognized a student's successes but also saw and responded to difficulties a student encountered. Students said that the faculty made themselves approachable, encouraged students to address them by first name, and greeted students when they met them outside class. "Because people listened to you, you felt like you could explore." Older, more experienced students seemed less likely to be surprised by an egalitarian faculty. They also considered it the preferred and appropriate style of interaction between adult learners and teachers. An alumna recalls, "It wasn't just their positive feedback, but the personal feeling that they seemed to show us. 'You're really a person to me' is what they were saying."

Educating for Learning That Lasts

It was not unusual for an alumna to say that she had not truly understood the curriculum abilities until she was out of school and in the workplace, trying them out as solutions to self-defined problems. It appeared these abilities continued to develop after graduation, provided that the graduate persisted in referring back to the conceptual models she had learned in college. The evidence is that graduates do not forget what they have learned when they actively use it as models for performance. There is reason to expect such an outcome. People in general seek ways to organize their experience and formulate efficient strategies for managing the many requirements of their lives. They are likely to grasp and hold onto symbolic or conceptual representations that help them organize their social world and show them how to think and act effectively.

If the curriculum and culture at a college has made sense to a student, if it has met with understanding at the personal level, and if it is relevant to life after college, then it will become a lasting conceptual resource for that person. If students have learned and practiced curricular models for learning and performance, then as graduates, they can continue to use them in the workplace, community, and family life. Indeed, they can develop their fullest understanding of what they have learned about performance and themselves when they practice their abilities after college. A college education of this kind can be relevant, inspiring, and transformative for the overwhelming majority of students.

Chapter Four

Learner as Developing Person

In the previous chapter we listen closely to individuals, the student voice. Here we test developmental theory using a range of instruments as a way of describing learning outcomes and personal growth. To do this, we use ways of exploring complex causal relationships that may be more familiar to some than others, and so we provide guides to interpreting these analyses, making them accessible to a broad audience. The methods of this chapter address the statistical reliability and validity of our observations. The developmental inquiry provides distinctive grounds for understanding how students learn, grow, and realize their potential.

One enduring assumption of developmental curriculum is that education should develop the whole person's way of being in the world. In this view, the individual learner actively constructs meaning across a broad range of domains. Such meaning making becomes developmental when the person can construct and confront increasing complexity with greater integrity. Chickering and Associates (1981), Kegan (1982), Perry (1970), and others have argued that such development should be a unifying purpose of higher education. Educators have often seen the raison d'être of the liberal arts as the learner's movement from a conformist to a postconventional way of being in the world.

In this chapter, we explicate what we have found through a formal research program about the learner's long-term development. We describe the intellectual, moral, and integrated development of students and alumnae as seen through a battery of measures. We focus on the contemporaneous effects of college, and those up to five years later. Finally, we investigate potential causes of development: "How well," faculty ask, "do curricular and other variables account for differences in student and alumna development across time?"

Why Study Student Growth and Development?

Teachers who know something about how students learn and develop are better able to use their students' concerns and expectations to further their learning (Brookfield, 1995; Katz & Henry, 1988). As curriculum developers they also benefit from understanding general patterns of student development. By thinking seriously about student learning and development, faculty and staff can continually question their practice, drawing implications for revising curricular components and their own teaching approaches. Thus, developmental frameworks can support a faculty's continual learning about teaching (Riordan, 1993).

Developmental measures call attention to specific areas of what learners can achieve. Findings and theories that probe the meaning of growth on a battery of human potential measures can advance how educators understand student growth. We have found, for example, that faculty judgments of individual student growth correlate with these measures (Alverno College Assessment Committee/ Office of Research and Evaluation, 1983). This chapter shows that students and alumnae can become more differentiated and integrated persons as a result of their education. These and other findings suggest that educators who take a developmental perspective on how students think, reflect, and grow can create a curriculum that successfully fosters learning that lasts.

Frameworks and Instruments

Tennant and Pogson (1995) propose that development is multidimensional and occurs across several domains. Yet development often seems to be studied within specific domains. For example, Piaget (Inhelder & Piaget, 1958) describes intellectual development, King and Kitchener (1994) and Baxter Magolda (1992) write about epistemological development, and Kohlberg (1969,

1981a) and Gilligan (1982) examine moral development. Although broad theories of development suggest relationships among these domains (e.g., Belenky et al., 1986; Kegan, 1982, 1994; Loevinger, 1976; Perry, 1970), their substantive differences affirm the need for empirical studies that can clarify theory. Target constructs—such as critical thinking, epistemological development, moral development, or ego development—appear to be either theoretically distinct or overlapping, depending on the theorist (Westenberg, Blasi, & Cohn, 1998). For example, Kegan (1982) takes a neo-Piagetian stance and argues for a single overarching developmental process, while Loevinger (1976) sees cognitive and ego development as related but distinct processes.

Other investigators have studied many of the human potential measures we have used; they have explored their relationships to background variables, college education interventions, and the hypothesized consequences of the constructs (see Kurfiss, 1988; Pascarella & Terenzini, 1991; Rest, 1979a, 1986). However, how these measures relate to and overlap with each other has not been as well investigated. Empirical studies have so far been generally limited to the discrete relationship between pairs of measures (e.g., Loevinger, 1979; Rest, 1979a; Watson & Glaser, 1964).

Because of the differences among theorists and the limitations of existing research, a broad, integrative study of development holds the promise of enabling educators to extend their thinking about college outcomes into the integrative realm of human development. A fuller understanding of the complex relationships among constructs and instruments requires both rigorous study and integrated analysis.

Sources of Data

We administered the human potential measures discussed below to the same participants at three points during the college years and again approximately five years after graduation. Sample sizes vary by analyses and included as many as 286 participants. Fully longitudinal analyses included only participants who had valid data on an instrument at each of the four times of assessment. Multivariate analyses that required fully longitudinal data most drastically reduced the sample. For longitudinal comparisons of mean trends, sample sizes generally ranged from 153 to 126 (exceptions for certain instruments, which further reduced sample sizes, are noted).

Human Potential Measures

Analysis of development focused on eight instruments that provided a range of measures of human potential. Pascarella & Terenzini (1991) give a fuller description of most of these measures and their underlying theories. (Appendix D reports estimates of reliability.)

Sentence Completion Test

The SCT is based on Loevinger's theory of ego development (1976), which comprehensively subsumes moral development, cognitive development, interpersonal relations, character development, and personality development under the construct of ego development, specifying nine stages. The test consists of thirty-six sentence stems, such as "My mother and I . . ." or "Education . . . ," which participants complete (Hy & Loevinger, 1996; Loevinger & Wessler, 1970; Loevinger, Wessler, & Redmore, 1970). The response to each stem is independently rated as manifesting one of the nine levels.

Measure of Intellectual Development

The MID is intended to assess epistemological development as described by Perry (1970). Participants write three short essays (denoted A, B, and C) describing a best class, a recent decision, and their career choice (Knefelkamp, 1974; Knefelkamp & Slepitza, 1976; Widick, 1975). The rating procedures and criteria, initially developed by Knefelkamp (1978), were extensively modified and validated during use at Alverno College (Mentkowski, Moeser, & Strait, 1983; Reisetter Hart, Rickards, & Mentkowski, 1995). Most refinements by researchers have focused on the nature of knowledge and learning (Mines, 1982; Moore, 1983), but the role of the self and the decision-making process also emerged as important (Reisetter Hart et al., 1995).

Defining Issues Test

The DIT is intended to be a measure of moral reasoning (Rest, 1979a, 1979b, 1986); it is based on Kohlberg's theory of moral development (1969). Rest departs from Kohlberg's "hard stage" model, arguing for a more complex model that presumes "stage mixture." Participants are presented with six moral dilemmas; for each, they are asked to choose among alternative considerations for making a moral judgment. The resulting "P percent" score, which we used in our analyses, denotes the relative importance the person gives to principled or other postconventional moral considerations. In trend analyses of aggregate change, we used scores that met Rest's criteria for consistency and meaningfulness. This reduced the fully longitudinal sample size ($n = 91$), but might help ensure the validity of our substantive interpretations.

Critical Thinking Appraisal

The CTA (Watson & Glaser, 1964) is a measure of critical thinking abilities that has been widely used to measure college outcomes. With a recognition format, the instrument tests for several components of critical thinking skills through a series of multiple choice exercises. We administered three of five subscales: Inference (Inf), Recognition of Assumptions (Rec), and Deduction (Ded).

Test of Cognitive Development

The TCD, developed by Renner et al. (1976), focuses on Piaget's most complex stage of cognitive development, formal operations (Inhelder & Piaget, 1958). Participants completed five paper-and-pencil tasks—two in proportionality, two in conservation, and one on separation of variables—and provided written justifications for their answers. The scoring key was provided by McBer and Company (Klemp, ca. 1977) and was revised for rescoring at Alverno College (Schwan Minik, Rogers, & Ben-Ur, 1994).

Test of Thematic Analysis

The TTA (Winter, 1984; Winter, McClelland, & Stewart, 1981) is a measure of the kind of intellectual ability expected to develop through liberal education (also see Schwan Minik & Rogers, 1994). Participants compare and contrast short essays, and their responses are scored for nine criteria. Rogers and Schwan Minik (1994) describe their derivation and scoring of three scales from the criteria: Clear and Direct Contrasts, Develop and Articulate Categories, and Egocentric Affect.

Picture Story Exercise

The PSE was modeled after the Thematic Apperception Test (Morgan & Murray, 1935), eliciting written (instead of oral) stories to ambiguous pictures in order to measure tendencies in habitual modes of thinking. McBer & Company scored the instrument for three dispositional motives: need for achievement, need for affiliation, and need for power (Atkinson, 1958; Heyns, Veroff, & Atkinson, 1958; McClelland, 1975; McClelland, Atkinson, Clark, & Lowell, 1953; Winter, 1973). In addition, they scored the PSE for the four developmental stages of adaptation proposed by Stewart (1977, 1982). They scored motives and stages separately. A word count was also used as an indirect measure of verbal fluency.

Moral Judgment Interview

The MJI (written form) is a measure of moral development based on Kohlberg's stage theory of moral development (Colby et al., 1987; Kohlberg, 1981a, 1981b; Kohlberg, Colby, Gibbs, & Speicher-Dubin, 1978). Participants write answers to a structured set of questions that probe their reasoning in relation to moral dilemmas. We used the continuous Moral Maturity Score, weighted average, in our primary analyses. Subsamples of those completing the entire battery of instruments also completed the MJI at each time of assessment in college ($n = 41$) and at all four times of assessment ($n = 32$). Two forms of the instrument were used in an A/B/A/B sequence, across the four administrations.

Rescoring

In 1983, Mentkowski and Strait presented analyses of results from the battery of instruments during the student years. When data collection for five-year alumnae was completed, we rescored all longitudinal data from the open-ended instruments, except the SCT, with protocols from different times of assessment interleaved (see Appendix D). External expert scorers were used for the MJI and PSE. A construct of Self-definition is also scorable from the PSE (Stewart, 1978), but attempts to rescore it were unsuccessful.

Some protocols from the first assessment of the TCD were accidentally destroyed, precluding rescoring and reducing the sample to thirty-eight for analyses that required both comparisons of means and fully longitudinal data. Nonetheless, some crucial analyses (for example, factor analyses) were insensitive to rater drift, enabling us to use original scores and maximum sample sizes.

Student and Alumna Domains of Growth

Research into the relationships among overlapping constructs and measures has evolved but still is insufficient to specify completely how these measures relate to a description of the whole person. At the same time, we felt the need to integrate theory, measurement, and analysis by specifying a plausible multi-indicator, latent-variable model. We have used exploratory factor analysis to help develop such a measurement model. (Factor analysis is a statistical tool for determining how separate measures are related to one another, potentially revealing underlying constructs.)

Two domains of development have emerged from factor analysis of the battery of human potential measures. Table 4.1 shows the resultant two-factor solution for each of the four times of assessment: Critical Thinking and Integration of Self in Context. One of the most striking features is the relative consistency of the relationships among measures and factors across all four times of assessment. (The most notable exception is that the Sentence Completion Test does not load clearly on a single factor at Time 2, but this is a minor inconsistency alongside the general stability of the factor-analysis solutions across time.) In effect, the four separate factor analyses provide cross-validation. The consistency of the factors across time is all the more compelling given the different aggregate trajectories for the component measures across time. This structural consistency provides a statistical foundation for understanding change within and across distinct domains of growth and argues for the robustness of the finding.

Critical Thinking

As Table 4.1 shows, one stable factor underlies the three Critical Thinking Appraisal subscales and the Test of Cognitive Development, a measure of Piagetian formal operations: the ability to reason with propositions and hypotheses. The respective literatures

Table 4.1. Factor Loadings for Human Potential Measures by Time.

| | Time of Assessment | | | | | | | |
| | Time 1 (n = 237) | | Time 2 (n = 258) | | Time 3 (n = 127) | | Time 4 (n = 208) | |
Human Potential Measure	Critical Thinking	Integration of Self in Context	Critical Thinking	Integration of Self in Context	Critical Thinking	Integration of Self in Context	Critical Thinking	Integration of Self in Context
Critical Thinking Appraisal, Inference	.54	.10	.57	.19	.52	.21	.54	.15
Critical Thinking Appraisal, Recognition	.54	.00	.59	.17	.49	.30	.56	.08
Critical Thinking Appraisal, Deduction	.68	.15	.65	.03	.82	.03	.68	.15
Test of Cognitive Development	.53	.31	.55	.14	.52	.17	.58	.11
Defining Issues Test	.39	.37	.52	.38	.32	.39	.53	.41
Sentence Completion Test	.05	.40	.23	.24	.15	.51	.09	.48
Measure of Intellectual Development, Essay A	.06	.47	.26	.58	.13	.56	.06	.67
Measure of Intellectual Development, Essay B	.26	.51	.04	.58	.17	.70	.22	.52
Measure of Intellectual Development, Essay C	.13	.67	.14	.61	.16	.64	.13	.45

Note: Orthogonal factors were extracted using principal components analysis and rotated through varimax. The two-factor solutions explain between 33 and 38 percent of the variance in the battery of measures. Critical Thinking was the first factor extracted for three of the four times of assessment. The Time 1 and Time 2 factor loadings use scores from original scoring of the TCD and the MID. This maximized sample size across measures, which is our primary concern when the statistical analyses are independent of the sample mean or time of assessment. The Time 3 and Time 4 factor loadings use the recent rescoring. The Test of Thematic Analysis also loaded on the Critical Thinking factor, along with the CTA and TCD, but was dropped from the analyses because it did not load as strongly as the other indicators. Because the Learning Style Inventory and the set of measures derived from the Picture Story Exercise did not correlate robustly at the bivariate level with the human potential measures, we did not include them in the factor analyses.

on critical thinking and Piagetian formal operations are so distinct as to lead those synthesizing research on college outcomes to treat them separately. At the same time, many have recognized their common link to a broad construct of critical thinking (see Pascarella & Terenzini, 1991; Kurfiss, 1988). The factor analyses suggest that the theoretical distinctions that these communities have articulated may not, however, translate into meaningfully different constructs at the point of their measurement.

This suggests a key question: How distinctive are the cognitive processes that underlie these different theories? For example, would formal operational capacity substantively support performance on the cognitive tasks implicit in the Critical Thinking Appraisal items? We can note a common domain of cognitive processes implied by the theories supporting the measures. Both focus on the soundness of reasoning; for example, each intends to tap deductive reasoning (cf. King & Kitchener, 1994; Kurfiss, 1988). Thus, it is not surprising that programs specifically designed to increase formal operations have increased scores on the CTA (Tomlinson-Keasey & Eisert, 1978).

We conclude that there may be a substantial overlap in these measures of higher-order thinking. The underlying latent construct would necessarily be a higher-order reasoning ability. We chose to label it a Critical Thinking ability factor, intending to convey the ability to think independently through the representations of a situation and to evaluate systematically what one believes in relation to evidence. Others might prefer to limit the definition to formal reasoning, with the observation that some other postformal reasoning capacities are not included (see Commons, Richards, & Armon, 1984); the term *creative thinking* is sometimes contrasted to *critical thinking* for a somewhat similar purpose. Still others might suggest calling this a verbal ability factor, acknowledging the effect of reading skills on performance.

Each label can suggest different teaching interventions and imply different assumptions, so we are obliged to label our constructs carefully and tentatively. For example, the term *verbal intelligence* offers another theoretical perspective, but is also likely to evoke a popular misconception of intelligence as not only a general but also an innate and unmodifiable ability—despite the strong evidence for "modifiability of intelligence at any age" (Anastasi, 1983; Neisser et al., 1996; Sternberg, 1996).

Integration of Self in Context

Underlying the second factor that emerged was the Measure of Intellectual Development (drawn from Perry's theory of intellectual and ethical development) and the Sentence Completion Test (an empirically derived measure of Loevinger's theory of ego development). Although these two developmental measures are theoretically distinctive, there is sufficient overlap to posit a single underlying construct. Loevinger (1976) herself has drawn a stage-by-stage parallel between the two theories, and both she and Perry (1970) see a developmental rethinking of the authoritarian personality (identified by Adorno, Frenkel-Brunswik, Levinson, & Sanford, 1950) as a key contribution of their work. Both theories address the development of the adult's capacity to integratively construct a personal stance in relation to complex life situations. Fundamentally, both theories shed light on different aspects of the same large process of increasing intellectual complexity and self-differentiation, which corresponds to the individual's self-defining and integrative relationship with the wider world. We therefore defined the second factor as Integration of Self in Context.

A factor analysis of the subsample that included the Kohlbergian Moral Judgment Instrument clarified the moral aspect of this factor (it was not included in the primary factor analysis due to its limited sample). The MJI loaded on the latent construct of Integration of Self in Context. Although Lee and Snarey (1988) attempt to make fine distinctions between moral judgment (the MJI) and ego development (the SCT), their data also reveal close correspondence between the two constructs (see also Commons, Armon, Richards, & Schrader, 1989). We concluded that the SCT, MID, and MJI are generally measuring the same deep structural construct.

Moral Reasoning Versus Moral Development

Is there a distinctively moral domain that is irreducible to the intellect? Rest (1979a) reports several different lines of evidence that support a distinctive moral judgment domain as measured by the DIT. He has also persuasively argued that such a domain should correlate with developing cognitive ability. He has summarized correlational findings across studies to show that the DIT correlates moderately with general intelligence ($r = .36$ averaged across fifty-one studies)—and, as expected, slightly higher with other measures of moral judgment ($r = .49$ in twenty-three correlations). As another important line of evidence, Rest reports a study in which a targeted intervention aimed at moral reasoning increased scores on the DIT but not on the Cornell Critical Thinking Test. In sum, he suggests that this moral domain is distinct from but empirically overlapping with cognitive ability.

Considering our results across instruments, however, we are unable to conclude that the DIT distinctly measures a moral sphere relative to an intellectual one (cf. King, Kitchener, Wood, & Davison, 1989). We found that the DIT ambiguously loaded on both the Critical Thinking and the Integration of Self in Context factors (see Table 4.1). In contrast, we did find compelling evidence that the MJI might be measuring a moral sphere distinct from the domain of reasoning, as it loaded on Integration of Self in Context (.61) rather than Critical Thinking (.20). For this subanalysis, we ignored time of assessment in order to create a virtual sample of 175.

We conclude that there is a distinct moral realm that is a fundamental and integral aspect of Integration of Self in Context. This deep structure of the self entails a particular kind of a moral self (Loevinger, 1976). The MJI appears to tap into the moral aspect of this deep structuring of the self, an individual's way of morally constructing and being in the world. This *moral development* construct contrasts with a more narrow *moral reasoning* construct, which we locate in the DIT, as somewhere intermediate between critical thinking and moral development.

Student and Alumna Patterns of Growth

How do students and alumnae develop intellectually, morally, and as integrated persons during college and up to five years later? What are their long-term developmental patterns? In order to examine the patterns of development statistically, we analyzed the longitudinal data for each instrument separately, using a trend analysis strategy. Based on aggregate mean scores, this analysis produces a broad picture of longitudinal change. More technically, aggregate linear, quadratic, and cubic trends were analyzed for four population groups and four times of assessment through a Population Type (4) × Time (4) repeated measures multivariate analysis of variance (MANOVA) for unequal interval lengths and n's.

Post hoc analyses focused on determining whether effects occurred in the student versus alumnae years and how population groups differed. Analyses of the student years—the first three times of assessment—have been reported earlier (Mentkowski & Doherty, 1983, 1984a, 1984b; Mentkowski & Strait, 1983; Mentkowski, 1988). The findings in this chapter add alumna data (Time 4) and use more advanced multivariate and causal analyses.

Student Population Groups

We wondered whether different population groups might show distinctive patterns of growth. To address this question, we broke down the sample into four population groups based on age at entrance to college, prior education, and work experience:

Directly from high school (fully longitudinal sample, $n = 80$). These women entered college (mean age = 17.7) immediately after high school. Relative to the mean of the other groups, they were more likely to reside on campus, be nursing majors, have high precollege GPAs, and come from families with higher socioeconomic status. They were less likely to be first-generation college students, to be married, or to have children. Their mean high school GPA was 3.2.

Delayed college/new life task ($n = 32$). These women entered college (mean age = 29) with few, if any, college transfer credits, work histories in jobs not requiring college preparation, and a mean high school GPA of 2.8.

Transfer student/returning task ($n = 30$). These women (mean age = 30) also entered with work histories that did not require college preparation, but they entered with more than ten units of transfer credit. Their mean high school GPA was 2.7.

Preestablished career ($n = 15$). These women entered (mean age = 37) with employment histories at a level often requiring some college preparation and with a mean high school GPA of 2.5.

These groupings call attention to a range of background differences as they existed in this sample, going beyond the default of age groupings as a between-subjects factor in the trend analyses (MANOVA).

Growth in Critical Thinking

Throughout college and five years later, participants demonstrated continuous overall growth in the intellectual domain. Significant upward linear trends were observed for all subscales of the Critical Thinking Appraisal (all p values $< .001$) and the Test of Cognitive Development ($p < .06$). Trend analyses for both instruments in the Critical Thinking factor indicated that students grew on these instruments during the college years and that alumnae were continuing to grow in this domain five years after college (see Appendix C). No differences were found by population group. Thus, students and alumnae in general continued to develop what many refer to as higher-order thinking skills: the ability to reason abstractly and to use evidence effectively in their analyses. A number of investigators have demonstrated growth in critical thinking during the college years (see Pascarella & Terenzini, 1991). Our findings for continuing postcollege growth in Critical Thinking extend this empirical base.

Some qualifications need to be made. One scale from the Test of Thematic Analysis (the Clear and Direct Contrasts scale) also loaded weakly on the Critical Thinking factor. Across time, however, we found no change on this scale. The other two TTA scales did not robustly correlate with any measures in the factor analysis. One of these scales, Develop and Articulate Categories (DAC), even suggested a downward trend (see Appendix C). Post hoc tests seemed to clarify that alumnae performed worse than students on this scale, yet across time, older participants had higher scores than younger ones. Rather than dismiss these somewhat ambiguous findings, faculty are using them to reflect on how the curriculum can better ensure that students develop habits of precision in their thinking.

Growth in Integration of Self in Context

Although the factor analyses suggest that the instruments included in Integration of Self in Context factor are measuring the same construct, when we look at the aggregate patterns for each instrument separately, we find a different trajectory for the MID and MJI relative to the SCT.

Measure of Intellectual Development

Trend analyses revealed linear upward growth over the ten-year period ($p < .001$), with students and alumnae showing continual development on all three essays (classroom learning, decision making,
and career decision making). Students gradually shook off their
original tendencies to approach learning and decision making as
a necessary function of black-and-white factual truths (what Perry
calls Position 2) and became increasingly open to at least considering alternative and multiple understandings (Position 3), though
they exhibited features of both ways of thinking throughout the
student years. Alumnae tended to weigh multiple perspectives
more rigorously in their essays (Position 4) though such rigor was
not uniformly present. Relatively few alumnae (less than 10 percent) demonstrated in these short essays the more complex capacity to make reasoned judgments in contextual relativism
(Position 5). Our impression was that this kind of complex thinking was more frequently expressed in their interviews.

For each MID essay, we found a main effect for population
group: Post hoc analyses indicated that those who came to college
directly from high school generally began at a less complex level
of commitment to growth and learning than did their older peers.
Because this is the youngest group of students, one could surmise
that maturation related to broader life experiences accounted for
these initial group differences. The post hoc tests also suggested
that students who delayed college (the delayed college/new life
task group) demonstrated an intermediate level of commitment
to growth and learning. All population groups, however, showed
comparable growth in their stance toward knowledge, learning,
and the self. This finding was robust across the scored essays and
suggests that returning students, as well as students entering directly from high school, can benefit developmentally from college.

Moral Judgment Interview

Similar growth was observed on the MJI (Colby et al., 1987;
Kohlberg 1981a, 1981b; Kohlberg et al., 1978). Trend analyses revealed a significant linear upward trend ($p < .05$). Due to the limited sample size, we did not test for population differences.

Sentence Completion Test

Ego development is a key construct defining Integration of Self in
Context. The role of college in fostering ego development has

been controversial, especially for women. Loevinger et al. (1985) found that women may even regress during the college years, while other research merely suggests no impact (Loxley & Whiteley, 1986). Research using the Sentence Completion Test has more generally established the self-aware stage as a stable level of ego development, typically reached by early adulthood (Cohn, 1998; Loevinger & Wessler, 1970). On this instrument, we observed that students showed no growth during college. Throughout all four years, they remained stably self-aware, the adult norm.

Alumnae, however, made a statistically significant leap in ego development after college ($p < .01$, quadratic trend test). They most typically shifted from the self-aware stage, the adult norm, to the conscientious stage. From the entering student's preoccupation with defining herself as separate from the group and its conformist social roles, participants moved over the ten-year frame to a more sophisticated postconformist capacity for detachment, empathy, complex reasoning, and taking responsibility for their actions. We are unaware of any comparable postcollege longitudinal studies using Loevinger's measure (cf. Cohn, 1998).

Interpretation of Gains in Integration Across Measures

Although we interpret these three measures as indicators of a common latent construct, they appear to have substantive differences. Most notably, the Measure of Intellectual Development showed aggregate growth during college, while the Sentence Completion Test did not (see Appendix C).

It appears that the MID, created in the college context, was particularly sensitive to expressions of development in that setting. It requires an essay and therefore is more congruent with college teaching strategies than are sentence completions. More substantially, the Perry-based measure may be sensitive to points in epistemological reasoning about certainty and sources of knowledge, a traditional focus of college teaching and learning, and to a deeper process of commitment—taking responsibility for one's growth and learning. This sensitivity to growth during college did not, however, restrict its ability to measure postcollege development.

Conversely, the Sentence Completion Test, despite the apparent narrowness of its task, may measure a more pervasive style of meaning making—perhaps due to the broad array of topics, their more challenging subject matter, and the way scoring focuses on close analysis of linguistic strategies. Change at this deeper level of integration, a professed goal of most liberal education curricula, may not actually occur for women during the college years.

Other measures showed less similarity with this construct than expected. On the surface, the theoretical formulation underlying the stages of adaptation seems related to this construct of Integration of Self in Context. But the four-stage scores derived from coding the Picture Story Exercise for this construct generally did not correlate with any of the other human potential measures in the study; the only significant correlation was negative. Analyses of three of four stage scores suggested no change during college, but interpretation of a quadratic effect for the highest stage of "integration" suggested a decline in college (see Appendix C). These results did not support including this measure, which has only a short validation history, in our causal analyses.

Nonetheless, from our more validated measures, we conclude that students and alumnae experienced deep, structural growth during college and beyond. In the student years, this personal growth may be narrowly located in the curriculum learning context. After college, however, a leap in personal growth becomes more apparent on a broader measure of ego development. Alumnae made deep structural changes in relation to their thinking about the self and their very identity. They seemed to integrate their personal identity, achieved in college, into the complexities of their lives. Given that these women call to mind higher education's newer populations, the development of the whole person may be an achievable promise.

Growth in Moral Reasoning

Formal education has often been associated with growth in preference for principled thinking about moral issues (Pascarella & Terenzini, 1991). We found that students grew in their moral reasoning, as measured by the Defining Issues Test, with a linear upward trend in student preferences for principled thinking, mean P percent score from 39 percent at entrance, to 46 percent two years later, to 50 percent near graduation ($p < .001$). For comparison, other studies have identified the adult norm for students with some college as about 40 percent and for graduate students as about 50 percent (Rest, 1979a). We conclude that these women grew remarkably in their capacity to take a broader approach to moral dilemmas and to resolve them from a principled perspective. The alumna mean remained at the students' graduating level, 50 percent. In other words, growth that occurred in college was maintained five years later. Our finding of a plateau after college is consistent with other research using this instrument (Rest, 1986; Rest & Deemer, 1986). The finding of strong upward growth during college reaffirms the meta-analytical conclusion that principled thinking about moral issues is just as much a concern for the growth of women as for men (Thoma, 1986; Walker, 1984).

Student Growth in Relation to Curriculum

Students may develop intellectually, morally, and as integrated persons, but what are the causes of this development? Studies of college outcomes have shown that college as a whole changes students (Astin, 1977, 1993; Chickering & Reisser, 1993; Feldman & Newcomb, 1969; Heath, 1977; Jacob, 1957; Pace, 1979), but few studies have demonstrated change linked to a particular curriculum (cf. Pascarella & Terenzini, 1991). Therefore, we were especially interested in how well curricular and other variables statistically account for differences in student or alumna development across time.

Specifying a Measurement Model

A statistical causal analysis based on correlational data requires specifying both a measurement model and a structural equation model (Blalock, 1982). We used the LISREL 7 statistical package (Jöreskog & Sörbom, 1989) to conduct our structural equation modeling. An often-stated advantage of structural equation modeling is that it forces us to make our theoretical and measurement assumptions, and the bases for them, explicit. A common feature of the models that we present is that they deal separately with change during the first two years at college and change from graduation to five years after college. We modeled the data in this way for a number of reasons, including the distinct differences between college and alumna environments and the ratio of sample size to the number of parameters we are estimating. Each model also accounts for correlated error among the indicators (see Appendix D).

Domains of Growth

Across all the models we tested, we specified three latent constructs of human potential. Besides the two factors supported by factor analysis, Critical Thinking and Integration of Self in Context, we specified the construct of Moral Reasoning (represented solely by the Defining Issues Test). Because this definition of Moral Reasoning was not necessarily distinct from either Critical Thinking or Integration of Self in Context, we allowed for correlated errors in the prediction equations. Of course, there are other distinctive aspects of development that we were not measuring, such as the newer constructs of postformal reasoning (Arlin, 1975; Commons et al., 1989).

Progress in the Curriculum

In Alverno's ability-based assessment system, the amount of student progress in the curriculum is fundamentally measured in the ability validations that students accumulate. As students complete courses, they are assessed for eight abilities integrated in the disciplines and are validated for specified levels of performance (Loacker, Cromwell, & O'Brien, 1986).

We are not equating curriculum ability level with a measured level of the performance (Rogers, 1994). If we were, we would have to address two sources of potential conflict with common measurement assumptions: Validations for higher levels of performance become available only later in the curriculum, and validation levels, as defined in the curriculum, cannot decrease through time.

We conclude that a student's accumulation of validations simultaneously represents (1) the student's degree of involvement in the curriculum across time—its accumulation does not decrease through time—and (2) the student's levels of achievement demonstrated so far in this performance-based curriculum. We have chosen the term *progress in the curriculum* to represent this measurement construct. During the first two years of college, students sufficiently differed in accumulated validations to test for curricular impact, offering some purchase on the issues addressed by control group designs. By graduation, however, student validation records tended to look similar, because all students are required to achieve specified levels of curricular abilities. So at least during the first two years, accumulated validations can statistically function as an aggregate measure of progress in this developmentally sequenced curriculum.

Prior Ability and Accumulated Role Responsibilities

In order to model statistically the curriculum as a potential cause of change during the first two years of college, we needed to identify, measure, and statistically model other causal influences that determine progress in the curriculum. Progress in the curriculum is potentially a systematic function of at least two classes of variables that occur before beginning college: prior ability and previously accumulated role responsibilities that limit a student's ability to fully commit time to college learning.

First, in what sense can prior ability be a cause of development? We might begin by noting that the student's capacity at entrance is a valid resource for further learning (Winter, McClelland, & Stewart, 1981). So even though faculty and advisors are committed to identifying and addressing barriers to learning wherever possible, prior ability might still moderate the rate of student progress in the curriculum. In order to model the potential effect of prior ability on curricular progress, we investigated statistical paths from ability at entrance—as measured in the latent constructs of Critical Thinking, Integration of Self in Context, and Moral Reasoning—to our measure of progress in curriculum.

Second, we expected that students with prior commitments and role responsibilities would make progress in the curriculum at a slower rate, taking fewer courses and thus fewer assessments of their abilities. As a result, they would accumulate fewer validations in the first two years after entrance, even if they performed as effectively as their peers did. Age seems to be a good indicator of accumulated commitments and role responsibilities, which might include marriage, children, financial obligations, job duties, and volunteer activities.

Resident Versus Commuter Status

A traditional assumption is that living on campus, immersed in the norms and activities of residential life, can be a powerful source of development, but this urban college attracted a relatively small proportion (17 percent) of resident students. Nonetheless, we examined the covariance potential of "a resident versus a commuter." Residential versus commuter status did correlate positively with progress in the curriculum, r (218) = .18, $p < .01$, perhaps because resident students are likely to be younger and thus full time. It did not, however, correlate with any measures of the developmental constructs; the absolute magnitude of all r values was less than .11.

Specifying Error in Measurement

When there are multiple indicators, LISREL can estimate the error for the indicators for a latent construct, but for a latent construct where there is a single indicator, we must estimate the amount of error in the indicator. This means taking a stance on how well the measure represents the latent construct, as well as estimating its reliability (Hayduk, 1987). Because such estimates of error cannot be made with complete confidence, we conducted sensitivity analyses—testing the effects of different plausible estimates on the measurement and structural models (cf. McAdams, 1986). We graphically display our final models but also report on alternatives in Appendix D. In the final model, we specified 35 percent error in the measure of progress in the curriculum. We were less confident in the measurement properties of role responsibilities and specified error at 54 percent. When prior research has established estimates of test consistency and test-retest reliability in similar populations, we can set estimates of error with more confidence (McAdams, 1986). For the Defining Issues Test as a measure of the Moral Reasoning construct, we specified error at about 21 percent, which implied test reliability at about .79.

Specifying the Student Causal Model

We focused on change from college entrance to two years later because the progress in the curriculum variable showed greater variance during this interval. We tested all causal paths from entrance measures to two years later and tested whether progress in the curriculum was an intervening causal variable. The total sample size for the two-year student model was 312, with no fewer than 247 observations for estimates of pairwise relationships between measures.

Interpreting the Causal Model of Student Growth

Figure 4.1 is a guide for reading and evaluating causal models. We intend it as a tool for readers with only a minimal background in statistics, but even those with no background in statistics may find it useful. Figure 4.2 displays what we found were causal explanations of student growth during the first two years of college. Only the paths that are different from zero with some stability are displayed. For example, Moral Reasoning at entrance directly affected neither progress in the curriculum nor growth on any human potential measure, and so no straight line connects it with these constructs. A dashed line indicates that a path only reached a p value of less than .10 rather than a conventional level of statistical significance. These path estimates are unbiased and can be relatively high, which gives them theoretical and practical interest. Nonetheless, a dashed line indicates less confidence in these estimates. (For a discussion of the overall fit of the model, see Appendix D.)

Curriculum as a Cause of Student Growth

First, it is useful to look at the most proximate causes of growth in Moral Reasoning. In Figure 4.2, the key finding from the statistical test of the curriculum is represented in the arrow from the latent construct "progress in the curriculum" (top middle of graphic) to Moral Reasoning two years from entrance. The statistically significant causal path from the curriculum to growth in moral judgment at the end of two years provides strong evidence for curricular influence (cf. Mentkowski & Strait, 1983). The path is statistically significant across all of the sensitivity analyses. This growth in moral reasoning reflects a deepened capacity to use principled or other postconventional justice frameworks to think broadly through moral issues, enabling students to take a moral perspective that extends beyond their own concerns or rigid applications of societal rules (Rest, Narvaez, Bebeau, & Thoma, 1999).

Although the statistical significance of the path is robust, its size (.18) is not overly impressive. It should be recalled, however, that the progress in the curriculum variable was limited in its sensitivity to the most conceptually relevant aspects of the curriculum. DIT researchers have typically made comparisons via effect sizes, which prevents comparisons using causal coefficients. Alverno's effect sizes are relatively large (see McNeel, 1994).

We conclude that progress in this developmentally sequenced curriculum does lead to growth in moral reasoning—the capacity to think through and embrace abstract concepts of justice. This unqualified conclusion adds to those reported by others (Rest,

Figure 4.1. How to Read a LISREL Causal Path Analysis.

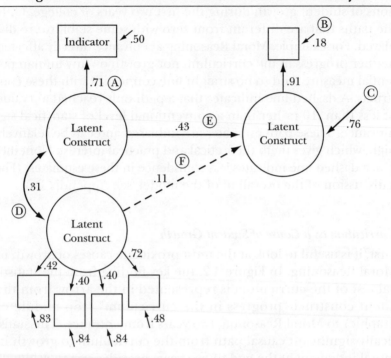

Causal path analysis investigates potential causal relationships among constructs. Both the theoretical specification of the model and its results can be evaluated for their plausibility. Results provide an empirical test of the causal model and estimates of the size of proposed causal relationships, which reflect on the plausibility of the causal model, but do not directly prove it. Causal modeling enjoins researchers to be clear about their statistical and theoretical assumptions. A theoretically meaningful construct is called a latent *construct (represented by circles). The investigator's primary interest is generally the causal relationships among latent constructs (unidirectional arrows between circles, also see E on facing page). Every causal model requires a measurement model, a way of relating actual measures to latent constructs (see A and B). Such measures are called indicators (represented by boxes) of the latent construct.*

1979a, 1986; Rest & Narvaez, 1994), again demonstrating a broad link between formal education and the development of moral judgment. It extends prior research by representing the causal mechanisms as they occur in relation to the well-articulated core curriculum of a liberal arts college, integrated with the professions and its value traditions. We note that our measure of progress in

Figure 4.1. How to Read a LISREL Causal Path Analysis, cont'd.

(A) A short arrow from a latent construct to an indicator represents the degree of its relationship to the indicator. The estimated value for this connecting path should not be close to 0 nor can it exceed 1.

(B) An arrow from "nowhere" to an indicator reflects error in measurement for the indicator as a measure of the construct. When multiple indicators are specified, LISREL can estimate this error, providing evidence on the quality of measurement. Otherwise, the investigator must set the amount of error (ideally an informed judgment). Error in the indicator is inversely related to its relationship to the construct (see A). Mathematically, setting one determines the other. Error should not be close to 1 nor can it fall below 0, the converse of A above. As a point of contrast, ordinary regression analysis assumes no error at all, which limits its realism.

(C) An arrow from nowhere to a latent construct reflects its *disturbance* term, indicating how well this construct is explained by the causal model. It can range between 0 and 1. Lower values mean the construct is better explained.

(D) This curved arrow represents an unexamined correlation between the latent constructs, that is, it does not distinguish causal relationships from noncausal ones. By beginning the model with only observed correlations between latent constructs, the model acknowledges that it begins in the midst of ongoing processes. (Curved arrows may also represent disturbance terms for causal relationships between latent constructs or correlated error between indicators.)

(E) A unidirectional straight arrow between two different latent constructs indicates that we found the one construct was a statistically significant "cause" of the other. (We have elected not to display statistically nonsignificant paths.) A positive or negative numerical value indicates whether a cause has a positive or negative effect. If the investigator misspecifies the direction of the causal arrow, then the validity of the model is threatened. Where we have longitudinal data, however, we have been able to specify which variable precedes another with confidence. When a path connects the same latent construct across time, it represents the stability of that construct. A theoretically stable construct, such as an educational outcome, should generally have a correspondingly high and positive empirical value.

(F) In this chapter, we have used dashed lines to indicate causal paths that were significant only at $p < .10$ instead of $p < .05$.

Figure 4.2. Alverno Curriculum as a Cause of Student Growth During College.

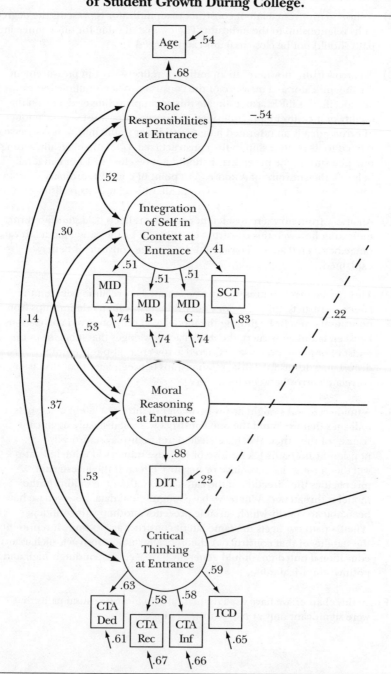

Note: Completely standardized solution is shown. Estimates of correlated error in

Figure 4.2. Alverno Curriculum as a Cause of Student Growth During College, cont'd.

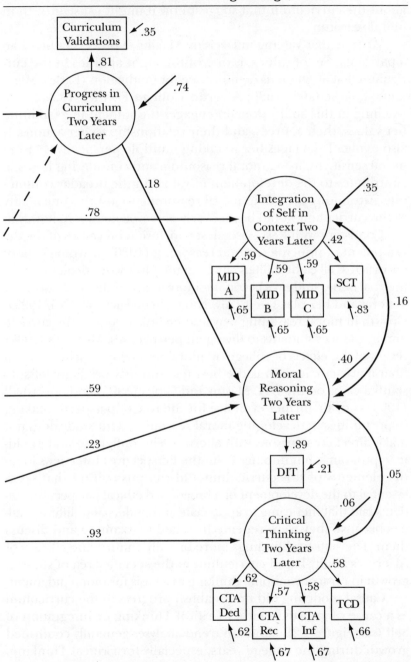

indicators are not shown. A dashed line indicates $p < .10$, and a solid line, $p < .05$.

the curriculum is tied to the college's developmental articulation of its entire curriculum. We can therefore make a few observations about the curriculum that suggest how it might cause growth in moral reasoning.

We note that Valuing in Decision-Making, a process rather than a particular set of values, is one of the eight abilities in the curriculum that all students demonstrate for graduation (Earley, Mentkowski, & Schafer, 1980; Alverno College Faculty, 1992). The teaching in this ability domain engages the student in examining her values, their sources, and their relationship to her actions. It also explicitly engages her in taking multiple perspectives, using moral sensitivity, using moral reasoning, and considering how she contributes to the development of values in the broader community. Attributing growth in moral reasoning to just this one ability in the curriculum would be an overly narrow conclusion, however.

Consistent with Rest's broadest conclusion on causes of the development of principled moral reasoning (1986), learning experiences across all eight abilities taught in the Alverno curriculum reflect the goal of the student's becoming more aware of the social world in general and her place in it (Alverno College Faculty, 1976/1992). Growth in moral reasoning may also be linked to how the curriculum introduces students to divergent perspectives. McNeel's (1994) review of the effects of college on moral reasoning concludes that a liberal arts curriculum is the best institutional predictor of substantial gains on the DIT. Mason and Gibbs (1993) and Sprinthall (1994) provide further evidence for the role of perspective-taking opportunities in developing moral reasoning. Our study does not make direct comparisons with alternatively configured undergraduate programs, but findings from the Perspectives Interviews identify elements of this curriculum and campus culture that seem essential to the development of a broadened ethical perspective. Students said that they came to appreciate and understand differing values because they were repeatedly asked to examine and discuss them. The statistical findings more broadly confirm the efficacy of Alverno's ability-based curriculum in the specific area of student growth in postconventional thinking as a basis for moral judgment.

Causal modeling did not establish progress in the curriculum as a cause of growth in either Critical Thinking or Integration of Self (see Figure 4.2), although trend analyses generally confirmed growth during the college years, especially for Critical Thinking.

Like most other higher education institutions, Alverno College is committed to developing critical thinking (Cromwell, 1986; Halonen, 1986; Loacker, Cromwell, Fey, & Rutherford, 1984). The lack of statistical linkage from progress in the curriculum to growth in Critical Thinking is especially puzzling, and so we wondered if the Moral Reasoning measure might actually be a more sensitive measure of intellectual growth than the indicator measures of Critical Thinking. We observe that student attributions, as summarized in Chapter Three, suggested that the curriculum caused growth in critical thinking abilities and that these were connected to how students thought through their values. Perhaps the puzzle can be partially explained by the narrowness of the underlying measures for Critical Thinking relative to the breadth of the curriculum. The imprecision of our measure of progress in the curriculum is another possible explanation. For example, all of the students in the study do progress in the curriculum, though some do so more rapidly.

Next, in order to probe the meaning of the causal model, it is useful to examine the predictors of progress in the curriculum. As we would expect, and as Figure 4.2 affirms, older students entered college with a range of role responsibilities and commitments that slowed their rate of progress. Figure 4.2 also suggests that the student's initial capacity to think critically was positively related to subsequent curricular progress (cf. Winter, McClelland, & Stewart, 1981). Although the path from Integration of Self to progress in the curriculum seemed nontrivial ($b = .28$), it was statistically nonsignificant. Despite our effectiveness in modeling these influences on progress in the curriculum, a fairly high disturbance value (.74) suggests that other causal or random factors are also present. Unmeasured curricular causal factors might include patterns of student coursework, levels of student and faculty contact, or differences among majors or programs. We also note that this causal model does not capture—as the interviews do—specific causal elements of the curriculum, such as how students learn to use feedback better, learn to self assess more effectively, and learn to take responsibility for learning more fully as they progress in the curriculum.

Role of Critical Thinking

A number of theorists have suggested that a certain level of critical thinking may be a precursor for development of Moral Reasoning and ego development (e.g., Loevinger, 1976; Kohlberg,

1976), and the student model tentatively supports the causal role of Critical Thinking in spurring growth in Moral Reasoning in the first two years of college. But Critical Thinking did not lead to Integration of Self in Context, $b = .09$, as theory predicts.

Curriculum as a Cause of Sustained Learning and Development After College

Given the difficulty in creating a causal model of how college learning affects student growth and development, we should expect that generating a model of how alumnae continue to benefit from their college learning would be especially difficult for both conceptual and measurement reasons. What is needed is a model of sustained learning that connects college learning with learning that lasts.

How might a curriculum support sustained learning? One possibility is that college learning is sometimes naturally self-sustaining. By this we mean that continued learning might arise directly from persistence of the identity as a learner that students have developed in college. As Pascarella and Terenzini (1991) note, an important part of college's long-term influence is that it builds "an interest in and receptivity to further learning" (p. 107). Another possibility is that sustained learning beyond college is mediated through involvement in a broadening range of activities. Research suggests that reading widely, continuing one's education, and remaining informed about social issues are activities that college fosters (Pascarella & Terenzini, 1991). Reading is a good example. It is generally recognized as one of the learning strategies well developed in college, and the habits and skills of reading are commonly expected to transfer beyond college. Other activities after college may have a similar learning potential. Alverno's curriculum and many others, for example, explicitly offer experiential learning in community settings and encourage similar involvement after college in professional, volunteer, and civic activities.

These considerations suggest three self-directed components of sustained learning: the persistence of a broad commitment to learning, alumna involvement in a wide range of postcollege activities, and pursuit of postbaccalaureate degrees. All of Alverno's eight outcome abilities connect to this dynamic view of sustained, self-directed learning. Some—such as Effective Citizenship, Global

Perspectives, and Aesthetic Responsiveness—address specific domains where learning is expected to continue. Others—such as Problem Solving and Communication—address broad domains of learning and performance that are expected to grow because they undergird most life activities.

We have also considered other possible influences on alumna growth. Educators have often wondered whether the effect of a college education would be swamped by after-college influences. For this reason we modeled three major elements of a graduate's life: major stressors and role changes, the degree of support offered by her primary environment, and the challenge and stimulation offered by her career.

Specifying a Measurement Model

To measure other constructs, we relied on participant reports through two questionnaires. Near graduation, students completed an extensive questionnaire on their learning and preparation by Alverno (Mentkowski & Bishop, 1981). As five-year alumnae, they completed another extensive questionnaire on their learning, preparation by Alverno, career history, further education, and other life experiences (Alverno College Office of Research and Evaluation, 1985). The sample size for the alumna causal model was 170, with no fewer than 145 observations for pairwise relationships between measures.

Sustained Learning: Breadth of Alumna Activities

We hypothesized that breadth of alumna activities would mediate postcollege learning and development. As five-year alumnae, participants reported on how much time during the most recent two years they had devoted to each of a list of activities. To create an index of breadth, we summed the reported levels of involvement in each of twelve activities: (1) volunteer work, (2) personal interest or skill development, (3) continuing/graduate education, (4) self-analysis/reflection, (5) providing civic leadership, (6) discussing current events and issues, (7) cultural activities, (8) participating in politics, (9) friendships, (10) spiritual growth, (11) professional activities, and (12) reading for pleasure or enhancement. For this single indicator, we estimated error at 51 percent in the model.

Sustained Learning: Breadth of Alumna Learning Goals

The participants also reported for nineteen broad learning goals how important each was to them as five-year alumnae. Based on the empirical associations among reported goals, we created alumna goal indexes for each of four learning domains: interpersonal or social ability (SOC); civic and cultural participation (CIV); cognitive ability (COG); and learning to learn, or self-directed learning (LRN). In the alumna model, each of these domains was considered to be an indicator of breadth of learning, the latent construct.

Sustained Learning: Advanced Degrees

Completion of a master's degree or above was used to represent the potential effects of further formal education; however, relatively few alumnae had completed an advanced degree by the time of the five-year assessment.

Breadth of Preparation by Alverno

While breadth of alumna activities and learning goals are each considered to be college learning outcomes (cf. Pascarella & Terenzini, 1991), we wanted to link them statistically back to the curriculum as well. We therefore created a latent construct for breadth of preparation by Alverno that included four focuses parallel to the four alumna learning goal domains, with identical statement items. Breadth of preparation was measured at graduation.

Career Stimulation and Work Centrality

Part of our alumna research has focused on coding career level from position title in paid employment (Ben-Ur & Rogers, 1994). Following Kohn and Schooler (1978), we used career level as an indicator of career stimulation, which corresponds to the intellectual stimulation of work in the position. We used first position after college as a single indicator. The other construct, work centrality, reflects the degree to which the five-year alumnae both worked full time continuously since graduation and perceived paid employment as the activity where they devote most of their time and energy. We estimated error at 31 percent and then as a sensitivity test at a fairly high 59 percent.

Environment Support and Life Stressors

Five-year alumnae were asked to identify the primary environment where they had spent the greatest proportion of their time in the previous two years. They then rated their primary environment for how well it supported them on twenty-two variables, such as "recognition and respect for effective performance, achievement, or contributions," "encouragement and support for women to aspire to their highest level of ability and potential," and "opportunities to think independently." We created an environmental support index based on a summation of the twenty-two items. Factor analysis and item analysis supported this decision (alpha = .94). We specified measurement error at 25 percent.

Five-year alumnae also were asked to report on nineteen categories of life experiences (including marriage, financial difficulty, moving, selection for leadership role) and to rate the extent to which these changed their broad professional and personal goals. To represent the degree of stressors in an alumna's life, we created an index that summed these life experiences and their impact. Because a moderate amount of stress might support development, we investigated effects of both low and high stress. We specified measurement error at 25 percent.

Interpreting the Causal Model of Alumna Growth

The statistically significant paths for the model of curriculum as a cause of sustained learning and development after college are displayed in Figure 4.3. (For a discussion of the statistical specification and evaluation of the model, see Appendix D.)

Alumna Environment as Cause of Growth

We modeled environmental support, life stressors, advanced degrees, career stimulation, and work centrality as potential intermediate causal variables; not one was related to Critical Thinking, Moral Reasoning, or Integration of Self, nor to change on them. They were neither a cause of breadth of alumna learning goals nor related to seniors' breadth of preparation. We dropped them from the model. Many have speculated on the influence of these kinds of environmental variables. For example, life stress has often been postulated to be a potential cause of development, but statistical

Figure 4.3. Alverno Curriculum as a Cause of Sustained Learning and Growth After College.

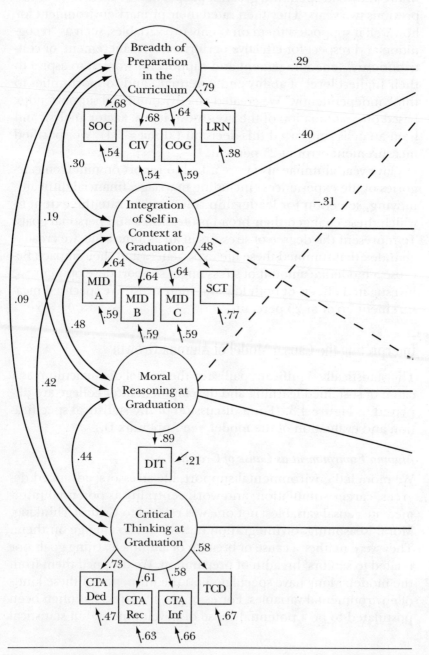

Note: Completely standardized solution is shown. Estimates of correlated error in

Figure 4.3. Alverno Curriculum as a Cause of Sustained Learning and Growth After College, cont'd.

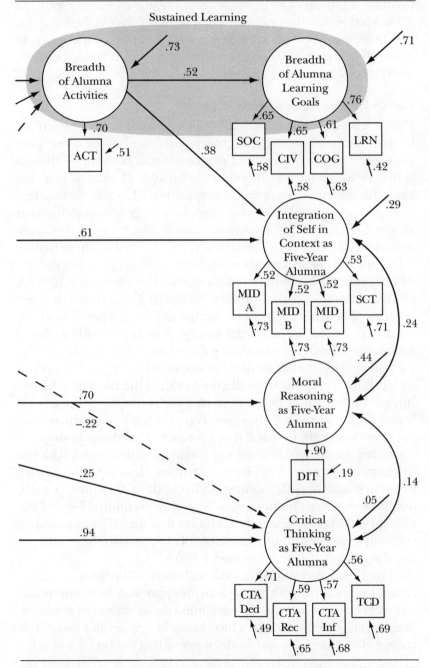

indicators are not shown. A dashed line indicates $p < .10$, and a solid line, $p < .05$.

support is slim (Helson, Mitchell, & Hart, 1985). In contrast to our findings, some research suggests that career stimulation does cause continued growth in moral reasoning (Rest & Deemer, 1986). We acknowledge that the graduate's first position after college is a limited indicator of career stimulation over a period of five years. In general, however, the range of environmental variables did not seem related to alumna growth.

Curriculum as a Cause of Alumna Growth

Figure 4.3 suggests that breadth of preparation in the curriculum leads to lifelong learning and growth. First, there is the direct path from the reported breadth of preparation to breadth of alumna activities, which itself is linked to the breadth of alumna learning goals. Breadth of alumna activities appears to play a mediating role in sustaining breadth of learning goals from graduate to five-year alumna. This finding is consistent with and extends the argument that Pascarella and Terenzini (1991) make for the persisting influence of college. Interestingly, breadth of preparation did not directly support breadth of learning goals five years later. Instead, alumnae sustained their broad learning goals through their breadth of activities. We conclude that college prepared students for and oriented them toward engaging in and learning from a wide range of civic, personal, social, and intellectual activities and that these were the cause of their sustained learning. Consistent with this interpretation, the degree to which the student achieved Integration of Self by graduation also had a positive influence on breadth of alumna activities (see Figure 4.3). The graduate's capacity to reason about moral issues seemed, if anything, to suppress somewhat the positive influence of broad preparation and achieved Integration on breadth of alumna activities. However, this negative influence of Moral Reasoning on breadth of activities, $p < .10$, might be doubted. It does not achieve a conventional level of significance, and prior research has found that the DIT was positively correlated with composite indicators of civic responsibility and political awareness (Rest & Deemer, 1986).

Figure 4.3 also shows that the influence of breadth of preparation on breadth of alumnae activities may also have important indirect consequences on the continued development of alumnae. Recall that alumnae showed a broad leap in ego development after college. The alumna causal model suggests that the breadth of activities that results from the curriculum was an important causal influence for this surge in development, providing evidence for the lasting influence of liberal learning (see Appendix D). Robin's alumna interview illustrates the kind of openness to challenge that a developmental education needs to foster:

> I'm the producer of a musical this year. Now there is no reason in the world why I should have said yes to that job because it certainly has nothing to do with science, they never taught me that in education class, and, yet, it was a need. And why did I respond to it? Partly it was the challenge. I thought, "I can do that." Then I looked at my skills: "What do I need? I can communicate with people. I can write press releases. I can communicate orally, in written form, if I have to, and if I can't, I have resources that can help me." I said, "Ask me in two months if I'm glad I did that." But that's the kind of possibilities that pop up that we may not anticipate, but that we can contribute to and that can challenge us, help us to grow.

We found that the influence of college was far from overwhelmed by postcollege influences (cf. Feldman & Newcomb, 1969). Indeed, environmental supports and life stressors had no aggregate effect on continued development. Instead, the quality of liberal learning in college continued to influence the quality of the alumna's interaction with the environment, spurring personal growth.

Relationships Among Domains of Growth

During college, progress in the curriculum was a cause of growth in moral reasoning. The student's capacity to think critically may have also supported this growth. Our test of causal effects for the alumnae years, however, suggested that the path after college is more likely to be from moral reasoning to critical thinking (see Figure 4.3). Theorists and researchers have suggested that critical thinking might be the precursor to the development of sophistication in moral reasoning (see King & Kitchener, 1994), but the assumed primacy of critical thinking as a precursor to moral reasoning needs to be reconsidered in the light of where growth occurs. Further, development of moral reasoning may not by itself lead to gains in the deeper moral development of the whole student, as evidenced, for example, by the lack of any significant causal paths between Moral Reasoning and Integration of Self in Context (see Figures 4.2 and 4.3) and by the possible tendency of Moral Reasoning to suppress breadth of alumna activities (see Figure 4.3).

The factor analyses reported at the beginning of this chapter suggested that the DIT, our indicator of Moral Reasoning, could be equally related to either Critical Thinking or Integration of Self in Context. The causal analyses suggest that Moral Reasoning is more related to Critical Thinking and, by inference, has in common with it a focus on thinking with abstractions. And so we have distinguished this moral reasoning construct from a deeper moral development that is embedded in the fullest integration of self and all that that means. In this deep moral development, capacities for reasoning about moral issues are assumed to be integrated with the structure of the whole self into a moral stance in the world, as indicated by the strong relationship of the MJI to the latent construct of Integration of Self in Context.

The different context after college seems to be a key feature in explaining the pattern of some of the causal relationships we see. In college, progress in the curriculum was linked to the capacity to understand, think through, and embrace the meaning and logic of abstract principles of moral reasoning. We looked to see if breadth of preparation had any long-lasting influence after college and found that it continued to support further Integration of Self. But these two curricular effects were distinct. Both in college and afterward, Critical Thinking and Moral Reasoning were causally linked, but without a positive relationship to Integration of Self in Context. In college, the path from Critical Thinking to Integration was at least positive, although not near statistical significance. After college, higher Integration of Self in Context actually appeared, if anything, to suppress the tendency for alumnae to continue to develop their Critical Thinking abilities, as indicated by the *negative* value for the path in Figure 4.3, $p < .10$. This tentative finding seems analogous to the negative, if also tentative, relationship between Moral Reasoning and breadth of alumna activities. Together these causal estimates suggest that development is a highly complex and diverse phenomenon. Not only may it not be as uniform across domains as most developmental theories suggest, it also may involve competing domain-specific developmental tasks (Labouvie-Vief, 1992).

It is tempting to conclude that during college, the development of abstract reasoning capacities is one key feature, occurring alongside development of a capacity to take greater personal responsibility for oneself. From the student's perspective, the capacity to think abstractly was a precursor to independent learning. But it is also tempting to conclude that graduates might sometimes face sharp choices after college between focusing on further development of precision in thinking (perhaps through career specialization) or broadly developing their whole perspective on life. The crucial effect of college may be its difference from and interaction with the postcollege context. For alumnae, growth in Integration of Self in Context appears to be supported by the complexity and ill-structured characteristics of the environment after college, as evidenced by the role of breadth of activities in mediating continued growth in the integration of the whole person. Thus, the deepest and broadest integration of self after college may be linked to the perplexing complexity of everyday problems, which insistently demand an integration of thinking, intuition, and judgment.

We might doubt the speculation that precision and breadth become divergent after college, because the corresponding estimates do not reach conventional levels of significance. But at best, the evidence would suggest no supportive relationships between Critical Thinking and Integration of Self in Context. Extant theories generally emphasize uniformly supportive linkages across developmental domains; consistent with prior research, we did find substantial correlations between these latent constructs across domains (represented by the curved bidirectional arrows in Figures 4.2 and 4.3). However, breaking these correlations down through causal modeling did not suggest any supportive relationship between Critical Thinking and Integration of Self. These findings challenge theory by creating a new empirical base. There are relatively few longitudinal studies of development that extend beyond the college years. Moreover, we are not aware of any that have measured the necessary range of variables with large enough samples to model these cross-domain relationships effectively.

In summary, structural analysis of the relationships among the battery of human potential measures identified two domains of development: Critical Thinking and Integration of Self in Context. A third construct, Moral Reasoning, overlapped with these, but seemed narrower than the deep moral integration of self. Causal analyses showed that during college, Alverno's curriculum and the capacity to think critically supported growth in moral reasoning. Afterward, critical thinking and moral reasoning remained linked, although the causal direction may be different than emphasized by prior theory. In contrast, Integration of Self in Context not only remained a distinct domain of development but may even have split off further from Critical Thinking. The potential for these domains to become more like alternative focuses—alongside the firm link between Critical Thinking and Moral Reasoning—sheds new light on the sequences of development across domains. Perhaps more important for educators, the evidence suggests that colleges can influence postcollege integration through their breadth of preparation in civic, personal, social, and intellectual learning. This is consistent with the historical case for the liberal arts.

Taking a Developmental Perspective to Foster Learning That Lasts

It has become popular to dismiss developmental theories, especially stage theories, as overly simplistic. Our findings, however, support their ability to describe student gains in intellectual and personal development. In particular, we see gains across the domains of development through time and in relation to the kinds of broadening experiences suggested by developmental theory. Although we have challenged some of the predictions from developmental theory, the theories turn out to have been precise enough to be tested and refined. Indeed, our findings suggest that abstract reasoning (with its precision in thinking) and integration of self (with its breadth and ambiguity) may have distinct roles in development of the whole person. The implications of this sharpened understanding of learner development remain positive.

Educators who take a developmental perspective can create a curriculum that is developmental and fosters learning that lasts. Breadth of perspective is already at the heart of a liberal arts education. We found that an integrated liberal arts and professional curriculum did develop moral reasoning. We found too that the breadth of an education is causally linked to alumna involvement in a breadth of activities, such as reading, professional activities, and civic leadership. In and of themselves, these activities benefit society. And when they are broadly pursued, they become a cause of continued growth for integration of self, as well as for sustaining breadth of learning. A student can develop breadth of perspective and become a more integrated and differentiated person through a liberal arts curriculum that emphasizes a professional career as well as individual development.

Chapter Five

Graduate as Performer and Contributor

Undergraduate institutions powerfully influence society through their graduates. The abilities and perspectives of the graduate become a sustained contribution to the wider world, revealing not just the individual's character but also that of his or her education. Chapters Three and Four give evidence for the key proposition that graduates can transfer their deepest learning to postcollege contexts. Now we more firmly propose that a renewed and deeper vision of liberal learning can be summoned from the graduate as performer in work, personal, and civic life. We make the case that performance can be intimately united with the liberal arts, the professions, and a college's value traditions, redefining the meaning of the undergraduate degree for students, faculty, and the wider society.

In this chapter we show that learning in the various disciplines can serve the student's pragmatic, moral, and personal goals without sacrificing the full and distinctive spirit of a liberal arts degree to the marketplace. In a renewed vision of the liberal arts, an undergraduate education reaches fruition not at graduation but in an educated citizenry and workforce, realizing its collective potential by empowering the full emergence of the individual in community and family.

We believe that broadened demands that employers are making of higher education signal an opportunity for liberal arts educators to move nearer to the dream of a more enlightened society. An educated society, rather than just an educated elite, is higher education's most compelling project. Like Boyer (1987), we see the major field deeply enriched by connections to general education and the performance of its graduates (see Armour & Fuhrmann, 1993; Berberet & Wong, 1995; Stark & Lowther, 1988).

In this chapter, we illuminate these convictions with statistical and qualitative data on the performance of five-year alumnae. We have found that graduates can firmly connect performance with prior learning in the academic disciplines, when, as students, they learned them in ways that could inform their own stance and talents after college. When graduates continue to enact learned attitudes, values, beliefs, skills, and knowledge, they give them the vital breath of life—in work, home, and public settings. The graduate's daily performance nourishes learned habits of mind and heart, invigorating them with ongoing learning.

The Call to Connect Education, Work, and Citizenship

Historically, higher education has remained committed to the ideal of the educated citizen. Thomas Jefferson and John Dewey built their ideas for democracy on this bedrock. Putnam (1995), however, finds a "decline in social capital," which may be a key cause of a range of societal problems, from uncivil discourse, to unresponsive government, to the decline of local economies. In *Habits of the Heart,* Bellah, Madsen, Sullivan, Swidler, and Tipton (1985) also put forward the case for renewal of community as a main societal goal. They suggest that a pervasive language and perspective of individualism threaten our ability to think and act collectively toward the common good. Many educators are already working under the banner of service education to revitalize higher education's contribution to the practice and spirit of citizenship (Gabelnick, 1997). But some graduates will need to lead through their service (Greenleaf, 1970/1991, 1976), drawing out the best from others, envisioning collaboration, and practicing the difficult and very human art of evoking harmony from discordant and distinct voices, interests, worldviews, and individualistic habits.

Alongside this call to citizenship, employers plead as a chorus for more talented workers who can fill the evolving posts of a constantly restructuring workplace. These business leaders must navigate among cutting-edge technologies and their almost daily obsolescence to succeed against global competition. They have convinced public leaders that investment in education is an engine of economic progress, but as governments and employers struggle to adapt to an accelerating and unprecedented pace of change, they are increasingly critical of the response time of educational institutions. Some even predict that communication technology will make existing institutions obsolete.

Still, the future workplace will require much more complex abilities. Not only are employers calling for more competent workers (Carnevale, Gainer, & Meltzer, 1990; Secretary's Commission on Achieving Necessary Skills, 1991; Sheckley, Lamdin, & Keeton, 1993), but workforce analysts are projecting that economic restructuring will increase the value of cognitive and interpersonal skills (Berryman, 1993; Berryman & Bailey, 1992; Goldstein, 1993; Hunt, 1995; Parker, Wall, & Jackson, 1997; Zemsky & Cappelli, 1998). Teams, quality circles, and just-in-time manufacturing have spread the need for self-direction and collaborative problem solving across the factory floor; workers are responding by taking on professional responsibility for their effectiveness, leading to a decline in quality control jobs (Hunt, 1995).

With this expansion of an educated and professionalized workforce, graduates will have to perform at ever higher and more complex levels. Customers and clients at all levels of scale will continue to demand more specialized and responsive service, even though workers are already facing paradoxical challenges: to do more with less and simultaneously perform at greater speed while thinking further into an increasingly unknowable future. At the same time, they are being asked to work more in teams and across functional boundaries, even across national borders. The best jobs will go to those who can comfortably perform as restructuring quickens: making sound judgments, communicating ideas, appreciating diverse perspectives, interdependently defining and pursuing their own purposes, and simultaneously enabling others to see new horizons (see Senge, 1990; Senge, Kleiner, Roberts, Ross, & Smith, 1994). Such complex, multidimensional abilities will distinguish professional performance. Any projection can be easily doubted, of course, but as educators, each of us must broadly envision the future; the very act of teaching commits us to it.

Some fear that educational institutions will end up supporting the shallowest corporate notions of what is effective (Mohrman,

1983; Shore, 1992). They are concerned that higher education will become co-opted by bottom-line ethics and narrowing self-interest. But a productive performance orientation entails a relatedness to others and to the world, best characterized by respect, which simultaneously establishes our individuality (Arendt, 1958; Fromm, 1947, Senge, 1990). Colleges, universities, and related institutions can enable each student to forge a broadened identity distinct from—but connected to—workplace performance and a sense of competence. Educational institutions do, of course, need some boundaries in their relationships to the workplace and should resist superficial demands for commodifying education. For example, Bloland (1995) notes that the widening consumer culture also puts pressure on higher education to deliver prepackaged educational units (cf. Marchese, 1998). But it is up to us as educators to manage the creative tensions that a relationship to the workplace and the community produces. We cannot flee—neither into a cloistered and silent existence, nor into an unthinking accommodation to the demands of the marketplace.

Performance and Competence

With the term *performance,* we intend to call attention to effective and dynamic action in a situational context. Performance can also connote public displays of effective action, as in a learning and assessment context (for example, "performance-based assessment"). This is an important educational use of the term, but, as Schön (1987) observes, "If, however, we use *performance* to mean the execution of any skillful *process,* public or private, then it is clear that all professional practice consists in performance" (p. 211).

Performance invites an emphasis on effective action, implying standards of excellence in discretionary action that rise above the everyday or merely adequate. It cannot be understood simply in behavioral terms. Effective, excellent performance integrates the whole dynamic nexus of a learner's intentions, thoughts, feelings, and construals into a dynamic and enduring line of action. This stands in stark contrast to automated behaviors, regurgitated thoughts, or uncoordinated feelings (Eraut, 1994; Harris, 1993; Perkins, 1995; Schön, 1987). Nor can it be equated with "skilled behaviors" that might be the focus of some vocationally oriented models. Narrow definition of specific and desirable behavioral tasks, such as the steps a nurse takes setting up an intravenous line, eventually obscures the dynamic character of professional action with oceanic lists of "competencies." In contrast, *performance* usefully brings forward how discretion and situation interact, how the scene unfolds as a protagonist acts.

The related concept of competence is often raised in the narrow frame of how it will be assessed in certification, licensure, or program evaluation, but it also connects vitally with broad teaching, learning, and curriculum issues (see Alverno College Faculty, 1979/1994; Loacker, 1991; Mentkowski, 1991). Newer conceptions of competence often take into account broader domains of performance, without dismissing the role of knowledge and basic cognitive processes. Some have expanded the concept of knowledge to include the procedural or tacit knowledge that underlies effective performance (Sternberg, Wagner, Williams, & Horvath, 1995). Other educational theories have called attention to how dispositions, attitudes, values, and beliefs crucially undergird competence, for example, in how they incline the individual to use his or her capacity to think critically (Perkins, 1995; Senge, 1990). Similarly, new understandings of distributed cognition (Salomon, 1993), social intelligence (Gardner, 1983), and emotional intelligence (Goleman, 1995, 1998) call attention to the importance of fostering interpersonal abilities.

Connecting the college curriculum to a vision of professional performance raises empirical questions from educators and others. Are there particular abilities that most distinguish outstanding professionals? What abilities can students take with them that transfer across a range of settings and occasions? These questions connect to larger educational questions educators all share: What do we teach? What should students learn and be able to perform? For both educators developing curriculum and students seeking to develop themselves, abilities need to be specifically and descriptively defined so that they provide a picture of the performance (Alverno College Faculty, 1979/1994).

Research on Multidimensional Performance

Cognitive researchers have come to identify metacognitive abilities as the key to learning and transferring broadly useful skills (Campione & Brown, 1979; Pressley, Borkowski, & Schneider, 1987;

Sternberg, 1986). For example, Perkins (1995) characterizes reflective intelligence as knowing your way around a very broad and critically important realm: the domain of thinking. Reflective intelligence includes broad strategies for approaching problems and explicitly suggests that positive attitudes and dispositions toward thinking are part of what makes up competence. Perkins argues forcefully that reflective intelligence can be developed.

Alverno's ability models suggest that interpersonally charged dispositions and interpersonal abilities also transfer across a wide range of settings (e.g., Alverno College Social Interaction Department, 1994). A large body of research in practice settings strongly suggests that interpersonal abilities have considerable generality and substantively contribute to general competence (Boyatzis, 1982; Bray, Campbell, & Grant, 1974; DeBack & Mentkowski, 1986; Fivars & Gosnell, 1966; Howard & Bray, 1988; Huck & Bray, 1976; Klemp & McClelland, 1986; Spencer & Spencer, 1993; Thornton & Byham, 1982; Van Scotter & Motowidlo, 1996; Yukl, 1989). Cognitively oriented theories tend to overlook the role of some human motives and emotions (Wyer & Srull, 1989). Sometimes performers themselves may overlook these critical interpersonal abilities, especially when specific skills distinguish their professional expertise. For example, pilots have undervalued interpersonal abilities, even though inadequate team coordination, communication, and leadership are among the most frequent causes of modern aviation accidents (Helmreich, Wiener, & Kanki, 1993). The research that supports the centrality of interpersonal abilities tends to use assessment strategies that include time-intensive human judgment processes, taking into account how interpersonal abilities involve adjusting performance to a specific and evolving context. At the same time, interpersonal abilities may be dramatically limited by situational constraints on autonomy, such as a narrowly defined job position (see Barrick & Mount, 1993).

Educationally sophisticated models move beyond specifying job requirements or licensure exam content to include articulated dimensions that individual employees can use to guide their own performances and learning (e.g., Boyatzis et al., 1995; Helmreich et al., 1993; Thornton, 1992). Boyatzis's model (1982) has been particularly important in framing educational issues, because it details how skilled competence is connected to the individual's values, self-image, and underlying motives.

A Depth Model of Multidimensional Abilities

Boyatzis's work (1982) on abilities was informed by David McClelland's perspective on the motivational bases of performance (1971, 1976). Many educators will recognize the way students develop habit structures around the broad characteristics of the goals they seek, but underlying motives by themselves are not a sufficient basis for competence (McClelland, 1987; Spangler, 1992). Boyatzis (1982) imagines "motives at the unconscious level, self-image at the conscious level, and skills at the behavioral level" (p. 27); in his "onion" metaphor, characteristics of performance are progressively easier to develop as they are closer to the observable surface. Underlying motives, at the deepest level, are very difficult to develop (McClelland, 1987; Spencer & Spencer, 1993; Thorton & Byham, 1982). Our findings corroborate this; we generally found no longitudinal change in the power, affiliation, or achievement motives, as measured through the Picture Story Exercise (described in Chapter Four). (However, our timed administration may have reduced the validity of their measurement; see Lundy, 1988.)

Conscious self-image is dynamically related to underlying dispositional motives. For example, a culture's values can channel the expression of an achievement motive away from individualistic striving and toward an energetic collaboration toward excellence (McClelland, 1987) and educational exercises in role responsibilities can channel a power motive away from irresponsibility into effective prosocial performance (Winter, 1973, 1988). Thus, the onion model suggests that a student's collaborative self-image can be developed, even though it lies relatively deep.

Closer to the surface is what Boyatzis (1982) calls "skill," or "the ability to demonstrate a system and sequence of behavior that are functionally related to attaining a performance goal" (p. 32). Curriculum definitions of abilities and research scoring protocols primarily function at this visible skill level of ability. At the same time, the effective behavioral display of a skill in context generally implies underlying self-image and dispositional habits, as well as necessary knowledge.

Spencer and Spencer (1993) suggest that knowledge and skill are both relatively easy to develop and similarly related to competence. By knowledge, they largely mean procedural or tacit knowledge (knowing how) rather than declarative knowledge (knowing that). Sternberg and his colleagues, in particular, have accumulated evidence for the criticality of tacit knowledge in a profession, which they link to a distinctive domain of practical intelligence (Sternberg & Horvath, 1999). Tacit knowledge, however, is generally believed to be highly context bound.

Closest to the surface are narrowly specific actions, which can be defined behaviorally (Boyatzis, 1982). Although specific actions are the easiest to develop, habitually focusing on them limits an individual's effectiveness. For example, Vallacher and Wegner (1989) have found that those who tend to describe actions in terms of their larger ends show more self-motivation, sense of self-understanding, impulse control, continuous uninterrupted action, and internal versus external control. At lower levels of agency, people conceptualize action more in terms of "how," rather than "why" and "to what effect."

Sources of Data and Method of Analysis

Following a method developed by McClelland (1978) and other researchers studying multidimensional abilities (Spencer & Spencer, 1993), we investigated five-year alumnae performance primarily by eliciting and then probing their recollections of specific, recent episodes (Mentkowski & Rogers, 1993; Rogers & Reisetter, 1989). In this two-hour Behavioral Event Interview, five-year alumnae gave confidential and detailed accounts of how they performed in each of six different situations. One of the advantages of this interview is that it probes how performers are conceptualizing their actions. Another is that the interview assesses both interpersonal and cognitive abilities, as do similar performance interviews that are also moderately structured. For example, Huffcutt, Roth, and McDaniel (1996) concluded in their review of the literature that this kind of interview has a generally strong relationship to measures of cognitive ability, and Campion, Campion, and Hudson (1994) demonstrated that such an interview has incremental validity beyond a battery of cognitive ability tests. In contrast to the interview method grounding Chapter Three, this kind of interview presumes that performers' recollected accounts to some degree resemble what happened. This assumption is not without foundation; reviews of research show that such probed recollections can predict future performance (McDaniel, Whetzel, Schmidt, & Maurer, 1994).

Conducting the Behavioral Event Interview

Participants were asked to "think of a time you were particularly effective" or—in an alternative prompt—"a time when you did not accomplish what you were intending, but still demonstrated your abilities." Once the alumna thought of a specific situation in the previous two years, the interviewer asked the following questions: (1) "What led up to the situation?" (2) "What did you do?" (3) "What were you thinking and feeling?" (4) "Who was involved?" and (5) "How did it all turn out?" The key to the Behavioral Event Interview is to focus on what the participant actually did rather than on what he or she usually did in such a situation, which would more reflect an espoused theory. This enabled us to study how intentions, feelings, and actions contributed to the construction of a coherent performance. As a whole, the set of questions serves also to distinguish what the alumna did from what others did in the situation and to clarify how she may have contributed to outcomes for herself and others.

Sample

Trained scorers coded 844 performances from 211 five-year alumnae. (Two of six events were systematically dropped from scoring to make the task more feasible.) Alumnae selected performances from the areas of their life where they spent most of their time and energy, a self-defined primary and secondary activity (Rogers & Mentkowski, 1994). We scored three of four performances from their primary activity, which was usually paid employment (75 percent). Analysis of workplace abilities focused on 471 performances from 157 alumnae. Family was the next most predominant primary activity (21 percent) and a frequent secondary activity (33 percent). We scored one of two performances from their secondary activity.

Developing Scoring Rubrics for Alumna Performance

A useful model of abilities classifies specific abilities into a set of meaningful and communicable categories (Fleishman & Quaintance,

1984). In the context of our research, we needed both to distinguish related abilities and to maintain these distinctions consistently as we scored alumna performances in a range of postcollege contexts and settings.

Source of Codes

Boyatzis (1982) demonstrated that the McBer and Company (1978) model of management competencies and its more specific criteria distinguished managers who were most highly rated by their supervisors. Subsequently, an Alverno management study (Mentkowski, O'Brien, McEachern, & Fowler, 1982) validated the usefulness of the competence model and its scoring system for one hundred effective women managers from fifty-three organizations who were *not* Alverno graduates. Schall and her colleagues (1984) concluded that the abilities in this model could be mapped onto Alverno's curriculum abilities. We then buttressed this competence model with Klemp and McClelland's (1986) competence model for outstanding senior managers.

Alverno College also developed a competence model for primary care nurses based on a Behavioral Event Interview study of eighty-three effective nurses who were not Alverno graduates, validating it in relation to professional experience and education (De-Back & Mentkowski, 1986). This model captured abilities more generally important to direct contributors in a service oriented profession (cf. Spencer & Spencer, 1993).

Research staff then derived codable language from the abilities that faculty defined for the general education curriculum (Alverno College Faculty, 1976/1992) and, more specifically, for the teaching major (Diez, 1990). Of particular note, we derived codes for *reflective valuing* from the general education curriculum and derived *diagnostic adjustment* and *social process conceptualization* from the education department's model of teaching competence. These curriculum ability definitions enabled us to include a liberal arts perspective and to set standards for alumna performance commensurate with a college education. After critically evaluating our comprehensive alumna competence model (Rogers, 1999a) in relation to a draft of Spencer and Spencer's generic competence codebook (1986), we added *accurate empathy* to the codebook. We developed further specifications for the scoring criteria by reiteratively applying them to sixty performances from the overall sample. For the purpose of further statistical analysis, we categorized 125 coding criteria into 42 abilities, based on our theoretical understandings and coding experience. The codebook (Rogers, 1999a) makes distinctions among abilities with differing cognitive, social, proactive, and motive bases, but we describe here only key distinctions within intellectual and interpersonal abilities. By making these potential distinctions, we can empirically investigate if they make a difference.

Distinctions Among Intellectual Abilities

Theoretically we followed the prevailing distinction between two cognitive abilities: *diagnostic pattern recognition* and *conceptualization* (Boyatzis, 1982; Klemp, 1991; Spencer & Spencer, 1993). This distinction can be related to developmental levels. Individuals use their preexisting frameworks for understanding when they recognize diagnostic patterns, whereas they create such an integrative system for understanding when they conceptualize. One way performers might conceptualize something would be to identify key aspects of a situation in relation to its broader context and complexities. Frederiksen (1986) and others have linked pattern recognition to Anderson's (1982) theory of how individuals learn to chunk smaller processes into larger ones, which then function as automatized pattern recognition systems (Boyatzis, 1982; Klemp, 1991). Diagnostic pattern recognition may be a component of tacit knowledge and thus a relatively profession- or setting-specific form of expertise. The use of specialized knowledge to make decisions or assess situations might also be connected to expertise and be a form of pattern recognition, but we attempted to distinguish the use of a broad technical knowledge base from the use of more limited knowledge, such as might be gained through a relatively brief experience or instruction.

Klemp (1991) defines analytic thinking—distinct from diagnostic thinking—as "the ability to think in terms of causes and effects, to reason deductively from facts and assumptions, and to sequence activities according to rules of logic" (p. 11). We used much of Klemp's general framework for organizing the intellectual abilities in our codebook, but we also were careful to maintain conceptual distinctions that he might not maintain. For example, in our own analyses, we did not assume that the propensity toward "planning" would continue to conjoin with "causal thinking" as Klemp and McClelland (1986) found. We reasoned that the propensity to anticipate and plan for foreseeable events could be distinguished from the capacity to think systematically about multiple causes and possibilities. We made another key distinction between inwardly focused thinking and thinking that is about others or systems in the wider world. Both can be explicitly about effectiveness, but nonetheless self-focused thinking may entail distinct kinds of processing (Duval & Wicklund, 1972; Markus, 1977).

Distinctions Among Interpersonal Abilities

We distinguished some interpersonal abilities by the source of influence (cf. French & Raven, 1959). *Relational influence* uses warm or inclusive relationships as a source of influence. *Persuasive influence* uses valid and specific information, construction of a rationale, or, more rarely, appeal to one's credentials for expertise. We distinguished other interpersonal abilities by the goal of influence. In a study of nurses, DeBack and Mentkowski (1986) identified a "developmental" sequence in the goal of influence. Nursing faculty at Alverno have used this model to channel initial student preferences for *helping* into more proactive *influencing* abilities, and more complex *coaching* abilities, which entail strategies for encouraging others to take more responsibility for their wellness.

We observed that the kinds of influence noted above were often one-on-one and unidirectional in their primary intent. When interpersonal influence involved a larger set of individuals and emphasized a receptivity to influence, we identified abilities such as *collaborative organizational action* and *social process conceptualization,* which in their execution tended to be more extended in time and complexity. Collaborative organizational action often required alumnae to seek input from others and to think interactively with them.

Inter-Rater Reliability

Estimates of our inter-scorer reliability for the forty-two abilities suggested relatively low convergent agreement, average $r(71) = .42$, but high discrimination, average $r(71) = .05$. To mitigate the effects on measurement implied by low convergent agreement for individual abilities, we used factor-level scores for most analyses.

Factor Analysis

We used factor analysis to summarize what coded abilities tended to appear together in the sample. From distinctive ability factors, we then made further inferences about alumna performance in postcollege contexts, its character and underlying processes. (Of course, factor analyses and their interpretation are influenced by the setting and populations they generalize across, as well as by the kinds of abilities included in the analysis.)

To study patterns of abilities with factor analysis, it is best to create an index that reflects the relative strength of the ability. For alumnae with paid employment as a primary activity ($n = 157$), we tallied for each ability the number of times the ability was demonstrated—for at least one scoring criterion—across three performances. This assumes that the strength of the ability for the person would be reflected in how often it was displayed.

Performance of Five-Year Alumnae

In general, more abilities were demonstrated in paid employment settings than in family settings, although there were exceptions counter to this pattern. We concluded that the alumnae were likely to bring different combinations of abilities to their family versus paid employment performances. Because of sample sizes, we present here factor analyses only for alumna performance in paid employment. Even so, we can unequivocally report that the vast majority of alumnae consistently projected a collaborative self-image. The depth of this self-image might be illustrated by Amanda, an alumna who fired an employee in her office. "I consider it to be more successful," she told the interviewer, "when you can find an inappropriately placed employee and provide a win-win situation." Backing up this claim, she maintained a friendly relationship with the former employee across succeeding months, engendering his continued respect for her. Congruent with this collaborative self-image, alumnae often demonstrated strong teamwork skills.

Alumna Ability Factors

We extracted four ability factors from five-year alumna performance in the workplace. The factors suggest four different kinds of effective alumna performance:

Ability Factor I: Collaborative Organizational Thinking and Action. This factor contains a set of abilities that appear to be associated with effective participative leadership. It includes strong independent conceptualization and action abilities and collaborative leadership abilities, where alumnae take responsibility for being collectively effective within the context of the interdependencies of an organization.

Ability Factor II: Balanced Self-Assessment and Acting from Values. An alumna who scores high on this factor is sensitive to her own strengths and weaknesses and personal values and is attuned to the meaning of interpersonal cues in the situation. The abilities in this factor suggested that alumnae may use self-reflection to construct integrity in their action, as well as to improve their performance. The factor potentially relates to lifelong learning and the development of the whole person.

Ability Factor III: Developing Others and Perspective Taking. The core set of abilities in this factor explicitly advances the development of others. An alumna high on this factor is sensitive to differences in individuals and concerned about their needs. She trusts others, believes in their potential, and is respectfully aware of differences in perspectives on issues. At the same time, she directly addresses crucial problems in their performance.

Ability Factor IV: Analytic Thinking and Action. An alumna who scores high on this factor emphasizes rational approaches to problem solving and the persuasion of others. One potential cognitive marker for this factor is the use of specialized knowledge. This ability seems to distinguish intellectual abilities in Factor IV from similar ones in Factor I, such as diagnostic pattern recognition and systematic planning (see Appendix E).

These four factors account for 30 percent of the observed variance in the individual abilities, which may reflect contextual variability in the factor structure as well as level of achieved measurement. Alumnae often demonstrated abilities from more than one factor, and so we treat the factors as prototypes of how abilities go together in the person rather than as a tool for classifying individuals into types of performers. (Appendix E displays the factor loadings for individual abilities.)

Most Effective Alumna Abilities

When researchers scored five-year alumna performances for specific abilities, their judgment entailed the conclusion that alumna actions were effective in the context. But how valid are these judgments, and which abilities most distinguish outstanding performance? We compared the researchers' judgments of alumna abilities against two kinds of criteria: (1) faculty judgments of alumna performance effectiveness and (2) three separate indicators of alumna career achievement (career level, position autonomy, and full-time salary). Career level (job title) and position autonomy (scaled interview protocol) were independently scored for five levels (Ben-Ur & Rogers, 1994). In the faculty-judgment validation studies, pairs of faculty independently sorted written descriptions of ten alumna performances into "most effective," "effective," and "least effective" sets (see Rogers & Mentkowski, 1994). Faculty judged performance within a specific professional field or other activity area such as family. In all, fifteen faculty judged the effectiveness of 120 performances from ninety-seven alumnae.

We found that faculty judgments were significantly correlated with the researchers' independent scoring of abilities for Factors I, III, and IV but not for Factor II, Balanced Self Assessment and Acting from Values (see Table 5.1). This latter finding might be qualified, because faculty did judge alumnae performances with *self assessment of abilities* as more effective (Rogers & Mentkowski, 1994), which is, of course, an ability within Factor II. One explanation for the relative effectiveness of this self assessment ability is that we developed stronger scoring criteria for the level of this ability compared to other abilities in Factor II. Research staff scored *self assessment of abilities* only if the alumna took a balanced perspective and if she spontaneously abstracted her ability beyond the current performance.

Table 5.1. Correlations of Alumna Ability Factors with Validating Criteria.

| | | Ability Factor | | | |
| | | I | II | III | IV |
Validating Criteria	N	Collaborative Organizational Thinking and Action	Balanced Self Assessment and Acting from Values	Developing Others and Perspective Taking	Analytic Thinking and Action
Correlates with faculty judgment	97	.32***	.16	.33***	.27**
Correlates with career position attributes					
Career level achieved	157	.29***	.04	.27**	.09
Salary	92	.41***	.22*	.14	.24*
Position autonomy	151	.39***	.13	.27**	.18*

Note: Paid employment positions most represented in the sample were in the fields of nursing and business and management. Technically the validation correlations were with ability scales, informed by factor analysis. In the scale constructions, weighting of the abilities within each ability factor was conceptually based. Abilities deemed more developmentally advanced were assigned a higher weighting. All correlations are for alumnae in paid employment positions, except for the faculty-judgment validation study, which included family, personal development, and civic settings. Factor-informed ability scores were summed across three performances in paid employment. But for the faculty-judgment validation study only one performance per individual was used.

*p < .05.

**p < .01.

***p < .001.

Table 5.1 shows that each ability factor was related to at least one indicator of career achievement. Collaborative Organizational Thinking and Action (Factor I) correlated with all three indicators of career achievement. This factor appears to include some of the most crucial abilities for effective performance. For Ability Factors III and IV, two of three indicators of career achievement were statistically significant (see Table 5.1). Subanalyses for these factors suggested that Developing Others and Perspective Taking related to career achievement in business and management and that Analytic Thinking and Action related to nursing career achievement. Factor II, Balanced Self Assessment and Acting from Values, was weakly associated with career achievement, correlating only with salary (see Table 5.1).

We can speculate on the meaning of the somewhat overall lower "validating" correlations for Balanced Self Assessment and Acting from Values. On the one hand, there are some methodological caveats. First, it seems likely that the criteria for these codes may simply need further development. Second, performance effectiveness seems to be a less appropriate criterion for an ability factor that is largely about learning from performing. For example, Huck and Bray (1976) found that a similar factor, which they labeled Sensitivity, was also somewhat less associated with ratings of effectiveness, and yet it related well to potential for advancement.

On the other hand, several substantive explanations also seem plausible. First, less effective alumna performances may themselves have prompted more self-reflection (Duval & Wicklund, 1972). The *reflective thinking* codes associated with Factor II (see Appendix E) explicitly included searching for self-insight following mistakes. Second, a relative lack of experience or capability might lead one to emphasize a willingness to learn rather than to focus on performance. Goffin, Rothstein, and Johnston (1996) found that "willingness to learn" was the only assessment center performance dimension they assessed that was not related to supervisory rating of performance. Third, Factor II's association with a concern with affiliation raises other possibilities. An affiliative orientation might either undermine task goals or reflect anxieties about possible rejection, rather than a readiness for close interaction with others (McAdams, 1992; McClelland, 1987). In contrast, the implicit emotional warmth involved in participative leadership (Factor I) or in developing others (Factor III) might be more self-assured or task oriented.

Sustained Learning in Alumna Performance

For each ability factor, we were able to infer a distinctive form of ongoing learning connected to the performance. The abilities featured in Factor I, Collaborative Organizational Thinking and Action, suggest a connected and collaborative learning process, where the alumna constructs her learning as a mutual enterprise with others. The highest loading ability on this factor is *developing organizational influence* (see Appendix E), suggesting learning through collaboration. One criterion for this ability, for example, is "seeks input from others strategically located in the system or institution." The more moderately loading abilities of *social process conceptualization* and *collaborative organizational action* even more strongly imply this kind of learning from and with others. Such an orientation toward collaborative learning might strengthen group performance in a number of ways. For example, Kim (1997) concluded from one experimental study that team problem solving was improved when individuals sought from the beginning to find out what each group member uniquely knew and speculated that this understanding prevented premature cognitive commitments.

Possible links between other ability factors and distinct forms of learning can be briefly noted. Balanced Self Assessment and Acting from Values (Factor II) can be seen as a factor primarily related to reflective learning from performance. Factor III, Developing Others and Perspective Taking, is also manifestly about learning—in this case, facilitating the learning of others. As educators know well, teaching others leads to one of the deepest kinds of personal learning. The learning implied in Factor IV, Analytic Thinking and Action, seemed more analytical, for example, involving *diagnostic information seeking*. Here the alumna is learning from independent analytical inquiries, gathering useful knowledge for decisions and actions. Other evidence suggests that learning consolidated in the curriculum and its effect on the alumna's ongoing learning is responsible for the overall structure of the four ability factors (Rogers, 1999b). These integrations of performance with learning in the ability factors empirically clarify the relationship between competence and what Stephenson and Yorke (1998) have called capability, a more future-oriented construct.

Alumna Integration of Interpersonal and Cognitive Abilities

Consistent with a depth model of competence that simultaneously assumes emotional, dispositional, and cognitive foundations to performance, we found evidence that interpersonal and cognitive abilities were integrated in alumna performance. This was often evident in the individual performances (Mentkowski & Rogers, 1993; Rogers, in collaboration with Kleinman, Wagner, & Schwan Minik, 1994). In addition, each of the ability factors includes distinctively cognitive and interpersonal abilities.

Collaborative Organizational Thinking and Action

Traditional models of competence might suggest that cognitive abilities saturate Factor I. On the one hand, we would agree that *conceptualization* may be central to defining the factor (see Appendix E). On the other hand, we found that alumnae distinctly connected their conceptual abilities to the task of participative leadership; indeed, abilities in this factor resemble Ford's (1986) description of the layperson's prototype of "social instrumental skills." Consider how Greta, a five-year alumna, thinks through the system-wide implications of applying participative management principles to the budgetary process of an institution she has just joined:

> Creating the budget for the division was a significant piece of my responsibilities. Prior to providing budget data for my division, I went to find out all the elements that would be needed, because I was new in this organization and didn't know what their sequence and process was. I talked to several executives who were involved in the budgetary process, to find out what each of the pieces were that they were going to need and how this whole process was going to fit together: what data they needed, their time frames, how it all meshed, what they did with it.
>
> The people in nursing management had never truly participated in budget preparation before. Because I feel very strongly about participative management, I set up a framework within which all of the nurse managers were given education coursework, within

the hospital, on how to create the budget. You can't have a responsibly professionally participative person if they're not informed. I asked the education director to put together a one-day seminar that would cover all they needed to appropriately participate in this budgeting process and to do that in a collaborative way. There was a lot of expertise within the hospital. I had her go through literature and find good materials that we could give people, so they came into the seminar with some reading done, so they had a foundation, even to raise questions. And I asked her to also talk to the executive vice president of finance. I wanted him to set a tone for this seminar. I also wanted to impress him with how committed we were to really carrying out this major end of our responsibility.

After the seminar, I approached the nurse-managers I supervise very much as a teacher-mentor, because I wanted to make it a learning process. I asked a lot of questions. I asked them, "Tell me what you think and why. Tell me—describe—what you are doing, particularly in relation to staffing, which is where the big dollars are," saying, "Have you thought about . . . ?" "What about . . . ?" As they talked, I put it on the flip chart with colored pens so they could see it. While we were talking we could say, "It would seem to me that there's an alternative here." It would become a very spontaneous mutual generation of ideas.

I want them to have positive feelings about this because it was their first time through it. If they thought this was a negative experience, every time the budget rolls around, they're going to start having some fear in their heart, and that's not a healthy way to think about this. Then, we were starting to amass all the information we needed for the total division budget and pulling that together. When that was done we had our staffing costs. Corporate-wise, they decided our FTE [full-time equivalent] numbers were too large. We called everybody in and said, "You'll have to make some cuts." In our discussion we had already identified things that were soft, so it wasn't a big shock. We had talked about the potential of having to reduce further, and so on. As a result of that process, people really bought into the goals and objectives.

This five-year alumna evidences one of the most effective performances on this factor. She is systematically integrating her thinking with the thinking of others and taking responsibility for the implications of doing something new in the organization.

Independent Initiative in Collaboration

Collaborative Organizational Thinking and Action also requires strong independent contributions that interweave social, emotional, and cognitive performance. For example, sometimes an alumna needed *ego strength* in order to stick to and take responsibility for her own judgment in the face of confrontation. Most alumnae (75 percent) demonstrated *initiative,* another ability loading on this factor (see Appendix E). Initiative involves taking discretionary action to accomplish a task, making a judgment that a particular action is appropriate, and going beyond standing procedures or scripts. Effective *achievement action* is a sophisticated form of initiative, where an individual pursues an explicit standard of excellence or a unique achievement.

Participative Leadership and Positional Limitations

We found that the participative leadership abilities within the factor *(conceptualization, collaborative organizational action, social process conceptualization,* and *developing organizational influence)* were common to management positions across fields. About half of the alumnae demonstrated one of these abilities (Rogers et al., 1994). Although the *social process conceptualization* ability was somewhat distinctively defined in relation to the Alverno curriculum, studies by business and consulting firms have often related similar leadership abilities to superior performance by midlevel and senior managers in a range of organizations and countries (see Klemp & McClelland, 1986; Spencer & Spencer, 1993).

Studies show some differences across positions in what abilities are most effective and needed, but these differences are often not very dramatic (see Thornton & Byham, 1982). In our own study, entry-level staff nurses (with direct professional responsibility for patient care) demonstrated these integrative leadership abilities much less than did alumnae in other fields who were also in entry-level professional positions. At the same time, nurse managers demonstrated this set of leadership abilities just as often as advanced managers in other fields did (see Table 5.2). One explanation might be that professional staff nurses are granted less autonomy. Nurses demonstrated many other abilities in this factor, such as *ego strength, diagnostic pattern recognition,* and *concern with achievement,* about as frequently as those in management; these seem most related to their nursing responsibilities, such as patient advocacy. But statistically removing differences in autonomy through analysis of covariance did not eliminate the statistically significant interaction displayed in Table 5.2.

Valuing, Perspective Taking, and Persuasion

Valuing, perspective taking, and persuasion each involves the integration of cognitive and interpersonal abilities. In that sense they are alike, but each loaded on separate ability factors (see Appendix E). *Reflective valuing* combines inwardness with interpersonal concerns. Balanced Self Assessment and Acting from Values also included *reflective thinking*, which is clearly inward thinking, and *affiliative orientation*, which is just as clearly relational (see Appendix E).

Factor III, Developing Others and Perspective Taking, adheres closely to what Ford (1986) found was the layperson's intuitive understanding of "prosocial skills": (1) sensitive to the feelings of others, (2) respectful of others and their viewpoints, (3) socially responsible, (4) responsive to the needs of others, (5) genuinely interested in others, (6) emotionally supportive, and (7) trustworthy. We did not score trustworthiness, but every other prosocial skill was represented in the component abilities of Factor III. For example, *perceptual objectivity*—a management term for perspective taking—loaded highest on Factor III (see Appendix E). Although it is an interpersonal ability (Spencer, 1983), such relational abilities are indeed also cognitive in the broadest meaning of that term.

Factor IV, Analytic Thinking and Action, more than any other ability factor brings to mind the abilities most often associated with college learning. Here we saw five-year alumnae conducting independent analyses, seeking information, and *using specialized knowledge* to clarify a situation. In contrast to the participative leadership of Collaborative Organizational Thinking and Action, the alumna's contribution through Analytic Thinking and Action was distinctively her own throughout her performance. Analytic Thinking and Action may be a cognitive factor, but it also reflects a multidimensionality and depth. For example, this ability factor includes two kinds of influence strategies: *use of unilateral power*, which means legitimating a request through reference to rules, procedures, or personal authority, and *persuasive influence*, which means

**Table 5.2. Profession by Career-Level Means and
Standard Deviations for the Collaborative
Organizational Thinking and Action Ability Factor.**

	Profession	
Career Level[a]	*Business and Management*	*Nursing*
Professional	8.5 (5.9)	4.6 (3.3)
Advanced professional	10.3 (5.5)	11.1 (7.3)

[a]For nurses, a position of entry-level nurse with direct responsibility for patient care was considered to be professional career level ($n = 31$) and a nurse manager was considered an advanced professional ($n = 27$). For business and management, the distinction between professional ($n = 33$) and advanced professional ($n = 25$) corresponds generally to the distinction between entry and middle manager. Alumnae who were not in at least a professional-level position or were in other fields were excluded from this analysis. The advanced professional category collapses distinctions we sometimes make between higher position levels (Ben-Ur & Rogers, 1994).

providing rationales or information that effectively persuade another. Of course, effective influence requires contextually adjusting interpersonal actions (Falbe & Yukl, 1992; Yukl & Tracey, 1992).

There may be some interactions between field and level of job positions that affect how five-year alumnae attempt to influence others, although this is beyond what we can statistically demonstrate. In particular, nurse managers may use *persuasive influence* more than professional staff nurses do, who have direct patient care responsibilities. Both staff nurses and homemakers used *relational influence*—where a warm relationship is the basis for influence—as one frequent influence strategy. Alumnae in their family settings used both *relational* and *unilateral influence* in their efforts to develop others. In contrast, those in business and management almost never used *relational influence* in their paid work, while staff nurses used *persuasive* and *relational influence* about equally.

Performance as a Distinct Domain

What is the relationship between multidimensional abilities and the intellectual and developmental capacities discussed in Chapter Four? We found that Collaborative Organizational Thinking and Action (Factor I) had the strongest relationship to our battery of measures of human potential (see Appendix F). The career essay from the Measure of Intellectual Development correlated with all four ability factors, but only one other human potential measure was significantly correlated with ability Factor II, III, or IV. Factor II correlated with an *integrative* stage of adaptation, as measured in the Picture Story Exercise (see Appendix F). Why does Factor I have a stronger relationship with the human potential measures? One explanation might emphasize its level of measurement and its strong proactive character.

Nonetheless, the weakness of these relationships seems to call for careful distinction between seemingly overlapping constructs, such as self-directedness and proactivity. For example, we would say that *self-directedness* is one focus of the human potential measures that loaded on Integration of Self in Context, a deep developmental construct, but that *proactivity* is what is explicitly required for almost all of the intellectual and interpersonal abilities explored in this chapter. Another explanation for the stronger relationship of the human potential measures to Factor I might focus on the strong intellectual abilities of Collaborative Organizational Thinking and Action. But then we would also expect Critical Thinking to be related to Analytic Thinking and Action, and this is not what we found (see Appendix F), which itself raises additional questions about the relationship between cognitive ability and performance in context.

The theoretical relationship between intellectual capacities (see Chapter Four) and performance may be complicated by several considerations. Rest (1986) observes that moral action is dependent not just on moral reasoning capacities but also, for example, on sensitivity to moral concerns and ego strength. Another related explanation for why Factors II, III, and IV do not correlate with the human potential measures might point toward the distinct character of the performance domain—for example, the way it brings forward both the interaction between the person and situation and the deep dispositions of the person, which are difficult to measure when responses are constrained.

In order to see if the performance domain was distinct from the factors found for the human potential measures (see Chapter Four), we conducted another factor analysis for the subsample of participants who completed both the Behavioral Event Interview and the primary battery of human potential measures, excluding the Moral Judgment Interview to maximize the sample size ($n = 117$). This factor analysis extends those in Chapter Four by including Collaborative Organizational Thinking and Action. (It made no sense to include the other ability factors because they did not correlate substantially with the human potential measures.) The results replicated those in Chapter Four, except that Collaborative Organizational Thinking and Action loaded (.74) as a distinct third factor. We also tried adding word count from the Picture Story Exercise as a measure of verbal fluency and found that it weakly loaded (.29) on this third performance factor, which is consistent with the substantive character of the ability factor. Thus, performance emerged as a distinct domain, along with Critical Thinking and Integration of Self in Context. More pointedly, this finding favors the distinct meaning of proactivity and intellectual skills in the performance domain.

Curriculum as a Cause of Alumna Performance

The alumna ability factors and the individual performances show a resemblance to the Alverno curriculum and its specific abilities, but can we go beyond this impressionistic appraisal and statistically link alumna performance to the curriculum? We addressed this question by extending the LISREL alumna causal model described in Chapter Four. We treat this as a subanalysis because adding the alumna performance data to the model reduces the pairwise sample size ($n = 116$).

Specifying the Causal and Measurement Model

In our investigation of the causes of alumna performance, we chose to focus on Factor I, Collaborative Organizational Thinking and Action, because it seemed to be the ability factor most associated with effective performance in the workplace and it has especially strong conceptual links to the integration of liberal arts and the professions. As in Chapter Four, the estimate of the graduate's breadth of preparation in the curriculum stands in for the curriculum as a potential cause of alumna performance. In addition, we included constructs related to the question of the alumna's career in the workplace. Here we investigated change in the alumna's career level from her first position after college to her job position as a five-year alumna, with Collaborative Organizational Thinking and Action as an intervening variable. We reasoned that participative leadership may be a cause of both career advancement and alumna growth and development. At the same time, the model acknowledges that the level of the alumna's initial position might already represent prior career advancement because of her established abilities or the opportunity and discretion to perform participative leadership, or both. Completion of a master's degree related to neither career advancement nor growth on the latent constructs and so was dropped from the model.

Interpreting the Causal Model for Alumna Performance

The tested alumna model overlaps with that presented in Figure 4.3; for the purpose of clarity, Figure 5.1 highlights in boldface type the causal model solution in relation to the new constructs. Two of these boldface lines suggest the key determinants of alumna performance. First, there appears to be a notable link between curriculum and five-year alumna performance: breadth of preparation led to effective Collaborative Organizational Thinking and Action five years later. Second, initial career level after graduation also directly led to greater performance in Collaborative Organizational Thinking and Action. However, performance did not conversely lead to career advancement. In fact, this path was near zero. Ben-Ur and Rogers (1994) also tested a regression-based causal model on the same data that posited Collaborative Organizational Thinking and Action as a cause of career advancement. That model supported this path, but unlike this model, it did not control for initial level of career as a cause of participative leadership.

Despite a few differences, overlapping estimates of causal paths are similar to those reported in Figure 4.3. Figure 5.1 does not show a path from Integration of Self at graduation to breadth of activities, because it is no longer statistically significant. The path drops from .40 to .34. This difference does not affect our overall interpretation. However, another two-fold difference suggests a different twist from Chapter Four, where we speculated that a broader

Figure 5.1. Statistical Causal Model Linking Curriculum and Alumna Performance.

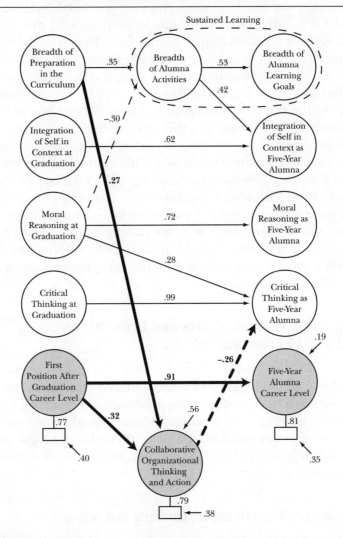

Note: Boldface lines indicate statistically significant causal paths that in this chapter extend the alumna causal model displayed in Figure 4.3. For solid lines, $p < .05$; for dashed lines, $p < .10$. Latent variables in gray indicate new variables relative to the alumna model in Chapter Four. For simplification the figure displays only the measurement model and its indicators for constructs not displayed in Figure 4.3. The new exogenous variable, first position after graduation career level, correlated less than .18 with the others. See Figure 4.3 for comparable values for undisplayed path coefficients in the measurement model.

integration of self might slow further growth in precision thinking. In the expanded model of Figure 5.1, the path from Integration of Self at graduation to Critical Thinking is deleted. Relative to Figure 4.3 it has dropped in absolute value from $-.22$ to $-.14$ and is no longer even near statistical significance. However, the boldface dotted line in Figure 5.1 suggests an alternative negative path from Collaborative Organizational Thinking and Action to growth in Critical Thinking, $p < .10$. In effect, this may be another way of expressing the potential divergence of breadth and precision as alternative alumna focuses. In this version, breadth of preparation leads to a kind of broadening of performance, Collaborative Organizational Thinking and Action, which then leads to less interest in pursuing precision in thinking. (The estimate of the path from Critical Thinking to performance was opposite in sign and of equal magnitude, but just misses the cut-off for statistical significance.) In any case, these tentative path estimates suggest that the relationship between Critical Thinking and performance may be complex and also dependent on differences between college and postcollege environments.

Integration of Liberal Arts and Professions in Alumna Performance

Analytic Thinking and Action (Factor IV) resonates to the oldest traditions of both liberal and professional education. Abilities such as *use of specialized knowledge, diagnostic information seeking, hypothetical/causal thinking,* and *persuasive influence* would be quite at home in the medieval trivium of grammar, rhetoric, and logic. But the task of integrating liberal arts and professional education goes much deeper.

Collaborative Organizational Thinking and Action

We should not be surprised to find that Collaborative Organizational Thinking and Action resonates with leadership factors identified in organizational research. This factor includes both Boyatzis's (1982) leadership cluster, which is marked by strong conceptualization and oral presentation skills, and his goal and action management cluster, which is marked by efficiency orientation and diagnostic use of concepts. Boyatzis's ability clusters, however, do not capture the distinctly participative leadership of Collaborative Organizational Thinking and Action. In this vein, Collaborative Organizational Thinking and Action is also somewhat similar to a combination of two factors that Thornton and Byham (1982) identified across a set of studies: Interpersonal Skills and Administrative Skills.

Although Collaborative Organizational Thinking and Action is reminiscent of other ability factors, it seems to point to a specific contextual blending of thinking and interpersonal abilities into a kind of participative leadership, one that broadens frameworks for understanding and crosses boundaries within organizations. This blending seems to be one key to the integration of the liberal arts and professional education, and it well represents some of the most challenging intellectual and civic goals educators have. At the same time, participative leadership, and its civic virtues, may distinguish star performers in the new workplace (see Klemp & McCelland, 1986; Morrow & Stern, 1990).

Balanced Self Assessment and Acting from Values

Sophisticated performers can sometimes adjust their ongoing actions, based on their learning, without disrupting their flow of action—what Schön (1983) calls "reflection in action." Often, however, the issue is whether performance subsequently leads to reflective learning that improves future performance. The whole problem of transfer of abilities can be conceived of as one of continued independent learning, but time demands for performance in some professions seriously limit time for self-reflection (Eraut, 1994). *Self assessment of abilities* may be one way that alumnae fluidly integrate self-reflection into learning from performance.

In the educator's vision, the liberal arts graduate will show a sensitivity to the nuances of moral questions and continue to develop a moral identity. Alumnae in family settings, as compared to paid employment, were twice as likely to relate their actions to explicit values they hold. Perhaps our greatest challenge as educators and employers is to assist others to examine and integrate their values in the context of the workplace communities they serve. For example, globalization of work is challenging corporations to define their own values more explicitly and is creating opportunities for individuals who can figure out how their moral compass works in distinct cultures (Donaldson, 1996). Indeed, *reflective valuing* was occasionally a key quality in the most sophisticated performances in paid employment (see Mentkowski & Rogers, 1993; Rogers et al., 1994). When five-year alumnae demonstrated reflective valuing, they tended to demonstrate many other abilities as well. Consider how Kate, a primary school teacher, approaches a challenging student:

> He started throwing temper tantrums to the point where the whole class would be disrupted. I found out that this child was diagnosed with attentional deficit disorder. I was not aware he was on medication. Knowing this child was hyperactive helped me understand him a little bit better. I felt a little bit sorry for him, so I tried to work around that. Then it got to the point, though, where I was overcompensating, and I was trying to make excuses, but it wasn't working because it was disrupting the rest of the class. I couldn't let one child do whatever he wanted. After a little while, I began to think, "Well, you're breaking your neck for one person who is getting away with everything in your room, and all the other kids are seeing that, and that's not fair." I'd be teaching, and all of a sudden the pencil would go on the floor or the paper would go on the floor. The outright, "I don't want to do this."

To prevent the needs of one student from having a negative impact on others, Kate goes to workshops on hyperactivity, reads about it, sends daily reports to the parents, and so on. At the same time, she remains committed to her teaching ethic of reaching every student and to her ethic of addressing her value conflict: "And of course, I didn't give up on him. We did have respect for each other, but it was hard, and he knew when I wasn't happy with him. It took us a good five months. . . . He improved in that he learned to control himself better. He achieved it for himself too. It's like a long, hard climb. I think we both did a lot of learning and growing, but it's not done yet."

This example of reflective valuing stands out because the alumna shows an intellectual and emotional commitment to realizing and addressing *competing* values. Holding on to the creative tension of an internalized value conflict for what it can teach can become a crucial component of reflective valuing.

Developing Others and Perspective Taking

Educators might have the greatest stake in a set of abilities related to taking another's perspective. Developing Others and Perspective Taking included several abilities that resonate to the vision of a society of broad-minded citizens and workers: *sensitivity to individual differences, accurate empathy, positive regard,* and *perceptual objectivity.* This suite of competencies is a needed but all too uncommon set of abilities in society. We found that managers needed these abilities to develop staff and resolve conflicts. In service professions, these abilities have to accommodate to fast-paced and understaffed settings. Consider how Anna, a nurse in a hospital emergency room, is sensitive to the feelings of an elderly man who is the husband of a critically ill patient: "He was just so afraid that he was going to lose her, and he blamed himself for what happened. He felt it was all his fault because he should have called the paramedics sooner. I said, 'Let's look at the things that you did that were really right. For example, when you noticed something wasn't quite right, you called the doctor, and you called other people and talked to them. And when you saw something definitely had gone awry, you called the right people.'"

Anna thinks through how she can help the man understand his wife's illness. She applies and adapts nursing theories she learned in college:

> I hadn't only read one theorist; I had read many. I tried to pull out the kinds of things that I thought would work the best. I knew that you need to identify with the person and let them know you understand how they are feeling. Then you need to look at the person's perceptions in relation to the reality of the situation and try to bring the two closer together. When the wife went to the ICU [intensive care unit], there were several people involved, including physicians, the primary care nurses who take care of the patient, the social worker, the priest. I wanted to know their perspective. For example, the physician: "What's your diagnosis? What do you expect? Is this person going to survive?" Being that this was an elderly gentleman, sometimes doctors and nurses are kind of abrupt; they're really busy. I often helped the husband formulate the kind of questions that he needed to ask. I also at times shared with them those things he was sharing with me. I'd say, "This is what he's really concerned about, and I want you to know that these are the

kinds of questions he is asking that he needs you to be able to answer for him." I tried to facilitate his decision-making process—from knowing his perspective, and appreciating him and what he had to say. He made the decisions that were probably the only ones that he could have made.

Anna seems conscious of how individuals construe situations differently and how bringing perspectives together can lead to new insights. She also demonstrates *positive regard,* which entails faith in the potential of others. The predisposition to see possibility in others touches the very core of what it takes to be a teacher (cf. Spencer & Spencer, 1993) and is a deep competence that must be nurtured over time. This faith in possibility was related to realistic appraisal. *Perceptual objectivity,* which involves a nonjudgmental understanding of two different perspectives, often enabled alumnae to bring a balanced perspective to a conflict between individuals in an organization. Of the forty-two abilities we scored, only *initiative* equaled the relationship of *perceptual objectivity* to alumna career achievement. Sessa (1996) has demonstrated that even short-term training in this kind of perspective taking helped workers depersonalize perceived conflicts. Senge (1990) argues further that the ability to harmonize differences in perspectives is the key to unlocking shared vision in an organization. Arts and humanities faculty have even more complex ideals for the performance of graduates, beyond what we have yet confirmed for our alumnae (see Mentkowski & Rogers, 1993). These faculty hope that alumnae will recognize the limits of their judgment, reaching beyond the current conceptual frameworks that shape their consciousness (Cromwell, 1986).

Some have argued that workplaces of the future need to become learning organizations to remain viable. The findings for Factor III suggest that the development of others in the workplace is a key part of learning in the workplace, requiring empathy, sensitivity to differences, and the ability to develop larger and more encompassing understandings. Some organizations are investing in long-term talent development. Many more are probably underestimating the degree to which the development of talent will need to be a mutually shared responsibility by everyone in the organization. If so, liberal arts educators can contribute significantly to defining and addressing the needs of a learning organization.

Redefining the Baccalaureate Degree

The ongoing restructuring of the workplace toward an emphasis on human talent creates new opportunities and demands for educators. The parallel trend in education toward more explicit definitions of curricular outcomes suggests that educators are already responding to the deep underlying currents in society. We have found that multidimensional, complex abilities provide a common language and a way of framing and discussing goals that connect educators, employers, and the public alike. Our findings can be used to clarify which abilities educators should teach for and why. For example, we found that a set of participative leadership abilities was often highly effective, supporting recent efforts of educators to develop models of collaborative learning. The task of developing others was another important area, requiring a number of often overlooked or undervalued competencies. Some findings are provocative in other ways. On the one hand, the structure of the ability factors suggested multidimensional integrations of abilities across cognitive, affective, interpersonal, and proactive spheres, blurring commonly held distinctions. On the other hand, carefully drawn research distinctions among cognitive abilities—such as systematic planning, hypothetical/causal thinking, use of specialized knowledge, and diagnostic pattern recognition—fleshed out broad differences among the ability factors. Liberal arts educators may be especially interested in the way certain inwardly directed abilities—for example, reflective thinking, valuing, and self assessment—came together to form a distinct aspect of learning in the domain of performance.

From a systems point of view, the true outcomes of college occur in the interaction of the college experience with the postcollege environment. There are many ways of asking what has happened to college graduates, but few as compelling as asking how they are contributing in their performance. The way graduates solve problems, interact with others, communicate, and express their values in action tells us about the quality of their education and how that education counts in their lives and the lives of those they touch. We found that our own alumnae sometimes had room to grow, for example, in how far they were integrating their values and perspectives with those of others. But we also found that they were deeply collaborative, sensitive to differences, caring, and balanced in how

they appreciated the perspectives of others. They often used a wide range of intellectual and interpersonal abilities to find and solve complex problems. By combining their interpersonal abilities and intellectual abilities in distinct ways, they kept learning through their ongoing performance, and they found ways to make meaningful contributions to the lives of others. In diverse ways, they lived out the ideals of a liberal education in their performance at work, at home, and in their communities.

We conclude that higher education can build explicit and feasible ideals for the performance of its graduates. As educators, we can create a unique vision of performance that simultaneously broadens our historic role in creating space for the life of the mind, the emergence of the individual, and the re-imagining of the community. We can redefine the meaning of the degree, so students and college graduates can plainly see how their education guides how they act, how they continue to learn, and who they might become.

Part Three

Interpreting and Envisioning Learning That Lasts

Part Three develops an integrated theory of learning that lasts inspired by our synthesis of theory, research, and practice. Chapter Six consolidates Part Two through an educational theory of the person: how individuals use transformative learning cycles to integrate domains of growth. Chapter Seven articulates what educators know about learning that bears on teaching by developing principles of learning and teaching in a cross-disciplinary language. It draws on the perspectives and evidence of Part Four. Each chapter builds on and extends the theoretical integration in the other. Educators can use both chapters for interpreting and envisioning learning that lasts in their own settings.

The educational theory presented in Chapter Six integrates the long-standing theories and research of the Alverno community of educators with the work and theories of leading researchers and educators from many fields. It builds on this achieved wisdom by using a wide range of inquiry paradigms to explore a multifaceted mountain of evidence generated by the college's longitudinal research. These are strengths. However, Chapter Six remains accountable to the paradigms of this programmatic research, so it is not fully accountable to the deeper and wider experiential understandings, evidence, and research of this college's community of educators. In effect, we need both an integrative theory built on coherences found in the unrelenting skepticism of disciplinary inquiry and one built on the coherence of enacted and informed commitment developed in practice. For us, a methodology of belief has become as rigorous as a methodology of doubt. Both are equally necessary to thinking (Elbow, 1986), especially in a learning community.

To integrate fully the evidence for learning that lasts from a community of educators, its members need to consider what they know, blending the evidence from day-to-day experience, years of reflective practice in fostering learning that lasts, and more abstract theory and evidence. In Chapter Seven, we ask, "What do we know about learning when we broaden our reach to further probe its meaning for teaching?" Here, conversation and interaction with others vitally sustain an achieved wisdom about learning that lasts. It means that educators develop ways to capture their formal and informal conversations as they construct their theory of learning that lasts. Because these conversations are a first step in creating and influencing educational policy, we make clear how readers can initiate them and the role of language in sustaining them on campus. For any theory to tap creative thinking and also be useful for affecting policy, it follows that each group has to create and use its own theory.

Chapter Six

Integrating Domains of Growth Through Transformative Learning

The previous three chapters explored growth by listening to student and alumna voices and examining statistically analyzed outcome data. Now we pull together a map of our exploration by creating a theoretical model. The model can help us think together clearly, and if we remember that the map is not the territory, it can stimulate divergent, creative thinking as well as consensus and synthesis. To focus and encourage discussion, this chapter offers a cross-disciplinary, empirically based model of how a person grows in relation to educational processes. So far we have followed our students and graduates—in their learning, development, and in their performance. We now take on the task of integrating what these learners have taught us.

We began our collaborative inquiry hoping to understand better the "what is learned" of learning that lasts. We identified three domains for exploration: *learning, development,* and *performance.* In our attempt to integrate the findings in Part Two, we found ourselves grappling repeatedly with how to understand these domains and their relations to one another. From the beginning we felt that the term *learning,* as used even in the title of this book, seemed a more global, universal term, while *development* and *performance* denoted a more specific domain within our overall topic, learning that lasts. Out of the interpretive struggle between data and theory, we came to a new understanding that clarified what kind of learning lasts and how it is fostered.

On the way to this new understanding, some key empirical findings formed the bedrock for rethinking learning and growth. First, we found a persistent statistical distinction between critical thinking and integration of self. Personal integration arises from the meaning-making and ethical capacities of the learner as he or she seeks integrity or *development*. Critical thinking involves distinctive higher-order thinking skills, closely resembling the *reasoning* abilities traditionally identified as central to higher education. It too is "developmental," but not in the deep sense of reflecting the learner as a "whole person," with achieved structures of self-awareness. Next, we found that *performance* was also statistically distinctive, with its contextual complexity represented by four ability factors that span conceptual, collaborative, principled, empathic, and multiperspective ways of being effective in action. Still, something was missing, and so we returned to our interview findings to take account of the student's distinctive self-reflective voice. Of course, the crucial role of *self-reflection* in learning had also been identified by the faculty long ago in their earliest curriculum discussions.

Figure 6.1 summarizes how this chapter calls for a shift from the heuristic understanding used in the prior chapters to a new way of thinking about which domains are integrated in learning that lasts. Each of these empirically derived domains corresponds to four long-standing aims of education: (1) developing thinking skills in relation to the declarative knowledge structure of the disciplines, (2) developing the whole person's capacity to make meaning, (3) developing self-reflection and cultural identity, and (4) developing capacity to perform in work, family, and civic settings. We believe each is ultimately indispensable to an expansive educational theory of the person.

This chapter builds on the research in Part Two by describing how learners extend and transformatively integrate the singular powers of each of the four domains of learning and growth. This way of understanding learning and growth suggests a larger view of the whole person than developmental theory alone. Developmental structures of the person are complemented by distinct domains of reasoning, performance, and narrative self-reflection that the learner weaves together into a unique and emergent whole. We see the learner's growth as dynamic: incorporating stages, re-

Figure 6.1. A Shift in Thinking About the Domains Integrated in Learning That Lasts.

Three Domains Are Integrated in Learning That Lasts:	Four Domains Are Integrated in Learning That Lasts:
Learning Development Performance	Reasoning Development Self-Reflection Performance
Learning Is One of Three Domains Integrated in Learning That Lasts.	Learning and Growth Permeate Learning That Lasts.

versals, and cyclical patterns, while also taking into account the learner's unique identity and heritage within a wider culture, as well as growth's holistic nature. The domains of growth and the integrating learning processes clarify how, why, and what kind of learning lasts.

Dimensions Organizing the Domains of Growth

The complex geography of the whole person begins in the enduring present of the individual's awareness and perception of the world and his or her lived relation to it. In the map of the domains, we place the active learner at the center. The educational theories and constructs we have examined seem to differ along two main dimensions, and it is in the center, in the concrete lived experience of the learner, that they intersect and blend (see Figure 6.2).

The domains are organized along two metatheoretical dimensions: *direction of attentional focus* and *relationship between person and context.* A north-south dimension—"direction of focus"—acknowledges that the learner's focus normally varies between the internal world of the self, where existential *meaning* is essential, and the external world, where successful engagement yields *competence.* Thus, both *self-reflection* and *development* involve focus on the self, but the self that is focused on is different. Near the internal pole (southern)

Figure 6.2. Dimensions Organizing Domains of Growth in the Person.

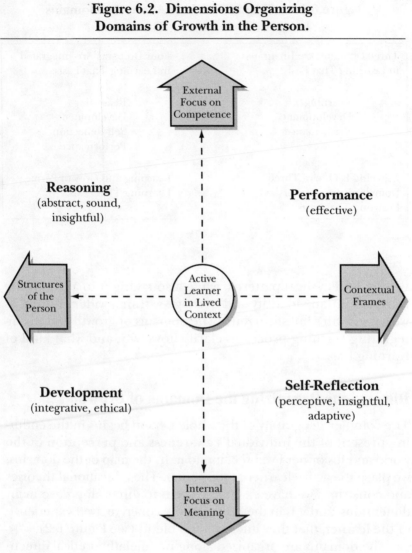

of the axis, the focus of attention is either on the self as the active process of awareness (cf. Loevinger, 1976) or the self as narrative object (cf. Bruner, 1986), as the individual orients toward *development* and *self-reflection*. Approaching the external pole (northern), the individual orients awareness toward *reasoning* and *performance* and away from the self as either construer or object.

The east-west dimension—"relationship of person and context"— characterizes those organismic and environmental forces that guide a learner's growth. To the left, *structures of the person* organize an individual's thinking, feeling, and ethical deliberations. (*Reasoning* and *development* are the domains associated with structures of the person.) To the right, growth is more contextualized, involving interactions of person and contexts. As a result, *contextual frames*— with person and context thoroughly interwoven—become more central to describing the domains of *performance* and *self-reflection*. Contextual frames are cognitive, affective, and behavioral resources appropriated from extant worldviews, organizational cultures, and professional practices and constituted in interactions with individuals, groups, institutions, and the built world (cf. Boyatzis, 1982; Cole, 1996; Mezirow, 1991; Salomon, 1993). In contrast, structures of the person are achievements of internal congruence in ways of perceiving, thinking, and making ethical judgments as described by structurally oriented developmental theories.

Although Figure 6.2 represents only two dimensions, showing how the domains relate to each other and expand, we like to imagine this figure as a cross-section of a third dimension, integrative growth, which occurs across a fourth dimension, time. Such growth involves both increasing complexity and integration, but we assume that it is neither linear nor simplistic, especially because it gives rise to new transformations. Of course, growth also involves adaptations that may be unique to a specific context.

Four Domains of Growth in the Person

We believe that educators can use these domains and their relationships as a way to consider how teaching and learning can address the learner as a whole person. In particular, we have found it effective to consider how learning activities might better facilitate the breadth of student learning within and, especially, across domains of growth.

Reasoning as a Domain of Growth

Educators often emphasize the role of thinking skills in relation to the disciplines. *Reasoning* is linked to (1) declarative knowledge structure; (2) formal, abstract, and systematic reasoning; and, more generally, (3) basic cognition and its underlying structure. We believe it is also linked to underlying dispositions to pursue thinking with intellectual rigor (cf. Perkins, 1995), though our instruments were not designed to measure this. Indeed, reasoning done well is passionate (Fromm, 1947). Nonetheless, reasoning can be distinguished from the other domains by its tendency to separate from those affective processes that are highly interpersonal. Productive reasoning is abstract, sound, and insightfully aware of particulars.

In the domain of reasoning, as in the others, we ask how one might extend oneself beyond the habitual processes that most often prevail. This is not to denigrate the power of habit; in a very real sense, we "inhabit" our lived experience. The skilled reasoner relies on the productiveness of everyday habits of inference and on the learned ability to see effortlessly the most relevant issues and patterns in a complex situation. But one can also actively extend beyond everyday experience. Extensions appear to take on a different character for each domain, but all challenge the learner to broaden his or her scope of awareness.

In the domain of *reasoning*, the learner extends from the concrete particulars into abstraction. We see reasoning as the manipulation of ideas and abstractions—the realm of what is possible and necessary. The learner's ability to extend thinking systematically into hypothetical possibilities is the hallmark of formal reasoning (Piaget & Voyat, 1979). For many students, learning to think independently or in close collaboration with others also represent extensions. In discourse, reasoning involves what Ohlsson (1995) calls the epistemic tasks of describing, explaining, predicting, arguing, critiquing, explicating, and defining.

Theories of postformal reasoning extend cognitive developmental theory into the adult tasks of problem finding (Arlin, 1984) and critiquing one's epistemological assumptions (Baxter Magolda, 1992; King & Kitchener, 1994). Arendt (1978) emphasizes in her philosophical analyses that thinking takes nothing for granted; this perspective recalls *recognition of assumptions,* one of the skills in the Critical Thinking factor. Many learners perceive improvement in their reasoning as especially significant. A senior, Wanda, seems to identify the self-critical character of thought and other features of reasoning as she describes what she believes are the key outcomes of her college education: "I believe that the goals of this school are to strengthen the thought process, to encourage critical thinking, to encourage analysis, and to be aware of where the limitations of your responses might lie. At least that is what I gained from it."

Performance as a Domain of Growth

Dewey (1916, 1938) brought *performance* to the center of the discussion about educational aims, emphasizing the interaction of person and situation. The alumna ability factors helped define this domain. Performance is imbued with interpersonally charged emotions and dispositions; each ability factor involves integrating interpersonal and cognitive abilities. Performance sustains learning through teamwork, developing others, and analytical inquiry. There is one fundamental criterion for performance: effectiveness. Yet effectiveness implies the values of a productive orientation and, as it expands, collaboration. We found that professional performance is connected to the liberal arts and its values traditions; each of the ability factors reflected a particular integration of liberal learning and professional abilities.

In the domain of *performance,* the learner extends experience into an envisioned future. The performer envisions and acts in the face of contingency and actively revises his or her actions in the light of their consequences. Effective performers envision a distant future, though it can be only partially influenced by action and the consequences cannot be fully foreseen (cf. Jaques, 1989). At higher levels, performers conceptualize action in terms of purpose and end—"why" rather than just "how" (Vallacher & Wegner, 1989). Recent theories of situated learning and professional education have highlighted the role of increasingly complex participation in a community of practice (Lave & Wenger, 1991; Schön, 1987). Pursuing excellence in organized practices may extend performance into broader meaning and values (MacIntyre, 1981). In Chapters Three and Five, we saw how alumnae extended their notions of effectiveness to include collaborative success. Performance appears to be extended by the integration of cognitive and interpersonal abilities, for example, balancing perspectives and perceiving empathetically. We found that students direct from high school often experienced the demand for performance as something new in their education. In her second year, Julie Lynn puts it this way: "Before, it was just studying for a test, but now you are constantly reading a book or reading an article or listening to a lecture to aid you with doing performance. Because later on, after I graduate, I'm not going to be able to take a test and give it to a patient. You have to be able to do certain things. And in talking or working with your fellow employees, there are certain things that you have to be able to demonstrate every day."

Self-Reflection as a Domain of Growth

Construction of meaning in personal experience lies at the heart of this domain. *Self-reflection* involves distinctive affective processes (see Markus, 1977; Pintrich & Garcia, 1994) and necessarily views the past but also envisions a future self. For example, the act of self assessing one's abilities congeals reflection on past actions for the purpose of improvement. Self-reflection also involves thinking about one's learning. We found that students perceived themselves as embracing more abstract and active ways of learning, as evidenced on Kolb's Learning Style Inventory, in effect, embracing a greater diversity of approaches to learning, a finding confirmed in the learners' narrative accounts (Chapter Three). Self-reflecting learners become engaged in a narrative or storytelling mode of making meaning, with a focus on their own attributes and accomplishments (see Bateson, 1989). We found that self-reflection was often directed to personal values and identity.

Learners extend their *self-reflection* by judging how episodes in immediate experience relate to their ongoing personal story. As with performance, extension is into wider contexts. This was often reflected in a broadening identity, such as becoming a professional or connecting to one's heritage; such learners intentionally wove their personal story into a wider narrative history. Meredith imagines at the end of her first year the ideal college graduate: "I think of a person that would be self-assured, who knows herself and basically where other people are coming from. Knows values. Is aware of not only her family affairs, as they may be, but also her community and national and international affairs."

Self-reflection is not entirely private. It involves a kind of judgment, and as Arendt notes, "judgments, and especially judgments of taste, always reflect upon others and . . . take their possible judgments into account" (1978, p. 266). Balance seemed to characterize effective self assessment of abilities. We found that immersion in this college's shared "language of learning" also encouraged productive self-reflection in learners. Students and alumnae experienced the liberal arts as a spur to self-reflection. Given the narrative basis of this domain, we might surmise that opportunities to listen to the stories of others could extend self-reflection. Questioning personal assumptions is another extension (Brookfield, 1991), as is critical reflection on learned cultural frameworks (Cranton, 1996; Mezirow, 1991). Emmy, an older student, says at the end of her first year, "Coming here forces you to think about your life—where you've been and where you're going, and where you want to be and why you want to be there, and why you're where you're at. I never really got into philosophical thinking about the things that I did before. Okay, I have a job and I'm really career oriented; I want this promotion. But why did I want it? Did I want it because I thought someone else would think it was glamorous? It's just forced me to think about my decisions and to really put them in perspective."

Development as a Domain of Growth

Development is characterized by deep, enduring structures of the self: how the learner engages issues of personal integrity and purpose. It entails a view of the self in process and a focus on the ethical or spiritual dimensions of life. Many educators regard it as the most crucial goal of higher education. Even in its narrower strands, development looks toward deeper personal meaning. Student growth in independent learning seemed to be a key component of this domain. Theorists such as Kegan (1982), Perry (1970), and the authors of *Women's Ways of Knowing* (Belenky, Clinchy, Goldberger, & Tarule, 1986) inform our understanding of how growth is expressed in the intermingling of the intellect with the interpersonal and intrapersonal. As the learner's development moves toward autonomy, grounded in a sense of interdependence, it becomes increasingly integrative and ethical.

Development extends immediate experience into broader purposes, meanings, and commitments. As such, it also can lead toward synthesis as the learner becomes increasingly able to unify capacities and awareness into a sense of personal mission, imbuing even mundane actions with a whole philosophy of life. The distant future and past can seem immanent in the lived moment, making such moments pregnant with meaning. The call of developmental wisdom is the call to the meaning of a lived life.

Developmental theorists articulate different visions of this trajectory into individuation and deepening relations with others, yet development of a deep sense of self does not appear inevitable in contemporary culture with its emphasis on consumption, conformity, and a passive happiness (Cohn, 1998; Josselson, 1987). After graduation, we found alumnae moving steadily further from the conformist posture and into their own personal stance. Virginia, at the end of her second year in the college, describes her early efforts to develop a personal perspective:

> This philosophy course I'm taking, covering dying and other people's philosophies—I think I'm developing a different philosophy of life for myself, and understanding death and things like that a lot better. I think that class has changed me a lot, in my thinking. Just the way people approach death, the idea of euthanasia, all those ideas of kidney transplants, when a person is legally dead— thinking that all over has changed me a lot. I've changed a lot of my views according to the books we've read, especially when I read a book about the Jews in the concentration camps, and the program I was watching last night, and we studied guilt and things like that; I think of the times when I felt guilt in my life and I relate them to what the author says in the book and the different responses by different philosophers. I get a different view on guilt and I change my feelings on guilt and forgiveness. I just relate the things that we're learning to myself and change myself. I never really thought about them before we read them in the book, and once you read them you think about them and you internalize them.

These longitudinal findings confirm that these women develop their capacity to construct personal meaning and integrity in ways that others have shown occur for men (Perry, 1970; Valliant, 1977). It also shows that in developing their own voices, these women often emphasized connection with others, though it does not address whether they emphasize connection more than men do, as many have suggested (Belenky et al., 1986; Gilligan, 1982; Josselson, 1987).

The Whole Person as the Interdependency Among Domains

We offer a theory of the integration of four domains of growth that attempts to bridge models of competence (e.g., Perkins, 1995; Sternberg, 1998) and of meaning (e.g., Mezirow, 1991; Perry, 1970). Increasingly, other theorists have also sought to bridge these divergent concerns (Boyatzis, 1993; Kegan, 1994; Kolb, 1984). We have found confirming parallels to our empirically informed domains of growth in a number of philosophical works. We will briefly consider just one.

Kenneth Burke (1969) uncovered in his analysis of the grammar of language five terms that express distinct stances in relation to human action: *agent, agency, act, scene,* and *purpose.* According to Burke, these terms function as grounding metaphors for all philosophies and psychologies. Interestingly, these five terms map directly onto the domains of growth. The "agent" is the active learner. Reasoning functions as a tool-like "agency" used by the learner. In performance, the learner "acts" with some discretion. Self-reflection draws forward identity's "scenic" background. Development calls the learner toward some "purpose."

To aid clarity, we have presented the four domains of growth as separate entities. Although they are distinct, they entail each other, just as Burke's terms do. We now turn to considering more active relations among the four domains as the learner transformatively cycles across these imagined boundaries. We believe the whole person grows from, and is most expressed in, these vital interdependencies.

Transformative Cycles of Learning

From integrating the research reported in Part Two, we recognized three transformative cycles of learning, in which the learner moves from one domain to another: (1) using metacognitive strategies,

(2) self assessing role performance, and (3) engaging diverse approaches, views, and activities. Figure 6.3 begins to break open each of these three cycles according to their key elements (boldface in the figure), with the cycles identified by these key causal elements. These cycles are powerful learning strategies, enabling learners to become more aware of, and in control of, their own learning, a kind of metacognitive learning. Teachers serve a crucial role in shepherding students toward this kind of awareness and the integrated learning implied by these cycles. The development of specific curricular features can play another crucial role in fostering these transformative cycles of learning. For example, as implied by the arrows labeled "breadth of learning" in Figure 6.3, a number of lines of evidence suggest that such learning in an ability-based curriculum can lead to both metacognitive performance and engagement in a breadth of activities and learning.

We have been impressed by the consistency of evidence suggesting that the four domains of growth mutually reinforce one another. This suggests that an instructor may be focusing a learning experience on one domain and still be supporting growth in the others.

Using Metacognitive Strategies

When learners connect *reasoning* and *performance,* they get an integrated sense of "what I know and how I can do this." But they may often need to develop their conceptual abilities before they can link the two. We found that the students who floundered in classroom assignments tended to have difficulty using abstract concepts; coaching and practice in the conceptual thinking demanded by the general education curriculum was critical to their success. Eventually they were able to connect the curriculum abilities with their assignments, courses, and own growth. Even so, women coming to this college with high reasoning abilities did not necessarily understand the curriculum immediately. Once students connected abstract knowledge to meeting performance demands, however, it set in motion a transformative learning process.

A five-year alumna, Justine, still recollects the dramatic effect of pulling her learning together. First, she describes what her learning was like before she entered an ability-based curriculum:

You know, I was able to, with very little effort, pull down a B, so it was no major deal. So, it's not as if anyone was pushing; no one was pushing me hard. And, you know, I really feel that what I learned primarily was how to coast, how to pull out the most important parts, and just skim along. And that's okay; that's a useful skill. And I happened to have the kind of memory that makes test taking and those kinds of things very simple. So, you know, I was always smart. I wasn't thinking; I was parroting. But I didn't know that—and nobody ever told me that—and everybody told me I was smart, and I could do whatever I wanted because I was so smart. So I said, "Okay, I can do whatever I want to do."

Justine recognizes that being smart was not enough. We note that she came to college with high moral reasoning skills (P percent = 62 on the Defining Issues Test) that she does not acknowledge in this excerpt. She delayed college, as many women do, but once at Alverno, she was asked to do something difficult for her: enacting her thinking in performance. Her assignments were asking her to integrate her knowledge and analyses into coherent action, even as the contexts tugged at her values, capacity to make aesthetic judgments, and accustomed ways of approaching problems and relationships. Then, "like a bolt of lightning," she finds that she is independently integrating her learning in one of these assignments:

When I started at Alverno, I didn't understand what it was that they were asking me to do. And I didn't understand why I didn't understand it. . . . I can remember very specifically when it did mesh for me, and it was the third-semester assessment. . . . There was a film that we had to watch, and then there was a slide of this building for this group task, and we had to do some aesthetic comparisons. It was Victorian and very gingerbready and all kinds of things. And it was like a bolt of lightning, and I was pulling things from all over the place and putting them on this paper, and I laughed because I knew how good it was. And I knew that it was exactly what they wanted, and I knew—I knew what it meant, and it was like "Ta-dum! Here it is!"

Now that's something that I had never been able to do. I had pieces of information over here and pieces of information over here, but I didn't necessarily have a connection between those two pieces of information. I had all these little discrete bits of knowledge, because that's what they teach you in school. They teach you

Figure 6.3. Transformative Learning Cycles Integrating Domains of Growth.

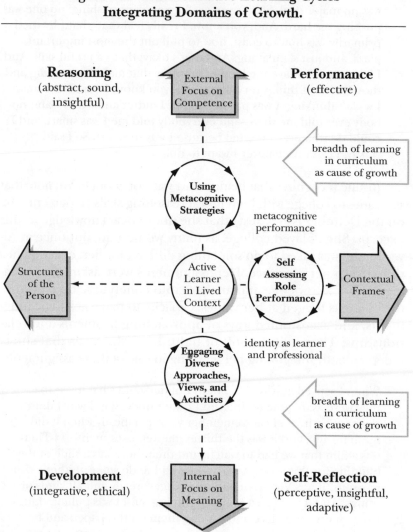

Figure 6.3. Transformative Learning Cycles
Integrating Domains of Growth, cont'd.

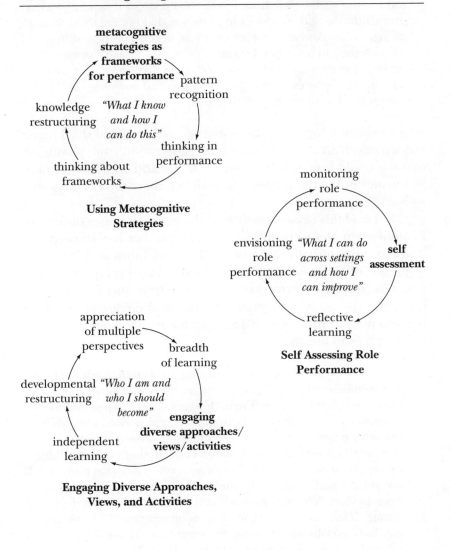

history over here, and they teach you math over here, and they teach you science over here, and they have nothing to do with each other. And so, the flaw in my intellectual process, if you will, was in not synthesizing these things in some way that related them to anything, to life! And all of a sudden, there were all of these things that meshed in my brain. I mean I could almost hear the gears grinding as they came together. And it was marvelous! Instead of going out of that exam room dragging, as had been the case in past years, I went out higher than a kite.

When Justine integrated her aesthetic and analytical thinking, it was a transformative experience, revealing to her the possibility that she could internalize learned abilities and combine them in action and in the disciplines and could connect this "to anything, to life!"

Most students came to believe in the major premises of the curriculum when they were able to put concepts they had learned into practice. They initially understood the curriculum as specifying a sequence of steps for performing, more like a recipe than as a guide to creating a performance. But with time and practice, they learned metacognitive strategies for performing. As Justine says in her second-year interview, taking up a theory becomes connected to how one can use it:

That was once my approach to learning: to skim through the book and memorize the highlights. I now analyze—I probe deeper, perhaps beneath the surface. I'm no longer content to just understand or know facts or figures. I want to understand reasons why this is true—for example, what is the relationship between sender and receiver? This is the communication concept that we were talking earlier of—sender/channel/message/receiver—and at one time, I would have said "sender/channel/message/receiver" until I had it down perfect. Now my approach to that would be, "What does that mean?" "How does that relate to my communication—to my communication skills—to building my communication skills?" "How can this concept serve me as a communicator?" Okay, it is much more an attitude of, "How can I make this work for me?" rather than "This is what it is."

In Chapter Four, progress in the ability-based curriculum was found to be a cause of growth in moral reasoning, a capacity also closely linked to critical thinking. While Justine was perceiving her growth in abstract thinking, she also was showing growth in principled or postconventional moral reasoning. Her second-year principled thinking score was 68 percent, similar to estimates of typical scores for graduate students in moral philosophy (Rest, Thoma, & Edwards, 1997). In the aggregate, learners' moral reasoning developed during college and was maintained afterward.

Figure 6.3 represents a generalization of this transformative learning-and-doing cycle (cf. Kolb, 1984). Research on expertise has shown that immersion in the thinking and practice of a specific area, such as a discipline or profession, is key to the quality of performance. Such participation develops strategies that are frameworks for performance and that enhance pattern-recognition abilities in performance. Because experts immediately grasp patterns that the novice can perceive only with effort or support (Feltovich, Ford, & Hoffman, 1997), they are able to use their cognitive resources for thinking in performance (see Figure 6.3). These strategies rise far above pattern recognition, transforming the performer's capability in the setting. The participative leadership abilities in Collaborative Organizational Thinking and Action appeared to operate at this strategic level. Learners use these strategies for constructing performance; cycling back from performance, they then think critically about their knowledge frameworks, now informed by strategic performance in context. Through this thinking, which inquires into assumptions and connections, the learner deepens his or her understanding, restructuring and expanding a personal construction of knowledge. This completes what can be thought of as a cycle of assimilation and accommodation, from assimilating experience through one's current understandings (pattern recognition) to critically thinking about and using frameworks as ways of understanding and performing (see Figure 6.3). As learners reiteratively experience using a range of frameworks, they master metacognitive strategies for selecting and flexibly using them. Achieving this capacity releases creativity and further energizes this learning cycle.

During college, several features of the curriculum seem vital to supporting this transformative process. Initially, students may need mechanical "recipes" for how to perform. Teachers can be effective by coaching learners through their performances and providing opportunities for students to try out their learning in realistic contexts. This college's shared culture of learning is another support. But students also need to be pulled into more fluid and discretionary performances that reflect professional expectations. Study in the liberal arts and collaborative work with peers is one key to meeting these expectations. Asking for performances that call forth critical thinking about disciplinary and professional frameworks provides another effective challenge.

Self Assessing Role Performance

When students integrate performance and self-reflection they get a sense of "what I can do across settings, and how I can improve" (see Figure 6.3). As they develop their self assessment capacities, they take charge of their own learning (cf. Loacker & Jensen, 1988; Marienau, 1999). We found that students used their growing understanding of abilities as frameworks to construct criteria for self assessing and improving performance. As a result, they transferred their college learning from one context to another, so that performing after college generally became a relatively smooth transition. Through a cycle of metacognitively monitoring performance, self assessment of performance, reflective learning, and re-envisioning performance in some specific role, students and alumnae gained a sense of self-confidence grounded in their capacities (see Figure 6.3). The Balanced Self Assessment and Acting from Values factor described in Chapter Five statistically demonstrated a link among many of these elements that transformatively link performance and self-reflection. This factor included self assessment of abilities, reflective thinking, reflective valuing, commitment to improvement, and diagnostic adjustment of performance. Factor analysis cannot, however, demonstrate how these elements work together as a lived process, and so we probed students' perspectives on their learning.

In distinct voices, learners described how self assessing role performance transformed their learning. To get a sense of the whole person, we return to Justine, who says, "The better I understand what the purposes of the program are, the ability-based learning, I think it is real important at first, to make a conscious effort to apply those strategies and those ways of looking at things, the problem-solving method, and the task-oriented role model, and analysis. I think at first you need to consciously think about carrying those strategies into your life, your career, family, whatever. Because, eventually, you reach a point where they're so much incorporated into your thinking that you don't have to think about applying them."

As we found for most others, Justine's insight also involved her reconfiguring her identity as a learner and performer, which is connected to her more grounded self-confidence. A belief in one's capacity to learn and grow is associated with a positive attitude toward challenges and momentary setbacks. Bandura (1997) describes a cycle of self-regulation from a cognitive-behavioral perspective, emphasizing the difficulty of transferring self-regulation to new contexts. He nonetheless acknowledges the transformational effect of developing belief in one's capacity to be effective. We too have found that students came to develop a belief in their potential for personal growth when they experienced growth. Justine says when she came out of that fateful assessment, where she put it all together, she "was high as a kite":

> And I laughed and had a wonderful time and wrote pages and pages and pages, and I knew it was good and nobody had to tell me it was good. And that was another thing that they were trying to get me to do, to be able to recognize, to self assess, and not to need those external clues to the extent that I had in the past. And I knew that it was good, and in fact one of my instructors said to me later, right before graduation, as he had looked back over everything that I had done, "I looked at this first year stuff and that's not the you that I know." And I said, "Yeah, I know that." And he said, "Well, why? What is the explanation?" And I said, "You know, this whole process, this ability-based learning stuff was so foreign to me that it took me that long to catch on to it—it really did—to begin to make connections between literature and art, and my job, and economics and history." And it was like a flash.

Here we see that students can connect their integrative experiences to the rationale for self assessment. We found that learners described their capacity to self assess as key to their ongoing learning and their transfer of abilities to new contexts. The connections Justine makes between her school work and her job illustrates again the importance of the work context as a key element in experiential validation for these women, a confirmation that they have grown. As a result, students become more self-aware of themselves as learners. Justine notes:

> In retrospect it probably didn't arrive on that day. It probably had been building. I felt very confused. I felt very threatened by the system here, but at another level I must have felt challenged. You know it was simply unfathomable to me that I could fail at school. And by fail, I mean not be the best. I must have been a semester into it before it occurred to me that being the best wasn't what this was about. It was being the best me, and doing the best I could. But it wasn't about getting a higher score than the person sitting next to me. That absolutely did not figure into the process in any way, shape, or form.

Some students could not reach an insight into self assessment as a transformative learning process until they reconfigured their understanding of the purposes of self assessment toward personal improvement. For students like Justine, good grades in high school can primarily serve as self-validation, proving that one has worth by being better than one's peers. "By not having grades," she said, "I didn't have anything to prove that I was good, which was very difficult for me. Because I had relied very much on those external clues." When learners indulge in a tendency toward global self-evaluation, they do not energize the connections between their performance and self-reflection on their performance. A tendency for global self-evaluation and comparison with others has another downside for the learner: it can lead to debilitating negative self-evaluations. In her sophomore interview, Justine contrasts her experience during the college's entrance assessments with new understandings about effective self assessment:

> The attitude of the faculty toward the student is not judgmental. It's more, "This is what is happening. This is why it's happening. So what?" and it does not go on to say, "This is right or wrong." It just stops there. This is what is happening, and this is why it is happening. Now you have to deal with what that means to you, and I will deal with what it means to me. This more realistic view

is the self assessment process, so continuous here. When I did that first self assessment, I was extremely hard on myself. I saw the flaws, which there were plenty of, and was therefore unable to see the virtues in that particular piece of work. So I didn't look at the overall picture and say that this is balanced by that. I looked, "Oh, this sentence is very bad, and therefore the whole thing is just a loser."

We have made the case for how performance and self assessment sustain learning during and after college. We understand performance and its educative value somewhat differently in a pedagogical context versus a postcollege context. In pedagogy, the value of performance is found in its capacity to call students to demonstrate what they know and can do. In this pedagogical sense, students are asked to perform, so that feedback and self assessment can be brought together in assessment. After college, we say alumnae are *performing* in any situation where they are acting with some discretion to achieve effective outcomes. A number of theorists in the workplace have discussed what we have called transformative learning through performance and self-reflection (e.g., Senge, 1990; Schön, 1987).

When individuals reconstruct performance in a role, they may rethink both their understanding of the role and how to perform in it effectively. This second transformative learning process enables a learner to learn about how performance and self-reflection work together. The learner begins to critically observe himself or herself performing in context—actively using abilities as frameworks for performing. Following the performance, the learner self assesses his or her performance in relation to an internalized construction of effectiveness. Through this cycle of reflecting, envisioning, performing, and self assessing, students increasingly self-identified themselves as learners, gaining confidence in their own capacities and increasing their understanding of criteria and standards for professional performance. This self-identification emerges in reflective learning where students connected their values to their goals and self-images.

A number of educational theorists have pointed toward the transformative power of self-reflection (e.g., Brookfield, 1991; Mezirow, 1991). Boud, Keogh, and Walker (1985) describe reflective learning from experience in a similar way to our own. They describe a process of imaginatively returning to experience, constructively attending to the feeling it engenders, reevaluating the experience, and rehearsing new learning with a "view to subsequent activity." O'Connell Killen and de Beer (1994) and Palmer (1983) describe a parallel reflective process from a theological point of view that resonates with both secular and nonsecular value traditions.

Several features of the curriculum seemed critical to the student's internalization of the cycle of envisioning, performing, and self assessing. Ironically, faculty empathy, attention, and coaching provide support to students' taking hold of independent learning. In this context, we found that students steadily grew as learners, in both their ability to articulate the role of criteria and their internalization of professional standards for role performance. The developmental sequencing of the curriculum enabled students to use criteria in more flexible ways.

Engaging Diverse Approaches, Views, and Activities

When students integrate self-reflection with the call to development they get a sense of "who I am and who I should become." Engagement with diversity in learning, perspectives, or activities seems to kick-start independent learning and further development of the whole person (see Figure 6.3). Other researchers have come to similar conclusions. For example, college students who perceive more opportunities for exploring diverse perspectives demonstrate more sophisticated intellectual and ethical development (Belenky et al., 1986; Perry, 1970), moral development (Mason & Gibbs, 1993), and maturity (Heath, 1991).

We found that as students developed a broader perspective on what and how to learn, their frameworks for independent learning—in this curriculum and beyond—consolidated. A more sophisticated framework became a habitual orientation that they brought to every context. We use the term "self-directed learning" to distinguish this developmentally consolidated form of independent learning. In becoming self-directed learners, alumnae came to understand tacitly their role in constructing their own experience, an essential step to becoming their own person.

In Justine's case, a flash of insight into this curriculum came when she could pull the breadth of her learning experiences together in an assessment. This assessment seemed to create the conditions for her to grab hold of the conceptual model of the curriculum. This became the fulcrum for her development of her identity as a learner. Justine describes her transformative insight into the independent learning foundation of the curriculum:

> It was real freaky, because I've never had that problem with schoolwork. And so I would sit and look at it for a long time: "I don't know what they want. Now this. I don't know what they want," and I would sit and sit and sit and stew and stew and fret, and finally I would sit down and say, "All right, I don't know what they want, so I'll do what I want. I'll take my own approach to this." And it was very interesting then, to come in and compare my approach with someone else's approach, because they were often very, very different. Then I would immediately go, "Oh no, I must be wrong. I should have done it that way. I didn't even think about doing it that way. I did it this way." Well, then I discovered that the instructor didn't think that that was necessarily wrong, if, in fact, I could justify the approach that I had used. And, I went, "Okay, you mean there is more than one way to get from here to there?" And it took a long time for me to feel absolutely comfortable with taking an individual approach to a task. It was like, "Give me more direction. I have got to have more guidance here: give me a clue, tell me what you want." When it finally dawned on me that that wasn't the point at all, oh boy, that was a giant leap. Life became so much easier for me when it dawned on me that that wasn't the point, and it didn't matter what they wanted. What mattered was that I took a position, that I extended that position, and that it was logical and clear. So I guess that that, more than anything, changed my whole approach to learning, to problem solving, maybe to life.

As Justine expressed above, it was common for students to emphasize how they learned from experiencing a range of approaches to learning and performance. They confronted more than one kind of diversity, however. Inevitably when individuals engage in deep self-reflection, they confront questions about their own values, identity, and personal agency. As in the case of Justine, the ability to think in abstractions is often connected to independent learning.

Justine thus pulled her thinking forward into performance and pulled her performance forward through self-reflective processes. When learners self-reflect on deeply held personal beliefs and assumptions, they embrace a transforming developmental challenge, pulling their self-reflection into an awareness of themselves in a wider world. Next Justine describes how the curriculum challenged her to think by confronting her with multiple perspectives:

> The whole challenge of stretching my mind in new directions— concepts that were absolutely foreign to everything I had ever thought, believed, heard. The challenge of putting myself inside that situation enough to understand its validity in that situation. It's not enough to learn that cultural relativism means that things are, okay, "acceptable in this culture, are not acceptable in this culture." Okay, fine. That's the concept, so what? How can that be? How can it be that, for example, in the Tibetan culture, it was traditional for the queen to marry her brother and in Western culture that is abhorrent. Where did that come from? Cultural relativism gave me a lot of problems. Situational ethics! There have been some class discussions on moral issues, ethical kinds of things, where I have been unable to accept a certain position and yet unable to justify my own position. That is extremely unsettling. So what happens is that you just have to keep examining and reexamining your own position and the other position, and either justifying it or changing it.

Justine's reflection on the differences between her own values and those of others led her to appreciate the value that the perspectives of others have for her own learning. Of course, Justine met this challenge when she was developmentally able to confront it. The safe and nonjudgmental atmosphere of the curriculum made this kind of challenge hospitable to self-reflective thought and personal growth. As Perry (1981) so eloquently says, "It may be a great joy to discover a new and more complex way of thinking and seeing; but yesterday one thought in simpler ways, and hope and aspiration were embedded in those ways. Now that those ways are to be left behind, must hope be abandoned too?" (p. 108).

Our findings argue that the curriculum scaffolded the students' development of independent learning, giving them a safe space from which to explore their aspirations. Self-directed learning then becomes the sustaining engine of this developmentally transformative learning process. Once the cycle becomes self-sustaining, self-directed learning becomes both a cause and an effect. Students and alumnae who appreciated, or came to appreciate, the value of multiple perspectives on a topic seemed also to take more charge of their learning and to have broader learning goals. They began to enjoy exposure to different perspectives as a way of learning about others and the world.

We found that students first came to appreciate liberal learning as they connected it to expanded understanding of professional role identities, laying a foundation for their development of a sense of purpose. The liberal arts exerted a long-lasting influence on the integration of the person, and the way the individual enacts values of compassion, collaboration, continued learning, open-mindedness, and integrity.

One of the exciting things we learned from our alumnae is how college can exert a continued influence on their learning. Their persisting desire to continue transformative learning was woven into the breadth of their daily activities. Our statistical causal analyses unexpectedly confirmed one of Dewey's most central theses: high-minded goals that are unconnected to the pursuit of activities are unproductive, while human conduct, pursued with deliberation, preserves and enlarges meaning in our lives. Expanded endeavors became a basis for a recommitment to a breadth of learning goals and for further integration of the person. As Justine perceives it, "I find that a lot more things are grabbing my attention, and rousing my curiosity and making me want to delve into them further—whether it's a television program, or a newspaper article, or something that one of my kids brings home, or something that happens at work. For example, entirely on my own, I have done considerable amounts of research into the economics of the tobacco industry."

We found that as alumnae expanded their roles, they developed a greater sense of personal integration. On the one hand, focusing on a particular role, such as the family or work, enabled alumnae to develop specifically in that role. On the other hand, when such a focusing persisted for an extended period it was experienced as confining (Mentkowski, 1983). As they grew, they came to see themselves as more than the roles that they enact (cf. Kegan, 1982). While expanding their careers, these women expressed a developmentally sophisticated care for others, ensuring that any changes in family roles enabled others to develop as well, appreciating and understanding how others perceived the situation. Justine enacted her growth in this way as well, realizing its potential for disrupting the basis of her relationships with family and friends. She had been through similar struggles before and had been able to reconstruct her relationships so that they still made sense.

Figure 6.3 summarizes this transformative learning process. Living out their passion for a breadth of learning, well-rounded individuals engage a diversity of activities and views, developing their capacity as independent and self-directed learners. As they experience growth, they consolidate a developmental restructuring of how they perceive the world, which gives them an appreciation for multiple perspectives and reignites their passion for learning.

As educators, we can prepare students to develop broader meaning and purpose in their lives, but we cannot, nor should we, do it for them. What we can do, we have found, is to assist them in engaging a diversity of approaches, views, and activities, so that they become active agents in their personal meaning making. Faculty and staff can coach students in independent learning and encourage them to self-reflect on who they are. These scaffolded supports may be especially necessary given the nature of such transformational challenges.

The Call to Development

Developmental theory generally suggests and finds that formal reasoning capacities are a precursor to later structural development of the self (Brabeck, 1983; King & Kitchener, 1994; Loevinger, 1976). Although we found that moral reasoning and critical thinking seemed mutually supportive, each seemed unsupportive of the development of a deeper moral structure of the self. Developmental theory and previous research findings did not lead us to anticipate that development and reasoning would, if anything, become diverging and alternative focuses after college. Graduates who focused on creating personal meaning may have been more inclined to pursue breadth of activities and their complexities, leading them to intuit and synthesize new meanings central to their life. We refer to our interpretation of this self-sustaining effect of development, through a broadened life into further development, as the "call to development." Breadth of learning in college appears to amplify such a call to development.

If there is a fourth transformative cycle of learning that connects reasoning and development, our empirical analyses have not so far helped us to describe it. Our longitudinal measures and qualitative analyses may not have yet extended into that kind of reasoning that is dialectically sophisticated at finding meaningful problems and that may be informed by development. We did find evidence that suggests something about the deeper wisdom of development. After college, the perplexing complexity of everyday problems, which present themselves differently across activities, seems to have called alumnae to a different kind of thinking, intuition, and judgment (rather than formal analysis or, even, dialectical reasoning alone).

Some Intrinsic Connections Among Domains

Two pairs of domains—reasoning in relation to self-reflection and performance in relation to development—share neither a focus on the pursuit of meaning or competence nor a common characterization of the relationship between the person and context. Nonetheless, these pairs of diagonally juxtaposed domains are intrinsically connected.

Developmental Connections to Performance

In some ways, seeking personal development and seeking effective performance seem to be different focuses. Individuals often strive for external achievements or personal meaning, but seldom, it seems, for both at the same time. For example, Boyatzis (1993) observes the phenomenon of highly competent and effective business leaders who "step off the ladder of success." Parallel to our factor analyses, McGregor and Little (1998) found that individuals clearly distinguish happiness, which is associated with instrumental efficacy, from meaning, which is associated with personal integrity (see "competence" and "meaning" in Figure 6.2).

We believe that development and performance overlap at the most macro levels of strategic choice and action. Thus, one's effectiveness as a performer may relate more to one's developmental sophistication in choosing a meaningful career direction than to one's general capacity to reflect on meaning in other contexts. We found that the developmental sophistication of an alumna's career decision making was correlated with each of the four ability factors discussed in Chapter Five (see Appendix F). No other human potential measure was this robust in its relationship to performance. Of course, structural change may also connect across domains. We can see how Justine's deliberation about her career brings forward her understanding of how life leads to changes, which is emblematic of an individual's potential to extend and unify forms of meaning making into a persuasive structure of awareness:

> I'm asking myself questions about, you know, what are you going to do with the rest of your life? Is it time to grow up? Do I have to grow up now? I don't really want to. I am asking myself the same questions that I always ask, and the answers change, you see. "Is this the job I want to be doing?" "Is this where I want to be doing it?" "Am I satisfied with who I am, and, if not, why not?" Basically those are the questions I have been asking myself all my life, and the answers keep changing because I keep changing.

Reasoning and Self-Reflection as Complementary Modes of Learning

Self-reflection and reasoning often appear complementary. As a domain of learning, reasoning emphasizes clarifying ideas and gravitates toward a propositional mode of expression; self-reflection emphasizes personal insight and gravitates toward a narrative mode of expression. Teachers often design assignments so that they connect to both the disciplinary ways of understanding and students' personal lives. We found that students often used reasoning to support self-reflection and vice versa. As they develop their capacity to self-reflect, they may gain an appreciation of how ideas develop (cf. Basseches, 1984). As a five-year alumna, Justine says that during college, "I learned that life is a question of juggling priorities, from minute to minute. I learned to identify my own strengths and weaknesses—when to know that I don't know and how to go to someone else to get the answer. I learned how to think! I learned that learning is a process, and it's not isolated, and that if you stop learning, you're dead, only you don't know it yet."

Because self-reflection extends reasoning capacities into lived understandings of dynamic processes, it may be a key link in how self-reflection, performance, and reasoning support one another and lead to development. While critics of logical thinking often point to how its propositional structure seems to lead to static and timeless reasoning, the two domains actually seem to become usefully intertwined.

An Educational Theory of Integrated Learning and Domains of Growth

We offer an educational theory that acknowledges the multidimensionality, complexity, and integration of the person and his or her learning. Each of four domains makes a distinctive contribution to how we imagine the growth of the whole person; each entails all the others. Indeed, transformative learning may be the most powerful of four generic processes of growth because it builds on the integrating connections among the domains. Integrated learning is a hallmark for growth within the domains as well.

By describing the four domains of growth and their dynamic integration, we hope to encourage expansive and nuanced descriptions of college leaning outcomes. Others have also offered distinctive descriptions of college learning outcomes, identifying key abilities and how they are fostered (e.g., Boyatzis et al., 1995; Chickering & Reisser, 1993; Heath, 1994). Their book-length accounts offer compelling, descriptive insights into how students confront the developmental tasks posed by college. With them, we share a vision of describing college outcomes and how they are fostered. Our theoretical perspective is also congruent with theirs; one can usefully relate Chickering's vectors and Heath's dimensions of growth to what we call domains of growth, and vice versa.

In other ways, the theory we offer bears resemblance to Kolb's experiential learning theory (1984), presenting an integrated explanatory account of both structure and process. Kolb's developmental theory can even be usefully mapped onto it, although we have found that its domains and cycles seem to have distinct if not divergent meanings. The most concrete difference is how our analysis opens up three learning cycles, two of which uniquely relate to growth in identity and moral integrity.

Four Generic Pathways for Growth

Many educators are most interested in how growth happens within and across the domains. In this chapter, we have explored various processes that fostered growth. All along, the integrated growth of the learner has been an implied third dimension, an integration that goes beyond the two-dimensional extensions of the domains represented in Figure 6.3. Figure 6.4 builds on the prior graphic by explicitly imagining this third dimension of growth across the life span, with the undifferentiated point at the bottom of the cone representing the beginning of an individual's life. Figure 6.4 schematically posits four generic pathways for growth within or across each of the domains: (1) transformative cycles of learning, (2) foundations, (3) consolidation of strands of growth, and (4) extensions within domains. We use a cone to represent growth because we are distinguishing horizontal and vertical growth in the person, which roughly correspond to breadth and depth. In this chapter, we have described the horizontal growth of the person as broad extensions of each of the domains. Vertical or integrative growth involves the integration of specialized processes into an overarching system that organizes their combined complexity.

Transformative Cycles of Learning

One of our main theses is that horizontal and vertical growth are often accomplished through cycles of learning that transformatively connect the domains of growth. These connected domains have some overlapping characteristics in either direction of focus (external competence/internal meaning) or relationship to person and context (structure of person/interaction with context).

Figure 6.4. Schematic Model of Growth.

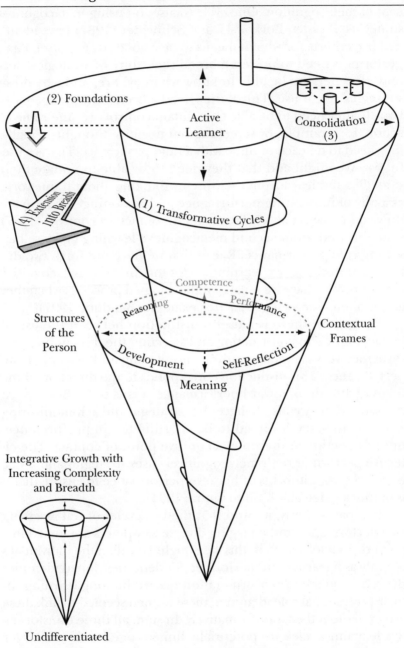

Two of these learning cycles are explicitly related to the concept of metacognition. One cycle focuses on using metacognitive strategies. Pressley, Borkowski, and Schneider (1987) have identified five criteria for what it means to be a good strategy user. First, performers need to possess a broad repertoire of strategies. Second, they need to be able to know when, where, and why these strategies are of use. Third, they need a broad knowledge base. Fourth, they need to be able to maintain control over their line of action, for example, by screening out negative thoughts. Finally, they need to do each of these with a fluid proficiency. This is a useful list. We might add that they need to be able to update their strategies and learn from their use by thinking about frameworks as a way of integrating performance and reasoning. We have addressed Pressley et al.'s fourth criterion of "action control" (1987) primarily under our second metacognitive learning cycle: self assessing role performance. Recall that we have put forth two distinctive transformative learning cycles that include metacognitive moments. Why have we separated these joined processes when they are so often seen as together (for example, Bandura, 1997)?

We believe there is a useful distinction between the use of metacognition in constructing and selecting the direction of performance versus metacognitively monitoring and learning from performance. This distinction corresponds to the direction of the focus of attention, toward performance versus self-reflection. At the same time, we also believe that strategic and self-monitoring metacognitive cycles need to be coordinated in performance, linked in action at their metacognitive point of contact. The effective performer both metacognitively uses strategies and metacognitively monitors his or her own performance to ensure that it is on track (Metcalfe & Shimamura, 1994).

In a parallel way, we find that the two cycles of self assessing role performance and engaging diverse viewpoints are linked in a point of contact, which in this case might be called the individual's identity as a learner and performer. Students developed identities that encapsulated their orientation toward lifelong learning. In their professional role identities, these women seemed to link these two cycles together transformatively. In sum, all three transformative learning cycles are potentially linked together into a larger transformative chain (see Figure 6.3).

In this linkage, the transformative cycle of envisioning and self assessing role performance appeared to play a key role. It served, it seemed, as a central link in the chain of cycles, securely connecting the pursuit of competence with a larger search for meaning. Figure 6.4 schematically depicts the linkage of the three transformative cycles as a spiral of growth that integrates the four domains of growth in the person. This spiral is numbered as the first of four generic processes of growth. In depicting this linkage as a spiral, we have taken some graphical license, since we have not claimed a fourth cycle linking the domains of reasoning and development. Nonetheless, no other image so compellingly seems to represent this integration of the domains of growth.

Foundations

Our aggregate statistical analyses suggested that the learner's critical thinking capacities grew at a steady rate during college and afterward. In many ways, the development of Critical Thinking seemed foundational to growth in other domains. For example, student constructions of their own learning suggested that the capacity to use abstractions supported their development of independent learning. The arrow numbered "2" in Figure 6.4 represents building these foundations. Evidence for abstract reasoning as a foundation for development was not, however, consistent across all analyses (see Chapter Four). Evidence for the role of building foundations seemed more secure within domains or where they overlap, for example, in the mutually supportive role of abstract reasoning and principled moral reasoning.

In our view, both discussion and solitude foster reasoning. Group discussion can often clarify, extend, and stimulate learning. At the same time, the internal dialogue that constitutes the restless criticism of the life of the mind may require a kind of self-imposed solitude that enables one to hear oneself think (see Arendt, 1978). It is useful to consider whether the learner who is in a mode of reasoning about something needs some time to pull his or her thoughts together outside the immediate presence of others. Nonetheless, there are strong social determinants of the development of thoughtful reasoning (see Kuhn, 1997; Lourenco & Machado, 1996).

Consolidation of Strands of Growth

Flavel (1963) has been a key pioneer in articulating developmental approaches. He notes that developmental stages, as abstractions, underestimate how much difference in capability an individual possesses across context. This emphasis on acknowledging that adult developmental capacities within the individual may be functionally different across context is consistent with developmental theory, but does strongly qualify some developmental abstractions. In particular, such variations may affect how educators think about the whole person and domains of growth.

Kegan (1994) makes powerful arguments for the relationship between development and performance. We agree with Kegan's main point that new demands of the workplace call for the development of the individual's capacity to be self-directed, but our data suggest that the performance domain is less correlated with the individual's development than Kegan's analysis seems to imply. Alumnae who showed the most advanced thought and initiative at work did not necessarily appear to be more self-directed in general (see Appendix F). So in contrast with this part of Kegan's analysis, we believe the performer can contextually extend his or her optimal level of performance beyond overall developmental capacities. Such extensions are limited. For this reason, we need to distinguish when an individual is self-directed in a narrow context from when an individual has achieved integrative self-direction in all of his or her functioning. Indeed from the perspective of approaches that emphasize how individual development and social context are intermeshed, we might go further and emphasize how institutions, professional practices, and the built environment co-construct the individual's capacities (Cole, 1996; D'Andrade, 1981; Lave & Wenger, 1991; Salomon, 1993).

More congruent with Kegan's developmental perspective, we also believe that vertical growth can first occur within narrow contextual strands that then both broaden and consolidate to become functional across contexts. For example, we have made the case that growth in independent learning was key to identity development during college and that identity as a learner became a key basis for broader identity later. We saw that particular identities—such as "learner," "well-rounded person," "effective performer," and "collaborator"— often fused in an emerging professional role identity.

Figure 6.4 schematically represents this third growth process—where these strands are consolidated into a new integration—as a bowl rising from the larger cone (number 3 in the graphic). The connections of the three cylinders in this cone might, for example, represent the integration of three strands of identity. In contrast, the lone strand-like cylinder on top of the large cone might then represent an ability like problem solving that the student has not yet integrated with interpersonal abilities. It is possible to imagine similar consolidations of strands of growth in other domains. For example, Justine, in a "bolt of lightning," synthesized topics from a range of disciplines in her performance on her sophomore assessment. To say that students actively integrate their breadth of learning in some sense takes a pass on describing how they accomplish this integration. Instead, it more modestly emphasizes the role of pursuing several areas of deep learning in a domain and opportunities to pull this learning together. A developmental emphasis on the need for consolidation cautions us to be careful about expecting students to grasp an educator's most sophisticated developmental stances, such as the most up-to-date postmodern perspectives, just as these students are learning to become self-directed (Kegan, 1994).

Extensions Within Domains

As Figure 6.4 implies, when learners expand reasoning, performance, self-reflection, or development horizontally, they also develop vertically. Examples of horizontal extensions include questioning assumptions in one's own thinking, envisioning performance into the future, reflecting on how one's values have changed, and committing to the implications of one's own philosophy. They differ from vertical strands of growth by being expansive from the start. While sustained horizontal extensions into the breadth of a domain entail vertical growth in a domain, the converse may not follow, as we have noted under the topic of strands of growth. There is, however, one corresponding caveat. Whereas vertical strands need integrative insight to imply personal growth, horizontal expansions need to be sustained and organized to imply integrative learning. For many of Alverno's students, the liberal education core of the curriculum led them to extend their thinking into abstractions and collaboration. In the domain of performance, alumnae appeared to make the furthest extensions through participative leadership, taking a larger view of their organization and its objectives. In the domain of self-reflection, students profited from immersing themselves in a shared language of learning and reflecting on their identity as a learner and performer who holds certain values. In the domain of development, students benefited from engaging multiple perspectives and making lived commitments to self-identified purposes and ethical stances. In general, these extensions within a domain can also become moments in the transformative learning cycles that connect and cross the domains of growth. The extensions within these domains are congruent with social constructionist perspectives that emphasize the intermeshing of person and context and with developmental perspectives that simultaneously emphasize differentiation and integration.

Performance and Liberal Learning

It is worth recalling in a sweeping glance what our findings have suggested about performance and liberal learning, two topics that seldom mix. Chapter Five made the case for an integration of professional and liberal arts curricula. We have suggested that the meaning of the degree can be defined by alumna reasoning, performance, self-reflection, and development—and their integration through transformative cycles of learning. An education that fosters these facets of learning simultaneously reinvigorates the values and perspectives of the liberal arts and meets the challenges of the new workplace (cf. Heath, 1994). We have made the case for how civic educational goals are linked to performance and its emotive depths. We are struck by how consistently our findings support the pivotal role of liberal learning in education. We also found strong evidence for the collaborative orientation that students and alumnae developed and carried out in their everyday lives.

The educational model of growth that we offer, like those of some others (Boyatzis et al., 1995; Chickering & Reisser, 1993; Heath, 1994; Kolb, 1984), concerns itself with the whole matrix of the developable person. In our view, a maximally holistic education balances its collective efforts across the range of domains of growth in the person. Based on the depth and comprehensiveness of these longitudinal studies of student and alumna growth, we have concluded that an educational program can simultaneously develop each of the four educational aims that are so often promised by higher education: mastery of thought in the disciplines and professions, meaningful self-reflection, development of the whole person, and performance in work, family, and civic settings.

Education can also be about a greater whole person, one that actively integrates all of these domains of growth into a complex unity of personhood characterized by dynamic and deeply felt inscapes of individuality and integrating ties with others. In our inquiry, we have been impressed by how students have taken on and integrated a professional identity with humanistic ideals. We have seen many instances where alumnae have risen to acts of courage born of commitment to personal integrity and a concern for the greater welfare of others. At the same time, their lives and ideals are still unfolding. They are still broadening themselves and developing a sense of their capacity to make a better world by envisioning it in their daily interactions. As educators, we share Justine's sentiment:

> I wonder who I will be ten years from now, because it's happening, evolution is a reality in my life. And, it's really neat; I can't wait to see who I'm going to be.

Chapter Seven

Creating the Learning-to-Teaching Connection

Learning-centered education does not mean replacing an emphasis on teaching with one on learning. It does mean taking up the complexity of educators' envisioning the learning-to-teaching connection by making explicit the intuitive bridge from their knowing to acting. When building such bridges from learning-to-teaching in conversation, educators benefit by using learning principles—cast in a usable, transferable language—as bricks and mortar. Once on the bridge, however partially completed, they are free to brainstorm collaborative action principles for learning that lasts—that is, evidence-based guidelines for teaching and advising, two roles that faculty and staff embrace as part of the teaching-learning interaction.

The persistent effort at Alverno College to deeply rethink the learning-to-teaching connection resulted in an educational theory of learning that lasts: a theoretical model of the person—a map of how individuals use transformative learning cycles to integrate domains of growth—and a parallel expression: principles for learning and action. Together, Chapters Six and Seven yield new meaning for learning-centered education. Part Three is another way readers—and their colleagues—can bridge "what educators know about learning" (Part Two) and "what educators know and do about teaching, advising, curriculum, scholarship, and institutional culture" (Part Four).

Building bridges from learning to teaching is an abiding concern for educators as they move from student learning, as a starting point, to rethink teaching. As they formulate what they know about learning-to-teaching, educators imagine or plan what to do with what they know in their own setting. We propose that educators initiate a conversation about learning that lasts as it bears on teaching. To frame it, we provide three tools for helping it along and a design for how the conversation might flow. Such a conversation can be long or short, broad or in depth, begun with expert or novice educators—inspired by the intent to understand their students' learning.

The three tools or strategies can help initiate the conversation because they unpack the complexity of the learning-to-teaching connection. The tools are a practical part of Alverno's theory of learning that lasts, making it understandable and usable to other educational communities. First, we explore the complexity of jointly forging an educators' language of learning-to-teaching to foster awareness of some of the concerns in that endeavor and the benefits of gradually addressing them. To advance a usable language, we offer a second tool: the learning principles for learning that lasts. They reflect the four ways of knowing about learning—including the experience, intuition, and informal reflection that characterizes learning by educating in a learning ecology, as well as formal research, collaborative inquiry, and review of literature and practice (recall Chapter Two). Third, to illustrate the use of learning principles, we pair each with action principles for teaching-advising. The pairing is based on a recent cross-disciplinary conversation about those learning principles on our own campus, using aspects of a design that acknowledges key turning points in such a discussion. We close the chapter by elaborating this design to capture important questions and processes that would constitute a more extended conversation about learning that bears on teaching across different roles, on any campus.

The process of starting with learning in making the learning-to-teaching connection can build on a group's own learning principles, those articulated here, or from other sources. Although this chapter focuses on the need and context for starting this conversation and then extending it across roles, we know that sustaining it is necessary to making learning that lasts a reality. With that in mind, the chapters that follow in Part Four explore how this kind of conversation can become a significant dimension of any institutional culture.

Framing a Conversation About Learning That Bears on Teaching

Educators deepen their understanding of learning and teaching through discourse, which is shaped, consciously or unconsciously, by the participants' knowledge and concerns about learning. Each individual and group frames what they know in different ways and comes to different solutions. Differences and commonalities will emerge across disciplines.

When a group takes up a conversation about the learning-to-teaching connection, interesting challenges arise at once. If a challenge is to integrate different voices in discussion, then one tool is the development of awareness of a need to forge a common language for discussing the learning-to-teaching connection. If a challenge is to integrate different sources of ideas and evidence about learning, then a second tool is thinking through learning principles that probe the learning-to-teaching connection. If a challenge is to integrate different contexts of practice, then a third tool is generating action principles that illustrate teaching *for* learning.

A design for collaborative inquiry can organize the three tools into a process for initiating a conversation about learning that bears on teaching. In a beginning conversation, such a design primarily encourages the flow of conversation from thinking through learning principles to generating action principles, with the emphasis on moving from learning-to-teaching and advising. Using this design, faculty and staff might ask each other to consider explicitly what their own students are learning currently, within various disciplines, across different contexts, outside class, and after college, sparking change from within by drawing on the very knowledge, courage, and understanding that makes teaching and advising possible. This implies consciously using language that can break the ice in a cross-disciplinary conversation and ground the discussion in evidence.

Forging a Language of Learning-to-Teaching, Integrating Different Voices

Beginning a discussion about learning often evokes a request for a definition. For our purposes here, learning emerges from educational practice as an integrative, recursive, heuristic activity. In the fullest sense, learning involves thinking through the personal, disciplinary, or contextual frameworks that bear on a situation. It involves engaging in multiple experiences and performances to explore, demonstrate, and consolidate one's learning. It also means ongoing assessment that opens performances up to observation, analysis, judgment, and insight. It means embracing a range of other reflective activities that increase understanding of performance and support the integration of learning into one's overall makeup (for example, making meaning across situations, planning for future action, taking action in a range of contexts). A definition of learning and its revision may be a product of a conversation, but definition is not the primary purpose.

To move beyond a definition to a discussion of learning as it bears on teaching, educators benefit from jointly forging a living language to capture the elusive learning-to-teaching connection. For example, as we started to share and probe the connection across disciplines, issues of language were immediately on the table—and the dictionary and "using plain English" did not seem to help! We were reminded that to study in each of our disciplines also means to learn the language of that discipline in order to participate in disciplinary discourse. The language must change when new ideas come into being. For a group's conversation to serve their dialectic inquiry about the learning-to-teaching connection, we found that their language must steadily become more accessible across disciplines, roles, and educational settings.

Five kinds of language are germane to the proposed conversation:

- *Context-specific language, to discuss across disciplines what is observed in students' learning* (for example, "experiential validation of abilities" in and outside of class; students "self assessing in relation to criteria"). A conversation in a different setting would equally need to clarify specific terms.
- *Terms and methods that reflect the modes of inquiry used to test educational assumptions and learning principles.* These are grounded in various disciplinary paradigms—for example, approaches to studying learning such as deliberative inquiry, cultural psychology, or causal analysis, each with its respective terms (document analysis, thematic analysis, statistical terms).

- *Disciplinary and role language that encompasses concepts, terms, and methods that have different meanings.* For example, the term *hermeneutics* has a different meaning in the social sciences than it does in theological studies. The phrase "impact of teaching on student learning" is more common to conversation about policy at the institutional level; in the classroom, faculty refer to "interactive influences of learning and teaching."
- *More abstract language that encompasses education as a discipline.* Educators across disciplines who teach undergraduates are likely to meet this language because they reference particular learning and teaching theories and strategies, educational values, philosophies and assumptions, or issues about what is valid inquiry in teaching and learning—for example, "development," "perspective taking," "assessment," "personal growth," "scholarship of teaching." Because education is also a profession, it includes the language of commitment and belief.
- *The formulation of what educators know about learning as learning principles.* Recently learning principles have been derived from collaborative discussions conducted by national associations, which see benefits to formulating principles in order to take more collaborative action toward improving student learning (American Psychological Association Presidential Task Force on Psychology in Education, 1993; American Association for Higher Education, American College Personnel Association, & National Association of Student Personnel Administrators [AAHE, ACPA, & NASPA], 1998; Astin et al., 1992; Engelkemeyer & Brown, 1998, p. 11; Lambert & McCombs, 1998; McGovern, 1993; Mentkowski, 1998).

This chapter extends the national effort to formulate learning principles as part of a language of learning-to-teaching. We also use the strategy recently created by AAHE, ACPA, and NASPA to pair learning principles with collaborative action principles. Thus, the language of learning throughout this chapter is intentionally transferable and cross-disciplinary. It extends the more abstract language of educators' theory building in Chapter Six; and educators can also use it, as a prompt in conversation, to build bridges to action more easily. We rely primarily on the fourth and fifth kinds of language for the sake of accessibility, while cautiously including the first, second, and third. In this chapter, we amend the learning principles we have previously offered (Alverno College Faculty, 1979/1994) to incorporate new ideas and evidence and to provide a sample of action principles for teaching-advising. Even so, conversations about learning are likely to remain both broad and context based, formal and informal, potentially highlighting the obstacles to using a language of learning-to-teaching. Resolving these problems led to directly transformed student learning, enhanced collaboration for educational purposes, and the promotion of cross-disciplinary talk about evidence for student learning.

"New Language" as a Learning Strategy

As Alverno faculty tried to adapt their language of learning-to-teaching for wider discussion, on and off campus, they realized that it was rooted in their experience of teaching. It was difficult for them to discuss the processes and consequences of learning, or their emerging ideas about the nature of teaching, apart from the contexts with which they were familiar (Riordan, 1993). Thus, amending the learning principles for this chapter meant renewed efforts to craft a language that makes explicit the learning-to-teaching connection. We expect that readers who use the principles initially to reflect on their own knowledge about learning and then to study learning as it relates to their teaching will transform our language into their own context-specific dialect. Thus, the language of learning is constantly evolving and adapting, as conversation communities pull apart or overlap.

Faculty at this college persisted in developing a common language of learning because it began to serve a pedagogical purpose. The studies on student as learner (Chapter Three) showed us that the faculty's language, unfamiliar and abstract though it first seemed to students, explicitly enabled students to integrate their learning. Clarifying that language helped students build their own concepts. As they internalized the language of learning, students carried its constructions—"process," "models," "frameworks," "self assessing," "integrating"—with them into future learning situations even as they evolved their own language for these ideas. In so doing, they taught faculty this insight: *Language fosters transfer of ideas. The language of learning can become a resource that is independent of where the language was learned.*

Mastering, transforming, and using one's language of learning (Mezirow, 1991) fosters learning that lasts because it provides linguistic tools for concept development. To learn a field of study, a student has to learn about how to learn it; the content-process dichotomy is a false one. At the same time, a language of learning moves beyond the typical discourse of the disciplines. It includes expressing how to make metamodels in the discipline explicit (theories, frameworks, heuristics, methods), how to demonstrate learning outcomes in performance in the major field (using performance criteria), how a practitioner in a discipline "thinks, does, and feels" the discipline. Faculty and staff began to see the implications for themselves: *Learning effectively means developing, revising, and depending on mental models about learning.*

"New Language" and Collaboration

As educators, we are continually testing idioms and usages that work well to build consensus across disciplines, but we also need context-specific, technical terms for our discourse to become more deeply meaningful (cf. Harris, 1985). A broadened and deepened language also serves communication among colleagues across higher education, because meaning making requires attention to a number of fundamental issues and common tasks in the field. Then, tensions around terminology (for example, *judgment* or *action, design* or *implementation*) can become dynamic and productive rather than barriers. For example, educators struggle to develop a language where learning and teaching are not immediately bifurcated, but each informs the other. They are unlikely to separate learning from its context, for example, while interacting with students. They do not separate "ability" from "content," "content" from "process," or "process" from "outcome" while they are teaching. Neither do most educators separate knowledge from performance, theory from practice, or emphasis on the disciplines from emphasis on learners. Nor do most educators, in practice, sever the "is" from the "ought" or divide the ideal from the feasible. Rather, they link what learners are actually learning with what ought to be learned, in order to project what can be learned.

A language of learning also helps faculty to connect contexts and colleagues across undergraduate education. Merging our own and others' disciplinary and pedagogical scholarship can help us reconstruct our knowledge; it can help us reflect on and self assess our role performance, supporting the interdependence of research and teaching. We expect, along with Mezirow (1991), that ongoing exploration and development of a language of learning, in conversations for envisioning learning that lasts, will serve all educators.

"New Language" and Evidence

Jointly developing such a language means that much of the conversation ("What is *learning*? *What* can be learned?") becomes a search for definitions, concepts, and evidence. Once a cross-disciplinary conversation turns to comparisons among various sources of ideas, then the nature of evidence, its form and epistemology, becomes a topic. Faculty and staff who uncover outside advances in learning theory and practice also create such advances themselves. To do either requires an evidence base in a language of learning that integrates emerging evidence from cognitive scientists as well as from teaching-advising practice. The need for evidence arises in part because claims for causality permeate an educator's language of teaching. Even so, that assumption of causality encounters constant challenge from each discipline, because each has a different perspective on what is good evidence. Causality in a collaborative conversation implies using a range of sources of ideas and kinds of evidence if participants are to generate principles that anticipate collaborative action. A benefit is that participants can begin to formulate, use, or revise learning principles for integrating different sources of evidence.

Thinking Through Learning Principles, Integrating Different Sources

To elaborate their ideas about learning in a usable form, many educators translate them into a set of learning principles—the "transferable" part of the learning-to-teaching connection—because they integrate many different sources of substantive ideas about learning (for example, theory, experience, inquiry, understanding of current students). Some educators may not yet have formulated their learning principles and may initiate their conversation by using principles from various sources that resulted from collaborative inquiry (American Association for Higher Education, American

College Personnel Association, & National Association of Student Personnel Administrators, 1998; Lambert & McCombs, 1998). We also offer a set of learning principles here, as a way of initiating a conversation. *Learning that lasts is integrative; experiential; self-aware and self reflective, self assessed and self-regarding; developmental and individual, transitional and transformative; active and interactive, independent and collaborative; situated and transferable; deep and expansive, purposeful and responsible.*

The learning principles in this chapter have a two-decade history in Alverno faculty and staff collaborative inquiry. They are most often in revision, with periodic published updates (Alverno College Faculty, 1979/1994). Structuring a process that anticipates the revising of learning principles by educators with different roles, levels of expertise, and experience requires a systematic method if it is to integrate the many ways educators learn about learning, probe what key learning processes and experiences enable learning that lasts, and surface, explore, critique, and expand learning principles. We have used a deliberative inquiry method where a smaller group works ahead of time incorporating new ideas about learning into evidence-based learning principles to make a large group conversation feasible using a design. This method is a common one in developing principles of good practice at the national level (Chickering & Gamson, 1987). (The deliberative inquiry process that undergirds the update in this chapter is described in Appendix G.) We assume that any educators, whether using their own, ours, or others' principles, will challenge the worth of any set of learning principles as part of generating action principles. We also anticipate this benefit: Sooner or later, participants will revise any set of principles to adapt (not adopt) them for their own use, and those learning principles will better reflect the nuances of the learning-to-teaching connection.

Thinking through learning principles can guide our action as educators. This is no simple matter of listing theoretical principles or applying research results to practice; even the term *applied learning* seems too unidirectional and narrow to describe this process. Recall that learners go through distinct, transformative learning processes or cycles to connect reasoning and performance, and self-reflection and performance. This process is complex and challenging for students and alumnae; we can expect it to be no less so for ourselves. During this transformative conversation, each of us can expect to take our restructured knowledge about learning back into our teaching and advising situations and reconstruct that knowledge again in our situated performing.

Generating Action Principles, Integrating Different Contexts

Learning principles often do not suggest more than very broad learning conditions. Corresponding action principles for teaching and advising are a necessary part of the conversation. Educators do not dichotomize learning and action principles in practice. However, learning principles are intended to be more comprehensive and transferable than action principles; the latter are much more situated yet transportable. The benefit is that action principles are closer to actual practice. As axioms, they reflect how educators integrate different contexts of practice as well as a host of day-to-day teaching and advising experiences.

Bridging Learning Principles and Action Principles

In creating an action principle from a learning principle, educators *perform an act of individualized and collective interpretation,* orienting their understanding toward a future action. Action principles represent educators' integration of their current perspective with their long-term, empirically based picture of learning that lasts. They join their past and most recent inquiries with their current teaching practices. "If-then" statements, formulated as action principles, can capture the dynamic between teaching and learning; they are at the heart of what enables effective teaching. Learning and action principles reflect conscious understandings that the faculty or staff member keeps focused on while planning, carrying out, and reflecting on teaching or advising. Of course, action principles are only a beginning for design—an anticipatory action—and only one outcome of the interpretive act of constructing connections to a theory of teaching from a revised theory of learning. In a particular setting, such principles are further mediated by the thinking, judging, and acting of each educator in response to that of the students (see Chapter Eight).

By making learning and action principles explicit, the educator also demonstrates an awareness that he or she is a bridge in a larger and shared program for educating the student. The educator is responsible for setting up the connections between learning principles, his or her own teaching, and the learner's learning, and these relationships are imbued with an awareness of the whole curriculum. In conversation, a clinical educator in nursing put it this way: "If learning is integrative, I am responsible for knowing what other faculty have taught and what this student has learned, so that I can create connections to what the student can be learning in a new situation." She also notes that she uses shared beliefs, assumptions, or principles to guide her teaching (cf. Donald Schön's "theory in use," 1987): "What I consciously say to myself and to my students as a teacher becomes key in creating practice. For example, I 'voice' theoretical perspectives from nursing and observations gathered from my former practice to my students—while they are observing me working with a client. I model my synthesis of nursing and learning theories. This is how I integrate my discipline as a framework for student learning, with the principle, 'learning that lasts is integrative.' It's one way I am mindful about how disciplinary learning interacts with teaching."

Learning and action principles should meet several criteria. They should bring together the maximum diversity of voices, sources of ideas and evidence, and contexts of practice. Further, they should integrate what *is* learned and what *ought* to be learned with what *can be* achieved. They should be constructed in an iterative, interactive process and expressed in a usable language that connects learning to teaching, and should be amenable to continual, evidence-based adaptation with a concern for transferability or transportability to other groups or settings.

Learning and Action Principles for Learning That Lasts

Learning principles realized through action principles, together with relationships among the domains of growth and transformative learning cycles, make for an educational theory of learning that lasts. And so we explicate principles of learning that lasts in relation to the in-depth inquiry in both Parts Two and Four, giving these principles more meaning because they are grounded in an integrated theory, research, and practice. We elaborate action principles with direct quotations to reflect selected, individual voices from the 110 faculty and staff members who contributed to twenty-one group conversations (see Appendix G).

Learning That Lasts Is Integrative

The learner begins to integrate, to continually make connections and create new wholes out of multiple parts: his or her knowledge and ability, individual abilities needed in a given situation, and abilities and the situation or context. The learner is enabled to integrate and develop historical, scientific, and artistic concepts and frameworks by thinking with them and interacting with them in specific situations. Students learn to integrate by challenging themselves to continually differentiate, to break open ideas and concepts in their development of understanding. Some begin with the whole, others with parts in varied orders, pulling things apart to come to different ways of reconnecting them uniquely. Such learning creates a more sensitive and complex understanding of differences and how things fit together. Integrative learning that lasts extends, deepens, and secures the learner's knowledge and ability.

In designing developmentally appropriate learning experiences, educators recognize the affective or emotional dimension as central to learning. They do not segment learning as a cognitive process or set aside the development of empathy or a tolerance for ambiguity. Emotional development is not just a condition, input, outcome, or consequence of the learning process; it is something educators deliberately plan for. A sound learning process involves the learner's career and personal aspirations, prior learning and experience, maturity, subculture, and family situation, to name a few. As students process what they have learned, they are making connections and constructing new, related understandings. Student and alumna interviews showed various forms of integrative learning that students constructed as they interacted with the curriculum and took up postcollege challenges.

To think of learning as performance is often to think in terms of acting out, or applying, what is learned. This misdirects. Performance is the integration of knowing and doing—in class and off campus. It is a kind of learning in which a student is actively engaged and involved, whether it be in creating a painting, solving an experimental design problem, or developing a public relations strategy for a business. Students see integration of knowing and doing as an ongoing interactive process in which both knowledge and experience are repeatedly transformed, and so it encourages transfer of learning. Thus, learning as integrative is intertwined with learning as experiential. Developing as a competent performer means internalizing curricular abilities. And so, faculty expect students to integrate curriculum abilities in their performance as they advance.

Educators can create conditions that enable learners to integrate domains of growth (reasoning, performance, self-reflection, and development) through transformative learning cycles. First, learners are able to integrate knowing and doing (that is, reasoning and performance) when educators provide experiential learning opportunities that simultaneously require integrating concepts in the disciplines and integrating abilities in performance. For example, the learner can gain an effective awareness of how historians take stances, explore the evidentiary bases for interpretations, and interact with the broader community by doing the inquiry into differing primary sources for a particular historical event and then interacting with others around alternative interpretations. Second, students are able to self assess their strengths and weaknesses in their work (integrating self-reflection and performance) when educators consistently insist on this and create learning opportunities that develop self-confidence, self-awareness, professional identity, and performance capabilities. Feedback develops and extends self assessments, enabling students to evaluate and think through their actions and more broadly envision roles and responsibilities. Third, learners can effectively integrate awareness of their particular roles, responsibilities, and social identities with an understanding of independent and interdependent learning (integrating self-reflection and development) when educators create diverse, safe, and challenging opportunities for students to explore their horizons through new approaches to learning and new perspectives. Effective learners find courage to make distinctive commitments within their vision of collaboration.

Based on this synthesis, the Alverno faculty and staff have developed, through discourse, a few examples of action principles.

They tuned in to the several forms of integration that learners use to connect knowing and doing: synthesizing concepts; combining knowing, feeling, and doing to consolidate knowledge and abilities; integrating curriculum abilities in performing.

If learning is to be integrative so that it lasts, then:

- Curriculum abilities need to inform and connect teaching, learning, and assessment and be expressed through a coherent educational system.
- A curriculum needs to include opportunities for self-reflection, especially on how learning in multiple contexts affects who the learner is becoming as a professional and a person.
- Learning strategies need to emphasize doing what one knows, so that learners can experience the process and come to see their own performance in all its dimensions. Learning strategies also need to involve students in exploring the many dimensions of themselves in relation to the different dimensions of their fields of study.
- Faculty need to collaborate within and across disciplines, creating developmental experiences that move from the more discrete to the more integrative.
- Faculty need to develop learning and assessment strategies that create opportunities for students to make connections across a variety of contexts, incorporate new ideas, break open prior connections, and make new ones.
- Faculty need to encourage a developmental outlook—and approach integration developmentally—by connecting theory to data, then data to theory, examining what is consonant and what is dissonant over a number of semesters and courses.

In generating the "if-then" action principles as a group, faculty and staff as individuals also articulated several corollary insights in conversation. As one noted: "In thinking about a course, major, or program, faculty strive to create coherence. However, integration is fostered by coherence within diversity. So I also work with the multidimensionality of a concept, issue, or situation; draw on diverse sources; and engage students in exploring the complexity involved." Another group member said: "I ask students to look at different perspectives. Sometimes they understand their own perspectives better after examining others', so it's important to make the environment challenging as well as supportive." Said another: "Continually ask questions that encourage students to reflect on the relationship among the various concepts they are learning." Another commented: "Learning experiences should include explicit periods of reflection for students to analyze the expression, demonstration, or use of their abilities in varied contexts." Said another: "Integration is developmental, and novice students need multiple opportunities to grow in their ability to integrate." One faculty member noted, "Students experience knowing and doing more as discrete moments in their learning, even though faculty encourage their integration." Therefore she suggested organizing learning experiences for intermediate students so that they have some fidelity with future performance settings and more directly guiding beginning students to consider how their disciplinary learning connects to doing something with it.

Learning That Lasts Is Experiential

The learner learns experientially by connecting knowing and doing, theory and practice. Experiential learning is both active and situated, as well as integrative. It begins with experience but does not stop there; experience becomes the basis for students to develop abstractions reflectively based on familiar content. These abstractions become experiential hooks that students can consciously connect with disciplinary abstractions, which otherwise might have little meaning or purpose for them. Designing experiential learning asks educators to reconsider the principles of active learning and situated learning in the light of the need for reflection on experience. Experiential learning also calls on learners to think *during* experience. One way performers learn is by pursuing analytical inquiries in a problem-solving context, using their knowledge base to frame useful questions, seeking needed information, drawing conclusions, and persuading others. Individuals also learn from the experience of others. Students continually learn from observing and modeling their performance on that of peers and faculty. They learn by analyzing history, literature, consequences to the behavior of others, and the outcomes of world events.

Students described self-sustained learning as a process of experiencing, reflecting, forming new concepts, and testing their judgment and abilities in action. Alumnae also experienced learning as a continuous process. They tied knowledge, theory, and experience to productive action; applied abilities in action, asked for responses, and adjusted accordingly; self assessed and integrated and adapted abilities; and demonstrated a sophisticated integration of thinking and performing in context. Off-campus internships were key experiences for both older and younger students that validate these experiential learning principles and their learning in the ability-based curriculum. Important experiential features of off-campus learning situations are a complex performance-demand structure, in which students can test their ability to transfer what they have learned to actual work contexts; feedback from an independent environment; and the opportunity to observe oneself at work and to test the ability to appraise one's own performance. Through off-campus internships, students were able to articulate connections between their college learning and future professional expectations. They came to key insights on how to read organizations and what it meant to demonstrate professional responsibility. Experiential learning in the classroom and in internships confirms the learner's abilities and enhances individual identity. At the same time, experiential learning validates the meaning of curricular abilities for postcollege settings.

In the action principles, faculty and staff acknowledged that students use experience to ground disciplinary abstractions, to develop their capacity to think abstractly, to envision and internalize their future roles, and to develop interpersonal abilities for thinking collaboratively with others.

If learning is to be experiential so that it lasts, then:

- Faculty need to work with students to support them in actively constructing their learning, by moving from a specific and concrete context toward broader principles and reflecting on their experiences and abstractions in relation to disciplinary understandings.
- Faculty need to take responsibility for coaching students in the art of developing and using abstractions in the disciplines and in effectively organizing their knowledge for action and understanding.
- Faculty need to create structured reflection guides, encouraging students to stand back from their experience in order to

probe all aspects of learning—affective and cognitive, social and individual.

- Faculty and staff need to help students recognize that varied situations, in and outside the classroom, provide opportunities to experience and reflect on their application of disciplinary concepts and their practice of professional behavior, and on-going development.
- Faculty need to create opportunities for students to identify real-life applications of concepts and to interact with community resource people and agencies in order to gather and try out new ideas.

Given the evidence for the role of abstract thinking in student performance in the curriculum, faculty and staff emphasized that "Students need practice in relating examples that connect abstractions to concrete experiences that are meaningful in their lives. Teachers take on a corresponding responsibility for keeping in touch with current cultural idioms, and for inquiring into students' experience and upbringing." Another educator concluded, "Teachers need to guide students deeper into the discipline and encourage them to relate abstractions to experience outside their own milieus sooner rather than later." Because students do not find disciplinary abstractions meaningful in the same way that faculty do, faculty suggested being explicit in class about how abstractions connect to the student's current experience, internships, and future roles. The role of reflection on internships in relation to discipline knowledge and outcomes is essential. One educator argued, "We need to assist students to move between concrete contexts and broader principles. This implies bringing broader principles to bear on actual experiences and drawing broader principles from actual experience. It involves inductive and deductive reasoning."

Learning That Lasts Is Self-Aware and Reflective, Self Assessed and Self-Regarding

In order to take more and more responsibility for developing abilities, learners need an increasing understanding of what they are doing in relation to what they aim to do. Being aware is thus an essential part of learning. If a learner understands what was clear and meaningful about an explanation of a biological theory or a sociological framework, she can determine future strategies for effective presentations. If another understands why he was unable to hold a group's attention, he can work on improving. A successful active and reflective learning process includes learner engagement, self assessment, and feedback. Reflective self assessment helps learners to shape future performance, based on understanding both their past and present work and their intellectual processes.

Curricular elements support self assessment and awareness of self in a variety of ways: the use of explicated abilities, performance criteria that integrate knowledge and ability, discussions with peers and faculty, the use of feedback on performing and learning progress. Assessing multiple performances—in diverse settings with supervisors and faculty, in groups, and in reflection—leads to a different kind of mindfulness about learning. Such a structured awareness operates as a learning cycle. By making the interaction of performance and self assessment an object of the student's learning, the faculty give students more opportunities to be reflective, that is, to consider thoughtfully their growth as learners and performers who are developing a professional identity.

Curricular structures for judging performance, and their common language, make learning in disciplines and professions more visible to students. Their efforts to learn to think, in varied disciplinary frameworks, interact with their performances; this interaction results in clearer understanding of a field of study. As students work with their experiences and new forms of reasoning and analysis, they engage in learning at levels of increasing sophistication. Even as they move into denser and more complex material, their expanding awareness of curriculum abilities (including constructing and monitoring performance) enables them to navigate the rapids.

Students develop confidence that they can transfer their knowledge and abilities to new settings through performances, when they see themselves do it. Knowing what they can do across settings leads to self-regard in that learners appreciate their own ways of doing things. Similarly, self-reflection and individual development interact as students actively engage the breadth and diversity of approaches and views they have encountered. More generally, the faculty's attention, empathy, feedback, and coaching support students' taking hold of their learning. For example, through coaching, students learn to focus on self assessment for improvement. Reflection on past performance and envisioning future performance provide a transformative link that enables students to develop a learning identity and begin to connect their values and goals to who they are and can be, as professionals and persons. Asking students to reflect systematically on their own values and those implicit in the views of other individuals, cultures, organizations, and professions leads them toward a valued self-awareness and developmental transformations. These learning cycles persist past graduation.

If learning is to be self-aware and reflective, self assessed and self-regarding so as to last, then:

- A curriculum needs to provide opportunities for reflective self-awareness and feedback on that awareness; it needs to encourage balanced self assessment of identified strengths and weaknesses in performance and focus on how abilities are manifested.
- A curriculum needs to connect the process of becoming self-aware with future professional roles and goals, and encourage critical attention to the explicit and implicit criteria for practicing within professional roles.
- A curriculum needs to incorporate a range of self assessment modes in order for students to gain many different types of views of their performance (for example, listening to themselves, reading their own work, viewing themselves on videotape, giving solo presentations, and interacting in groups).
- Faculty need to fulfill various roles: providing context for self assessment, guiding discussions, encouraging responses, offering resources, modeling the value of self assessment (for example, articulating the principles that inform their teaching behavior, monitoring their own approach publicly, referring to sources in relation to their own personal thinking).
- Self assessment needs to be taught and learned developmentally; it needs to become more and more sophisticated and complex as students move on.
- Self assessment needs to incorporate students' goal setting over time (including projects, majors, professional planning).

- Curriculum needs to facilitate moving students toward an increasing integrity in self assessment. It does this through insisting on the credibility of the evidence offered (if the student provides no evidence, the self assessment cannot be considered adequate). Students are held to standards of credibility; they meet criteria. Faculty should make sure that the standards for credibility are in published criteria where kinds of criteria ("format," "content," "performance") are differentiated.
- Faculty members must fulfill various roles: providing context, articulating frameworks, guiding discussions, encouraging responses, valuing the self assessment process, offering resources.

The interacting groups discussed how students grow in their capacity to observe, interpret, analyze, and judge their performances in relation to planning future performances and ongoing development. Students' perspectives reinforced the faculty's realization that self assessment was central to the student's growth as a learner. In generating action principles, faculty and staff focused on their active role in fostering self assessment and self-awareness in student learning: "Create self assessment prompts that reflect the learning experience; ground self assessment in a specific content/framework/context; include self assessment in learning; and teach the principles of self assessment as well as the meaning of criteria and their value." Another noted that "It is important to create settings that are communal, conducive to risk taking, open-ended." "Yes," said another, "the goal of peer assessment is 'making the other person better.' It is then nonjudgmental and nonthreatening, and results in more honest critique. Assist learners to balance self assessment between attention to development of skill and a holistic attention to personal development, intellectual and emotional." A member of the group added that curriculum should *not* require that an entire self assessment framework for learning be laid over every self assessment. For example, planning future performance is not appropriate to every self assessment. Commented another, "Because intuition and intuitive actions are based on integration of past learning, a series of disciplinary frameworks to draw on is essential in order for a student to arrive at a performance."

Learning That Lasts Is Developmental and Individual, Transitional and Transformative

Learning is an ongoing, advancing process. Learners build on what they already know and can do, reconstructing their knowledge and ability with new learning, then carrying it forward to another level, which becomes a next potential starting place. This calls for a sequencing of learning goals, outcomes, and tasks, as well as a developmental, coherent course structure. Since this structure is a pedagogical framework and not a matter of how each student learns, it also means building in the kind of flexibility that enables a student to find and fashion an individual pattern of learning. That learning is developmental is a self-evident idea for educators. This means that they take responsibility for making learning meaningfully developmental in the curriculum. In part, that means clarifying outcomes to create multiple points of entry into the learning process for varied learners at varied stages and styles. Individualizing learning requires ensuring that students actively participate in the process by creating learning experiences that demand their individual involvement and their explicit incorporation of how new learning builds on existing knowledge and understanding.

Learners master more than knowledge. Both they and the object of knowledge are transformed. Learning in one domain of the person may parallel or diverge from another; the dynamic fosters what a learner knows and can do. The learner tends to experience this development as psychological; the faculty tend to experience it as pedagogical.

Learning advances in a more spiraling than linear fashion; it is often more differentiating and transitional. Students make transitions, from entering an educational program to mastering it and from a more general education to a more specialized one. These more obvious transitions often give the appearance of more coherence than actually lies beneath these surface markers. More subtle ones emerge day to day and week to week, and they build gradually. It is only when new learning enters the fabric of thought and action, after repeatedly recycling through earlier forms, that learning appears to have a more stable character. Teaching is essential to learning when it is a means for planning and stimulating the transitions that are a necessary next step. Along the way, the learner creates an identity as a learner, performer, contributor, and professional, all of which contribute to constructing the self as a developing person. Cohorts of students also display unique characteristics over time. Some cognitive-developmental patterns are relatively stable, yet differences surface year to year in each group of students. Consequently, a curriculum is always in process. Moreover, a faculty's concern for learning, its assessment and validation, is distinctly individual. This means respecting individual differences in how students approach learning and assessment and drawing out the learning potential from the diversity of individual experiences and performances.

We have learned that embracing the various meanings of the learner's development is essential to a language of learning. The term *development* often means that student performance is scaffolded to greater sophistication through a curriculum and that learners' capacity to profit from or achieve certain experiences relies on their progressive mastery of ideas more likely learned in a program of study. Teaching must support students in moving from addressing individual criteria in particular performances to understanding how criteria apply across situations and how situations require broader and more complex frameworks. This faculty's description of learning and its performance characteristics such as integration, independence, creativity, awareness, and commitment—each modified by habituality—also opens up the learner's development as a person and a professional (Alverno College Faculty, 1979/1994). Faculty find these kind of characteristics more evident in advanced student performance.

The learner's developing capacity to integrate knowing and doing in this curriculum with reflective awareness is transformative. Teaching beginning students can be highly challenging because learners at first do not share the same assumptions about their roles and responsibilities in the learning process. As they progress, they develop their own personal sense of integration in their engagements with the broader community. First and foremost, they take increasing responsibility for their own learning, gradually developing the capacity to hold onto personally felt tensions. Such conflicts may arise from taking multiple perspectives on issues in the disciplines or from struggles in their personal life. Along this path, they begin to connect a growing identity as a professional and as a learner to concerns and issues that are larger than their specific career choice. They evidence a complementary dynamic among school, work, civic, and personal relationships, with self as the integrating factor. A transformative learner is concerned with his or her personal future and sees the self as linked inseparably with the future of the human community. Such a learner comes across as a lucid interpreter of life consonant with his or her own experiential background. Reliance on authority and tradition is meshed with a personal synthesis of one's own experiences. Educators who take a developmental perspective on transformative learning acknowledge that restructuring of the self, and how one constructs the world, is neither easy for the student nor complete at graduation. These educators nurture a breadth of perspective and a commitment to a lifelong process.

If learning is to be developmental and individual, transitional and transformative so that it lasts, then:

- Faculty who work with students at a range of developmental stages of learning need to learn from each other about the interconnections between developmental stages and how to structure learning experiences so they are meaningfully developmental across the curriculum. Students need to engage in multiple approaches to learning and in multiple perspectives with flexible supports.
- Teachers need to expect that students take responsibility for developing their learning—discerning its complexity and inferring patterns, seeing relationships, and setting priorities. All of these enable the learner to spiral through learning experiences by which development becomes increasingly cumulative.
- Faculty need to provide students with many diverse modes of learning to help them learn that there are many ways to do things and interpret things—and that there is seldom just one right answer. They need to help students to engage in constructive dialogue around controversial issues. Students need to be guided to accept that the process of engagement is a higher goal than the immediate issue and develop a tolerance for the conflict, ambiguity, and delay that come with learning transitions.

- Teachers need to recognize that each learner has an individual purpose for learning; planning for a curricular outcome should allow for variations in student intentions and goals.
- Teachers need to respect each learner's unique role and investment in the learning process while holding all students to appropriate standards and criteria for achievement.
- Teachers need to incorporate opportunities for students to articulate connections between course and college outcomes and their personal goals.
- Teaching needs to involve considerable diagnostic activity, based on expertise in the discipline and familiarity with learner differences and the clues that signal a learner in transition.
- Faculty need to recall that learning does not move at the same pace across multiple areas; they must therefore work to interpret needs individually and build bridges with students among learning areas.
- Teachers need to take responsibility to know as much as is appropriate about the diverse cognitions and affective experiences of students and to use that knowledge in designing learning activities.

Insights from the discussion of action principles support the idea that student performance is guided so that it becomes more sophisticated and complex by attending to the specific prerequisites and conditions for growth. "Teachers must understand the role of core skills in the discipline, how to teach these as developing abilities, and then model these as ways to take up academic work—often in advance of current learning activities." Another noted that "The curriculum must enable a student to begin education where he or she is in terms of prior experiences, ability, knowledge, attitudes, emotions, and expectations. Learning calls for faculty to recognize the developmental needs and knowledge of individual students in order to create learning opportunities that are useful to each student. This means that teachers need to ask how criteria make explicit the kinds of scaffolds, transitions, and leaps that students need at various points." Said another, "Teachers may be dealing with performances that represent the lower edge of an ability level, and students may not be ready to move to the next level, even though they meet criteria for a particular performance. Teacher expertise involves knowing the extent of performance data that warrants judgment or validation." At the same time, this faculty and staff also commit to supporting students' overall capacity to take responsibility for their own learning. Faculty and staff take on a role in guiding students toward confronting their obligation for this—a kind of transformative development in the learner's way of being in the world. A faculty member noted, "Learning is a responsibility shared with students. How that plays out is very individual." An advisor replied, "Students must learn to work in self-directed ways."

Learning That Lasts Is Active and Interactive, Independent and Collaborative

Another principle central for student development of ability is that learning is active. Students cannot learn to think or solve problems just by listening to the most informed professor or reading the most erudite text. They test and develop their thinking by thinking aloud; that is, they learn principles of effective problem solving by addressing business problems or designing plans for civic action.

Students also cannot fully learn in isolation; learning is interactive. Today most problem solving is collaborative. In addition, thinking becomes reflective only when confronted by perceptions other than one's own, when educators set it forth in a context where the learner can question as well as be questioned, can affirm, supplement, and extend his or her understanding. In learning interactively, learners develop their knowledge and understanding, their critical thinking, their ability to solve problems and to think and speak credibly on their feet, as well as their ability to interact with others effectively.

A student's learning has to become independent if he or she is to sustain learning and performance as conditions and settings change. Students must take hold of the disciplines and learn to take stances that lead to further learning. Learning is constructed individually, yet it is also based on individual and collaborative performances. In our observation, collaboration means something different from, and more than, interaction or even cooperation. It means an effort as individuals to understand the perspectives of coparticipants and to share with them a mutual responsibility for work, products, and leadership.

We found that collaboration with others symbolized the college years and postcollege life. Many alumnae practiced a distinctive kind of participative leadership, linked to strong independent thinking abilities. Independent learning appears to have its most striking origins in the interactive engagement of diverse perspectives, approaches, and views. Encountering this diversity serves to propel this transformative learning cycle, connecting self-reflection with the development of independent learning.

When encountering novel situations, advanced learners prepare to develop an independent judgment based on their breadth and depth of understanding in the setting. They gradually work through the implications of their line of thinking and become capable of making a case for their views when others are not well prepared to understand or accept them. Because effective learners can act as individuals and in team collaboration, across roles, they take on leadership responsibilities in situations where learning is achieved in a group or corporate sense. Many thus come to view learning within interactive and collaborative settings as more important than they had thought—something that they need to understand better. Group activities begin as an important basis for learning cooperative action, but learners increasingly value them as opportunities to work across multiple perspectives. This function becomes critical as students learn to regard diversity with respect, use it as a means for testing ideas and constructing alternatives, and think critically and argue their own positions. For alumnae, breadth of activities serves a similar role. More recent studies at Alverno have underscored the significance that students and faculty place on class discussions and other group work as a basis for thinking critically and working with diverse frameworks.

If learning is to be active and interactive, independent and collaborative so that it lasts, then:

- Students need repeated opportunities to work in significant projects that are defined and executed by the group.

- Students need time for collaborative interaction with others and time for individual reflection on their own perspectives in relation to alternatives.
- Many beginning students need to learn a kind of appreciative listening. As they advance, this becomes the basis for synthesizing a group discussion.
- Teachers need to assist students to establish and evaluate collaborative processes.
- Teachers need to encourage learners to make connections between their individual learning experiences and the collaborative process, by providing learning opportunities that invite multidimensional problem analysis.
- Students need repeated opportunities to practice what they are learning in multiple disciplines; this also implies multiple opportunities for evaluation of performance.

Faculty explicitly balance their goals for students' collaborative learning—and related skills and orientations—with independent learning. "Teachers must provide opportunities for students to set goals for their own learning." Another said, "Faculty need to create opportunities for students to give service, and help them to understand both the value of service and its potential for learning." In contrast to the call for independence, some said, "We must foster a capacity for connectedness among teacher, subject matter, client, and student. Students need to develop social interaction skills for collaboration and learn to value collaboration, while teachers need to be flexible in activity design and physical class space and frame the learners' collaborative work to help them make connections beyond immediate tasks."

Learning That Lasts Is Situated and Transferable

Learning is most secure when it is situated in the context of its ultimate use. Practice settings, internships, apprenticeships, mentorships, and simulations can embody needed rationales, means-ends relations, and other situational dynamics that become particularized resources for the learner. In situated learning, learners learn strategies that effectively use the concrete resources of particular settings. They draw on their relationships with other learners to create valued contributions in recognizable fields of practice and construct professional identities that are emotionally and intellectually sustaining.

Students can readily appreciate learning in context, and yet they also can learn to construct models of performance that unify their learning across diverse situations. Although a performance is bound to the specific situation, learning from the situation can be unbounded. The learner comes to perceive his or her abilities both in and beyond the immediate situation; the net effect is that the learner develops a capacity to address and appreciate the uniqueness of each situation, while developing a sense of personal competence and readiness for new and ambiguous situations. Thus, a student's integration of knowledge and ability must be transferable.

Each student needs to make his or her learning part of a personal repertoire, something he or she can exercise in varied situations. Because it is often unclear exactly which aspects of learning transfer, educators try to provide multiple opportunities for students to develop their learning in varied contexts, so that both they and learners can gradually discern what they can depend on to carry from situation to situation. The primary pedagogical concern for transfer is not linked to specific learning alone, but also to the learner's perception of the whole array of abilities. An advanced learner has developed a criterion-specific picture of his or her effectiveness in demonstrating ability, a picture that is congruent with external standards while highlighting what is unique to the individual.

A closer analysis of transformative learning cycles makes the work of transfer even clearer. Students ground their performances in a particular context, learn to construct effective interpretations of their roles and evolving situations in that context, and begin to connect disciplinary learning to real-world performing. By also practicing across diverse settings, undertaking field experiences, and completing various performance assessments in the same ability in different disciplines, they are then able to internalize curriculum abilities as a metacognitive framework for constructing and improving performance. As a result, students can transfer college learning from one context to another, so that performing after college usually becomes a relatively smooth transition.

As students consolidate their learning, they also develop an integrated sense of themselves as learners and performers that helps them function effectively. This identity as a learner and performer enabled alumnae to transfer their college learning to new contexts. Students come to believe in their potential for personal growth as they experience it, developing a constructive attitude toward difficulties and setbacks. Students who actively think about and believe in transfer do transfer college learning to after-college performance. They come to have a strong sense of their own learning, which allows them to shape and reshape performances as situations change.

While learning is situated, reflective learning and a metacognitive awareness seem to be key to abstracting learning beyond the situation. This awareness leads to consolidating relationships among their learning experiences and their individual constructions of themselves, their values, and their vision of personal contributions to the cultures they inhabit.

If learning is to be situated and transferable so that it lasts, then:

- Students need to learn through experience in high-fidelity simulations and practice settings.
- Learners need concentrated practice in specific professional contexts to give depth and agency to their learning.
- A curriculum needs to provide varied contexts in which students can, with meaningful feedback, practice and demonstrate their abilities. As with integrative learning, such experiences need to include explicit periods of reflection so that students can analyze the expression, demonstration, and use of their abilities in varied contexts.
- Learning experiences need to include assignment and assessment prompts, to help students learn what is consistent about a particular ability demonstrated in varied contexts and what is different about it. This feedback enables the learner to develop depth of understanding of the ability and flexibility in using it.
- Teachers need to take responsibility for integrating the frameworks of the discipline's knowledge base into their teaching, so that these frameworks encourage continued learning.

- Teachers need to help the student come to understand that abilities are the mechanisms of transfer to settings external to college. They need to help mature learners see and attend to the connections between abilities they are developing on campus and their development as a professional.
- Self assessment strategies need to assist students to recognize elements of what they have learned that can be transferred to other contexts.
- Faculty who are teaching within a series of courses need to know what is taught when and where, in order to introduce, reinforce, and extend learning. They build learning situations that are highly related to the actual situation so what is intended to be learned is then directly applied.
- Because transfer occurs best when courses are purposefully structured to ensure it, faculty need to create a shared understanding of ability development and a language of learning that enables them to talk across a curriculum.

In these action principles, faculty and staff link the transformative learning cycle that connects reasoning and performance with the one that connects performance and reflection. Another focus is the dynamic of situated and transferable learning. "Transfer is more likely when faculty are very explicit about connections between real world need, new information, and skills to be learned." Another emphasized that "learning must be transferable to nonacademic situations. Experiences in academic settings must move from knowledge to action in a variety of settings, must encourage connections to the learner's life, must engage and 'demand' participation." One reflected on implications for faculty: "Ironically, the necessity of making one's field meaningful to such a broad and diverse audience of learners actually requires a greater mastery and facility with the essentials of the field than when one is addressing mostly specialists or future specialists." Another noted, "Both student and teacher contribute to envisioning the essentials of the field. The student claims a contribution by framing the relevance of the concepts to everyday living and future professional roles."

Learning That Lasts Is Deep and Expansive, Purposeful and Responsible

As we have reviewed and extended these principles, a prominent theme began to unfold that we introduce here as an emerging learning principle: *Learning that lasts is deep and expansive, purposeful and responsible.* When learning endures, a learner has the habits of deep inquiry, delving into meaning, developing further levels of expertise, and letting imagination serve productive creativity. Such learning means looking beneath the surface for hidden causes, exploring larger systems, and appreciating nuances. Learning is also expansive when learners broaden their horizons by inquiring into different purposes and perspectives, trying out different approaches, and diversifying their contributions. From such learning comes commitment with integrity to their own and other purposes, which translates into integrating the self after college.

Learning that endures is more likely to be intentional than unintentional, and yet this does not mean that all learning is immediately self-aware. Rather, the learner deliberately thinks through experiences, identifies what he or she has learned, and with this developing awareness, pursues experience for glimpses of insight and tacit knowledge. Most educators acknowledge that learning happens constantly and that much of what is learned does not happen in the classroom. Further, "unlearning" previously held ideas and assumptions becomes a prominent part of college-level learning for both teacher and student. Learning becomes most purposeful when learners not only show learning to learn but also learning to unlearn, deliberately replacing old learning with new. A clear theme is that advanced learners can articulate how they go about learning and purposefully choose what they are needing to learn now. The more common phrase, "learning is goal directed," is closely allied with the educational assumption that education should be purposeful.

Learning that lasts is also responsible, in that learners are responsive to others and take up the implications of what they have learned. What the learner knows and can do implies considering what moral obligations and imperatives are shareable ideals. Learning becomes responsible as the learner gains appreciation for the complexity and value of his or her connection with community, individuality, and human spirit. Learning that lasts is a step toward the kind of learning that many educators believe is true of themselves: that we inquire, broaden, intend, and care.

If learning is to be deep and expansive, purposeful and responsible so that it lasts, then:

- Students need to work with the multidimensionality of a concept, issue, or situation. Educators need to draw on diverse sources of ideas and evidence and to engage students in exploring the complexity involved.
- Educators need to ask students to look at different perspectives and then help them consider the merits of each without having to decide among them immediately. Educators should encourage enlightened stances but also leave the deepest paradoxes unresolved, encouraging students to have concern over how to make ideas useful and to find joy in the sheer appreciation of ideas, self-understanding, and human relationships.
- Students need to examine their own values, intentions, and purposes for learning in order to make thoughtful connections to more general curricular goals and value frameworks.
- Students need to articulate how they integrate course and curricular goals into their personal reasons for studying specific concepts and disciplines in order to realize their responsibility in the learning process and to the learning community.
- Educators need to acknowledge to students, and reflect in their teaching, the idea that learning happens continually in all settings. Further, as educators build learning experiences, they need to probe for learning that is unintentional on the part of the learner. When they make educational goals explicit, they need to consider what learners may know but cannot express. Then students see the goals as more attainable and can more readily negotiate them with faculty.
- Educators need to model interdependent commitment to these goals, continually making a case for them with the learner. This means challenging what learners have already learned and devising ways for learners to "unlearn" as well as to learn attitudes, values, and commitments.

- Higher levels of learning are visible only within the more so-phisticated structures of a discipline or knowledge area. Field-work, clinicals, and other advanced learning activities elicit students' learning as well as their developing sense of role and responsibility, providing a context that pulls on deeper forms of integration that can lead to lives of meaning and commit-ment to others. Faculty need to analyze learning activities—including fieldwork sites—for their potential to engage and challenge students.

Using each of the seven learning principles to generate exam-ples of action principles is a bridge to taking more concrete actions in a particular setting. Generating action principles within and across roles is a necessary next step in moving from abstract prin-ciples to considering how an educational program on any campus is learning-centered.

Extending the Conversation Within and Across Roles

On any campus, a conversation about learning-to-teaching is es-pecially useful for improving student learning when faculty and staff join it from across diverse roles and disciplines. The resulting dynamic prompts them to engage and influence policy within and across departments, expanding their role as educational policy-maker beyond the classroom, advising department, residence hall, or dean's office. Generating joint action principles is a way of con-structing educational policy that can lead to improving educational programs. The dialectic of strengthening within roles and con-necting across them through conversation can lead to crucial in-sights about program elements that make changes probable.

Generating Action Principles in Role and Context

In the previous section, how faculty, academic, and student services personnel shape their roles in a cross-disciplinary conversation about learning that bears on teaching is a subtext. Most conversa-tions about learning-to-teaching begin in a particular department. Often they are more informal, targeted, and in depth than a con-versation across roles. For example, when generating action principles at a department meeting, faculty in cognitive or developmental psychology will bring forward a depth of understanding about a learning or action principle, both as it affects their teaching and as it reflects their understanding of learning as a specialty in their discipline.

Seven professional staff advisors at a year-end retreat probed just one learning principle in the context of advising beginning students who are negotiating the transition from entrance to college, and later, the transition into the major field (Alverno College Advising Department, 1998). Advisors' conversation yielded action principles for each facet of one learning principle ("Learning that lasts is developmental and individual, transitional and transformative") rather than the broader statements that characterize a conversation across roles. As a result, they were especially cognizant of the need to conceptualize development as a complex phenomenon *(developmental)*; celebrate different purposes, backgrounds, and capabilities *(individual)*; develop trust as a bridge *(transitional)*; and challenge students to grow as active, independent learners who show personal growth *(transformative)*. By the end of this conversation, in Exhibit 7.1, these staff advisors were generating action principles that have implications well beyond their role, because they see their role in relation to that of the faculty. When advisors join roles in conversation about student learning, it is a signal that the conversation is turning to actually making concrete improvements to programs.

Sustaining a Conversation Across Roles

In our experience, educators both initiate and extend their conversations by raising specific questions that relate most often to instructional design or the problems they see regularly in the classroom. These practical problems vary depending on the way educators understand and experience them in a particular role and context. Such questions often say a good deal about an educator's learning theory, and a group can quickly probe for it. To discuss learning as it bears on teaching releases the educator's creative flow. For example, a conversation that starts with, "How can we improve class atmosphere so that more students come to class and turn work in on time?" can advance to, "How do students develop

Exhibit 7.1. Generating Action Principles in Role and Context: A Discussion by Professional Staff Advisors.

If learning that lasts is developmental, then educators have responsibility for knowing where the learner is beginning. But learning is an interactive process. Advisors argued that it is important to communicate to learners that "you are at this level, and now you're going to try to get to the next level"—but that "you will not experience this as chiseled, continuous steps up a mountain." Advisors are particularly aware that different learners blossom at different points in the process. One learner will make progress in a short time at one level, and then "it may take a very, very long time to get where she can make the next leap." For other students, "you can see the light bulb go on—for example, for a transfer student who did poorly in another setting and then finds this curriculum a good fit." Since learning is not linear, advisors need to "celebrate persons where they are, recognize that there's a fuzzy and not distinct starting point, that students are at different points. If something clicks, the learner makes quick progress, but then might plateau, or cycle back through earlier ways of learning."

If learning that lasts is individual, then educators help the learner to think about various consequences to potential actions a student plans to take, rather than direct that learner in one direction instead of another. For each student (direct from high school, or older and work experienced), taking on responsibility for her own learning—whatever shape that responsibility takes—may mean coming to the advising office and saying, "I can't handle this." Advisors don't say, "No, you can't drop that class," or "You have to take this other course first," nor do they turn to the computer and enter a corresponding change in the student information system. Having a conversation about consequences means helping learners find information for making their decisions. Advisors also take responsibility for helping the learner to move on if this setting is really not a good fit. Learning that is individual calls students to take control of their education in relation to the realities of their whole lives, "in spite of external forces that might undermine or even devastate them." Learners, not advisors, ultimately have to make choices in relation to events in their lives and their own values, and "those values may be quite different from ours. What we hope to do is strengthen them in thinking through all of their options instead of limiting themselves to other people's opinions entirely, including ours!"

If learning that lasts is transitional, then educators who are trustworthy themselves develop trust in the learner. They continually recognize

Exhibit 7.1. Generating Action Principles in Role and Context: A Discussion by Professional Staff Advisors, cont'd.

that, at some point, students do have to have confidence in this kind of learning. If students imagine that they are just going to take classes—sort of "renting seat time"—they will have to make more of a leap of faith in a curriculum that rests on the idea that learning is transitional but ultimately transformative. "Students who struggle with this idea might be especially bright or experienced, but not able to deal with the kind of dissonance that demonstrating abilities along with content implies: 'But I have always gotten A's in English,' or 'I give training workshops across my organization, so why do I have to demonstrate my public speaking in this science course?'" The advisor looks for the danger that students might leave college altogether, or return to a learning environment that's more comfortable but where they have not been successful. For a learner who has had particularly harmful experiences in early education, combined with deleterious life events, advisors expect changes in the way the learner views her world, but this can be much too challenging at first. "She may not be used to having a voice and the faculty expect that she develop that, and gradually learn to self assess and talk about her performance—that is very hard. But when she does find her voice, she makes a developmental leap." In seminars for new learners, advisors try to create opportunities to gain students' confidence, to talk directly to them about trusting. "One aspect of this trust comes when staff advisors successfully move students on to a faculty advisor in their major field." However, as another observed, "Some intermediate students have difficulty transferring their abilities from one context to another; they failed to grasp significant connections among concepts. Sometimes we leave them too early." Even as learners become both increasingly independent and collaborative in their learning, they usually begin with structured opportunities, modeling, coaching, and a supportive atmosphere.

If learning that lasts is transformative, then educators help students take an active role, rather than passively select—not just in their studies but also in student organizations, in meetings with faculty and other students, and in life events that happen on campus or in the community that could stunt or stimulate personal learning and growth. Learning that is transformative calls on learners to take up reflection and introspection around the quality of their Valuing in Decision-Making, and for advisors to elicit and support that. There has to be a payoff for spending time self assessing, for gaining knowledge, for improving yourself, if learning is to endure. "If learning that lasts works that way,

**Exhibit 7.1. Generating Action Principles in Role and
Context: A Discussion by Professional Staff Advisors, cont'd.**

---

then it implies that learners can easily have sensory overload because of
the variety and depth of what they feel is thrown at them, and what they
must wade through—how to make sense of it themselves." That means
providing opportunities for learning those skills. Expect students to
participate. If they are not engaged in learning that is transformative,
they will not succeed. Provide students with structured experiences
where learners take active roles, and where learners become seekers,
committed to learning new knowledge that is difficult. There are students who do not succeed, at least at that point in time. At registration,
advisors often see students who have gone on leave, return, and say,
"Now, I'm ready." Advisors admit that there are still some students who
might graduate without fully developing learning that is lasting: "That
can be painful for the learner and for the faculty. A more transformative kind of learning may not happen until later, well after college."

---

responsibility for learning to learn—and to unlearn?" The concern
"Why do so many students resist moving into groups?" can lead to,
"How do students develop skills and dispositions for working together?" The concrete question, "How do we assist students to
show their thinking behind their project design so we can facilitate
more creativity?" might benefit from asking a more abstract one:
"What is the role of practice, performance, insight, assessment, and
reflection in learning?" The evaluative concern, "Why do so few
theoretical frameworks from courses show up in student experiential logs?" can become, "What is the nature of transfer of knowledge and skills to internships and service?"

A discussion across roles on any campus can lead as easily to
new challenges as it can to new insights; without it, some consensus around concrete change is unlikely. Such an extended conversation has a number of turning points that require conscious
care. Thus, we elaborate a conversational design to acknowledge
those points, so that extending a conversation across roles can be
sustained. This extended conversation is likely to yield action principles (or policy) not only for teaching and advising, but also for
rethinking an educational program as a whole, and the educator's
role in that inquiry and reflection process. The shaded boxes in

the design, set out in Figure 7.1, primarily encourage attention to *thinking through learning principles* in order to *generate action principles*. In addition, Figure 7.1 opens up connections to *considering educational programs as frameworks for learning*. A further turning point is toward *considering educational assumptions*. As the group deepens the discussion of rationales for a program, educators can start to identify their own assumptions and the learning principles that underlie them. The degree to which a group becomes conscious of these turning points and comfortable with them can influence the viability of a policy discussion; it is a stepping-stone to making improvements.

As educators discuss how learning bears on teaching across roles, they often discover how much they share fundamental issues about learning. These issues are connected by a shared concern for what education is and can be, reflecting converging interests and commitments that generally define what it means to be an educator who takes up the common tasks that reflect cogent concerns in higher education (recall Table 1.1). For this reason, educators take up the broad task of thinking through an educational program for its learning-centered qualities with colleagues from various roles. Of course, each role (and each person within it) will differ in standpoint on these fundamental issues about learning, but if a few individuals recognize the turning points, they can help sustain most conversations about learning by tying specific concerns to broader questions and ultimately prompt policymaking. These fundamental issues, important to any educational institution, reappear as background questions in Figure 7.1. Here, we see how these issues are tied to the four shaded components of the design for a collaborative inquiry.

Educators who are asking each other what they know about the learning-to-teaching connection care deeply about the nature of learning ("What is *learning?*"). From their understanding of human potential, they constantly ponder, "*What* is learned?" in relation to the dialectic between "What *can* be learned?" and "What is *being* learned?" by students in their care (now, over a semester, in a major, in college, after college). This leads to *thinking through learning principles* that are bridges to action and to influencing policy.

In their move to forming policy, educators consider the abstract and concrete nature of learning and also its prerequisites, conditions, and processes ("How and why does learning happen?"). To

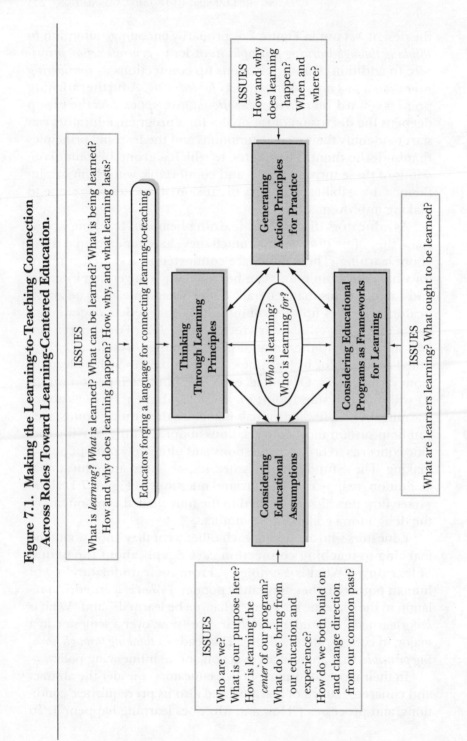

Figure 7.1. Making the Learning-to-Teaching Connection Across Roles Toward Learning-Centered Education.

ISSUES

What is *learning*? *What* is learned? What can be learned? What is being learned? How, why, and what learning lasts?

ISSUES

How and why does learning happen? When and where?

ISSUES

What ought to be learned?

ISSUES

What are learners learning?

ISSUES

Who are we?
What is our purpose here?
How is learning the *center* of our program?
What do we bring from our education and experience?
How do we both build on and change direction from our common past?

Educators forging a language for connecting learning-to-teaching

Thinking Through Learning Principles

Who is learning? Who is learning *for*?

Generating Action Principles for Practice

Considering Educational Programs as Frameworks for Learning

Considering Educational Assumptions

focus explicitly on *how* to learn, with students in various contexts and across time, means educators consider the center of the design: "*Who* is learning?" and "Who is learning *for?*" These questions raise the joint interests and commitments, responsibilities and rights of learners, faculty, and other academic personnel, as well as the many groups interested in higher education—a direct connection to *considering educational assumptions* (for example, "Educators are responsible for making learning more available to the learner by articulating expected learning outcomes and making them public") and a necessary step in shaping educational policy.

As educators develop an understanding of each new group of students, what students can learn now and what they intend to do with their learning, faculty commit themselves to exploring anew the consequences of an education. By exploring how a learner's goals, history, culture, and experiences shape learning, each educator engages with learners' aspirations and values and what it means for learners to enact them in various settings in and after college. By *generating action principles,* the educator reinforces his or her role in creating and influencing policy, designing and reflecting on practice, and evaluating learning outcomes.

In generating action principles or policy, educators are always implicitly (and often explicitly) engaged in a dialectic with students about "What *ought* to be learned?" in relation to "What *are* learners learning?" This is the implicit meaning of a course syllabus, of every comment on every paper; it is the focus of challenge and feedback from instructor to first-year student, or from mentor to apprentice. Its innate tension energizes every lively learning discussion: in a classroom, hallway, counseling office, or on the Internet. The dialectic is a stimulus for considering educational programs as frameworks for learning (for example, general education, disciplines, student assessment, career development) at the level of the course, curriculum, and cocurriculum. In examining these, educators as policymakers are also considering educational assumptions that undergird different programs, and how those curricular and cocurricular frameworks are changing.

As one educator suggested during a conversation about learning as it bears on teaching: "This design is centered on the learner, with the tension between '*Who* is learning?' and 'Who is learning *for?*' A lot of educational assumptions may or may not begin with learning at its center. So I can see that the question, "How is learning the center of our program?" might easily become part of a conversation about learning that bears on teaching. Too often, learning theories and strategies as they are often taught us are overlaid, and learners are molded to them, rather than the individual learner molding them to him or herself." "Yes," commented another educator. "Usually it is starting with a theory or teaching method and fitting it to the student rather than looking at 'Where are the students, what do they intend, where do they need to go, or what do you need to do to assist them?' In this design there is not necessarily a beginning or ending; one could jump into the questioning at any point. This makes sense philosophically, because, in practice, we certainly consider who learners are as unique individuals and we tailor things to them." A professional staff advisor jumped in: "Initially, however, learners themselves are not savvy enough to reach out to our assumptions and principles about learning. So as advisors, we are working with learners in a pretty prescriptive, directive way at first so that after they have a foundation, they can be creative and start reaching out."

Note that the participants immediately reflect on their concrete experience in their own setting. A conversation about learning flows among the many practical problems, questions, and tasks that frame the conversation on any campus and make the fundamental issues about learning concrete. Eventually a conversation about learning that bears on teaching can become part of educators' expertise on any campus, provided it acknowledges the diverse voices, sources of ideas and evidence, and contexts of practice that participants bring to the table, and honors their role in shaping educational policy across an institution. Action principles give life to learning principles by honoring the learning and teaching dynamic; they connect what educators know about learning-to-teaching. Being aware that learning should be integrative, for example, can lead to very different pedagogies depending on the specific teaching context. In this sense, theory, research, and practice become more of an interwoven tapestry than a linear application of one to another. The entire theory of learning that lasts embraces such parallel constructions. Taking teaching seriously involves inquiry on the relationship between student learning and educational processes. Such scholarship will be all the more significant and productive when there are structures and processes in place that support it.

Part Four

Fostering Learning That Lasts

Part Four takes up a challenge familiar to all educators: fostering learning. We turn to this familiar ground in order to see it anew, probing the meaning of fostering learning that lasts from the vantage points of Parts Two and Three. In Part Two, we explore learning from the standpoint of the student as learner, the learner as developing person, and the graduate as performer and contributor. In Part Three, our educational theory of learning that lasts brings students and faculty together to build a common enterprise: bridging learning and teaching. Our goal now is to capture the rhythm of daily practice as educators endeavor to realize individual and collective visions of an educated graduate.

In broad sweep, Part Four moves from how individual educators have broadened their teaching role to how they have changed curriculum and how institutions are transforming themselves. As educators focus on the larger outcomes connected to a concern for enduring learning, they find that they need to think beyond their classrooms, coordinate their teaching with others, and work to ensure that a curriculum maximizes coherence within diversity. Chapter Eight illustrates how a focus on these larger outcomes has led individual educators to reconstruct their educational inquiry and scholarship. Here, we explore the character of collaboration and inquiry that educators have experienced as they focus together on student learning across a curriculum. Subsequent chapters then demonstrate how conceptualizing an entire educational program as a curriculum and rethinking a college as a learning community become more central to the role of individual faculty. Chapter Nine explores how assumptions and learning principles already guide practice within a wide range of alternative curricular approaches. To meet the practical concerns of faculty who are working to rethink their curriculum, we also set forth curricular elements that lead to lasting learning. Chapter Ten proposes using the character of faculty discourse and teacher reflection to construct a model of collaborative inquiry that can be sustained and that will improve teaching and learning. Chapter Eleven focuses on negotiating the changes in institutional structures and culture that may be needed for a campus to organize itself around learning that lasts. The key message is that a commitment to learning-centered education transforms the faculty and staff role, the curriculum, the nature of inquiry, institutional structures, and ultimately the college culture for fostering undergraduate learning that lasts.

Chapter Eight

Integrating Theory, Research, and Practice

Postsecondary educators face an enormous challenge in integrating ever in-creasing information, new knowledge, and complex ideas about learning into their practice. Making meaning that integrates diverse sources seems particularly characteristic of their emerging roles. Yet this is seldom a mat-ter of direct or obvious applications, whether dealing with field literature and research or faculty and staff conversation around findings from their own students. It involves creating tools and resources for using a transfor-mative learning process. This applies to an individual, a major depart-ment or campus committee, or a faculty team teaching a multisection or capstone course. It also means probing the reflective practices by which a faculty and staff shape inquiry and then integrate what they have learned into their teaching expertise. In describing these processes, we are building on the documentation from extended faculty and staff collaboration that has been part of our studies of learning from its inception. This chapter op-erates on three levels: as an exploration of learning outcomes interpreted through educational practice; as a study of one faculty's experiences in in-tegrating practice, research, and theory; and as an argument for the role of reflective practices and the structures that support it.

Charles Dickens, in *Hard Times,* created an enduring—if problem-atic—model of teaching and learning in the urban, industrial age. Embodied in the character of Thomas Gradgrind, knowledge was a commodity, a sum of facts that a teacher poured into the minds of students: Gradgrind's "little pitchers" waiting to be filled. Even as a negative stereotype, the image calls up the tensions that un-derlie the teaching-learning experience, including the interaction of concerns for disciplines and for students as learners. A century later, William Perry interviewed students who echoed this image in their descriptions of the expectations that many college students bring to their early classes. At the same time, to see teachers as flow-through systems of disciplinary knowledge grossly underrepresents the roles and responsibilities that they assume for understanding their students, interpreting their own disciplines, working with the teaching systems that are their areas of expertise, and building and implementing their courses as learning experiences (Edgerton, Hutchings, & Quinlan, 1991; Shulman, 1989).

Given this complexity, we can understand why increased information and complex ideas about student learning seldom lead directly to practice. Yet this same complexity enables faculty members to respond thoughtfully and professionally to the range of challenges they face. When faculty encounter findings from more formal inquiry (for example, regarding cognitive development or a transformative learning cycle), they are also integrating a wealth of student information and pedagogical expertise that they have developed through experience. The act of thinking through theory and research findings is thus not a simple or direct process of application; it is subtle, repeatedly cyclic, and complex. The process, however, can be made more visible in ways that provide an understanding of learning enlivened by a teaching and advising perspective.

Reflective Conversation in a Community of Educators

Presumably individuals approach the task of constructing their roles as educators in highly different ways. In the context of a campus and a community of educators, this process takes form as a sustained, reflective conversation—a teaching discourse or a faculty discourse. Examples throughout the prior chapters suggest the importance of taking up the discourse itself and understanding its form, role, and implications in postsecondary education. The more we know about how faculty reflection operates—and the seminal role that it plays in educational practice—the better we are able to understand relationships among reflection, inquiry, and practice and, from this base, to use research in effective ways. In this chapter, we ask, How do faculty integrate diverse perspectives, expertise, and sustained inquiry in their practices? How do these affect the construction of their roles? Having raised these concerns in the abstract, it may be useful to see them in a particular situation with implications for the rest of the chapter.

Rethinking the Teaching Role: An Illustration

Alverno College has always had a clear commitment to teaching as the primary faculty responsibility, and faculty regularly and systematically discuss and evaluate one another's teaching. Before 1990, they had not publicly articulated developmental performance criteria for teaching effectiveness. Expectations for other categories of faculty performance, like professional scholarship, were spelled out in specific developmental terms. For the category "Teaches Effectively," there were some operational norms and benchmarks but no more formal expectations at any academic rank. As a faculty that believed strongly in making learning expectations public for their students, they thought it important to do the same with respect to their expectations for one another, particularly for their central responsibility of teaching. Faculty formed a committee with representatives from across the college to create potential developmental criteria for teaching effectiveness at each academic rank for review by the entire faculty. That committee met regularly during the next two years to plumb their collective experience. They studied narratives from faculty annual reviews for a local base of teaching descriptors and analyses and engaged in several workshop discussions with the entire faculty about teaching, creating a full set of criteria for the teaching role (Table 8.1).

A consensus emerged that effective faculty members work to integrate frameworks of disciplines, knowledge of students, and the college's curriculum and mission and that this integrating work would develop in particular ways. New assistant professors would be expected "to bring disciplinary expertise and a concern for students to their teaching." As they increased in experience, they would "develop a more comprehensive view of the curriculum, which they are able to incorporate into their teaching," along with expanded "awareness of students and their needs" and feedback from peers and students about their teaching and assessment practices. At the

Table 8.1. Selected Statements and Criteria for Effective Teaching by Faculty Position.

Position	Effective Teaching Statement	Performance Criteria
Beginning Assistant Professors . . .	. . . are expected to bring disciplinary expertise and a concern for students to their teaching. They develop in their understanding of the ability-based curriculum and the implications for pedagogy. They provide direction for students and develop an understanding of the curriculum and assessment processes.	• develop understanding of ability-based curriculum and assessment • teach for appropriate abilities in disciplinary context • provide direction, clarity, and structure for students • provide timely and helpful feedback • are available for and respectful of students
Experienced Assistant Professors . . .	. . . develop a more comprehensive view of the curriculum which they are able to incorporate into their teaching. They expand their awareness of students and their learning needs. They integrate feedback from peers and students into their teaching and assessment practices.	• create learning experiences and assessments that reflect integration of discipline and generic abilities • organize learning experiences that assist students to achieve outcomes • provide feedback directed toward specific abilities and individual need • respond to students in a variety of settings with sensitivity to background and learning style • generate student enthusiasm for learning • refine teaching practice based on self assessment and feedback

Associate Professors . . .	. . . use an integrated approach in their practice. They combine frameworks from the curriculum and their disciplines with developmental learning theories. They respond resourcefully to unanticipated learning situations. They are flexible in using different modes of assessment and can adapt and individualize their instruction. They actively serve as resources to other teachers.	• integrate disciplinary/professional learning with teaching experience to shape teaching practice • apply developmental frameworks and teaming theory to teaching practice • organize learning experiences to allow for flexibility in responding to students • engage in dialogue about teaching in the higher education community
Full Professors . . .	. . . extend the range of perspectives they integrate. They take leadership in exploring the teaching enterprise within and across disciplines. The results of their scholarship are seen in teaching practices within and outside the institution. They provide direction in identifying and addressing significant teaching concerns.	• extend scope of scholarship to include new areas/other disciplines to inform learning-centered teaching practice • take leadership in developing materials, presentations, workshops, and publications that address significant curriculum concerns • influence professional dialogue about teaching scholarship in the higher education community

Source: Alverno College (1997).

associate professor level, they would "combine frameworks from the curriculum and their disciplines with developmental learning theories," and, at full professor, they would show leadership and an integration of perspectives as they address teaching concerns in the institution and beyond. In essence, the faculty said, developing as a teacher involves a continuous inquiry into and participation in community discussions about teaching. These statements and the process by which they were developed illustrate the faculty's commitment to a discourse on learning—that faculty should be doing this individually and collectively—and, more specifically, this college's cultural norms for assimilating and consistently applying complex knowledge about students and their learning.

Faculty Work: A More Complex Understanding

College teaching is too often defined in uncomplicated, minimalist terms, for example, as hours spent on the task of teaching subject matter. This industrial view emphasizes workload and masks issues of substance and quality and the range of essential roles. Yet in the face of changing enrollment, public concerns about the role of higher education, new technology, funding concerns, and a host of other factors, it is imperative to come to better understandings about the complexities of faculty work (American Association of University Professors, 1995; Elbow, 1986; Menges, Weimer, & Associates, 1996) and about integrating research on faculty and their roles (National Center for Educational Statistics, 1996).

In part, coming to such understanding involves constructing more accurate ideas about faculty work and, in particular, the depth of expertise involved in teaching. Further, faculty integrate a diversity of roles into their performances. Although individual faculty members may not be assigned the duties of others (for example, deans, advisors, provosts), their understanding and sense of responsibility regarding these roles are necessary for the campus to function. This means that individual faculty members carry some understanding of the broader frameworks that characterize a campus and its practices into their work, building the whole into all parts (cf. Senge, 1990).

A pedagogy for higher education based on increased understanding of undergraduate learning—and the ways in which such understanding becomes part of the work of faculty—is a relatively recent development (Katz & Henry, 1988). Groups such as the Carnegie Foundation for the Advancement of College Teaching and the American Association of University Professors (AAUP) have helped to document the complexity of faculty practice. In 1990, Ernest Boyer's Carnegie Foundation report, *Scholarship Reconsidered: Priorities of the Professoriate,* which called for a broader understanding of faculty scholarship, served as a catalyst for many national discussions. The notion of how different aspects of scholarship— advancing knowledge, synthesizing and integrating knowledge, application, and teaching—interact was followed by *Scholarship Assessed: Evaluation of the Professoriate* (Glassick et al., 1997), which further articulated the notion of scholarship and explored vocabulary to define its common dimensions. A growing number of authors have focused more closely on how faculty members construct their teaching and reflect on their own performance (Angelo & Cross, 1993; Bateman, 1990; Brookfield, 1995; Cowan, 1998; Cross & Steadman, 1996; Elbow, 1986; Schön, 1983; Weston & McAlpine, 1996). The recent Carnegie Scholars program provides another venue for understanding the study of teaching (Hutchings & Shulman, 1999).

As the studies proceeded at Alverno College over the past two decades, faculty have been particularly concerned about how their reflective practices are developed and enacted in a community made up of both learners and colleagues. As we saw in the studies of learner perspectives (Chapter Three), students experienced strong effects from participating in a coherent curriculum and the coordinated actions and explanations of faculty. In developing reflective practices, then, the faculty worked to integrate curriculum and program perspectives with those of individual members. This responsibility to function as a teacher and scholar in a community of educators adds to the integrity and complexity of practice.

Faculty Reflection and the Scholarship of Teaching

Reflection provides a broad category of action in which the processes of individual and group problem solving become visible and subject to review. It is the place, as Stephen Brookfield (1995) notes, where we as educators can find the connections between our operational assumptions and our behaviors, decisions, and plans; where we can construct our identities and integrate different frameworks of practice. Working between abstractions drawn from practice and theories in use—between pursuing one's practice, theorizing about that practice, and examining its fundamental assumptions and principles—fuels professional development (Eraut, 1994; Schön, 1983). The increasing understanding of how students construct their own learning experiences becomes an important element in thinking through curriculum issues, course design, and assignments and helping to elicit the desired performances. Integrating an understanding of transformational learning processes with the design of teaching and learning activities can mean a different emphasis on performance criteria and students' own reflection. These actions have particular meaning for the development of educational practices.

In the experience we describe in Chapter Seven, faculty and advisors were engaged in thinking through what they know about learning and its bearing on educational practices. Their discourse is stimulated by a complex framework of relationships and a revision of their own learning principles integrated with empirical descriptions of learning. Out of their conversation they generate action principles that can guide practice within and across disciplines. An extensive and integrated program of research, theory, and practice framed those conversations; however, across contexts, the discourse of educators covers a range of topics and formats with differing degrees of sophistication and content. These distinctions have great implications for the reflections of the participants and how these might be supported. At early levels, this may mean bringing increased information or new knowledge—such as might develop within a discipline or in regard to learning theories—into discussions. At other levels, it may mean interpreting findings from one's own inquiries and taking up complex ideas about student learning and patterns of performance. At higher levels, it will involve integrating complex ideas about student learning with advanced disciplinary frameworks and across different forms of educational practice.

As the faculty continued to take up the inquiry process and its findings as part of their ongoing work, they asked: How does this reflection affect the scholarship of teaching? To what extent does a process integrating practice, theory, and research function developmentally across a career and with developing expertise? How do individual reflections become public, so that faculty can participate in discussions and shared understandings of the meanings of relevant information? The process of developing criteria for academic ranks is important because it captures the spirit of the faculty's reflective practice and its contribution to vitality across a career. Faculty were able to come to a collective sense of the issues over the years because they met regularly to discuss issues of teaching and learning. Unless faculty create opportunities for substantive discourse on teaching, they are not likely to take the initiative in pursuing questions like this one. In fact, in the absence of an ethic of inquiry and discourse, there is no scholarship of teaching—only a claim for its value.

Faculty Perspectives on the Discourse on Teaching

The sustained inquiry into teaching and learning also led to a differentiated structure of ideas about teaching. Tim Riordan's (1993) synthesis of the Alverno and other faculty work over several years identified specific domains of teaching that could serve as a basis for continuing inquiries. At the center of this formulation is a fundamental concern for learners: for student learning styles and needs and the assessment of student learning. Disciplines as frameworks for student learning and curriculum coherence for student learning are examined as organizing educational frameworks. The work of teaching is more directly addressed in the study of particular pedagogical strategies and through the collaborative inquiry of a community of educators.

From a faculty perspective, what shape does this kind of reflection take? How does it affect the life of the mind and the roles faculty pursue in this context? In their observations, faculty have often focused on the interactions among disciplinary approaches to scholarship, increased understanding of student learning, and their individual constructions of teaching.

A professor in sociology characterizes working at this college as an experience that blends the reflective, contemplative aspects of traditional scholarly inquiry with the satisfactions stemming from more immediate integration of ideas into teaching practice.

He describes three different intellectual activities that seem to converge when this bridging function as a teacher-researcher is working well: "Faculty have to be able to 'start from where the students are,' discern their needs, and figure out ways to talk with them about things in ways they *both* can access. Faculty need a sort of ethnographic ability to 'research' student thinking and experience by inducing them to open up, and on our part we need to hear the complexity in their explorations of their experience and training." From another direction, faculty members must be learning about research in their own and other fields and looking for patterns that students must address as part of their college education. Finally, they need to analyze how ideas translate into concrete activity in the world in matters "like social policy, ethics, social change movements, professional practice. I assume that our students will be in the world and thus will have to use their education. This is not vocationalism, but rather a way to evaluate the worth of thinking."

For a professor of philosophy, faculty discourse forms a prominent, distinctive aspect of campus culture. The intellectual life of the faculty tends to emerge at the intersection of their disciplines and their teaching, and the primary emphasis of their scholarly reflection lies there. In practice, he proposes, faculty think of their disciplines as frameworks for student learning. That is, the discipline operates as a particular scheme through which to make observations, pose questions, think critically, and act analytically: "Faculty are interested in how students should be able to think because they have studied a particular discipline. This necessarily involves faculty in serious reflection on and discussion of the methods, concepts, theories, and processes of discourse in their respective disciplines and of how they can help students learn to practice the disciplines themselves." This is complicated by the fact that students will practice the disciplines in very different contexts when they graduate. Part of faculty reflection, then, has to do with the role the disciplines will play in the lives of a wide variety of students, and this leads to different perspectives on disciplines and their contributions to learning.

As a professor of history put it, "Both *what and how* faculty teach and *what* students take in and *how* they transform that into knowledge are variables in the learning process. Just as faculty work to expand our understanding of their individual disciplines and the interdisciplinary connections among them, they also work to understand the dynamics of student learning. Both are acts of scholarship." The challenge, as he saw it, has been "to overcome the perceived dichotomy between disciplinary scholarship and pedagogical scholarship in order to integrate my professional responsibilities. I believe that my focus on student learning is helping me to create a unified scholarly discourse. Whether I am examining the methodologies of history as ways of thinking, exploring theories of adult learning and development for insights into my students, or whether we as a faculty and staff are carrying out formal and informal empirical studies of our students' learning, I see myself engaged in a common scholarship that has a direct impact on the learning environment."

To a great extent, this culture of faculty life has been shaped by carrying out a sustained and reflective discourse of practice, inquiry, and curriculum development. How faculty and staff study teaching and learning points us toward considerations for faculty development. Different campus applications are useful to the extent that they explore different possibilities for supporting practice (cf. Cowan, 1998; Gibbs, 1996; Hativa, 1995).

The Changing Construction of Faculty Life

As Alverno College underwent changes toward outcome-based teaching and learning (recall Table 2.1), it was critical to have structured opportunities in which educators could talk in depth. To this end, college-wide institutes were held three times a year and faculty meetings in various configurations convened every Friday afternoon. These forums still continue and provide regular sessions for discussing issues of teaching and learning and for exploring teaching practices and roles. They are a means for integrating more formal research and inquiry into the faculty's reflective practice. Faculty study research findings from a range of sources, including the college's own studies, along with those of other researchers in higher education and adult development.

The essential foundation of these sessions is educational practice and the shared understanding of assumptions and principles. The sessions developed from the work and concerns of groups of faculty and staff, in committees, offices, and departments. These groups (for example, for curriculum, student retention, or assessment) cross office, department, or administrative lines, and their members brought broader perspectives on how a curriculum functions. In considering applications to other institutions, these are places where sustained discourse can occur, and they can be starting points for considering the integration of teaching, inquiry, and reflection.

Over time, such involvements led faculty and staff to conceptualize inquiry as a dynamic perspective that could be *standing in* teaching, *standing beside* it, and *standing aside* from it, and sometimes doing all three simultaneously. They were moving toward seeing inquiry as a direct part of their teaching and as a critical, reflective tool for observing themselves in practice. This shift shows two of the major themes in the faculty's development: rethinking relationships between teaching and inquiry and valuing public discourse about teaching. To better understand the shift, it is fruitful to examine how the inquiries in this book were taken up by faculty and staff as tools for integrating theory, research, and practice.

Taking Up Learning That Lasts: Response and Responsibility

While complex ideas about student learning address some broad questions for faculty, an equal concern is how these ideas enter individual and collective consciousness, so they can contribute to efforts to shape curriculum and practice in the service of learners. Two requirements stand out for this inquiry. First, faculty need to be engaged in a public discussion about teaching and learning and their practices. This opportunity allows for critical analysis, where faculty explore their own observations, ideas, and concerns about student performance. Second, this work needs to engage a sharp comparison between one's practice and the frameworks that represent and inform it. This act of critique allows faculty to make abstractions and extend their thinking, and is a valued part of their development.

Thus, integrating theory, research, and practice is expected to be a process that engages the faculty through their discourse on teaching and learning. The processes differ by context and focus, but they also share some structural features familiar from studies of adult learning and workshop applications. Stimulus material—a conceptual framework, the results of inquiry, a narrative description, a transcript of a student interview—opens the discussion. Individually and in small groups, faculty draw on their own experiences to respond to the material and extend their thinking. This work then engages a deeper, more analytic discussion, comparing the presented material and the participants' guiding frameworks and observed practices. When there are no obvious standards of comparison, data or observations can stimulate discussion about expected outcomes and standards. Some sort of production task or product is then used to bring their thinking into a more public form: a summary of observations from a group discussion, a presentation of ideas around a particular theme (for example, a resolution to a stated problem or a poster describing the implementation of a theory in practice), or an agenda for future work. A final step usually is larger discussion among all participants, for summary and closure. Following are several specific examples of how material on learning, development, reflection, and performance played a role in the discourse on teaching.

Student Constructions of Learning, Faculty Constructions of Practice

The Perspectives Interviews gave the college a unique source of insight into the students' goals for learning and their experiences of the curriculum. Educational research and evaluation staff synthesized the interview texts for review within the college and presented these at all-college sessions and to selected committees or departments. As the interview data were analyzed and written up, faculty and staff then became involved in interpreting them from a variety of perspectives. For example, they took part in guided, analytic group processes to examine relationships between their study findings and their own practices.

Questions and Process

Because the college was dealing with relationships between students' experiences in the curriculum and the ongoing revision of learner outcome statements, questions about integrating teaching and advising concerns were emerging about helping enter'r.g students adjust to the curriculum and particular expectations. The college council for student assessment was already doing work on self assessment and feedback through a study of classroom practices; the research and evaluation members of the council broadened this discussion with multiple samples of student perspectives. Together they structured a series of meetings to read interview summaries and make observations about the characteristics of learners as they experienced them in their own work. The resulting observations became rooted in the languages of both the students and the faculty; this meant they would have a salience for *these students,* in *this curriculum,* with *these faculty.*

Observations and Outcomes

The result was an extended portrait of the student as learner, structured as a series of student-as-learner statements describing students as beginning, intermediate, and advanced learners. The categories differed to some extent in content and concerns, but each one covered themes such as "committing to college work," "becoming an independent learner," "using feedback," and "self assessment" (see Appendix H). This document became a basis for faculty conversations in a range of curriculum work, including assessment designs and performance criteria. The student-as-learner statements were also developed into an inventory that new students could use to focus on their own learning and orientation to the curriculum, in relation to the expectations of college work. Exhibit 8.1 provides selected examples from the inventory. (See Deutsch et al., 1995, for a fuller description of development and use.)

As faculty members read through the student texts, they found that they could view their own classroom practices through learners' eyes; they also found material that broadened their observations, interpretations, and expectations. They could then use this common resource to challenge their thinking about the curriculum—how it worked and how learners experienced it. Faculty and staff also continued to refine their understanding of student self assessment and its relations to learning. Statements about this from the Perspectives Interview data were clear and showed definite developmental patterns. The students' specific observations also provided useful cues to individual faculty work, as well as for acting collaboratively (Alverno College Faculty, 1979/1994).

Exhibit 8.1. Examples from the Student as Learner Inventory.

Instructions for Completing the Inventory

Most of the pages of this inventory consist of different statements regarding the behaviors that students display as they develop as learners. All statements are descriptions from students at various points of development. Read each statement, then indicate the degree to which it is characteristic of your current performance as a learner.

Circle One

	Not Characteristic	Partly Characteristic	Characteristic
Committing to College Work			
1. I follow concrete suggestions, explanations, and directions in my learning process.	1	2	3
2. I do more than expected.	1	2	3
Becoming Independent in Learning			
17. I develop my own learning goals, plan for them, and achieve them on my own initiative.	1	2	3
20. I express my own perspective in thinking and communicating with others (do not simply disagree or agree with others).	1	2	3
Using Feedback and Assessment Criteria			
27. I compare myself to myself rather than just myself to others.	1	2	3
28. My emotional response to feedback interferes with my analysis of my performance.	1	2	3

Source: Selected from Deutsch et al. (1995).

The assessment council members studied samples of performances from student assessments in relation to curriculum-based expectations to develop a more elaborated statement of self assessment that shows how students increase their capacity to self assess across more complex performances. The next result was a developmental self assessment framework, now in use across the curriculum, to assist in the design of student self assessment and feedback (Alverno College Faculty, 2000). The process of continually refining this framework included two all-faculty and academic staff sessions for review and analysis with follow-up work by the council for student assessment. As a result of more refined observations about the nature of self assessment and related practices, faculty generated a broader range of self assessment protocols. The prominent concern for self assessment—and for what became, in effect, a theory of self assessment—emerged as faculty and staff continually researched their practice and integrated their observations and conclusions with relevant data from student perspectives, performances, and faculty practice (see also McEachern & O'Brien, 1993).

Linking Research on Student Development with Local Practices

Using the battery of human potential measures in the longitudinal studies of learning provided a way of estimating relationships between learning in the curriculum and individual development. The initial questions were necessarily broad and oriented to discerning relationships, particularly those that would give generalized feedback on "how the curriculum is doing": Does development move at least in a positive or predictable relationship with the curriculum? What can we learn about development that will help us teach better? Research and evaluation staff reported analyses to the college community at a variety of levels over a period of years. Faculty discussed data summaries and written reports, and these consultative processes resulted in new layers of understanding (see Mentkowski & Doherty, 1983, 1984a, 1984b).

Because statistical reports alone can have limited value and influence for a community of educators, more active processes were needed to help faculty take up information about their students' developmental patterns and integrate this with their ongoing inquiries and teaching priorities. While students' own constructions of their experiences can seem very relevant for teachers, developmental frameworks are abstract, even if they are more generalizable. At the same time, making more analytical comparisons involving developmental models and practice draws faculty toward the edges of their understanding about their expertise and practical frameworks, encouraging them to think more complexly about their work. A recent series of inquiries and workshops illustrates such a process.

Emerging Questions and a Discourse Process

A department that has as one of its responsibilities facilitating inquiries into curriculum abilities raised a number of concerns about how specific abilities were developed in relation to students' individual and personal growth, as well as how the curriculum functioned in relation to different developmental needs. How, for example, does more sophisticated knowledge of development help faculty in the design of effective learning experiences for a range of individuals?

The group developed its plan of action in three phases: (1) increasing knowledge of relationships between models of development and what had been studied about the students and the curriculum, (2) conducting a workshop with faculty on developmental concerns, and (3) analyzing workshop results and how related work evolved at the department level. Department members first reviewed the college's work with developmental measures and aggregate trends in student and alumna development. The process was intended to provide a stronger background in developmental perspectives for teaching and understanding curriculum principles in operation. In a four-hour all-faculty workshop, participants listened to a lecture on the historical context, strengths and limitations, and implications of selected developmental theories, such as those of Loevinger, Kohlberg, Gilligan, and Perry. Next, they read selected articles on approaches to applying developmental frameworks and shared general observations from their own experiences. Subgroups worked with particular theories, preparing poster diagrams to explain one theory to their peers, followed by a synthesizing discussion. Thus, each participant thought through and discussed, wrote about and represented graphically, their constructed relationships among the various theoretical perspectives and their own work.

Observations and Integration

In the months following, several faculty members and research staff from departments and committees met to synthesize and critique the process and findings. Faculty members had responded to the theories from multiple perspectives (for example, by their disciplines, by relevance to their own experience). They had commented on ways in which various college practices seemed consistent with or derived from theoretical understandings of development.

For example, one might ask, "How does an understanding of development among different students help me frame questions to elicit more conceptual thinking?" But it was also evident from their responses that each brought an understanding of developmental frameworks derived from their own teaching practices.

Using these responses, the team drew relationships between participants' practice-based and discipline-based frameworks and the abstractions in the theories. One group came to the developmental models seeking explanations of or insights regarding the difficulties of particular students (for example, in making the transitions to more active learning, working more fully with conceptual content). Another moved between a developmental theory and the learner outcomes they had articulated at different points in the curriculum. Developmental theory helped them discuss the outcomes from an additional perspective and communicate better to students through performance criteria. For another group, the distance between "what we do" and "what this material means" was not traveled immediately or easily. Their notions of teaching—and their models or frameworks for representing these practices—were fairly concrete, but they had little previous experience with developmental models. In the discussion, they needed to spend time considering the models themselves, then move toward more abstractly describing their practices. For this group, the developmental models provided a different perspective to consider as they reflected on practice. For the others, the models could be more readily integrated with their own observations and inquiries and their own constructions of models of practice.

As the college committee on research and evaluation observed later, these workshops brought developmental frameworks based on a range of evidence to the faculty and staff and enabled them to make connections among theoretical models, local research, and their own teaching models. As faculty become comfortable working through their own practices in depth, data from their own students' outcomes acquire added significance. Using processes that elicit reflection thus becomes key for assisting faculty to think through their own frameworks for teaching and release the creative power that reshapes curriculum and revitalizes teaching and advising. These conversations are a way for faculty to reflect on problems out of their own pedagogy. As one said, "They may be related to developmental theory, but the specific focus of the discussion comes out of your experience in teaching students."

Working with Alumna Performance: An Institute Workshop

Alumnae described their performances in work, civic, and family life in extensive detail through Behavioral Event Interviews (BEI) (see Chapter Five). Early in the formal research with the BEI, faculty had contributed to development of competence models in nursing, management, and teaching. They coded interviews and compared what they taught in those majors with the abilities that characterized effective, practicing professionals (who were not graduates of this college).

The multistep analysis of alumna performance data from the Behavioral Event Interview has also engaged faculty at several levels. Faculty again participated in discussions around the codebooks used in the analysis and the interpretation of professional and alumna performance. Later, independent faculty judgments were critical in validating the four ability factors that resulted from the data analysis. Both the process and the findings of these inquiries are thus integrated with faculty perspectives. This interactive process resulted in new ways to interpret the data, and the pertinent questions have been extended. This has helped move the alumna performance findings toward an alumna abilities model that supports the faculty's inquiries and makes postcollege performance more accessible to their analysis.

Developing Questions

Faculty concerns about postgraduate effectiveness led to the initial efforts to describe alumna performance. The BEI as a method opened new, complex ways to monitor and explore that performance, but there were few direct comparison sources available at the start. The evaluative power of this approach would lie in its capacity to illuminate the performance of graduates—to make it visible, in expanded and systematic ways, with a vocabulary that would allow for more precise descriptions and enable reflective discussions by the faculty. What would faculty find in the analysis of graduates' performance? How could they link these findings to their own course and curriculum work?

Faculty Participating in a Complex Process

In January 1997, the educational research committee and office developed a workshop in which faculty and staff members would read a pair of cases describing alumna performance and some related statistical summaries, discuss their own observations and interpretations in a small group, and then prepare a brief written critique from their discussion (Rogers, 1999a). Separate materials were prepared for each of the four ability factors; they were distributed so that each group dealt with a single factor over two hours. Each group responded to the questions relating their observations and inferences and their own frameworks of practice (for example, disciplinary, higher education, curricular, developmental, advising).

Observations and Continued Questions

Faculty observations showed considerable variety in interpretation, often focusing on how the understanding of an ability is affected by the situational contexts alumnae described. For example, one pair of cases a volunteer mediator for disputes not accepted by the judicial system and an elementary school teacher—evoked a range of responses that recognized the power of each alumna's Valuing in Decision-Making ability but expressed some concerns. As a psychology professor wrote:

> The initial example [the volunteer mediator] seems to point to someone who would overwork for no reimbursement—it seems to support, though I know not in an intentional way, the need for women to devalue their own needs (that is, survival) in order to meet the needs of others. I do like example 2 [the teacher]. It's the most balanced and realistic—that this teacher involved herself more deeply in the discipline in order to meet her value goal of teaching to every student. Implicit in her information seeking was her own value of what education can give—to learners and to teachers as learners. I'm not sure the explanation of the case gets at this enough.

Faculty explored ideas about the relationship between the workplace and the Valuing in Decision-Making ability as taught in the curriculum, an analytic question that had been raised by the stimulus materials because the data were unclear on this point. An assistant professor in computer studies wrote: "Valuing makes a unique contribution in that it enables one to prioritize—what activities, affiliations are most important in your value system? This will enhance your professional development by enabling you to concentrate on those things about which you feel most strongly, and ultimately, in which you will be most successful."

Some faculty focused specifically on teaching and curriculum relationships, drawing on students' developing values. An associate professor in professional communications noted the importance of "building in time for sharing values with each other so that each student can develop her own values as she helps others develop theirs. Another implication for education is to be very careful about how we define success. It may not be simply a high salary or an important title; success may be measured by happiness, or by a balanced life." Dealing with more complex ideas about student outcomes, then, points faculty discussions toward the models that inform teaching and curriculum.

Becoming Educators, Supporting Reflective Discourse

Standing back from these examples, we see different ways that a deeper study of learning affects a faculty's practice: exploring the role of self assessment, the developmental foundations of curriculum, the role of particular abilities in advanced performance. There is also considerable material about the complexity of their own roles. The more faculty learn about student learning and about their ongoing construction of their work, the more important and possible it becomes to address long-range career development for faculty and professional staff. Reflective discourse operates as a medium for individual development as much as for sharing ideas across a community of educators, as a source of career vitality, and for developing professional integrity (National Center for Education Statistics, 1996, pp. 71–80). In addition to department meetings or campus workshops, faculty members can plan for a range of formal and informal means to sustain conversations (for example, colloquia, study groups, roundtables). The challenge is in realistically using the resources and opportunities of a particular campus.

Context for Reflective Discourse

Our experience in collaborative inquiry, as well as our more formal studies of teaching and learning, point to several considerations in supporting a discourse on practice. In the examples described earlier, we saw how:

- Faculty bring strong models of teaching and learning to their practice, developed out of their disciplines, expertise, and experience (for example, as assumptions, principles, and procedures).
- Research findings and new perspectives on student reasoning, development, self-reflection, and performance can be used to engage those models, deepening the faculty members' construction of their own work and the challenges they encounter.
- Collaborative, discursive processes support individual integration and serve as frameworks for the development of the participants' and the community's educational practices.

Reflective discourse builds on educators' own teaching and learning concerns and, at the same time, must fit within the realistic considerations of practice (scheduling, for example). Furthermore, faculty members experience distinct shifts as they develop and work through a curriculum centered on student learning—integrating disciplinary and pedagogical frameworks. Discourse and reflection can then be different experiences at different points in this process.

Trends in Educator Perspectives on Teaching

What are the antecedents of faculty discourse and engagement with these kinds of issues? In order to better understand the process of becoming a teacher within this college, Lucy Cromwell and Stephen Sharkey (1994) asked selected faculty a series of questions regarding their experiences in this curriculum and found some specific trends: that these faculty frequently experienced shifts in their conceptions of teaching and increasingly valued the public discourse on teaching and that they were rethinking relationships between teaching and inquiry and the language used to communicate their practices.

Novice teachers, Cromwell and Sharkey found, tended to see teaching as "coverage of material" and struggled to do this efficiently; experienced educators, in contrast, described themselves as student centered rather than content centered: "Our colleagues could often mark a turning point in their careers where they began to see that the focus of their work was on the student and her development" (p. 7). For example, looking across students' performances over time, one might see unique aspects of learning in a specific class that reshape teaching strategies. In this context, the empirical patterns of growth and development evidenced by one's own students creates a richer context for teaching and reflections on practice. As faculty shift in their thinking about teaching, they are reflecting a central idea: "that improving teaching is about learning how students learn, and using that knowledge to improve how we help them do it" (p. 17). As faculty learn about student learning, they also rethink their relationship to their disciplines, teaching practices, and own views of scholarship and inquiry.

The studies described in Part Two of this book embraced different inquiry approaches—in part, to engage faculty at different career stages and from a breadth of backgrounds. In discourse, newer faculty often bring perspectives that are greatly determined by their individual discipline's traditions; over time, they learn to work between different formats, deliberative and experimental, rather than automatically gravitating to those sources of evidence that are most prevalent in a particular discipline. More experienced faculty have come to define part of their responsibility as learning how students use a discipline as a way of knowing and helping students develop that way of knowing; these faculty seem to evaluate different forms of inquiry and evidence for what they contribute to this understanding and practice (Shulman, 1989).

Our understanding of the role of formal research in the faculty's inquiry has developed to encompass a simultaneous *standing in, standing beside,* and *standing aside. Standing in* respects the direct actions of practice—teaching, mentoring, advising. At the same time, one can be *standing beside* the activity, observing, supporting, studying the models of practice. *Standing aside,* stepping outside, one moves to broader frames of reference, such as the outcomes of a discipline.

Our practice suggests that simultaneously standing in, standing beside, and standing aside is an ability that each educator needs to develop. The individual faculty member in the classroom may simultaneously be teaching (standing in), observing (standing beside), and reflecting (standing aside). In a committee meeting, a team member in educational research and evaluation may be comparing student performance to external standards (standing aside), analyzing assessment data for change patterns that may need faculty attention (standing beside), and working with faculty as they redesign an assessment instrument (standing in). This elaboration supports a more productive relationship across professional teaching and researching roles. Thus, discourse and inquiry operate together, not dichotomously as elements in either theory or practice, but as a critical third aspect, a kind of standing beside (see Figure 8.1). In the active construction and interpretation of models of practice, educators are involved in the more generative work of theory integrated in their own cycles of learning and practice.

Perhaps most significant, Cromwell and Sharkey (1994) noted that faculty came to see that teaching is not a private affair but a public concern. The very act of discussing how they approached these issues helped faculty clarify what they understood. This has not been an automatic understanding for entering faculty. They have begun with different levels of readiness, but their success in the institution has involved some development in this direction. Alverno College's inquiries into student learning have played an important role in this growth. They have served to help faculty see the overlap among courses and disciplines; this perspective helps demystify effective teaching, showing that problems and successes are rarely unique. An integrated process of theory, research, and practice, then, creates a context in which faculty can report problems and "failures" and share strategies. When the climate is supportive, they can examine their teaching openly, sharing concerns and creating a language for interdisciplinary consultation.

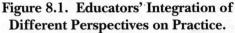

Figure 8.1. Educators' Integration of Different Perspectives on Practice.

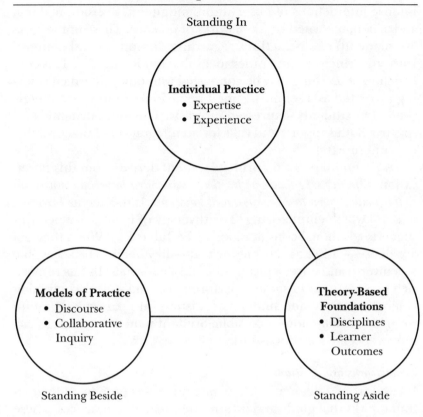

Toward Action Principles for Making Discourse Visible

Reflective practice involves both individual and group processes, although the interactive aspects are likely to be the focus of action. This inevitably takes the form of a conversation—intense, discursive, guided, oriented to a task—and ultimately a kind of deliberative process that leads to action principles for how to sustain effective reflection on campus about connections among practice, research, and theory.

Basic Engagement

Teaching is a multilayered and polyrhythmic activity that involves intense interactions of observation, judgment, decision making, and action, mediated by frameworks of practice. These frameworks are made up of abstractions regarding disciplines and content, learning principles, and other ideas that guide practice. This construction of teaching may be contrasted with others in which teaching is treated as a set of specified behaviors or more completely shaped by students' expressed interests. The more dynamic perspective both supports and calls for an integration of practice, theory, and research.

A preliminary action principle, then, derives from this observation: *Effective experiences with reflective discourse build on connections to the faculty's own tasks, issues, and questions.* If this seems obvious, it is still worth emphasizing. The diversity of faculty perspectives suggests additional considerations (see Table 1.1). When the data are dense—either as statistics or text—they need to be accessible to a diverse audience, typically in multiple formats. In this respect, rich presentations of student performance data—often combining video, narratives, and summary statistics—are particularly useful for making data more accessible. Student panels can engage faculty in specific learning issues.

Frameworks and Critique

Viewed from a deeper level, faculty members employ individual frameworks that guide and inform their teaching practices. These may be more or less articulated, but they are strong. Reflection makes these frameworks of practice more visible, subject to discussion, communication, and shared learning. Faculty development involves increasing understanding of the frameworks that inform individual practices, reflecting on these, and expanding expertise. Educational practice involves an ongoing reflection that integrates it with disciplinary and pedagogical expertise, and inquiry into the contexts of practice (for example, students and campus culture). Practice proceeds through a discourse about it with the application of frameworks, the needs of students, and so forth.

Therefore, a second principle deals with the analysis of frameworks and their underlying assumptions: *New and complex ideas about students (for example, reasoning, performance, self-reflection, devel-*

opment) enter practice through teacher discourse and become the stimulus for comparisons: What are the connections between empirical findings and the frameworks of practice in use? What are the assumptions, and how do they play out in practice?

Beginning Processes

Finally, frameworks for practice, because of their expression as principles, tend to act as guidelines for doing rather than structures for thinking about doing. Reflective discussions among teachers tend toward procedural knowledge and tales of experience; this is a realistic expression of how they encounter their work and represents the initial level for addressing frameworks of practice.

A third principle, then, addresses group process needs in a research discussion: *Processes must begin with clear means for actively engaging the participants in matters they perceive as significant.* These will often be linked to the reflective actions in the group's own practice (for example, making judgments about student outcomes, explaining their own practices and frameworks, addressing current priorities) but the discussion processes generally need to establish initial protocols for a dialogue. It may be impossible to plan for the directions that discussions ultimately will take, but there needs to be an adequate beginning. The ability to sustain and support this discourse can depend on knowing where and how the discussions can most efficiently and productively occur. These may range from ad hoc groups of faculty dealing with particular teaching concerns to department committees to more inclusive groups of faculty, staff, and administrators.

Discourse and the Construction of Educational Practice

Making meaning out of the study of learners is consistent with the effort to understand good teaching and the diverse challenges that face postsecondary education. At this point, we can put aside the "content transfer" model of Thomas Gradgrind and take up more complex images: James Hilton's Mr. Chips, struggling to construct coherent meaning out of the subjects he loves and the students who are his charges. Or Annie Sullivan, struggling to match her intentions and methods to the developing needs of her student,

Helen Keller, both of them refusing to be defeated. Or, more pointedly, Richard Feynman, in the early 1960s, thinking through the
physics courses that were to serve the multiple needs of each entering cohort of students at the California Institute of Technology.

Feynman's (1995) own chronicle of those efforts makes pertinent reading for insight into a teacher's processes. His colleagues
would later find a personal notation, written years earlier, in which
he seems to have expressed the substance of the conceptual discourse underlying good teaching in typically direct terms: "First
figure out why you want the students to learn the subject and what
you want them to know, and the method will result more or less by
common sense" (p. xx). In this brief statement, he names the constructs that we have seen teachers bring to these conversations: the
larger questions of why subjects matter (what do the physical sciences have to say to all learners?), what students must grasp (what endures in substance, epistemology, problem solving?), and what
teachers do with their own knowing and expertise to bring courses
and curriculum into life. This expertise, we would add, should include an understanding of students as developing learners.

From our own standpoint, then, these are discussions that need
to take place in the work of individuals and groups of faculty; these
are discussions that may embrace whole campuses. In practice
(and in contrast to Feynman's note) the depth and structure of
these conversations represent a kind of uncommon sense that precedes and enables the more fluid logic of instruction. In the case
of Alverno College, it has been important to organize workshops
and other types of discussions with broad participation across the
institution, but it has been even more important to work with sustained pockets of inquiry around particular concerns and questions. On most campuses, smaller groups of faculty with similar
questions and ongoing collaboration develop around capstone
courses, multiple-section courses, course sequences (for example,
arts and humanities, Western civilization), and curriculum planning (a major field, for example). These often become the starting points.

Discourse and Inquiry

In introducing this chapter, we described a process of developing
criteria for academic rank by analyzing more implicit norms and

connecting them with public criteria. The example is useful for highlighting the expectations for integrating multiple frameworks in teaching. "Taking up research findings" is not a faculty process distinct from raising questions about practice or the developing expertise that teachers bring to constructing their courses. The rank criteria illustrate that faculty are expected to be consistently engaged in inquiry about their teaching; they do not wait for the results of other research to reflect on their practice. In fact, as we have seen, raising questions in itself creates a mindfulness that exerts some effect on practice. At the same time, faculty are studying the research findings of others, from both the educational research and evaluation department at the college and other relevant research. This means, then, that faculty consider it their responsibility to create and practice forms of inquiry that allow them collectively to explore significant issues of teaching and learning. Findings from more local inquiry can help them continue to refine their sense of what makes for effective teaching and learning. From these efforts, they develop theories and interpretations of learning, teaching, and assessing. Finally, it suggests that for any institution, what it means to "take up research findings" should be shaped by the mission of the institution. If student learning is considered a central component of that mission, the processes of inquiry across the institution should reflect that.

Given the importance of various kinds of discourse, we need a range of methods for recording these conversations and monitoring their character and effectiveness. In the more elaborated single discourse described in Chapter Seven and several of the condensed examples presented here, the participants were producing written responses that could be tabulated, analyzed thematically, and compared with different explanatory models to test ideas and generate new understanding. In some of these examples, audio- or videotaping has served as a means for recording; the tapes can then be transcribed and the transcriptions analyzed from a variety of perspectives. Meeting minutes, notes, committee reports, and process documents have a place alongside interview texts as evidentiary bases for analysis in deliberative, collaborative investigations into teaching and learning. A final, critical dimension of the examples presented here is the way in which reflection is constructed as a public act and as a resource for the collaboration of faculty at a range of critical levels of practice.

Chapter Nine

Thinking Through a Curriculum for Learning That Lasts

For curriculum designers—any faculty or staff group who designs learning for students—the essential question is, "What elements of a curriculum could make a difference in our own situation, for our own students?" A broad range of educators need to struggle with such questions in order to advance an effective critique and continuing development of what to teach and how. As faculty and staff take professional responsibility for student learning, they also take responsibility for curriculum. In a curriculum that focuses on student learning outcomes, thinking through the curriculum is a continuing, essential activity, where educators question what ought to happen and how to make it happen in practice.

To foster learning that lasts, faculty and staff should conceptualize, design, practice, experience, evaluate, and improve curriculum— all as an ongoing process. Essential considerations are what students bring to it, how students experience it, what students should and do learn across a curriculum, and how graduates should and do learn, develop, and perform beyond college. To explore these complex expectations, we first develop the idea that educators need to be actively taking a curriculum perspective. The value of curriculum for learners depends on it because an effective curriculum functions not only for the time a student participates in it but also throughout the graduate's future as a learner.

Second, we define curriculum as an entire educational program that is a dynamic process with interactive elements; we explore this and other definitions later in this chapter. Because learning is situated, we do not assume that other educators should or would choose to replicate, idealize, or prescribe any one curriculum, given differences in college mission, culture, and dynamics. Nevertheless, learning is transferable and patterned, educators face common issues, and most work within a recognizable approach to organizing learning experiences. Thus, we explore a curriculum as a dynamic process by offering a set of six potentially usable elements of any undergraduate curriculum. Most educators can identify with these elements because we draw them from definitions, debates, and literature on curriculum, framed by an earned sensitivity to practice.

This dynamic understanding of curriculum can serve as a tool for thinking through what is currently in place. Because it is centered on learners and their learning, it points educators toward identifying educational assumptions and learning principles inherent in any curriculum. To illustrate, we analyze a range of current curricular approaches, inferring one assumption and one learning principle from each. A faculty group might use this analysis as another tool to clarify the ideas that ground their own curriculum and to explore the benefits of making conceptual frameworks explicit. This activity complements creating the learning-to-teaching connection: Educators benefit by considering educational programs as frameworks for learning and making explicit the educational assumptions and learning principles that ground them.

Third, we recommend analyzing a curriculum in order to foster learning that lasts. We offer an elaborated set of the six elements as essential to such a curriculum. This elaborated set is not that far removed from the initial one, but we extend each element to focus in on what works toward learning that lasts. To determine their essential character, we triangulated the elements that emerged from literature review, Alverno curriculum elements, and the empirical relationships set out in Parts Two and Three that link this curriculum to learning outcomes. For ease of use by faculty groups, we illustrate the essential elements with cohering evidence from student learning outcomes and faculty curriculum principles. Fourth, we discuss taking up the work of ongoing curriculum development when building on principles for learning that lasts. The chapter encourages ongoing deliberation rather than quick fixes by operating on several levels: as a discussion of critical curriculum processes that can serve a wide variety of groups, as an exploration of essential curriculum elements for learning that lasts, and as a probe of practical strategies.

Educators Taking a Curriculum Perspective

Analysis of the learner Perspectives Interviews emphasized the significance of the faculty and staff taking a curriculum perspective, underlining the connection between the core ideas of a curriculum and each educator's individual work. Students who took a curriculum perspective—who were able to articulate the rationale for and describe the curriculum while they were in college and could still do so five years later—tended to articulate their learning outcomes in a much richer way.

"Having a perspective on curriculum" differs from "taking a curriculum perspective." Each faculty or staff member at any college has a perspective on curriculum. Each could identify his or her own views about what a curriculum is or what it should be—the sequence of the courses, or how disciplinary perspectives shape a program's content—and could contrast this perspective with that of a colleague or with current sources for revisioning curriculum (e.g., Haworth & Conrad, 1995; Diamond, 1998; Gaff, Ratcliff, & Associates, 1997; Stark & Lattuca, 1997). Institutions that have created innovative curricula as they created a college are also enormously instructive (an example is The Evergreen State College, explored in Youtz, 1984). "Taking a curriculum perspective" means that an integrated understanding of curriculum is fused in one's work.

Most faculty and administrators imagine, explore, critique, and pursue various ways of thinking about the purposes and practices of a curriculum. By analyzing transcripts of our institution-level curriculum committee (see Exhibit 9.1), we found that taking a curriculum perspective was a critical first step in framing curriculum discussions that were intellectually stimulating and effective (Alverno College Curriculum Committee, 1998).

On any campus, taking a curriculum perspective might arise while conceptualizing the intent of a major, planning how students experience a range of methods across laboratory courses, or selecting a program of artistic performances on campus. It also arises

Exhibit 9.1. Taking a Curriculum Perspective:
A Faculty Conversation.

"A department, school, or college that explores its own assumptions may then reflect on what needs to be made explicit and how that informs teaching and learning. How these assumptions connect is an incredibly profound way to point to the need to examine teaching practice. I ask, 'What implications does this assumption have for what I do in the classroom?'"—*professor of philosophy*

"For me, taking a curriculum perspective is taking a perspective on the student's development as a person, not just as a professional. It is a more comprehensive, more global view than your own particular interests and responsibilities at a particular point in the curriculum. In a sense, you're responsible for the whole thing even though there will be a division of labor. You perform with a notion of a hand-off or a handshake from one curriculum element to another so that there is a cumulative and developmental effect. That view of curriculum is more likely to center on the student's learning rather than only on the specific dimension of the discipline that you represent. Each of us is responsible for more than our set of disciplinary constructs. When a student says, 'I have a question for you,' I don't say, 'Well, that's not my specialty; you'd better talk to Professor So-and-So down the hall.'"—*professor of history*

"For me, taking a curriculum perspective also means focusing on the student's interaction with the curriculum and how that works. I might think it's great to read Plato, but if the student doesn't respond, or can't make connections from that experience, then I have to look at how I use the material or even the selection of the material itself."—*professor of social sciences*

"What if we started with the definition of taking a curriculum perspective from the student's perspective? How is she aware of connections and relationships, not only for herself, but also for her fellow students, rather than, 'I learned this here, I learned this there.'"—*professor of nursing*

"A beginning student may see a curriculum as a series of courses: Abilities are separate, are extra work. As students experience abilities taught through the disciplines, they develop an integrated perspective on curriculum."—*professor of psychology*

"At graduation we say, 'All students with the bachelor of arts degree, stand up.' At that moment they are all sensing that, 'I may have been a

Exhibit 9.1. Taking a Curriculum Perspective:
A Faculty Conversation, cont'd.

management major and a psychology support, but the students next to me had some of the core or common experiences and values, as they have gone through their experience.' They sense that we've all been heading somewhere together, but we've had options in terms of how we focus on different disciplines."—*associate professor of physical sciences*

"Those of us who teach humanities courses to students who aren't our majors get to see the kinds of connections they're making. I don't know if students necessarily have the language to describe themselves that way, but I think they see themselves that way. There's a sense in which they know that they're distinct from many other people in their fields and that what makes them distinct has to do with the kinds of things they're able to do: These are the abilities. Abilities are very much contextualized within the context of their discipline and their major. I think that's how they would first define themselves and then within the context of that say, 'And as a nurse, I am able to do . . .' and then list off very succinctly the abilities that they bring to the career."—*professor of philosophy*

"I think students tend to define themselves in terms of the subject they studied, but I think that students do take a curriculum perspective when they see the commonality among abilities. Then they are able to do that and express it."—*associate professor of business and management*

"Employers take a curriculum perspective when they make judgments. 'You're coming from this school. I have perceptions and knowledge about your curriculum. I don't know all the courses you took, but I'm judging you by the curriculum of the school.'"—*professor of history*

"The question is, how can we describe curriculum perspectives a little more holistically so that students not only have all the right pieces at graduation, but the sense that somehow faculty were consciously making decisions about the whole thing? A faculty member should know what is going to happen to the student in the next course."—*academic dean*

"Taking a curriculum perspective is imagining and empathizing beyond what you do in your classroom and what is happening to your students right then, to what the student experiences cumulatively. It is thinking beyond the momentary experience that you have with your students and that your students have with you, and that's true for students as well."
—*associate professor of education*

in designing a student activity or an in-course assessment. Each example involves standing aside to consider one part of a program in relation to the whole, including others' views on curriculum. Faculty, individually or collectively, are called to take a curriculum perspective in a department meeting to resolve student advising issues, when interviewing potential colleagues or participating in resource planning, or during a visit by an accrediting team. This may not always be the reality, but most will recognize these situations as calling for taking a curriculum perspective. Indeed, so does almost every other involvement that a faculty or staff member has. We argue that taking a curriculum perspective frames curriculum inquiry and is also characterized by its consequences, which are themselves integral to liberal education.

Taking a Curriculum Perspective Through Inquiry

The idea of taking a curriculum perspective includes more than sharing responsibility for the curriculum. It also means following through, developing, and refining one's own curriculum based on the implications that flow from (and in turn stimulate) perspective taking. We defined taking a perspective on inquiry as standing in, standing beside, and standing aside simultaneously. Similarly, it means standing in, beside, and aside from one's own and others' roles and standpoints in curriculum—simultaneously—in order to see the curriculum holistically and define and debate the broader educational assumptions and learning principles that ground it.

Taking a curriculum perspective is further characterized by a range of comparisons that faculty make in curriculum meetings, comparing the perspectives and experiences of students, alumnae, and faculty; or comparing previously measured learning outcomes to those observed in current assessments. Faculty members might make explicit connections to external curriculum perspectives that appear to stretch their own. The work of curriculum inquiry requires sustained, extensive, deliberative inquiry by faculty and staff—those who are more directly involved in curriculum design and evaluation, as well as those who share a more general range of curriculum concerns such as determining learning outcomes.

Consequences of Taking a Curriculum Perspective

In the turbulent world of undergraduate curriculum reform, practitioners and curriculum scholars converge on several conceptual directions for improvement in the context of such challenges as degree completion, distributed learning, and satellite campuses. Joan Stark and Lisa Lattuca (1997) identify three challenges that faculty and staff face: incorporating diverse perspectives, increasing coherence, and meeting expectations for quality and access. Jerry Gaff (1997), summarizing the contributions of fifty-seven curriculum experts, argues that the current "renaissance of undergraduate education" should coalesce around the student, "putting students and learning at the center" (p. 691). Consideration of student perspectives can be a powerful catalyst, but it has generally been ignored (Stark & Lattuca, 1997, p. 380). It is our contention that taking a curriculum perspective can address concerns such as respecting learners' purposes for and experiences of their learning, determining student learning outcomes, clarifying the meaning of the baccalaureate, and contributing to faculty and staff vitality.

Respecting Learners' Purposes for and Experiences of Their Learning

Legitimizing students' purposes and experiences is an important factor in making a curriculum meaningful and relevant. Most colleges have used surveys of student attitudes and satisfactions to market education, and most faculty use student course evaluations and students' running commentary in courses to improve teaching and learning (Angelo & Cross, 1993). But students' in-depth perspectives on their learning are less well understood and are thus less often integrated by faculty into collaborative curriculum design.

What has emerged for us, in our inquiries so far, is a much clearer picture of what students consider essential to their learning and how they perceive the outcomes of that learning in relation to faculty curriculum design, the intent of their day-to-day teaching, and faculty experience of it. Fully appreciating student perspectives leads to taking a curriculum perspective. Faculty interpretation becomes paramount in the way faculty seek and use student perspectives—not just student attitudes and course evaluations—in evaluating and improving their teaching. By deeply analyzing student perspectives, faculty and staff also gain a more effective tool for evaluating student work and providing helpful feedback.

Determining Student Learning Outcomes

When curriculum is designed and practiced by faculty who are taking a curriculum perspective in relation to how students experience it, they are more likely to attend to student learning outcomes in their teaching and course designs. Obviously, how students construct learning cannot be the only important source for curriculum development; indeed, student perspectives may be quite limited initially. Other faculty efforts confirm the benefits of digging deeper into student views of learning (Erwin, 1991; Marton, Hounsell, & Entwistle, 1984). Further, taking a curriculum perspective also implies determining student learning outcomes. Joan Stark and Lisa Lattuca (1997) affirm this view. The intent, purpose, content, and development of curricula have been exhaustively debated by educators, they note, but the connection between learning as it is experienced by students and those students' actual learning outcomes continues to be unresearched in curricular studies (pp. 381–382). Distinguishing between student experience of a curriculum and the learning outcomes that accrue from it is difficult. Direct causal connections between particular learning experiences and outcomes often remain a puzzle. Nonetheless, considering student experience in relation to faculty-determined learning outcomes leads to revisiting curriculum intent, purpose, and content.

Clarifying the Meaning of the Baccalaureate

Faculty understanding of students' purposes, experiences, and their learning outcomes stimulates continuous rethinking of the meaning of the college degree. Faculty ask, "What should students know and be able to do upon graduation?" Stark and Lattuca (1997) state that faculty wrested curriculum development responsibilities from administrators in the earlier twentieth century and express a strong desire to retain that role. At a time when the question of what should be taught, learned, and assessed is on the public's agenda, insights about relationships among liberal learning, professional programs, and student learning outcomes are central to

educational policymaking. This broader agenda has been punctuated with arguments about what is common learning and what
makes up a liberal arts canon. For example, the call for reinstitut-
ing a core curriculum that has "integrity" has been part of higher
education discussions for some time (Association of American Colleges, 1985). Curricular integrity, which implies that the degree
represents what faculty intend and what students experience, requires that a curriculum demonstrate "coherence within diversity."
Designing it should, we believe, begin with the question, "Integrated for what and for whom?" The diverse interests and commitments among higher education's multiple stakeholders can
yield coherence when educators articulate a key principle: *Curriculum is for the learning of students.* Because centering on learning
illuminates the paradox that faculty aim for coherence within diversity, revisiting the meaning of the degree can be a bonding
rather than a divisive action for faculty and staff.

Contributing to Faculty and Staff Vitality

Faculty and staff vitality—sustained energy and productivity over
time—is essential to collaborative curriculum transformation; it is
also a by-product. Students can tell when faculty and staff demonstrate vitality and interdependence. When we studied student and
alumna perspectives, we looked for evidence that, in the student's
mind, faculty were taking a curriculum perspective. We probed students' beginning and advanced understandings of the rationale
they thought faculty had for student involvement and performance
across classes. Students' growing understanding of faculty rationale
influenced their motivation to stay in school, continue improving,
and apply and continue learning outside the classroom and after
college. When students became conscious of the design, process,
and coherence within the diversity of the curriculum, they reinforced and challenged these practices by expressing their expectations in class, and faculty responded with clarifications or
adjustments.

When faculty place student learning at the center of curriculum and build toward student understanding of their curriculum
perspective, they also stimulate their own perspective taking in directions that go beyond rethinking the meaning of the degree.
These include analyzing the impact of various social forces in shap-

ing curriculum, projecting new majors and the resources needed to develop them, and studying new disciplinary concepts and paradigms that enhance students' grasp of a major. Faculty also create a common bond with each other to support interest in student development. This bond, strengthened by disciplinary connections, fosters what Arthur Applebee (1996) described as *curriculum as conversation*. Faculty and staff, led by their own questions, consider curricular definitions, debates, and conceptual frameworks that stimulate and challenge their own interpretations. Ilene Harris (1991a) has called this *curriculum as deliberative inquiry*. Until recently, as Elizabeth Kamarck Minnich (1990) noted, an invitation to a department discussion on curriculum, mired in academic definitions and debates, would often drive away participants. However, given the fundamental role of interaction in faculty learning, it is all the more important to find the terms and elements that make for effective discourse about curriculum. This leads to a second emphasis: defining and debating curriculum.

Defining and Debating Curriculum

We define curriculum as a dynamic process with a set of six interactive, potentially usable elements of any undergraduate curriculum, drawn from the literature. These elements set the stage for debating the educational assumptions that characterize a faculty's own or other approaches to curriculum. Such a debate can illuminate learning principles, a bridge to the third emphasis of this chapter: a set of essential elements of a curriculum for learning that lasts.

Defining Curriculum as Dynamic Process with Interactive Elements

Educators often comment on how a designed curriculum is changing; this is natural and desirable once they perceive *curriculum as dynamic process with interactive elements*. "I envision curriculum in fluid terms," one social sciences professor says. "We change our curriculum, we evaluate it, we figure out what works, what doesn't work, the world changes, and we change it again." Recognizing curriculum—with its multiple interacting elements—as a dynamic process rather than a static set of structures challenges educators to understand the nature of curriculum change and to ask how and why they are continually shaping and reshaping it. They learn to situate a curriculum in relation to the defining characteristics of their institution, including its history of curriculum development, unique mission, values, and institutional culture. A designed curriculum, however dynamic, is not an entire curriculum. We think of a curriculum as practiced and experienced by faculty and also experienced by students. Observations about a curriculum as it is practiced reflect perspectives from each group. These can test the concepts that seem so important to faculty in the design phase and illuminate ideas that might otherwise be untouched.

Many experts concur that learners and their learning (who they are, what they intend, what they can do and become) should be at the center of how an educator thinks about an undergraduate curriculum (Gaff, 1997), yet this educational assumption may not reflect the ideology or organizational culture of a particular undergraduate institution or program. Organized learning experiences, the "practice" of curriculum, are usually arranged as courses or programs. Whenever faculty start taking a curriculum perspective as a working group, a department, or an institution, reaching a working consensus on content continues to be the most commonly perceived and central task, reflected in consensus on crediting ("consensus," of course, does not mean conformity or absence of conflict, and includes agreeing to disagree). Curriculum is more than learning experiences organized as courses and more than content; it also includes various interactive contexts and cultures (the cocurriculum, the family, and workplace; local and global communities and cultures formed around economic, ethnic, or other dimensions of human identity). Considering such interactive contexts and related subcultures, and examining the idea of hidden or latent curriculum, helps to make clear conceptual frameworks, which may be intended or unintended, explicit or implicit. These frameworks are often reflected in the mission, aims, and philosophy of a curriculum. Program evaluation and assessment are a common element where curriculum inquiry can occur. Figure 9.1 arranges what we found in the literature as key curricular elements into a set of ever widening, concentric circles; the broken lines indicate that each element blends with the others to form a dynamic whole, centered on learners and their learning.

**Figure 9.1. Curriculum as Dynamic
Process with Interactive Elements.**

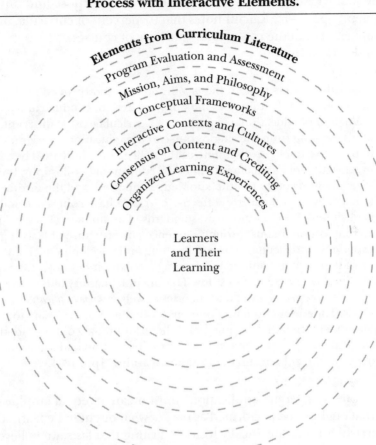

Organized Learning Experiences

With learners and their learning at the center of an undergraduate curriculum in Figure 9.1, the innermost ring addresses how faculty organize learning experiences for students. James Ratcliff (1997) sees an undergraduate curriculum as the formal academic experience of students' pursuing the baccalaureate or associate degree: "Such a curriculum is formalized into courses or programs of study including workshops, seminars, colloquia, lecture series, laboratory work, internships, and field experiences. Here, the term *course* is used generically, to designate a formal unit of an undergraduate curriculum. . . . What we call an undergraduate curriculum tends to be a universe of courses, each with its own purpose and environment" (pp. 6–7). Ratcliff notes that 97 percent of curricula, unfortunately, fall in the category of "universe of courses." He usefully extends his definition:

> Curriculum refers to both the *process* and *substance* of an educational program. It comprises the purpose, design, conduct, and evaluation of educational experiences. Curricula exist at different levels, ranging from the single course to the educational program to the department or discipline to the college or university. The organization of curricula is defined by educational philosophy, the structure and content of the knowledge imparted, and the institutional context and climate. Effective curricula have coherence and explicit definitions of aims and standards of attainment. They accomplish their aims through sequence and structure of learning experiences to facilitate student learning and development. They provide sufficient content and coverage to exhibit but not exhaust the limits of the subject of study. They include mastery of basic terms, concepts, models, and theories as well as *some application* [italics added for emphasis] of them to situations appropriate to the student, the learning aims, and the institutional context. Good curricula have the hallmarks of effective instruction and the evidence of the enhancement of student learning. [pp. 12–13]

In our view, "some application" must mean an equal emphasis on what ought to be performed as part of what ought to be learned. A curriculum that specifically fosters learning that lasts, we believe, must also relate structured experiences in the cocurriculum to organized learning experiences in the academic curriculum.

Consensus on Content and Crediting

Consensus on content is a bedrock curricular element, but it is also problematic. "What new content shall we *add?*" often prompts updating curriculum content by introducing newer ideas such as chaos theory (Gleick, 1987) or cultural diversity and gender studies (MacCorquodale & Lensink, 1995; Olguin & Schmitz, 1997); reinvigorating the canon (Bloom, 1987; Hirsch, 1988) or transforming it (Minnich, 1990; Nussbaum, 1997). When updating content means only adding electives or courses to a sequence, a concept of curriculum as bits and pieces may result. Today's challenge is not only, "What content do we include?" but also, "What do we mean by content?"

Content discussions once focused almost entirely on disciplinary knowledge, and faculty debates were more likely about relationships between general education and the major than the broader definitions that appeared in mission statements. More recently, content itself is being articulated as more than knowledge and its transmission. Content has now come to include values and attitudes (respect, tolerance, for example), intellectual capabilities and competencies (for example, critical thinking, problem solving), transition to college or work transition skills (computer literacy, time management, career planning), and interdisciplinary studies, as well as work in the disciplines (Chickering & Reisser, 1993; Doherty, Chenevert, Miller, Roth, & Truchan, 1997; Graham, 1998).

The enlivened debates on curriculum as content include whether and how disciplinary content, attitudes, and values are integrated with intellectual, emotional, and physical abilities and transition skills. These debates are changing the meaning of the degree by introducing a sometimes parallel "content" such as courses in critical thinking, study skills, or diversity workshops; or parallel interdisciplinary majors such as gender studies or cognitive science. Whether these should be or are integrated into a curriculum can lead to discussions about the purposes of undergraduate education and the purposefulness of curriculum design. William Tierny (1995) has observed that each discussion on curriculum can advance or deter a consensus on the meaning of a degree, depending on how content is framed by faculty.

As interactions between content and faculty obligations to student learning become more significant, Stark and Lattuca (1997) propose a view of *curriculum as an academic plan for a student's academic development in action* (pp. 9–10). They call for linking a curriculum's elements to student learning outcomes and report that few, if any, curriculum studies have accomplished this. Exploring these links immediately raises the issue of how learning is credited. When credits are achieved by a combination of time and participation in class and a faculty grade (however well that grade captures expert faculty judgment), it can be difficult to analyze patterns in learning outcomes across a curriculum or to ensure students' academic development. To ensure students' development toward maturity and service is one of the most demanding tasks in curriculum development today, given the changes in the locus of the college and its student body. To accomplish this means considering interactive contexts and cultures.

Interactive Contexts and Cultures

While learners' individual differences are emblematic of cultural, economic, and historical contexts, they also reflect the immediate conditions and events of their lives. Relationships between departmental-institutional mission and local and distant contexts affect a curriculum's potential as a vehicle for student learning. More pointedly, "Do students build on academic and life experiences in their internships?" or "How does the community benefit from service-learning?" Curriculum may also include broader contexts such as experimental colleges (Meiklejohn, 1942), learning environments (Schlossberg, Lynch, & Chickering, 1989), learning communities (Gabelnick, MacGregor, Matthews, & Smith, 1990; Hill, 1982), faculty communities (Kuh & Whitt, 1988), and knowledge communities (Bruffee, 1995).

These and other authors support a view of *curriculum as integrated with the cocurriculum and college experience.* Educators have long been raising questions about what both younger and older students are learning outside the formal academic curriculum. The cocurriculum may include learning experiences organized as courses (for example, transition to college, transition to career); it may include planned or ad hoc student activities, student governance, experiences in the workplace and family, civic commitments, and studies in other countries. Educators question how supportive and challenging the campus culture is for a more diverse population. *Curriculum as social context for learning*—whether on or off campus— becomes as important for the urban, commuter college as it has traditionally been for the residential college, and a goal for the virtual university.

Educators who debate educational intent, beliefs, and values while rethinking or reformulating a curriculum are likely to uncover what some scholars have called the "hidden" or "latent" curriculum. Originally, Benson Snyder (1971) referred to the hidden curriculum as the social or emotional surround of the "what to learn" in the formal curriculum. It included the "how to learn" engendered in faculty values and assumptions, student expectations, and the social contexts where ways of learning developed (p. 4). It involved the ways academic staff ensured sufficient interaction with students or even the nature of the encounters. Faculty and advisors also inferred it from student frustrations that might emerge in peer discussions or advising sessions ("Why doesn't she tell us how long she wants this paper to be?" "Why does he give surprise quizzes?" "Why aren't my views recognized in class?"). For Benjamin Bloom, the "latent" curriculum included student learning of the values implicit in interaction, a kind of learning ethic (as cited in Ratcliff, 1997).

The term *hidden curriculum* has come to imply that an institution's social learning context may be unintended but inherent in a range of student experiences in and outside class. Faculty, students, and others then ask questions about "what is really going on," and whether it is to good effect. A view of *curriculum as social learning process in a learning culture* means that curriculum is much more than learning experiences through which courses are put into practice. It includes the individual aims, philosophy, resources, and planning of the teacher and the "social process in which learning takes place, discoveries are made and [learners] come to terms with culture and [come] to learn independently" (Pring, 1995, p. 81). Learning is reinforced and extended by its culture (Bruner, 1990; Cole, 1996; Shweder, 1990); culture also extends curriculum. Alverno College Education Faculty "understand 'curriculum' as much more than a collection of courses. [Curriculum is] the sum total of the courses, the philosophy, and the ways students and faculty interact. It includes what and how students learn, what we do to promote that learning, and what our students are becoming" (1996, p. 4). Faculty and students are likely to perceive *curriculum as social environment—a planned social process for interactive learning.*

At a time when many groups are questioning the purposes and results of educational institutions, curriculum must explicitly include the cocurriculum and other interactive contexts that include patterns of relationships and norms among all members of a campus. Taking a curriculum perspective means discussing what the curriculum includes and thereby building trust, an essential value in relationships between learners and their teachers, as well as faculty and administrators, and between the institution and the public sphere. Conceptualizing curriculum to include all its interactive elements implies an expanded role for faculty, advisors, and student services personnel.

Conceptual Frameworks

A curriculum's conceptual framework is often equated with a particular curricular approach (core curriculum, great books curriculum). Faculty may already have consciously selected or evolved a curricular approach or gradually blended a group of approaches over time. In our view, a curriculum discussion is at its most effective when faculty probe the rationale for their curriculum. It is on *curriculum as conceptual framework,* then, that attempts at curriculum reconceptualization rest. Thus, educators make a habit of standing aside by studying other curricular approaches in the literature or by visiting other campuses to benchmark their own practices.

Any conceptual framework has assumptions, and we have found that a faculty's guided dialogue may make implicit assumptions explicit and specify the connecting principles that guide student learning. Thus, dialogue about assumptions can lead to curriculum change, setting the stage for thinking through educational assumptions that ground a curriculum for learning that lasts. Recent efforts to make assumptions explicit across institutions in problem-based learning (Albanese & Mitchell, 1993; Ravitch, 1997), student-centered and standards-based teacher education (Darling-Hammond, 1997; Diez, 1998), and ability-based learning (Alverno College Faculty, 1976/1992; Consortium for the Improvement of Teaching, Learning and Assessment, 1992; Otter, 1997) illustrate how powerful such discussions of educational assumptions can be in stimulating educational transformation that influences organizational culture (see Chapter Eleven).

In these efforts, faculty regularly touched on issues that are seminal in curriculum theory and research, are connected by disciplinary and philosophical foundations of education as a profession, and are reflected in diverse disciplinary or professional paradigms and worldviews. For some, articulating a set of operative educational assumptions and following their implications led to discovering incompatibilities and inconsistencies among the amalgamated approaches to curriculum that had been introduced and adapted over the years. That a shift in assumptions may lead to curricular reconceptualization is a popular topic among many faculty groups who are revising curriculum, as well as curriculum theorists (Pinar, 1999; Wraga, 1999). How educational assumptions affect and are affected by the selection and use of other curricular elements is fundamental to projecting how a curriculum might be experienced by students and which learning outcomes might actually accrue, especially outcomes that ensure learning that endures.

Mission, Aims, and Philosophy

In our experience, faculty are more likely to see an educational program as a curriculum with a conceptual framework that needs to be articulated and discussed when they include *curriculum as mission, aims, and philosophy* as a curricular element. Undergraduate institutions are expected by accrediting boards to have a mission statement; if faculty examine a *curriculum as a fundamental expression of college aims and convictions,* the operative meanings of the mission statement come center stage, particularly when discussing curriculum organization or revision.

Often, though, mission statements are so broad that they neither reflect the uniqueness of a college nor illuminate potential gaps between faculty intent, practice, and learner experience at the course or department level that might be helpful in curriculum revision. Aims or purposes and educational philosophy need to be clear as well. Hence, our emphasis on testing curriculum assumptions such as, "teaching leads to learning."

Program Evaluation and Assessment

Program evaluation and assessment functions more as a connecting element than as a large and embracing one. Historically, it has been oriented to the quantitative evidence of program documentation (for example, enrollment, retention, graduation, GPA). However, program assessment directions in the 1980s were grounded in part on the idea that graduation and grades were at best only proxy measures for learning; measurement and judgment would necessarily involve more sophisticated assessment procedures, as well as more integrated and coherent visions of curriculum. Evaluation activities, then, should serve as a means to a dynamic conceptualization of curriculum (Stark & Lattuca, 1997, pp. 266–268). So

considered, program evaluation and assessment are part of the lex-
icon of inquiry and connect the assessment literature to our theme
of taking a curriculum perspective (Astin, 1991; Banta & Associates, 1993; Erwin, 1991; Ewell, 1991; Gray, 1989; Loacker, 1988;
Mentkowski, 1998; Stark & Thomas, 1994; Taylor & Marienau,
1997).

Exploring Curricular Approaches, Assumptions, and Learning Principles

The dynamic interaction of elements defines a particular curriculum. We have found that exploring how curriculum functions as
a conceptual framework of educational assumptions serves as a
touchstone for deepening curriculum discussions. As a professor
of philosophy suggests, "A department, school, or college that explores its own assumptions may then reflect on what needs to be
made explicit and how that informs teaching and learning. How
these assumptions connect is an incredibly profound way to point
to the need to examine teaching practice. I ask, 'What implications
does this assumption have for what I do in the classroom?'" We recommend that a faculty group explore how these elements reveal
assumptions that may serve as organizing principles for thinking
through their curriculum. Where a group starts makes a difference. For example, *curriculum as course sequence* could start with a
debate about timing, scheduling, and faculty course assignments,
without ever clarifying concerns about content. *Curriculum as consensus on content* might begin with selecting texts, as in a great books
curriculum (Smith, 1983), but then gradually move to rethinking
assumptions about how to enhance learning from texts. Further
design work might focus on what a particular learned society has
set forth as essential for a major in its field.

The power of *curriculum as conceptual framework of educational
assumptions* is released when faculty focus on learning-centered education and articulate corresponding learning principles. For example, a primary focus on strengthening learning experiences
might lead immediately to redesigning a sequence of courses. Different curricular perspectives can lead to different discussions. Because they see *curriculum as professional problem solving* after college
or professional school, a faculty might begin by considering how to
construct cases so students must use the essential knowledge base

in the field, as in problem-based learning (Barrows, 1994; Barrows & Tamblyn, 1980). *Curriculum as social learning context* might start with identifying principles that foster interactive group learning, as in collaborative learning (Gabelnick et al., 1990). *Curriculum as mission, aims, and philosophy* might involve studying community needs, as in service-learning, so that students can practice contributing effectively in the community (Eyler & Giles, 1999; National Society for Internships and Experiential Education, 1990; Rothman, 1998; Zlotkowski, 1997–1999). *Curriculum as community context* might mean identifying underserved students with limited access to college or gradually increasing diversity in the student body so "all students can learn perspective taking."

Different curricular approaches have contrasting assumptions and principles. Some approaches are conventional; some are emerging, given a developing understanding of the challenges facing postsecondary education in general and undergraduate programs in particular. In reality, most programs integrate at least several approaches to curriculum. However, we have found it helpful to clarify the assumptions already in use because these often influence where a faculty might begin a conversation about curriculum. Here we offer a prompt for moving beyond defining one's own curriculum and its elements, toward external comparisons. We reviewed commonly held curricular definitions and approaches, drawing out educational assumptions and learning principles that underlie them. Table 9.1 lists sixteen approaches to curricula that have identifiable elements; we inferred only one implicit or explicit assumption and one principle from each approach to facilitate faculty discourse that explores the roots of current and potential conceptual frameworks *across* approaches. Each curricular approach actually contains multiple assumptions and learning principles. We selected some that may be embedded and hard to recognize immediately, in part because they rest on different meaning systems. For example, in a core curriculum (Table 9.1, approach 3), consensus on content, that is, common learning, is fundamental to specialized fields. Faculty might ask, "What is the nature of common learning that ensures that students gradually incorporate knowledge, skills, and attitudes over time?" Or, in a profession-based curriculum (Table 9.1, approach 5), "What common understandings about the profession are demonstrated via internships, so students learn them?"

Table 9.1. Inferring One Educational Assumption and One Learning Principle from Selected Curricular Approaches.

Curricular Approach[a]	One Inferred Assumption (Implicit or Explicit)	One Learning Principle (Implicit or Explicit)
1. Cafeteria or shopping mall	1. The content of the curriculum, purposefully selected by faculty, gives structure to the curriculum. Students make informed choices; they enroll prepared to take responsibility for their own learning. A collection of courses has an implicit conceptual framework or lack of one; the student can discern it, supply it, and use it to integrate learning across courses. Individual faculty emphases constitute the content of the curriculum.	1. Choosing is essential for individual motivation for learning. Learning is synonymous with content that changes endlessly.
2. Course of study as a set of sequenced courses (97 percent of curricula, Ratcliff, 1997)	2. Course sequence connects curricula for students; what is taught and learned earlier transfers to later courses in the sequence. Students can infer the philosophy and aims of the department, intended and not, from selection and sequence of courses. They learn coherent aims and learning outcomes informally, or through advising.	2. Learning builds over time; learning is cumulative. Curriculum connections are learned incidentally or individually created.
3. Core curriculum (liberal arts/general education component)	3. Common learning is fundamental to specialized learning in the majors and to a liberal education.	3. What is learned incorporates what has been learned.
4. Subject-matter curriculum	4. All general education requirements are not necessary in all fields (for example, communications, literature, and psychology are not needed in the study of engineering or languages). Coherence among individual theories of teaching and learning depends on the discipline.	4. Specialized content is the framework for learning.
5. Discipline or profession-based curriculum	5. Individual faculty create their own curriculum in courses, but teach out of both their individual and common understanding of what their discipline, as a dynamic field, requires.	5. The discipline and profession is the framework for learning.
6. Selective curriculum	6. Curriculum works when students self-select or are selected at entrance for their prior education, fit with the curriculum, or potential to graduate.	6. Learning potential is predictable.

7. Great books curriculum	7. Selected content or canon centers a curriculum.	7. Learning across selected, diverse texts yields cumulative understanding of liberal arts outcomes.
8. Credit for seat time	8. Credits that are awarded for attendance, prescribed time in class, and achievement represent learning in courses.	8. Rate of learning is constant. Ability to learn varies. Learning potential is predictable.
9. Time constant/learning variable	9. Curriculum units are awarded for mastery of course goals; unsuccessful students may repeat courses.	9. Each student's rate of learning is variable, so time to achieve is variable.
10. Writing across the curriculum	10. Individual faculty who create their own curriculum in courses have consensus on learning outcomes that are taught and assessed across courses.	10. Writing is essential to undergraduate learning.
11. Developmental education	11. Interventions challenge and support what students have learned and construct cognitively, so shifts in cognitive development occur.	11. Learning is deep, developmental, and structural.
12. Problem-based learning	12. Faculty hold assumptions and principles in common that ground curriculum and the teaching and learning within it. Predominant learning styles in a profession characterize formal learning.	12. Problem solving integrates learning.
13. Experiential learning	13. Curriculum includes real and simulated experiences that are reflected on, analyzed, and acted on.	13. Learning is experiential.
14. Ability-based learning	14. Curriculum is organized around integrated, explicit learning outcomes that integrate content and ability and are assessed in performance.	14. Learning is integrative and transformative.
15. Collaborative learning community	15. Curriculum is organized so students and faculty learn side by side or interactively in an established learning group.	15. Learning is interactive and interpersonal.
16. Virtual university	16. Curriculum relies on distributed or distance learning to enhance access to education. Learning is not tied to a particular place or time; both may vary.	16. Learning happens all the time, so accessible education provides choice.

aEach curricular approach has many assumptions and principles. This analysis provides a starting point for discussion rather than a comprehensive, inclusive analysis.

Most readers will be familiar with one or another of these curricular approaches and may recognize that each marks a shift in assumptions. For example, faculty might discuss approaches to curriculum and gradually articulate the assumptions and learning principles that underlie these approaches and, by inference, those in their own curriculum. Our premise here is that a conceptual framework for curricular revision should come primarily out of articulated frameworks for good educational practice. Articulating educational assumptions, begun in Table 9.1, can prompt questions about what learning principles a faculty group is committed to and what the priorities and implications are for their own curriculum. For example, specialized content as a framework for learning in a subject-matter curriculum (Table 9.1, approach 4) may work as one learning principle. But if a faculty expands specialized content to include broad abilities or outcomes that define a major field or cross fields, then the principle *learning that lasts is integrative* comes into play (Table 9.1, approach 14). The implication may lead to rethinking the role of subject matter in learning.

In our own case, the faculty began with a shift in focus from what they did as teachers to include what the student and, later, the graduate ought to know and be able to do. Once expected learning outcomes were clearer, the faculty developed student- and program-assessment systems to provide continuing information about progress and substantiate discussions about curriculum with information about actual student learning. This permanently shifted the faculty's focus to study student learning outcomes in relation to curriculum, as well as to alternative curriculum perspectives, structures, and the organizational culture (see Chapter Eleven). We now turn to the question of how curricular elements, drawn from the literature, are elaborated when a curriculum embodies a commitment to lasting learning.

Analyzing a Curriculum for Learning That Lasts

Probing the elements of a curriculum in relation to learning outcomes and elaborating them through learner attributions can provide observations about which relationships drive and sustain learning, one basis for inferring the potentially transferable curricular elements for fostering learning that lasts. The perspectives of learners—as students and alumnae—are a critical point of entry to elaborate curriculum elements. In pointing to the powerful and sustaining elements in the curriculum that account for learner outcomes, these perspectives serve a similar role.

Alverno's curriculum is grounded in a particular approach that has gone through extensive changes since its inception in the early 1970s. Further, the interactive relationships among its elements, outcomes, and consequent curricular principles may be quite different from those at any other institution. Recognizing this, we analyzed the Alverno curriculum—its practices, principles, and research—to determine those elements that were stable to a degree; ironically, each element also ensured change in the curriculum.

Essential Curricular Elements for Learning That Lasts

We offer an elaborated set of curricular elements as essential—that is, necessary and sufficient to ensure learning that lasts for a broad range of graduates (see Figure 9.2). They include and extend the findings from the analysis of the literature (introduced in Figure 9.1). These elaborated elements do not guarantee learning that lasts for every student. Rather, the elements, when joined and interactive, create a learning environment that has proved effective for most students in this setting; learners meet the standards set by the faculty and continue to develop and demonstrate them up to at least five years postcollege. If each of these elements is a part of a curriculum dynamic and realized in learner outcomes and attributions, a curriculum may successfully foster learning that lasts.

To obtain the elements we view as essential (Figure 9.2, bottom), we first identified interactive elements of undergraduate curricula from the literature (Figure 9.2, top) and then integrated them with their analysis of elements in the Alverno curriculum. For the latter, we analyzed Alverno faculty construction of practices and principles from their publications (e.g., Alverno College Educators, 1977/1998; Alverno College Faculty, 1976/1992, 1979/1994), including jointly published material from faculty membership in three consortia with other colleges and universities (Cromwell, 1986; Halonen, 1986; Schulte & Loacker, 1994). (See Appendix K for a list of institutions.) We used learner outcomes (examined in

**Figure 9.2. Curriculum as Dynamic Process
with Interactive Elements: Essential
Elements for Learning That Lasts.**

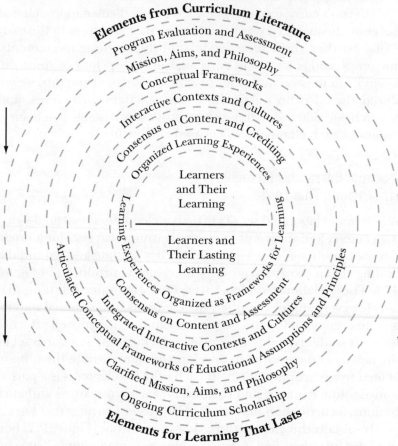

Parts Two and Three) to inform our analysis further. We then sub-
mitted seventeen hours of our taped, transcribed deliberations
(Alverno College Research and Evaluation Committee, 1998) to a
secondary analysis to clarify, synthesize, and confirm the essential
elements. In effect, we triangulated our review of the external literature with the literature on this college's curriculum—developed
experientially and studied for over twenty years—and the particular studies available in this book that link curricular elements to
learning outcomes.

How might a curriculum group use these results to analyze their own curriculum? We are mindful of Stark and Lattuca's (1997) caveat that the use of terms alone to describe aspects of a curriculum is often devoid of meaning. So to make the essential elements more useful, we created Table 9.2. The first column elaborates the essential elements through the context of the Alverno curriculum. Column 2 illustrates each of the essential elements through examples of cohering learner outcomes and causal attributions from Part Two, so a faculty group can see how these elements are reflected in student and alumna perspectives (see Appendixes H–J). Column 3 details curriculum principles that cohere to the elements; we inferred them after we had a picture of the essential elements.

Learning Experiences Organized as Frameworks for Learning

Rather than learning experiences organized only as courses, this curriculum's learning experiences are organized primarily as coherent frameworks for learning: (1) abilities integrated with disciplines and interdisciplinary areas of study and professions; (2) student assessment-as-learning; and (3) educating for learning to learn, maturity, and service. These frameworks undergird a level of coherence that balances the deliberately planned diversity within each, recognizing that theories of coherence have an "order bias, a consistency bias" (Quinn & Cameron, 1988b, p. 13) but that the concept resonates well with ineffable educational goals (Buchmann & Floden, 1992). Immediately, one thus confronts what makes liberal learning situated—how learning differs across contexts—and what it means to teach toward transferable abstractions such as abilities within disciplines, how students come to evaluate their own work credibly, and how to acknowledge and support the learner as developing person and contributor (Barrowman, 1996; O'Brien, Matlock, Loacker, & Wutzdorff, 1991).

Faculty see abilities integrated with disciplines as one "framework for student learning" (Loacker & Palola, 1981). Disciplines themselves are frameworks for learning, as are abilities (see Appendix A). Herein lies the challenge. A barrier to understanding of the concept of abilities integrated with the disciplines is the idea that, prior to integration, abilities and the disciplines can exist separately. Faculty

Table 9.2. Essential Elements of a Dynamic Curriculum for Learning That Lasts.

Essential Elements of a Curriculum for Learning That Lasts[a]	Curricular Elements as Realized in Learning Outcomes and Learners' Causal Attributions[b]	Conceptual Framework of Curriculum Principles
1. *Learning experiences organized as frameworks for learning:* Frameworks are elaborated as expected learning outcomes and experiences that include abilities integrated with disciplines and/or interdisciplinary areas of study, and professions; student assessment-as-learning; educating for learning to learn, maturity, and service.	1. Students and alumnae experience the curriculum as individualized and experiential; interactive and collaborative; coherent and diverse; structured and open-ended; designed for individual and group; and the result of a wide range of teaching, learning, and assessment strategies.	Faculty determine student learning outcomes that inform curriculum. Faculty define learning outcomes as complex and multidimensional abilities integrated with content, that are developmental and integrated in performance and in the person. Faculty designate the learning outcomes that are required for graduation and those that are expected but not required. A curriculum attends to both.
2. *Consensus on content and assessment:* Consensus on content means expected and required learning outcomes that integrate content and ability, abilities in situations, knowing and doing, personal and professional roles, and liberal arts and professions. Consensus on student assessment means student assessment-as-learning, with public, developmental performance criteria, feedback, and self assessment.	2. Public, explicit learning outcomes are developmental, ability based, and performance based. Learners express learning principles in various key components of assessment-as-learning: learning outcomes, criteria, feedback, self assessment.	What and how faculty teach are distinguishable from what students take in and how and when they transform that into knowledge, performance, and personal growth. Teaching, learning, and assessment are variables in the learning process. A curriculum attends to all three. A curriculum that includes distinctive performance outcomes and makes them explicit enables educators to better integrate disciplinary and interdisciplinary frameworks into a student's general education. A curriculum includes diverse opportunities for evaluation of individual performance.

3. *Integrated interactive contexts and cultures:* Contexts include challenging and supportive pedagogy, learning climate, community, and culture with integrated curriculum, cocurriculum, internships, travel abroad, service to community. Consideration of learners' lives and life events. Climate that encourages voice and trust.

3. A curriculum includes diverse opportunities for diverse learners to construct their own ideas, practice, reflect, validate the relevance of learning, and learn to perform. High expectations along with high acceptance, expectations for independent and collaborative achievement. A balance of curricular challenges and supports communicates a climate that encourages voice and trust and provides opportunities for learners to define and realize their own purposes.

4. *Articulated conceptual frameworks of assumptions and principles:* Frameworks include educational assumptions, learning and assessment principles, curriculum principles, and principles for learning that lasts.

4. A curriculum is learner and learning centered with positive regard toward students. Each learner is respected and can learn.

A curriculum provides for repeated opportunities for learners to construct, practice, perform, reflect on, and integrate what they are learning in multiple disciplines, interdisciplinary areas of study, and professions. Internships, advising, and instructional and student services are integral to the curriculum.

Curriculum integrity (the degree represents what faculty intend and what students experience) requires that a curriculum be coherent within diversity. A dynamic curriculum requires constantly rethinking and reformulating learning, assessment, and teaching/advising/inquiry/curriculum principles and continually validating educational assumptions.

Table 9.2. Essential Elements of a Dynamic Curriculum for Learning That Lasts, cont'd.

Essential Elements of a Curriculum for Learning That Lasts[a]	Curricular Elements as Realized in Learning Outcomes and Learners' Causal Attributions[b]	Conceptual Framework of Curriculum Principles
5. *Clarified mission, aims, and philosophy:* A curriculum is centered on learners and their learning. A curriculum is coherent within its diversity. It is developmental and requires students to meet explicit, common, and evolving expectations that maximize each student's potential.	5. Purposeful, connected curriculum is in the interest of learners. Curriculum is fair in that faculty and staff intent as communicated to students is generally realized in what faculty and staff do and how they interact.	Curriculum diversity yields coherence when curriculum is for the learning of students. A curriculum is designed, practiced, experienced, evaluated, and improved by faculty in relation to what students bring to it, how students experience it, what students learn and ought to learn across a curriculum, and how graduates learn and need to learn beyond college.
6. *Ongoing curriculum scholarship:* Faculty study the relationships between abilities, learning, and their disciplines.	6. Curriculum is continually improving for current and future learners; learners' perspectives on and experiences with the curriculum are considered and changes made. Learners perceive faculty and staff as experts in their fields, and in teaching, advising, and services.	Curriculum scholarship is ongoing, sustained, extensive, deliberative, individual, and collaborative with multiple methods and comparisons across disciplines. Scholarship in the disciplines or an integration of disciplines is shaped by and also shapes student learning.

[a]Elements of a dynamic curriculum emerge from a triangulated analysis. Essential elements of curriculum that lasts are based on interactive elements of undergraduate curricula derived from the curriculum literature; Alverno faculty perspectives and their current practice; consortia with outside faculty (Cromwell, 1986; Halonen, 1986; Schulte & Loacker, 1994); and by joining empirically derived student and alumna perspectives, performance, and other measurement-based findings. Rather than a uniform and idealized model of curriculum, the emphasis here is on the interaction of elements, and on those that are potentially usable in conversations about design and evaluation of curriculum. The premise is that some of these elements and relationships (for example, regard for the learner, performance assessment, experiential learning) may already be in place or may be implemented in stages in any one department or institution. It is the cohering relationships among these elements that make a difference for learning that lasts.

[b]See Appendixes H, I, and J.

know that this is a false dichotomy. Our way of explaining it away in the past has been to say that we cannot teach for abilities in a void. They must be taught in the context of something, and that "something" is the discipline or interdisciplinary area of study. But that dichotomy is false because disciplines as ways of thinking (particular organizations of procedural knowledge—facts, conventions, concepts, rules of thumb) are already, by this definition, composed of various ability components. The problem is not so much one of integrating abilities and disciplines, but of faculty recognizing and helping students to understand and perform the abilities that compose a discipline. This can be a challenge to faculty because they are generally so proficient at the practice of their disciplines (researching, writing reviews, and so forth) that their ways of thinking are almost second nature to them. Since they seldom articulate the processes underlying their thinking, all students ever notice are the products of faculty practice—the interpretations, the syntheses of current scholarship, the finished writings. What faculty have to do is to reflect upon and break open their professional disciplinary practice to rediscover the specific abilities and habits of mind that constitute them, and thus make them more explicit as they walk students through faculty practice, modeling the discipline for them.

There are various techniques for deconstructing a disciplinary practice; one of the most effective is for faculty to engage in professional dialogue about the meaning of their disciplines *across disciplinary lines*. Unable to rely on the common epistemological assumptions and shared language of a disciplinary community, faculty are forced to explain themselves, identify their assumptions, elaborate the informal rules that guide their thinking and decision making. Once they have done this, it is easier to teach the discipline (not just the disciplinary knowledge base) to students. Faculty must, however, be careful not to model their expectations for students on expectations for themselves. Faculty disciplinary practice is analogous, not identical, to the practice that they want to foster in their students.

Disciplines as a framework for student learning means that faculty make teaching choices based on the suitability of particular dimensions of their own discipline (in itself or integrated with other disciplines) for promoting student learning. They have also come to apply the term *learning framework* to their own thinking in the discipline and to the way they construct meaning through their scholarship. While their own disciplinary thinking differs from that of students in level of sophistication, faculty see their own learning as analogous to their students', and they tend to concentrate in their scholarship on questions about the method and nature of thinking in their disciplines. There is an ongoing interrelationship between the questions they raise about their fields and those that help them to refine student learning. Thinking, for example, about the way they present their discipline's methods for their students refines their own understanding of those methods. As one history professor puts it, "Our practice as teachers in an ability-based learning environment has led us to think differently, or at least more explicitly, about our disciplines. In order for us to help students learn to think in the disciplines, we have to pay serious attention to our own process of learning. Since we explicitly model disciplinary practice and explain this to students, we have to be very conscious of what we are doing."

Learners' outcomes and causal attributions provide additional insight here (see Table 9.2, column 2). Because learners apply what they know, frameworks for learning are *experiential*. An *individualized* curriculum is responsive to individual learners and provides for appropriate challenges from faculty. Extended, multiple interpretations of expectations and achievements express a plural, open-ended standard of excellence revealed in explicit developmental performance criteria; they encourage responsiveness to learning styles and *reinforce diversity* in learner perspectives. *Interactive and collaborative* learning experiences are a source of developing flexibility, as are *coherent and diverse, individual and group* learning experiences. They help to ensure an essential wholeness, continuity of argument, and integrity in the learner—a coherence across the curriculum that supports diversity, making the coherence robust rather than brittle. Learners experience a *wide range of teaching, learning, and assessment strategies.*

Consensus on Content and Assessment

In this curriculum, faculty come to consensus on content as expected learning outcomes and on assessment as an essential process for student learning. "Consensus on content" does not mean uniformity, total agreement, or lack of conflict, just as "ability" does not mean lack of content. Integration of content and ability is essential so that individual academic areas are learned in terms of the range of performances and abilities that represent their learning outcomes, and so that abilities are understood, developed, and demonstrated across multiple disciplinary and interdisciplinary contexts.

Coming to consensus on content as integrated content and abilities has led Alverno's faculty to raise questions about their broader role in student learning. For example, the same history professor asks:

> What is the relationship between faculty teaching and student learning? If we assume a complex epistemology, where subjective processing of experience affects what people know at least to some degree, then what faculty teach is not identical to what students learn. There is no objective transfer of knowledge from the mind of the faculty member to the mind of the student. The data that faculty have reflected upon and transformed into knowledge, through their scholarship, can be experienced by students as a more refined data set—but it will not become knowledge until students transform it into knowledge for themselves.

The language of abilities, integrated with content, has profound implications for learners because how they construct learning influences whether they can transfer it (Doherty et al., 1997; Evers, Rush, & Berdrow, 1998). The younger adult cohorts' experiences reflect what happens when a college is dominated by students directly from high school; the older, work-experienced cohorts reflect the broader adult population, including some young adults. Abilities integrated with disciplines constitutes a roadblock for both kinds of learners at first, but it poses a greater challenge for the eighteen- or nineteen-year-old who comes directly from high school with, in most cases, a less clear sense of career direction. The learner who has been a particularly high performer can stumble just as sharply as the one who has not ("Where's the content? How do I know I'm succeeding or failing?"). The discrepancy between their expectations and the curriculum has definite learning value, but with a major caveat: faculty and advisors must pay careful attention to retention, so their approach does not jeopardize particular kinds of learners. Of course, any college is a new environment, with a new language that the student has not been entirely exposed to before. It is discontinuous from that of the high school, and what appears to be resistance to the new culture may be the persistence of the old one. As Piaget and Perry suggest, when a challenge appears in the new environment, there is a heavy reliance on the prior environment for strategies. Work-experienced, returning, and transfer students are more likely to understand ability-based learning sooner. While similarly challenged at first (they, too, expect more traditional ways of learning), they engage with the complexity of the system sooner.

Performance assessment is inevitably linked conceptually to learning principles, and faculty have come to consensus on how to conceptualize and practice assessment, to the point where student assessment is a framework for learning: assessment-as-learning. With reflective self assessment, it assists learners to shape their future performance based on their understanding of their past and current work and their intellectual processes. A successful active learning process includes engagement, self assessment, and feedback. It must include public, explicit, and developmental criteria for judging performances, as well as feedback and self assessment. At the earliest level, such a framework for learning incorporates student development of self-awareness and self assessment by setting up a visual model (this level is like watching a drama). The next level provides opportunities for students to use the model (like rehearsing the play). At a still higher level, curriculum engages students in the process of self-awareness and self assessment (this would include seeing relevance, showing personal identification, and valuing the process). ("Developmental" does not mean relieving the learner of the obligation to meet standards, since each student must meet criteria in order to graduate.)

As realized in learner outcomes and attributions, an integrated consensus on content and assessment means *public, explicit learning outcomes* that have clarity for learners, faculty, and various groups (Table 9.2, column 2). The analysis of their observations points to the particular elements of the curriculum that they singled out as valuable: the ability framework and the integration of content, the orientation to performance (see Appendix I). *Developmental, ability-based, and performance-based learning outcomes* detail the nature and sequence of ability levels, interaction of abilities integrated with content, and how students might build them over time.

Interaction of course outcomes with the development of learners is appreciated (see Appendix J). Students show development in their *ability to express faculty principles in various aspects of assessment-as-learning, learning outcomes, criteria, feedback, and self assessment.* For example, an advanced learner has developed criteria as a picture of her effectiveness in demonstrating her ability, a picture that is congruent with external standards and highlighting what is unique to her (see Appendix H).

Aspects of the curriculum more associated with teaching behaviors and the delivery of the curriculum are student and alumna experiences of the powerful effects of assessment, self assessment, and the procedures for giving feedback on performances (see Appendix I). Recent studies with students in transition confirm these conclusions. Faculty find that students who have experienced problems progressing in the curriculum after two or three semesters are often those who have had trouble in working with curriculum frameworks—as in the structure of abilities and disciplinary theories—and in working closely with the feedback they have received. This becomes particularly problematic when, given this learning culture, students are likely to keep receiving greater quantities of feedback than they know how to use. Thus, assisting each student to use feedback to improve becomes the intervention faculty choose (Alverno College Intermediate Student Study Committee, 1994).

Integrated Interactive Contexts and Cultures

The multiple contexts that interact in this curriculum provide important opportunities for an appropriate balance of challenges and supports for learning. In this curriculum, faculty work toward integrating these contexts, so that educating for learning to learn, maturity, and service has become a learning framework. This framework connects the curriculum and cocurriculum in practice to learning that lasts through structured experiences in the cocurriculum (for example, transition-to-college programs, transition to career, learning support groups, residence hall meetings between counselors and residents; negotiating on-campus day care; internships, travel, and community service), as well as an awareness of students' lives and life events and the many subcultures that reflect the intentions and norms of a student population. Integrating interactive contexts has also meant finding ways to create a shared sense of the social process of education for the faculty and staff. The curriculum then provides multiple recurring opportunities for learners to construct what they are learning—and to practice and perform—in different disciplines, contexts, and cultures. Learners themselves come to see the *curriculum as a set of diverse opportunities to construct their own purposes, ideas, and criteria; to practice, to reflect, to validate the relevance of learning; and to learn to perform.* High expectations along with high acceptance, expectations for independent as well as collaborative achievement, challenges and supports—each dynamic is part of their experience, and each communicates a climate for encouraging voice and trust (see Appendix J). Considering climate can lead to rethinking the organizational culture (see Chapter Eleven).

Articulated Conceptual Frameworks of Assumptions and Principles

In this curriculum, educational assumptions—the ideas that generate frameworks for learning that shape teaching, assessing, advising, and inquiry—are explicit and discussed, and form a basis for generating curricular principles (see Table 9.2, column 3). A conceptual framework of assumptions enables a faculty to discuss what principles for learning that lasts imply for designing and evaluating curriculum. Such articulated conceptual frameworks open up the curriculum rationale for students—one that stays with them as alumnae (see Appendix J). Learners projected a strong sense of their own understandings of curricular principles and developed a regard for their own learning. Five-year alumnae who could articulate this rationale also tended to articulate their learning outcomes in more meaningful ways.

Clarified Mission, Aims, and Philosophy

The practice of clarifying mission, aims, and philosophy at this college and its relationship to conceptual frameworks reaffirms a commitment to serving learners and their learning. The focus on abilities integrated with disciplinary and interdisciplinary conceptual frames ties together the students' education, the degree programs, and the cocurriculum. Learners, then, experience the *curriculum as purposeful and connected.* It is purposeful in that faculty have deliberately defined purposes in understandable language rather than just naming them. Thus, learners can connect their learning across the curriculum. The mission, aims, and philosophy require that members of the college community respect each student. There is a democratic dimension to this experience—the sense that each participant is respected and expected to learn. While some curricula may foster learning that lasts but not be purposive, learners understood and experienced the democratic tendencies of this curriculum as a means by which faculty advocated the latent potential for all students to learn and to exceed what is required of them. Learners experienced the curriculum as fair in that faculty generally do what they claim (see Appendix J).

Ongoing Curriculum Scholarship

Reflective curriculum practice and inquiry means that faculty and staff, as a community of educators, engage in ongoing studies into the curriculum, student learning, teaching, advising, assessment, and inquiry itself. They also study relationships among abilities, learning, and their disciplines. The professor of history quoted earlier comments, "As great as the challenge has been to unify pedagogical and disciplinary scholarship, it has been an even greater challenge to explain to colleagues who have not experienced it what an integrated and collaborative scholarship discourse sounds like about curriculum because there is, at present, little common language to express the dialogue."

Faculty members' conscious emphasis on disciplines as frameworks for learning may have to do with the environment of a liberal arts college. If they are to have a significant and varied intellectual life with their colleagues, interdisciplinary dialogue is inescapable. Faculty are stepping beyond the comfortable epistemological boundaries of the disciplines. "We can no longer rely on our dialogue partners' automatic understanding of our basic assumptions. We have to be able to explain the structure of our thinking to each other," says the history professor. Accounting for integrated and collaborative scholarship in support of student learning in the disciplines does not, however, explain what it really means to say that disciplinary scholarship *is shaped by* and also *shapes* student learning. To explain this transformation of the disciplines and of student learning, we move to another example.

In a recent faculty fellowship paper, a professor of economics in this college's Business and Management Division explained her dissatisfaction with the assumption of standard economic theory that individual economic agents are autonomous beings who make organized and consistent choices that coherently refer back to a singular self-identity. She wrote that "this account of personal identity has always been problematic for me as a teacher—especially one who teaches adult women. . . . This account in no way explains the choices most of my students have made in their lives, thus making it particularly challenging for them to understand and internalize this theory." Although feminist economists have criticized this assumption of the autonomous individual and have emphasized the way social institutions like the family constrain individual choice, this faculty member went a step further to study the multiple-self literature in philosophy to understand how "individuals constrain themselves in their struggles between multiple selves as they choose between conflicting needs, desires, and values."

This example illustrates many of the characteristics of scholarship in support of student learning:

- Reflection on actual student learning is the stimulus for the examination of the adequacy of fundamental ideas in the discipline.
- The insights derived from this scholarship promise to improve student learning directly.
- The research goes beyond the boundaries of the discipline and presents opportunities for collaboration with colleagues in another field.
- Because the scholarship connects the discipline to the general liberal arts abilities of Analysis and Valuing in Decision-Making, it promises to influence student development of these abilities in courses across this college.
- The formation of method and theory in the discipline is directly addressed through scholarship in the way that term has been traditionally understood.

Curriculum scholarship provides for faculty to continue to develop in their disciplines and to craft cross-college studies as well. For example, learners perceive faculty and staff as competent in their fields—teaching, advising, or service—and experience a curriculum that is evolving in thoughtful response to their expressed learning needs and purposes, leading to the broader study of student outcomes. They also confirmed the power of various challenges and supports to teaching and learning that emerge from the faculty's assumptions and principles, and the opportunities to experience and perform in diverse situations on and off campus, as a dimension of a learning program, as sustaining elements for their continued learning and effectiveness, and for their development as persons (see Appendix I).

Confirming the Curriculum in Learner Outcomes

The proof of any curriculum is in learners' performance and their causal attributions (recall Part Two and Part Three). Learner perspectives on their outcomes confirmed essential elements of curriculum for learning that lasts. Most powerful perhaps is the finding that students constructed meaning from their education, with integrity and applicability, to the extent that they experienced a coherent and developing vision of education and learning from the curriculum; multiple, diverse perspectives on their areas of study; and feedback on their performance in a range of modes and contexts. Five-year alumnae linked learning to influential curriculum causes that enabled them to continue to grow. They pointed to the coaching, individualized attention, and positive regard that they experienced from teachers and the cooperative, collaborative work with faculty, external assessors and mentors, and peers as factors that have contributed to sustained learning (see Appendix J).

By integrating the statistical analyses on alumna performance, and student and alumna perspectives on their learning outcomes, the character of the curriculum emerges even more sharply:

- The ability framework serves as a metacognitive model as learners deal with work in context.
- Support from the curriculum and faculty teaching toward the learner's growing capacity for self assessment are foundational to becoming an independent and enduring learner.
- The diversity of preparation and the support for in-depth analysis leads to the learner's ability to work with and appreciate multiple viewpoints while effectively constructing and arguing her own position.

- The emphasis on performance and its attendant features (criteria, feedback, practice opportunities, for example) helps the learner integrate the knowledge structures developed across courses with performance opportunities in different contexts.
- Curricular challenges and supports combine to foster independence, and independent and collaborative elements provide for interdependence.

These findings from formal research are reflected not only in the student voice but in the faculty voice drawn from examples of collaborative inquiry.

Taking Up the Work of Ongoing Curriculum Development

Faculty dialogue about interactive and essential curricular elements bears on designing, practicing, reflecting, and deliberating on curriculum. *Designing* means making explicit curricular intent and conceptual frameworks, and planning the underlying structure of curriculum and how it is organized to facilitate particular outcomes. *Practicing* includes instructional interventions and their ongoing adjustments, observing the practices that become critical to their effectiveness. *Reflecting on experience* means using students' experience to learn about curriculum. *Deliberative, collaborative inquiry* means participating in constructing, implementing, evaluating, and improving the curriculum's relationship to student learning to ensure its impact and integrity. To do so, educators focus on how their roles intersect and how individual ideas become part of the practice of a community of educators. The ordering of these activities does not mean to imply serial curriculum planning. Rather, they are aspects of academic planning through which faculty gradually move beyond a view of curriculum as a set of learning experiences designed and organized as courses. They thus define content as "more than disciplinary knowledge," cross interactive contexts and cultures of the disciplines, and explore their more intangible assumptions, principles, mission, and philosophy and how they are carried out through curriculum. Dialogue that makes explicit the educational assumptions that underlie curricula, the values that bind a department or school together as a social entity, and the learning principles that undergird curricular principles are particularly helpful. Unarticulated conflicts can stop conversations about what is in the best interest of the learners, and faculty can miss the opportunity to be more accountable for practice.

Particular topics become critical to working on a curriculum: making the learning-to-curriculum connection, realigning faculty and staff roles, and sustaining discourse around activities and challenges. How are these supported by key mechanisms for reflection, deliberation, and inquiry, and how do these contribute to the development, implementation, and evaluation of curriculum?

Making the Learning-to-Curriculum Connection

A range of linking and integrating activities have made up curriculum work over the years:

- Shaping learning-centered curricula in the disciplines, while building opportunities for service-centered performance in the professional areas.
- Identifying, determining, and refining student learning outcomes as an integral feature of learning in the cocurriculum.
- Defining and pursuing problems in determining, revising, and teaching broad abilities or skills integrated with academic content, such as dealing with the "knowledge" problem, including different epistemological paradigms, or deconstructing content for ways of thinking.
- Engendering self-directed student learning through individual and group assignments.
- Modeling the learning gleaned from faculty experience in workshops for new faculty and integrating this learning in criteria for peer review and promotion.
- Using assessment as a tool for student and faculty learning, such as using self-directed learning and self assessment as tools for continuous institutional improvement as well as improvement of individual student performance. (For additional perspectives on such use of portfolio assessments, see O'Brien, 1990.)

Clarifying Roles

The work of curriculum spans a full range of educator roles. It involves the formal groups charged with designing curriculum and making decisions on content, course sequences, and full curricula, but it is just as inclusive of the ad hoc groups and the range of individuals who formulate and carry curricular ideas into program decisions and teaching practice. These activities enable purposive integration of transformative learning processes and learning and action principles into the curriculum. Given this broad involvement, it is all the more important that educators work to understand these roles and their effective interaction. Teachers need to understand their own roles in terms of modeling, building a rationale for, and setting up processes that engage academic work. And, finally, there is the need for processes that enable faculty, as individuals across the dispersion of roles, to take a curriculum perspective as part of their work. There are, as we will see, a number of challenges that emerge directly from this level of integration and collaboration, but it is an important starting point.

Design work that integrates major educational directions seems generally to occur through a committee or task group structure. At the same time, committees with designated curriculum functions may do as much overseeing of course and program policies as with testing the philosophical centers of educational practice. Even with a more or less stable core of educational commitments, much of the work of bringing a curriculum into practice occurs through ad hoc and even less formal group structures that reflect a wide range of college-wide and department meetings.

Creating Opportunities for Sustained Discourse

These meetings, by providing a sustained discourse on educational practice, help maintain the coherence of the curriculum—as a durable core of aims, commitments, and principles—and its flexibility. Revisiting emerging or expanded learning and action principles and educational theories is another part of reflection on curriculum practices. In this kind of context, the broad participation of faculty and academic staff contributes, individually and collectively, to their taking a curriculum perspective. One result is a better understanding of the controversies that can emerge from any structured, purposive endeavor and from curriculum in particular. These include questions of balance between intense collaboration and individual work and initiative; which commitments are shared and which are individual to academic freedom; and strategies for creating pockets of sustained curriculum discourse in a large, diverse faculty. Resource planning, including budgeting, gradually becomes a process that, rather than being delegated solely to a department chair, dean, or provost, is more open and participative, leading to sometimes painful changes in negotiating ways of doing things, including developing more participative strategies for conducting departmental review and self studies for accrediting visits. Thus, conversations about curriculum can lead to targeted, constructive individual and group faculty inquiry that pushes ideas into action.

Chapter Ten

Rethinking Inquiry That Improves Teaching and Learning

When discourse is critical to developing educational practices, educators confront how inquiries into student learning will be shaped accordingly. In this context, inquiry to improve teaching and learning—through a fuller understanding of student growth—must be constructed in relation to how it contributes to such discourse. Educators should ultimately be evaluating the success of inquiry programs, then, in terms that include the effective engagement of faculty and the consequences for student learning. The examples here come from analyzing inquiry activities over two decades and collaborating as a group of educators. By portraying a thoughtful faculty in action, we move toward creating a vision of collaborative inquiry. We provide an elaborated and complex picture of the ways theory, research, and practice-based inquiry become integrated in an institutional culture, helping ensure that student—and faculty—learning will last.

The prior chapters have provided strong evidence for the importance of inquiry focused on student learning, development, and performance and its integration with the work of faculty and staff. Now we ask how a program of inquiry, designed to meet such specific needs, can be constructed, pursued, and supported. A close look at most educational research reveals some types of collaborative action. Jon Wagner (1997) has noted that because of the inherently cooperative nature of educational research, educators need to give more attention to how to build and use cooperative processes effectively. From the perspective of one college's experiences, we would add that learning-centered inquiry is inherently a part of effective teaching and that it creates a need to explore and build on this dimension of scholarship; the work is too significant to be assigned strictly to academic researchers and too complex to simply import their methods. So having previously explored some examples in earlier chapters, why now focus on inquiry?

Relationships among teaching, research, and reflective practice, frankly, are difficult. Issues of tenure and faculty load and responsibilities remain large in the nature of academic life. Our concern here is on the nature of inquiry designed to serve critical teaching and learning needs. We recognize that as valuable as the integration of research, practice-based inquiry, and sustained reflection may be, it is also difficult to maintain. In elementary and secondary education, frameworks for collaborative inquiry interact and sometimes clash with ideas about school-university relationships and the validity and worth of teacher research (Cochran-Smith & Lytle, 1993; Feldman & Atkin, 1995). In higher education, the interactions among faculty role definition, disciplinary expertise, scholarship, teaching, and campus mission make collaborative inquiry even more problematic.

The institutional context creates additional complexities. An integrated inquiry is not easily or readily carried out in the midst of teaching and other faculty responsibilities. Often questions and answers arise in practice-based inquiry that can be worked through without the more sustained, rigorous data collection and analysis that have characterized research and can lead to more systematic accountability. Faculty become involved in practice-oriented research programs for a range of reasons—for example, accreditation requirements, institutional mission, or their own professional concerns—but the conventions of research and an unfamiliarity with interdisciplinary work can often become barriers. Clearly a degree of leadership and organizational support is needed for a sustained line of inquiry.

The nature of educational innovation creates additional challenges. Innovations are often implemented without clear, competing alternatives, making thorough evaluation difficult. New strategies in a college's practice need to be studied, but practically, they may need to proceed without precise, empirical comparisons among alternatives. There is as well a critical concern for evaluating the inquiry itself and its contribution to the improvement of education.

Considering Scholarly Inquiry

Earlier chapters have shown how educators build their work by integrating various forms of local inquiry grounded in diverse external frameworks and comparisons into the development of their teaching practices and curriculum. These examples—the long-term studies of learner perspectives, the longitudinal measurements of learning and development and consequent alumna performance studies, faculty discourse and inquiry to revise learning principles, and so forth—demonstrate diverse educational concerns and inquiry traditions. They have in common the effort to put inquiry in the service of teaching, learning, and student assessment in such a manner that faculty bring multiple levels of expertise to teaching: knowledge of students, expertise in their disciplines, and their participation in the curriculum.

Now, we reexamine and ultimately redefine our understanding of scholarly inquiry, in order to most fruitfully use the results of our collaborative, practice-based inquiry in an integrated practice. We also stand apart from our inquiry practices, critically analyzing relationships and characteristics that may serve as guidelines for new directions in higher education inquiry. This rethinking has strong implications for faculty life (for example, tenure policies and campus structures) and for the role of educational research in learning, teaching, and assessment (research policy and who does research). Examples in this chapter elaborate these themes, with a continuation of the lines of inquiry described in Parts Two and Three and a push toward institutional structure, the subject of Chapter Eleven.

Some of our consensual assumptions regarding the development of collaborative inquiry and its relationship to faculty scholarship are as follows:

- Serving student learning forms the guiding core of the educational program and becomes the basis for unifying the work of different disciplines and roles in the overall programs of a campus. This orientation moves the starting point of discussion less toward concerns of faculty governance and the conditions of teachers' work and more toward a focus on the effective conditions for student learning.

- The role of education is to support student learning that advances in the context of disciplines and professions, not just to select students most ready to move on. This being the case, the teaching and learning questions that then confront faculty—and link curriculum, practice, and learning—are unlikely to be sufficiently answered by distant inquiry (for example, by a survey of policies across a large sample of campuses). Curriculum work must build on local inquiry into one's own students, practices, and institutional programs.

- An educational researcher role in this context is to become an educator who understands how things are working and can enable informed judgments along with educator colleagues. At the same time, the effectiveness of programs designed to deliver education takes priority over basic research. By taking student learning as the central focus of action, inquiries are more closely focused on questions of teaching and assessment practice and the interaction of reasoning, performance, self-reflection, and development.

At the same time that these assumptions provide a foundation for the work, there are also areas where making assumptions is likely to be problematic—for example, in relation to how readily faculty and staff integrate inquiry into educational practices and how faculty develop teaching expertise. Inquiry is not enough in itself to ground or guide teaching actions. Nor are empirical findings a significant contribution to an educational system, unless they enter the reflective practices. Teacher reflection is not yet well enough understood for those involved in curriculum-based research—within the faculty or as professional staff—to make consistently wise use of research opportunities. But given the breadth of research approaches and a growing awareness of their applications in practice settings, it is just as problematic to push aside opportunities to learn from formal research and the fuller integration of research questions emerging from practice. Therefore, the more a study group knows about how faculty members encounter and make meaning from research results and inquiry in its various forms, the more the group is able to engage educators at multiple levels of practice and make good decisions about contributing to the processes by which faculty reflection is integrated into educational practice. The question, then, is how the research act can be most helpfully defined to further teaching and learning.

Emerging Definitions and Directions for Higher Education Research

As it was instituting a new curriculum and rethinking relationships among the disciplines and student learning outcomes, the Alverno faculty was also negotiating and rethinking relationships among teaching, curriculum, and inquiry. As the college confronted these issues within its own program, national concerns for higher education were moving in similar directions. Increasing information on college populations and adult learners and changing social expectations for postsecondary education has meant a different focus on teaching and related inquiries for the last few decades. For example, just the increase in the diversity of learners can call on different skills for faculty in entry-level courses. How do developing faculty members integrate their expertise in the discipline with their knowledge of students and courses, as well as with their developing abilities as teachers?

The Scholarship of Teaching

As colleges have sought to define their roles and questions of student learning have intensified, many have scrutinized the relationship between traditional scholarly productivity and teaching activities. As faculty move toward defining outcomes in learning terms—integrating disciplinary expertise, course content, and teaching with assessing—practice requires that they implement reflective inquiries (Heywood, 1989). The inquiry skills of faculty, shaped by their disciplines, are tools for learning, reflection, argument, creativity, and action—exactly the kinds of thoughtful, informed, and responsible activities envisioned for students in many college mission statements. Nevertheless, as played out in more dichotomous distinctions within faculty work, the articulation between research and teaching is far from clear (cf. Feldman, 1989).

Boyer and his colleagues at the Carnegie Foundation for the Advancement of Teaching (Boyer, 1990), in their review of higher education in this century, concluded that it was time to understand the work of faculty under "a broader and more capacious meaning" of scholarship (p. 16). The resulting publication, *Scholarship Reconsidered,* put forth a well-argued, fourfold vision of scholarship: as discovery, integration and synthesis, application, and teaching. This use of the concept *scholarship of teaching* has become a defining element for much writing on the challenges ahead for higher education. In this same vein, schools such as the DePaul University School for New Learning (Fiddler, McGury, Marienau, Rogers, & Scheideman, 1996) use faculty rank and promotion criteria that support a deeper approach to teaching and its scholarship. (For other approaches to application, see Davis & Chandler, 1998.)

A number of authors have pointed to a renewed focus on teaching as a response to changing enrollments and world needs (e.g., Halpern & Associates, 1994). Robert Menges and Mary Ellen Weimer (Menges, Weimer, & Associates, 1996) noted that the rethinking of scholarship and the closer study of teaching and learning are being shaped by a variety of factors, including the changing student body and their learning characteristics. There is more and more demand for lifelong learners.

But they are also candid about the problem of a vague notion of inquiry: "Scholarship of teaching has become part of our educational jargon . . . an amorphous term, equated more with a commitment to teaching than with any concrete, substantive sense of definition or consensus as to how this scholarship might be recognized" (p. xii). These authors and others (Astin, 1993; Pascarella & Terenzini, 1991) have published a range of studies on the impact of different educational frameworks. Even so, serious questions remain. How do their inquiries and findings become part of a faculty's discussion? What implications does this body of work have locally? Which work should be picked up at the campus level?

If we conceptualize our response only as a scholarship of application—for example, "How do these ideas apply to our students?"—we may limit the discovery element inherent in local inquiry and the opportunity to learn from particular disciplinary perspectives and their interactions in practice. In other words, we may be limiting the potential of a problem-driven inquiry to help us think creatively. We want to embrace but also move beyond an original problem definition to a fuller critique of current practices, with possible directions for future work.

Teaching Practice and Theoretical Inquiry

In practice, curriculum discussions on each campus are likely to blend observations from practice, knowledge of student learning, and a more or less eclectic range of theoretical models related to disciplines and teaching. However, when planning an inquiry, we need a more explicit understanding of the relationships between practice-based reflection and theoretical frameworks. As Donald Schön (1995) indicated, practice-based inquiry is both necessary and messy; the characteristics of practice settings—with issues of bureaucracy, tenure, and so forth—make it difficult to pursue; the work itself is often very problem based and can seem atheoretical.

We may come to think of practice-based inquiry more appropriately as *pretheoretical;* multiple theories of practice are often involved, but there is a sense of moving toward frameworks that will become the basis of fuller, theory-relevant communication and more coherent practice (cf. Eraut's perspectives on practice-based theory, 1994). All of this suggests that interactions between practice-based needs and epistemological and theoretical frameworks will need to be part of the scholarship of teaching—building on the frameworks of practice in use. These frameworks need to be understood from the perspectives of individual educators as well as organizing frames of curriculum. This interaction of priorities argues for a research approach that is local, situated in practice, deliberative, and rigorous in its capacity to produce substantive findings and results (cf. Greeno & the Middle School Mathematics Through Applications Project Group, 1998).

The Challenge: Integrating Formal Research and Collaborative Inquiry

The conventional distinction between research and practice-based inquiry is significant to a point but can become a false dichotomy. *Formal research* and *collaborative inquiry* have served us as better constructs because they can embrace a scholarship of discovery as well as application and teaching. But it is essential to also build collaborative inquiry as a sustained program, not just as an episodic and project-oriented phenomenon.

Perspectives on Collaborative Inquiry: Background

The literature of qualitative inquiry and program evaluation provides some important directions. Authors have dealt with such needs as working with communication issues, engaging a broad participation in a community of educators, and working on strategies to develop rigor and confidence in conclusions (see Harris, 1991b; Lincoln, 1995; Patton, 1990; Stake, 1995).

The challenges to developing inquiry in the service of teaching and learning in higher education bring to mind a primary lesson of program evaluation in the 1970s, as voiced by Lee Cronbach and his colleagues (1980): that evaluation inquiry is less a technical or scientific appraisal than work undertaken "to inform and improve the operation of a social system" (p. 66). Their ninety-five theses (pp. 2–11) echo clearly in a higher education context and emphasize the illuminative role that evaluation plays for a community of educators. For example, they noted that what is often needed is empirical support for discourse and negotiations rather than precise data on the "correct decision" (p. 4). The policy-shaping community, including those who plan and implement higher education, "must act in the face of uncertainty, settling on plausible actions that are politically acceptable" (p. 5). Therefore, and perhaps most pointedly, they note: "The evaluator is an educator; his [or her] success is to be judged by what others learn" (p. 11).

From a range of fields, the arguments converge on the need to develop more locally based inquiry in a variety of forms and integrate these findings in a larger practice. Teacher research, action research, and reflective practice at the precollege level offer significant models for rethinking inquiry to support teaching and learning (Cochran-Smith & Lytle, 1999; Gibbs, 1996; Zeichner, 1987). However, the more clearly we confront changing teaching and curriculum needs in higher education, the more pressing is the need for inquiry models that integrate the rigor of formal research approaches with response to contextual needs (Brookfield, 1995; Cross, 1993; Cross & Steadman, 1996; Schratz, 1992; Selden & Selden, 1993).

This need points toward an interaction between collaborative inquiry, which is situated and problem based, and formal research, which is anchored in specific discipline frameworks, that supports continued investigations into teaching and learning (see Greeno & the Middle School Mathematics Through Applications Project Group, 1998, regarding the integration of theory-oriented and instrumental approaches in a situated practice). At the same time, limiting the rigor of formal research in order to facilitate alternative forms of inquiry can diminish the definition of collaborative inquiry; a balance is needed. If research is to inform teaching and learning in a particular setting, then teachers must publicly pursue reflective inquiry (Cross & Steadman, 1996), and formal research must accommodate to teaching and learning settings (Deutsch et al., 1995).

Paradigms, Criteria, and Language: Issues in an Integrated Practice

The effort to construct an inquiry framework to serve the needs of an integrated practice means working through some issues that emerge in the interaction of different paradigms (for example, postpositivist, constructivist, critical theory). Paradigms are fundamental tools for structuring, advancing, and interpreting inquiry, and there will be a necessary merging in this integrative context. Paradigms become problematic when they preclude debate or create unnecessary dichotomies; collaboration means benefiting from individuals' different perspectives, frequently struggling with their underlying assumptions and terms, and using this discourse to improve practice. Over time, a line of inquiry must be rigorous and feasible, generalizable and usable. At different phases, choices will be made among multiple paradigms, but the general movement is toward a comparison and integration of perspectives (Alverno College Research and Evaluation Committee, Office of Research and Evaluation, & Additional Faculty and Staff, 1993).

An Institution's Perspective: Reflecting on Our Practice

At this college, different aspects of collaborative inquiry have emerged from different domains of practice. For Riordan (1993), it is most clearly implemented in the collaborative cross-disciplinary work of faculty as they mutually think through and construct their practices, in individual departments and as a whole curriculum, in their shared expectations for students and joint obligations. In such a context, the scholarship of teaching cannot take place in isolation; it must possess a pervasive collegial character in an integrated undergraduate experience for students (see also Barrowman, 1996).

In their reflective practices, educators integrate thoughtful, discipline-based frameworks with specialized expertise in their institutional curricular practices and expert knowledge of their students, suggesting particular relationships for reflection, inquiry, and practice. These observations are drawn descriptively in Figure 10.1. The central line of activity

educator expertise ➤ educational practices ➤ student learning

marks the basic territory of teaching and learning while recognizing the major role of faculty reflection in constructing actual practices. At some distance, the research knowledge base for higher education teaching is largely developed from field studies in different disciplines. The diagram in Figure 10.1 represents local, institutionally based collaborative inquiry as a nearer, stronger contribution to faculty reflection. But the processes that serve to integrate this kind of inquiry need careful consideration.

Wagner (1997) made a similar point about the collaborative processes involved in an elementary school's innovations, specifically that a planning team can begin by looking outside their own practices for ideas ("talking without looking") and move to studying their own processes and practices ("looking at the talking" and "looking at the school"). Reflective practice for higher education can be very similar, with an early deferral to research literature that underuses local knowledge and studies of best practices in context. Conversely, an overemphasis on the tacit, expert knowledge of teachers means limiting what could be learned from a more formal, empirical approach to inquiry. Consequently, constructing local inquiry as collaborative, and embracing the different empirical inquiry approaches available on a multidisciplinary campus, is critical to building more durable models and the transferability of findings.

As we explore the scholarship of teaching it becomes ever more significant to recognize what can emerge as the character of

Figure 10.1. Inquiry, Reflection, and Practice for Studying Student Learning.

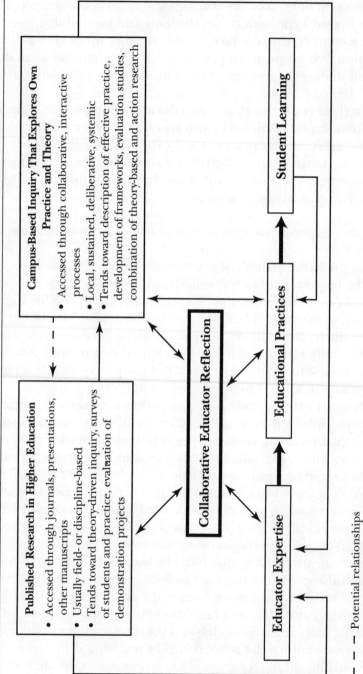

that scholarship. To simply name effective teaching as scholarship is as counterproductive as uncritically importing the frameworks and methods of behavioral science. As Brookfield (1995) notes about reflection, not all reflection is critical, yet it is the critical quality that leads to generative, transformative scholarship. As scholarship, the work on teaching should be building a line of inquiry, of argued and empirically based evidence to increase knowledge about teaching and to make it available to a community of learners, while connecting discourse to frameworks of practice.

Rethinking the Terms of Inquiry: A Substantive Proposition

In order to affect practice, inquiry needs to be pursued through faculty and staff reflection and discourse that functionally supports educational practice. Parker Palmer (1997) notes that faculty construct practice out of a dialogue with colleagues and develop new meaning through this community discourse. Here we identify some key elements that enable the integration of practice and inquiry. What considerations, actions, or operations can make this kind of inquiry workable, trustworthy, and credible? It is clear that instructional strategies seen only as guidelines or tips cannot support the kinds of change and persistent innovation that are called for, any more than can "research tips."

The more challenging questions here concern how the methods of studying more complex and situated understandings of learning can be integrated into the discourse of teaching. This represents a different kind of empiricism. It must, as conventional wisdom suggests, involve the sustained conduct of systematic empirical observations, analyzed in relation to a developing line of argument. And this activity must be integrated within the flow and character of the discourse of teaching and curriculum. In this sense, collaborative inquiry is powerful to the extent that it integrates different perspectives and ways of interpreting situations. This certainly involves the experience of individual educators and more formal, theoretical models of growth and development (as demonstrated in Parts Two and Three of this book); but it also means employing various means—from reviewing the literature of research and practice to working with colleagues within and across institutions—in studying one's own practices.

Building on Different Levels of Reflective Practice

Educators' conversations involve different levels of discourse and reflection, which typically involve different degrees of depth, formality, and abstraction. Three categories provide a useful basis for discussion: descriptive, framework oriented, and inquiry oriented (see Figure 10.2). These levels have characteristics with distinctive processes for movement among them. For example, faculty may review some description of their own performances, attending to particular procedures and comparing different actions; they can also refer to articulated principles of student assessment or educational practice as frameworks for interpretation and action. Sometimes the conversation stalls at one level and needs to be guided through to another, as when a colleague does not see beyond the procedural aspects of teaching or fails to integrate from research abstractions to the learning needs of current students.

Figure 10.2. Levels of Reflective Discourse.

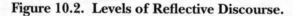

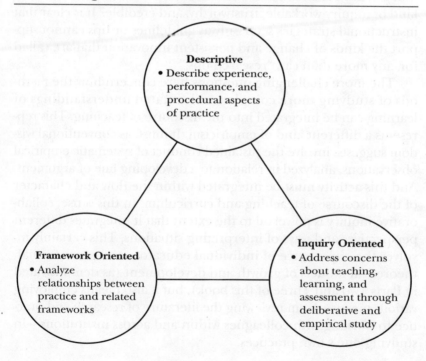

Descriptive
• Describe experience, performance, and procedural aspects of practice

Framework Oriented
• Analyze relationships between practice and related frameworks

Inquiry Oriented
• Address concerns about teaching, learning, and assessment through deliberative and empirical study

At the descriptive level, educators reflect on practice in a wide range of more or less informal contexts. These include the recurring conversations of daily work, as well as the spontaneous conversations that emerge in department meetings or other planned interactions. In these kinds of discussions, faculty build an understanding of their own teaching and transfer conceptual structures of a discipline into teaching and learning frameworks. These discussions are essentially descriptive of practice, but they are public; they involve learning how to use the language of practice, to communicate, analyze, and engage in critique with peers.

At the framework-oriented level, sustained discussions about teaching and learning involve the teacher in the powerful activities of working through a more complex and organized observation of performance, to analyze the frameworks that are guiding their own practices. This is difficult, messy, thoughtful work, but it often bears results. This is a different type of analysis and argument, linking educational practice with guiding frameworks rather than just matching instructor behaviors to broad expectations. In effect, as teachers develop the facility to move among frameworks and action principles, they begin to think more fully about behaviors or methods to evaluate their applications and generate their subsequent performances. This capacity also admits a fuller analysis of discipline-based frameworks and the frameworks of teaching practice. The resulting expertise, in turn, supports fuller communication and collaboration in shared work.

The broad pattern of discourse is an inquiry loop that draws on tacit knowledge, experience, and expert observation. The challenges that educators are facing (for example, enrollment, changing content, new ideas about learning outcomes) strain their professional resources. There is likely, then, to be a key point at which the need for a more systematic and a qualitatively different kind of inquiry emerges. The significant role of inquiry in this discourse—the inquiry-oriented level—is to bring in a new level of expertise, usually involving new levels of knowledge about student reasoning, performance, self-reflection, and development, as well as additional models of practice (as in the curriculum studies explored in the previous chapter). This is likely to involve situations in which there is some combination of elements: questions that require an extended analysis of student performance data; a sequence of data collection, analysis, and critique; shared learning across multiple departments.

A Generalized Process Model and Criteria

Process models or maps have been useful, interactive ways to understand working relationships; they can capture processes as they occur, make them visible for reflection, and model potential improvements. A number of inquiry loops for action research have been articulated, many with direct applications for teaching (e.g., Cochran-Smith & Lytle, 1993, 1999; Hakel, Sorcher, Beer, & Moses, 1982; Noffke & Stevenson, 1995). The model in Figure 10.3 is drawn from our experiences with collaborative inquiry and maps out relationships among major elements. It broadly reflects a planning-implementation-evaluation loop, with the elements arrayed to emphasize their dynamic and potential interactions—rather than a strictly sequential process—and to allow a focus on the unique aspects of pedagogical inquiry in a postsecondary context. In particular, this schematic emphasizes the significant roles of the close analysis of practice (that is, the fullest description of practices, such as in the classroom), the analytic work of relating frameworks of practice and teaching performance, and interpreting findings through a process of deliberations by educators.

When a process model is laid out in this fashion, it also connects with some of the assumptions and criteria that have emerged for collaborative inquiry and educational practice to help guide inquiry practices and become criteria for judging their quality, so that:

- Collaborative participation among faculty and staff leads to shared questions.
- There is an empirical foundation in the existing system of student performances as well as the learning of educators.
- There are multiple disciplinary approaches to inquiry.
- Findings are taken up through a range of processes, for individuals and groups, and that discourse or reflective practice is part of practice.
- Overarching questions such as validity and trustworthiness are addressed by the whole process while more specific criteria can apply at various stages.

Peter Senge's work (1990) has been particularly effective in mapping organizational processes and representing how inquiry-oriented activities operate to facilitate the larger directions of planning.

Figure 10.3. Elaborating Collaborative Inquiry in Support of Teaching, Learning, and Assessment.

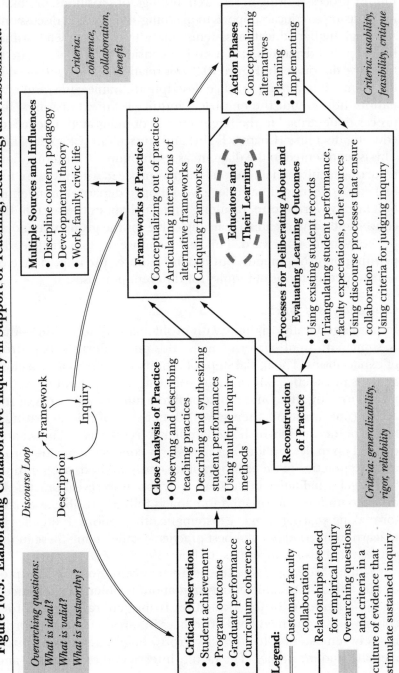

Inquiry processes bring in research findings, observations, or empirical thinking as critical supports to planning and decision discussions. Although higher education systems may not work completely within his proposed dynamics, it is useful to consider how these relate to reflective discourse. In Figure 10.3, this relationship is referenced in the interactions among practice descriptions, frameworks, and evaluation inquiry, but the empirical inquiry is an extension of the processes described in the larger models of integrated practice for educator discourse (Chapter Eight) and curriculum (Chapter Nine). This is represented in the diagram as a subroutine of customary and recurring faculty collaboration that may proceed without more formal data collection. In a college workshop, a department meeting, or a faculty work group, bringing in data changes the pace of the conversation and creates a learning curve for the group that moves the conversation forward. This may be more or less effective, depending on group needs, but it demonstrates the importance of using different forms of inquiry for different purposes.

Close Analysis of Practice

Inquiries generally originate with problematic observations—that is, some pattern of performance stands out against the backdrop of expectations. The initial steps of inquiry need to include a close analysis of practice. More than gathering background data, this means making the context of a problem and the practices of the actors (not the actors themselves) the objects of study, creating a frame of inquiry in which the familiar is treated as unknown and opened up to description. It is necessarily conducted in close proximity to practice in an ethnographic sense; methods are multiple but largely qualitative because the purpose is to reveal practice in order to understand the phenomena as fully as possible as a basis for making sharper or more systematic observations. It enables us to learn from good or even best practices, while seeing these in the context that also contributes to their effectiveness.

While observing students' performance patterns, a group of faculty and staff became concerned about problems experienced by some students in the transition from general introductory coursework to the next level of courses in various majors (approximately semesters 3 to 5). This group began a series of intermediate student studies. The faculty interviewed one another and discussed their observations to explore how they saw the students performing and what they were doing as teachers to support learning. As the studies proceeded, the group benefited from the different perspectives and method orientations of its members. General statistics on retention were combined with individual course performance and extended interviews with students. The college's earlier studies with learner-oriented Perspectives Interviews were considered as part of these analyses of student experience and, subsequently, in developing interviews with intermediate students. This extensive exploration of practice necessarily began to include students who were succeeding and a broader description of student experience, courses, and practices at this level. The early focus, then, was on students who were struggling, and committee members worked to develop a tentative description of characteristic problems as they encountered them in practice. As the project developed, the group shifted the focus to what could be learned from students who were successfully negotiating these changes and what faculty could learn about particular practices that would support the transitions at this point.

The close analysis of practice thus began with a group of faculty sharing similar observations and concerns. In other cases, the analyses have begun from more disciplinary or departmental perspectives. At one point, faculty who taught math classes at a range of levels had raised questions about the quantitative literacy of students across the whole curriculum. Their studies of teaching and learning in quantitative areas across departments, majors, and levels (for example, beginning and advanced coursework) led to a rethinking of quantitative literacy as part of the curriculum ability of Communication. Similarly, the nursing faculty's study of students' performance in key assessments led them to further study of curriculum expectations such as communicating with ethnically diverse clients. In all cases, the analysis of practice—how teaching and learning activities are constructed and experienced—is a critical step that leads toward abstractions that help faculty understand and even guide practice.

Frameworks of Practice

Research needs to proceed through an understanding and description of practice to a critical review of the frameworks that give it shape and durability. It serves as a necessary part of inquiry, in the interpretation and in thinking through the findings. But the frameworks are also subject to the inquiry process as faculty come to understand more about the frameworks that they presume to use, those that they carefully and actively cooperate to use (for practice), and those that are less articulate but meaningful within their experience and expertise (in practice). For example, the use of action principles requires a more complex analysis than describing teaching procedures. This is also a process that moves through critical study of field literature and research or theory-based models of learning and practice. There is a potential recursive loop between the analysis of practice and the analysis of frameworks; without a rich description of practice and its local foundations, there will be less integration.

Cromwell and Sharkey's study (1994) of Alverno faculty development illustrates this process. They began with some common ideas about teachers and teaching and the college's own ideas about the faculty's development. But as they interviewed faculty, they were asking the respondents to reflect on the different frameworks that were involved in their teaching, including those that were anchored in their disciplines and those that characterized the principles in the curriculum, as well as those that were built over time. The faculty would talk about their practices, but they were also constructing ideas about their disciplines and how meaning and understanding had changed. The findings gave a more complex picture of the changes faculty may experience and a better basis for targeting services for faculty at different points in their careers. Faculty came to understand teaching as a public act and a topic of general discourse, but it is also a topic contextualized by a coherent curriculum, the orientation to development and performance, and so forth. Any description of particular teaching performance moves toward those larger frameworks and their ongoing review.

Processes for Deliberation and Learning as a Community

To the extent that educational practices are supported by faculty discourse, it is all the more important to consider the processes that will best help faculty take up inquiry—as an activity and as findings (Mentkowski, 1991a, pp. 263–276). This point echoes the lessons of program evaluation made earlier. Working through a more elaborated picture of educational practice is a teaching-to-learning experience. Being effective, then, requires some analytic process to work with inquiry findings and, in the long run, a better understanding of how a particular group of faculty learn from different kinds of discourse. This may involve triangulating learning outcomes with perspectives from sources external to a program (as in the Chapter Nine curriculum studies). As noted earlier in the Wagner (1997) example, an educational team can also be "looking at the talking" to learn from their own processes and observations. Cromwell and Sharkey (1994) noted that not all faculty enter these deliberations with equal ease; as a developmental process they learn how to make effective use of discourse opportunities, to struggle with different paradigms and their underlying assumptions.

An event early in the intermediate student studies provides an example. As the faculty and staff group worked to understand the experience of students who were struggling, they identified a set of behaviors (for example, problems in transferring abilities across contexts, connecting prior and current learning) that seemed to distinguish these students in their approaches to learning (Alverno College Intermediate Student Study Committee, 1994). As an iterative process for the members, it represented their thinking at one stage, but they wanted broader input from their colleagues. In order to communicate their findings, they used an all-faculty-and-staff event in which they distributed a statement of characteristics for students struggling with intermediate coursework and wrote and presented a dramatic piece in which an encounter between a teacher and a student was portrayed by four individuals: one to represent each of the speakers in the dialogue and one to represent each speaker's inner thoughts as she spoke to herself. (These thoughts were reinforced by slides of cartoon-like thought balloons above each speaker's head.) The dialogue proceeded through a series of problems and superficial agreements, while the inner voices revealed the depth of anxieties, misinterpretations, and miscommunications for each participant. In small group discussions that followed, the participants critiqued the dialogue for accuracy, drew on similar experiences of their own, and added to the set of characteristics. As a result, the work group provided substantive knowledge about its findings, received feedback, and expanded its membership. They also established some base of knowledge within the campus community as a foundation for continued discussions about teaching, learning, and assessment in intermediate coursework.

One phase in the analysis of the Perspectives Interviews for alumnae provides a different type of example (Deemer, in collaboration with Alverno College Office of Research and Evaluation, 1993). The educational research and evaluation office prepared an initial synthesis of the data and then designed a process that was used with this college's committee on research and evaluation to elicit their interpretations and help in further uses of the data. The process involved the eight participants reading as individuals, discussing in dyads, and bringing their observations to a large group discussion. The whole process was implemented during a ninety-minute meeting. Its effectiveness and its feasibility required a structured process, with attention to the protocols that would engage participation in thinking through findings.

For example, statistical presentations, as elegant and accurate as they may be, are too cumbersome for general discourse unless they are linked carefully to priority questions and common tasks. Presentations of interview data can be extremely engaging with an immediate authenticity; however, without a synthesizing, guiding frame for the participant, it can be difficult to work through an effective group process and arrive at more than limited observations among the participants. Success depends on follow-up opportunities to reengage significant frameworks over time.

Building the Context for a Sustained Line of Inquiry

The vitality of teaching and learning inquiry depends in part on the grounding theoretical frameworks. The process model (Figure 10.3) addresses this by focusing on frameworks of practice as a step in the long-term work of theory building that should be taken up in each study. This is what makes inquiry—as a learning phenomenon—both situated in responding to the context of practice and transferable in the sense of having more durable meaning across contexts.

In general terms, the framework provides the basis for substantive, enduring contributions. Each inquiry arising out of practice, then, must also involve a critical struggle to understand the most meaningful framework. In general, the framework must put learning at the center of the inquiry. Such a framework must be larger than the epistemic character of an inquiry method (for example, survey research, developmental research), with operational links to practice, even if these are seen as pretheoretical and building toward a more integrated practice. Most important, the emerging framework should be the basis for subsequent questions and a continuing line of inquiry.

The practice of mapping out processes and relationships has helped in reflecting critically on the program as a whole, on individual operations, and on contributions. It has also helped to understand how to use collaboration as an element in a line of inquiry. System-level work like Senge's (1990) is likely to use some form of a mapping strategy to reinforce the understanding of how diverse elements interact. Maps become a reflective tool for research, describing how inquiry activities can be introduced at key points to enable work in an organization or institution. In this regard, interviews, meeting minutes and transcripts, progress reports, participant observation, and syntheses from multiple data sources were critical to evaluation and learning from the experiences described in this book. These different approaches point toward ways of defining collaborative inquiry that operate within an institutional context and build on the multiple perspectives there (see also Cowan, 1998).

To Sustain Inquiry in Support of Teaching and Learning

Our experiences in these studies of learning and higher education practice point toward some critical aspects of inquiry undertaken to improve teaching and learning. Fundamentally the inquiry must be constructed as part of the discourse of a community of educators; it has a life outside that discourse that is essential to its integrity and trustworthiness—just as faculty members have disciplinary perspectives—but that is part of the complexity of educator roles. This foundation, then, sets the basis for certain conditions:

- The primary questions that organize the inquiry should usually be anchored in faculty questions and concerns; they are

part of their investment in the work and contribute significantly to the interpretation in context.
- The inquiry must be pursued in a collaborative framework
  that integrates different perspectives and, to the extent possible, characterizes the diversity of the context of practice. The
  integration of different approaches—for example, deliberative
  inquiry with more formal, discipline-specific approaches to
  research—enriches the products and encourages an investment at the level of the group or community.
- In an integrated educational practice, faculty and staff must be
  able to stand beside their practice as well as inside and beyond
  it in order to perform most effectively. These roles represent
  enduring paradoxes as educators function individually and as
  members of communities, within disciplines and within a curriculum. Inquiry serves here as a means to constructing models of practice that can be studied and evaluated.

In building a case for an integrated practice of teaching, inquiry, and reflection, we have also tried to recognize the scope of
the challenges ahead. As educators themselves are learners, we can
address three action principles that can guide further action.

Building a Concept of Inquiry as
Part of Educators' Learning

While inquiry has had a conventional meaning in the professorate,
its role in the scholarship of teaching and learning needs to be addressed in direct terms. The examples in this chapter have explored how various inquiries become part of the learning process
in a community of educators. In many ways, these processes recall
the transformative cycles of learners, with analogies to the experiential and reflective aspects of learning. What most transfers may
be the importance of working at this notion of inquiry—centered
on learning and teaching—within a particular context. *Inquiry implies the close analysis of practice, the analysis of the frameworks of practice, and their critique in relation to student learning.* These action
elements have been significant in these inquiries and become considerations in other contexts. Two additional considerations deal
with the reporting and presentation aspects: *Communicating find-*

ings is viewed as iterative and layered and integral to the process of deliberation, not only as a final act or an obligation of accountability. This includes the processes for presenting findings in a conventional sense, as well as the processes by which the group takes up those findings as part of their reflective practices. Written publication regarding practices and inquiry should include these deliberations as part of a concept of findings. *Publication in all of its forms is an important consideration in working through key parts of an inquiry.* Whether on campus or through external sources, the concerns include how multiple paradigms interact and how the collaborative activities are represented in authorship, text, demonstration, a panel presentation, and so on.

Institutionalizing Inquiry to Improve Teaching and Learning

A program that enables and sustains inquiry-as-learning needs to be pursued through several kinds of support. Some of these are structural; some apply to the culture or norms that can develop among collaborating educators. But these have distinct implications for those in leadership and management roles for campus research programs. Questions of institutional support and the use of structures such as educational research offices and committees to oversee and conduct inquiry involve larger frames of reference for institutional action (Chapter Eleven).

Supports for inquiry are distributed through a curriculum system. Often such support is seen primarily as an administrative-level concern (for example, time, resources, places in the academic calendar, subsidy for study). But it is also a concern in terms of the educational program. If effective teaching is part of the mission, there is a shared stake in inquiry addressing teaching, learning, and assessment issues across all levels of faculty, advisors, and other staff.

Promotion and tenure issues are obviously important, as is the effort to ensure that educators are the driving force. However, little value can come of putting more emphasis on teaching in the absence of significant efforts to define good teaching, pursue a scholarship of teaching and evaluate it, and struggle with the issues of what would make this an effective commitment, given the complex responsibilities of departments to their students, colleagues, and the public. Evidence from the examples and cases we reviewed suggests that reflective discourse, inquiry, and evaluation are part of how individual scholarship contributes to joint educational practices.

Broadening Inquiry, Sustaining Conversations

Several kinds of support can encourage inquiry, and there should be concern for broadening and sustaining these studies. That is, while respecting the nature and urgency of problems and conditions as presented, what can help move the inquiry to the level of conceptual frameworks and models of practices? Engaging in critical review has been a way that keeps faculty and departments generating ideas. Inquiry that begins primarily around relatively immediate concerns can move into more long-term discussions through extensive data collection and analysis. Inquiry that begins with a basis in formal research may also have a different life by incorporating more deliberative approaches with interdisciplinary participation.

Taking Responsibility for Inquiry

Making decisions about using inquiry is part of the critical role of academic leadership. As the examples have demonstrated, learning-oriented inquiries open up and endure for a variety of reasons, but each involves a type of participative leadership responsibility. Different orientations to method or discipline seem less important here than the ability of educators to work with different perspectives on the role of inquiry: using evidence as a scaffold for moving to the next level of a discussion; teaching about different kinds of evidence and their meaning or, as appropriate, to support a collaborative effort to construct meaning; helping to formulate questions that open up a conversation or provide different lenses; and representing the collaboration in publications, presentations, or other reporting.

Developing Criteria to Support and Sustain Inquiry

In talking with colleagues elsewhere, we have found that asking faculty to participate actively in a community of educational scholarship produces a certain skepticism. How is it feasible in relation to the actual work of teaching? And how might it create problems for junior faculty in relation to tenure-related research requirements? These are not insignificant concerns, but they can also be distractions. Realistic questions of feasibility and resource costs need to be factored into developing a more complex understanding of teaching and the educational challenge that we all face (see examples in Gibbs, 1996; Menges, Weimer, & Associates, 1996). Similarly, there has been considerable rethinking of faculty work that can be advanced by sound scholarship addressing postsecondary teaching, learning, and assessment (see various American Association for Higher Education and Carnegie Foundation for the Advancement of Teaching initiatives). Ultimately the questions should begin with what is needed in support of teaching and learning. Then faculty support and judgments about the quality of work can be addressed most appropriately.

Scholarship Assessed

The diverse vision of scholarship in *Scholarship Reconsidered* (Boyer, 1990) was extended in a second report (Glassick, Huber, & Maeroff, 1997) that explored perspectives for evaluating faculty scholarship. The report presents criteria that follow a generic pattern, much like an evaluation of argument (for example, goals, method, analysis) that might help assessors from different disciplines deal with diverse scholarship in something like a promotion and tenure committee. These criteria represent a step toward making scholarship more accessible to review by emphasizing the contextual or consequential aspects of inquiry. For example, does a scholar's work involve finding appropriate forums for communicating with targeted audiences, does it add consequentially to a field, and does it provide for its own critique? These questions reflect significant expectations of work aimed at improving teaching and learning. At the same time, they are distinct to judging the work of individual faculty and relatively silent on the kinds of consequences (including presentations, workshops, curriculum materials) that would characterize more situated inquiry.

Taking Responsibility for Inquiry as Performance Criteria

Increasing understanding of the nature of faculty discourse and the contributions of inquiry leads to conclusions about the scholarship of teaching. An integrated conception of teaching, inquiry, and reflection points toward new criteria based on a fuller analysis of this practice context. In a related perspective, Pat Hutchings and Lee Shulman (1999) have posed rethinking institutional research to address questions of teaching and learning, integrating increased faculty leadership. As an example of possible strategies, Alverno's educational research and evaluation team has established criteria for their individual annual performance reviews and team evaluation (see Table 10.1). These criteria apply to two of six position descriptions fully focused on furthering inquiry at the college.

These criteria were developed by professional staff through analysis of the office's mission and planning documents as well as several years of annual reviews prepared by educational research associates at the Ph.D. level. This has led to articulating professional roles and criteria and a clearer understanding of inquiry-as-learning and a continuing development of the office role in this college. Abilities and developmental performance criteria for the level of research associate suggest that fulfilling a research program requires considerable leadership within a range of discursive formats, from ad hoc committees to formal workshops to specific research activities. Although these have been developed in the context of an academic office, they have application across faculty, staff, and administrative contexts in support of learning-oriented inquiry.

Collaborative Inquiry and the Character of Discourse

If educators accept the argument that the work of teaching and learning proceeds significantly from faculty and staff discourse and that inquiry-as-learning contributes most directly through its role in that discourse, then some of the criteria that characterize the best inquiry are going to focus on this interaction of discourse and inquiry. These criteria are both a projection of our knowledge of good practice and a basis for program evaluation. It has been useful to review Wagner (1997)—a university researcher—and his work with a complex school-based reform project. Because of the role of discourse in this collaborative process, he and his colleagues offer a related and emerging perspective on criteria. The audiences

**Table 10.1. Selected Abilities and Criteria for
Educational Research Associate Positions.**

Abilities	Educational Research Associate	Senior Educational Research Associate
Communication	Provides consultation with a range of faculty and staff on data collection and analysis involved in their studies of teaching and learning.	Engages national and international audiences of educators, researchers, evaluators, and assessment professionals in the inquiries of the educational research and evaluation office and the college. Interacts effectively with others around issues and findings that emerge.
Conceptualization	Uses interactive research and design and qualitative and quantitative expertise to develop and guide research and evaluation studies and analyses.	Collaboratively makes key relationships in a complex situation and creatively addresses conceptual issues and practical implications.
Productivity	Regularly produces primary documentation on the research and evaluation activities for which he or she is responsible.	Takes responsibility for moving projects forward in the context of office goals and college frameworks, and meeting multiple deadlines.
Collaboration	Assumes appropriate responsibility for engaging group members in consultation activities to achieve group investment and broaden resources (for example, seeking the perspectives of all individuals and integrating their feedback).	Habitually demonstrates a collaborative, interactive working style, shows collaborative thinking and performance on multiple projects where one is more fully and partially responsible for outcomes.
Problem Solving	Effectively uses formal and informal channels to ensure adequate breadth and depth of involvement in developing ideas, planning, decision making, and actions.	Works effectively with faculty and staff: division and department heads, the research and evaluation committee, and the council on student assessment. Projects goals and accomplishes joint objectives. Sustains and promotes institutional scholarship.

**Table 10.1. Selected Abilities and Criteria for
Educational Research Associate Positions, cont'd.**

Abilities	Educational Research Associate	Senior Educational Research Associate
Role Integration	Seeks to understand the research and evaluation needs of a range of faculty and staff and interprets his or her own role accordingly.	Elicits and sustains commitments through integrating diverse voices, ideas, and sources of evidence. Builds interest and commitment by initiating own and other contributions, providing effective feedback for improvement, and building on accomplishments.

Source: Alverno College Office of Research and Evaluation (1993).

for research reports in an educational context are frequently also coparticipants in constructing findings. Their collective thoughtfulness and informed decision making are as important as testing hypotheses or other propositions; research reporting therefore is a teaching and learning process and can be evaluated in pedagogical terms.

Wagner, Cronbach, Greeno, and their colleagues have made a strong case for the illuminative functions of inquiry, which itself can be evaluated by its contributions to a group's discourse. They also reinforce several points from the Alverno examples: the regard for the work of a practicing group and the use of processes for engaging educators in thinking through findings; that "use" may be judged by the nature of a discourse as well as by an influence on practices. Part of the context for these activities is the campus as a whole, and in Chapter Eleven, we turn to questions of institutional perspective.

Chapter Eleven

Transforming the College Culture Toward Learning That Lasts

As we probe what it means to foster learning that lasts, we are continually drawn to rethinking institutional culture. A curriculum—an entire educational program—functions within an institution and a larger college culture; it influences and is influenced by that culture. When the ongoing work of curriculum integrates a framework of scholarly inquiry and shapes the nature of that inquiry, the result is a constant push for change. Centering an institution on student learning can create a campus dynamic that propels institutional transformation from within. Building on a series of institutional partnerships, we now explore how discoveries by educators who have been organizing for student learning led to insights about learning at the organizational level. These insights are necessarily tentative, because they build on practice that is relatively recent in higher education; concepts, frameworks, structures, and language keep changing. Even so, some common tasks emerge. To deal with these, we synthesize insights and discoveries from recent consortia that engage a diverse range of institutions, including campuses that have purposes beyond fostering student learning that lasts.

Learning that lasts is fundamental for the entire college community—students as well as those who create and organize learning environments. For many educators, the terms *learning community* (Smith, 1993), *organizational learning* (Senge, 1990), and *transformative learning* (Cranton, 1996; Mezirow, 1991) provide direction and inspiration for transforming undergraduate education from within. Becoming clear about student learning outcomes in the context of broad educational goals, understanding the learner's and teacher's perspective, taking a curriculum perspective, engaging in inquiry about relationships between teaching and learning: each of these calls for reflection on what a higher education organization might learn about learning. Developing a curriculum for learning that lasts, and its attendant scholarship, creates an impetus for transforming institutional structures to reinforce learning. Some structures enable a college's institutional transformation by involving the whole college community.

The change processes that emerge influence a college's culture indirectly, so for any campus to engage in *transforming* is to experience ambiguity, reflected in the meaning of transformation, restructuring, institution, and culture. Defining these terms is a prelude to articulating the sources of potential change that drive transformation—factors that dot the more familiar literature on organizational change in undergraduate institutions. With that as backdrop, educators can turn to how institutional transformation works and take up common tasks for institutional transformation toward learning-centered education. We offer tasks that can serve as a tool for campus discourse because they integrate diverse voices, sources of ideas, and evidence from systematic analyses across contexts of practice.

The nature of institutional transformation differs at each campus; yet we expect to find transferable patterns as we turn to analyses of practice. To do so, we *stand in,* tapping the experience of our own institution for transforming acts, that is, critical connections that led to change in our own case and continue our institution's transformation. To *stand beside,* we move to analyses of practice from partnerships of a range of institutions in the United States and the United Kingdom. We limit our comparisons to five consortia that shared similar educational goals toward learning-centered education and where we had conducted or contributed to systematic analyses of practice and could also interpret what was learned from our experience as consortium participants. We sift through this ongoing dialogue for transforming acts: critical connections that lead to change toward institutional transformation. Finally, we *stand aside,* to learn from other consortia whose purposes and experiences are broader and where Alverno College was not a participant. These institutional partnerships independently engaged in conversations about institutional transformation itself, toward much broader renewal in higher education. Thus, we synthesize converging guidelines for institutional transformation toward wider institutional renewal as well as learning-centered education. To preserve the diversity of different perspectives, transformative acts and converging guidelines are on a somewhat different level. Thus, we revisit principles for learning that lasts and link them to what effective institutions might do that are transforming a college culture toward learning that lasts.

How can groups at any one campus use these ideas to address its own distinctiveness? Some may identify salient characteristics in their own institutional purposes and structures that cast particular guidelines or principles in this chapter as either supportive or obverse, given their own institution's intentions (see Appendix K for consortia and participating institutions to aid this judgment). We again propose focused and collaborative discourse on campus, so individuals and groups can make comparisons as they shape or renew their own unique educational goals.

What Is Transformation, and What Drives It?

At the institutional level, *transformation* is intentional, institution wide, deep, dynamic, and pervasive; it changes and is changed by institutional culture; and it is a process requiring time (American Council on Education, 1997; Eckel, Hill, Green, & Mallon, 1999). Examples of transformations that characterize higher education are a shift from teacher-centered to learner-centered learning (Barr & Tagg, 1995), from selective to open admissions (Cross, 1971), from research to a redefined scholarship (Boyer, 1990), and from stop-gap policymaking to institutional restructuring (Chaffee, 1984; Eckel, Green, & Hill, 1997; Zemsky & Massy, 1995). Attempts to make these shifts in assumptions have led to a call for institutional transformation—that is, a rethinking of the fundamental purposes of a college—rather than reform. "Institutional transformation" often signifies a level of discussion and thoughtful action in an institution that reflects a combined interest in and commitment to purposeful renewal by faculty, academic staff, administrative staff, and trustees.

Organizing for learning that lasts is a means to transformation. We use the term *transformation* to distinguish it first from *change*, an all-pervasive condition of global society. We mean to bring about a kind of evolution or metamorphosis in a college. Such transformation can enable a college to be much more assertive and responsive to its own call for action and the expectations and needs of the communities it serves. *Transforming*, as the term is used today in the higher education community, means a fundamental re-thinking of the ways an institution learns and works but also what it intends; both reducing discrepancies between its avowed beliefs and current performance and questioning those beliefs.

We also distinguish transforming from *restructuring*, that is, ob-servable, systemic reorganizations in function, such as connecting learning in classrooms with learning off campus through intern-ships. The difference between systemic restructuring and trans-formation, as we mean it here, is that transformation is deliberately connected to purposeful, explicit intent as expressed not so much in strategic plans as in the day-to-day activities through which an institution carries out its common purposes (for example, recruit-ing students; then teaching, advising, assessing, and graduating them). Thus, transformation, in contrast to surface or partial changes (capstone courses, a new building, course reorganization, integration of the library and information technology systems), is deep, dynamic, and pervasive.

For us, transformation becomes visible through recognizable and identifiable transformative acts, so as to judge that transfor-mation is occurring, and it continues to have a profound effect in that it becomes institutionalized or institution-wide. It gradually affects every component of a college and implies assessing, ac-counting for, and improving institutional performance. Perhaps a primary indicator of transformation is that a metamorphosis grad-ually becomes recognized by those who created it, even though it was not necessarily planned at the beginning. Faculty and staff thus begin to evaluate it, strengthen it, and test it. This kind of deliber-ative transformation necessarily takes time. Unintentional trans-formation becomes purposeful when administrators, faculty, and staff uncover primary values, assumptions, and principles that were implicit or unintended, and integrate these in designs for learn-ing. They decide whether the unintentional should become part of what is deliberately included, and if it should, how the effects of such transforming acts can be traced across the system for evidence that change is occurring.

Another test of transformation is that it is ongoing. An educational program is in a continual process of revision and refinement based on changing and stable elements of faculty practice and theory. "The problem . . . is one of continual learning under constantly changing conditions . . . continual learning is a requirement of the modern environment" (Vaill, 1996, p. xiv). For any college, attending to its cogent issues ensures continual learning. New questions continue to arise from active attention to diversity in the makeup of student body and faculty, new knowledge about learning and its outcomes, shifts in disciplines and their epistemologies, and societal forces outside the institution. This means rediscovering or rethinking some of the assumptions that faculty have held about a curriculum, such as the definition of coherence in the face of greater planned diversity in the student body. Mezirow (1991) confirms that transformative learning includes rediscovering the significance and importance of a value, assumption, or learning principle, as well as making shifts in these.

Shifting Value Priorities and Organizational Paradoxes

No one can review educational assumptions without feeling various tensions between one's own values and the inferred values of an institution (recall Exhibit 2.1 and Table 9.1). Transformation is rooted in awareness of these tensions. The interpersonal and intellectual conflicts that accompany them are often evidence that transformation is at hand.

A shift in educational assumptions spurs transformation because it usually means thinking through value frameworks and then shifting some institutional value priorities. These shifts in turn may create organizational paradoxes that drive institutional change because they change the roles, rights, and responsibilities of students, faculty, administrative and academic staff, and trustees. Contradictions include balancing access and achievement, high expectations and open admissions, coherence and diversity in curriculum, and fostering individual scholarship in relation to institutional mission. In their study of organizations, Denison and Mishra (1995) point out that conflicting needs for integrity of mission and for flexibility necessarily interact dynamically in the most effective institutions. Because paradoxes may be interpreted as dichotomies that lead to constant value conflicts, conceptualizing them as shifting value priorities by including rather than disregarding the competing value allows for much more flexibility in thinking about potential changes in college culture. Organizational paradoxes are not necessarily negative; they are creative tensions that are necessary for and enhance transformation (Harvey & Knight, 1996; Quinn, 1988; Quinn & Cameron, 1988a, 1988b). Competing value frameworks make effective organizations inherently paradoxical, because they must possess attributes that are contradictory, even mutually exclusive, and they must also pursue competing institutional performance criteria simultaneously.

For example, balancing access and achievement meant that Alverno faculty had to maintain sensitivity to students while also creating tensions for them if learners were to have lasting benefits. Students grew to be more independent, taking increased responsibility for their own learning and performance, because instructors paired affirmation and empathy with challenging feedback and provided flexible performance opportunities with firm expectations for students to meet graduation standards. Experiencing these conflicts was essential to learning that lasts.

Sustaining transformation requires that institutions use self assessment to develop awareness of organizational contradictions. This includes not only the structures that define a curriculum and institution but also culture in its symbolic sense: "as a representational system, the collective symbol systems and institutionalized meanings for the interpretation and organization of experience and action" (Much, 1995, p. 100). The emerging behavioral science of cultural psychology takes such "indigenous theories seriously" (p. 111); we have found that such studies illuminate shifts in value priorities and the particular paradoxes that drive and enhance transformation.

External Forces That Influence Institutional Transformation

Other external forces also influence institutional transformation. Consortia of institutions where Alverno was not a member provide a synthesis out of their own diverse experiences (American Council on Education, 1997; Eckel et al., 1999; Pew Higher Education Roundtable & the American Council on Education's Project on Leadership and Institutional Transformation, 1996). They argue that most American colleges and universities that formerly experienced growth, prosperity, and public favor now hear a call for institutions to adapt themselves to a number of new conditions:

- Economic issues that affect, among other things, tuition and student aid, faculty salaries, and the cost of producing new knowledge
- Changing public and legislative priorities for education, coupled with heightened insistence on accountability to students and various publics
- Increased demands for educational quality and excellent teaching, and their attendant implications for promotion and tenure policies and practices, teaching loads, faculty productivity, and the curriculum
- Explosions of knowledge
- Issues of race, gender, ethnicity, class, sexual orientation, religion, and other dimensions of human identity
- Changes in the nation's sense of time, distance, and space brought by technology and its cascading impacts on all areas of higher education

As the Pew report indicated, "The challenge is not only to change once, but to change repeatedly. . . . What is required for colleges and universities to succeed in today's environment is the ability to change, learn from that experience, and be able to change again (and again)" (p. 1). Those who study higher education argue that the elements of leadership and campus culture that encourage healthy responses to fiscal and other threats can be empirically identified and fostered (Cameron & Smart, 1998). Even if the differences among institutions are often the more prominent features to those from outside, one campus can learn from another's experience.

How institutional transformation works and becomes visible differs for any institution—its faculty, students, staff, trustees, and graduates. A college that is in the midst of a crisis (from enrollment or finances, for example) may experience the dynamic of transformation very differently from one that has only vague notions of why it should change. A university that has a broad set of responsibilities for graduate and professional schools may transform quite differently from a college that has more focused teaching and learning goals for undergraduates. A college that is already more learning centered than knowledge centered, and is intentionally transforming toward learning that lasts, will more likely build on structures already in place.

Educator Discourse and Transformation

Transformation, as we have defined it, does not occur by fiat or by drift. It is constructed out of processes that engage and depend on a high level of participation by faculty and staff. In effect, this is a kind of campus conversation, like the discourses we have described before, but one that integrates taking an institutional perspective—an awareness of the institution's dynamic nature—with a focus on learning.

In specific terms, we recommend at least three standpoints for comparing diverse voices, sources of ideas and evidence, and contexts of practice:

- Developing an integrated understanding of what kinds of learning frameworks, strategies, and structures work at one's own campus, arrived at through analyses of practice and campus documentation (*standing in*)
- A continuing analysis of practice in partnership with other institutions that can shape one's own transformative acts and guidelines for institutional transformation (*standing beside*)
- Tailoring literature and practice review to specific campus issues (*standing aside*)

Each standpoint can inform a campus conversation about institutional transformation toward particular educational goals. Together they sharpen discussion about an institution's theory, research, and practice about learning and how it is integrated, prompted by practical questions and problems that drive change on that campus. In this view, issues such as assessment, which have recently been the focus of accrediting agencies, are an important external stimulus. Such conversations might begin with experienced faculty and administrators, who gradually develop a facility with multiple discourses as part of their responsibility for organizational learning. Further, discussions among campus-wide groups can begin at different points within this triangulation of sources. Organizational learning through discourse is situated, and illustrative case studies that apply at any one institution differ. Yet they stimulate discussion. (For syntheses on the general topic from the higher education literature that are illustrated with case studies, see Birnbaum, 1988, 1992; Cameron, 1985, 1986a, 1986b; Ewell, 1985; Harvey & Knight, 1996; Haworth & Conrad, 1997; Levine, 1997; Morgan, 1986; Schlossberg, Lynch, & Chickering, 1989; Tierney, 1988, 1997; Zerubavel, 1995.) Actual participation in a consortium of institutions provides an external comparison for which there is no substitute.

Institutional Transformation Toward Learning-Centered Education: Common Tasks

Common tasks can prompt conversation about institutional transformation and also characterize individual campus efforts to organize for learning that lasts: identifying the "center" and its foundation in learning; integrating multiple perspectives for addressing student learning; identifying and acting on changing perspectives and value priorities; developing a language for learning that lasts; creating a reflective core; and developing shared responsibility and collective accountability. These tasks reflect the links between the transformative learning that happens for students and the processes of development for an organization. They address the different cycles of activities involved in conceptualization, planning, performing, assessing, and reflection. Discussions about these common tasks in the abstract must be linked to problem identification at any one campus.

Identifying the *Center* and Its Foundation in Learning

In order to create connections that generate transformative acts, it is necessary to identify a focus or *center,* that is, *making explicit the binding historical and value traditions and expectations of an institution.*

Often this core is reflected in a general mission statement. Such a statement of institutional value frameworks needs to be refined as a series of fundamental issues and questions about learning that are reflected widely in the campus community, including those that may emerge through drift (recall Table 1.1). This center then becomes a hub for organizational initiatives or synergy. Intersections among issues and questions have the potential to bring groups together around what is common to most faculty: a search for new knowledge, a dedication to the civic community, a commitment to students and their lasting learning.

Such questions reflect the ultimate purposes of an institution, yet developing an institutional identity means addressing fundamental questions of history and purpose: Who are we? What is our purpose here? What do we bring from our education and experience? How do we both build on and change direction from our common past? (Recall Figure 7.1.) These questions can lead to identifying a center and to asking, "Is this the center we want for ourselves and our students in the future, or will any center do?" Granted, many faculty identify their specific disciplines as their primary interest and commitment, and, particularly in larger research universities, they may turn almost exclusively to learned societies for opportunities for this kind of reflection. But this condition only further emphasizes the necessity for recognizing an organizational core enlivened by the diversity of interests. Building on the interest of undergraduate faculty in student learning, higher education authors have begun to explore what it means to develop commitments to teaching and to the learning community in which one lives and works (Palmer, 1997).

Integrating Multiple Perspectives for Addressing Student Learning

In our own case and that of various consortia, placing student learning at the center of an educational program means that student learning outcomes focus institutional change. Dealing with the implications drives institutional transformation. Addressing learning from particular perspectives is a way to understand these implications and to begin transformational processes.

Taking a Curriculum Perspective

We defined taking a curriculum perspective as sharing responsibility for curriculum and following through by developing and refining curriculum based on the assumptions and implications that flow from or stimulate this perspective taking. We concluded that transformation of learning-centered undergraduate education (in contrast to institutional transformation) moves from a process of curriculum reform to continuous improvement of that curriculum. When a curriculum is moving from fragmentation to coherence, for example, curricular transformation provides a primary impetus to institutional transformation. For our purposes here, an educational institution is an organization for student learning, made up of sets of learning environments and communities. Is it also a learning organization? Assuming that learning is transformative, what does it mean to move from the program or curriculum level to the institutional level?

Taking an Institutional Perspective

As faculty and academic staff are rethinking and reformulating curriculum, they also begin to rethink the ways learning is organized and how their institution supports—or does not support—student learning. In part, taking an institutional perspective means being explicit about how I as an individual or member of a group relate to the educational mission or goals of others, whether I own those goals, and how I contribute to creating and safeguarding a differentiated yet coherent perspective in my college community. This perspective includes a broader understanding of the college or university's place in higher education as a whole, as well as some distinctions and commonalities among the kinds of communities that make up one's own college culture or the culture of others (for example, academic, intellectual, social).

Taking an institutional perspective also includes engaging others in dialogue toward a common understanding of purpose, suggesting that groups also seek justification or confirmation beyond mere local agreement (Berkowitz, 1996). Such a broader criterion for consensus is often less easily met because those justifications are not so explicit in conversation. To be explicit, faculty in arts and humanities need to spell out relationships to the sciences for students. Or nursing faculty need to approach science faculty when they see a lack of clarity in their students' hypothesis generating rather than wonder privately whether the beginning science courses provide enough practice. When this happens, we have found, educators begin sharing mutual responsibility for the care of the entire educational program. They cross staff, faculty, and departmental lines to construct their practices from an institutional perspective.

Taking a College Cultural Perspective

Curriculum transformation and institutional transformation are distinguished primarily by the level at which change is occurring. Each indirectly influences and is influenced by college culture— the entire perceptual home and physical house of a college and its campus, its atmosphere, its past, present, and future. Culture would also include the norms, values, expectations, and interactive patterns that help members make mutual meaning out of shared experience. The elements of college culture are interacting, fluid, evolving, and porous, rather than mechanistic, hierarchical, or organized wholly in relation to the push and pull of the environment (Becher, 1984; Morgan, 1997; Schein, 1990; Senge, 1990). Taking a college cultural perspective in organizing for learning that lasts means that educators carry an understanding of the culture of their institution into the planning and implementation of educational practice. In Chapters Three and Nine, we probed for elements of college culture that may figure in patterns of learning-to-learn and development because they emerged as prominent topics in student or alumna interviews. They were expressed in terms like "an environment organized toward excellence" and "collaborative orientation of the college."

Most educators are familiar with the dramatic shifts in institutions that occurred as a result of broad social transformations such as the influx of students on the GI Bill after World War II, the emergence and primacy of the research university, and the expansion of state university systems and community colleges to increase student access. But unless educators take a college cultural perspective, they may not see the more subtle shifts in the learning atmosphere of a college. For example, it may be that students are not feeling as connected as in the past because the institution is growing rapidly. Perhaps an economic downturn has increased the time students spend working to earn tuition, and faculty feel the distance in class. Or long-awaited changes in physical plant lead faculty to say, "I used to know everybody in my department. Now we are in two buildings, and I hardly see half my colleagues and advisees." These changes that students and faculty sense may not have been created intentionally. But unless students and faculty notice and harness the changes into a positive transformational process, such shifts in the culture could become deeper and more pervasive, ultimately distracting from the core mission.

When taking a college cultural perspective, we consider it helpful to observe the ways learning takes place in a social context. For example, in a learning community, is learning taking place directly (as in conversation) or indirectly (as part of self-reflection on current and past experiences by a person learning alone)? The self-regarding learning community can enable educators to enact their deeper values, ones embedded in the heart and mind of the culture. The community can also enable its members to read what is beyond the college culture yet is part of it. Demographic, economic, or ecological pressures (for example, population distributions, the availability of jobs for the college's primary disciplines) may appear to overwhelm a culture at first. These can combine to influence learning that lasts at any one point in time. Therefore, it is essential that educators continue to sample and observe relationships among learner patterns, student/graduate/faculty/staff/administrative/trustee perspectives, and curriculum structures.

Taking a college cultural perspective is likely to be reinforced when the many faculty in the disciplines and professions who have studied culture as a concept bring their ideas to bear in developing perspectives on their own college culture. Historians may focus on cultural history, anthropologists on local or organizational culture, behavioral and social scientists on the social context for learning, and education and management professionals on purposeful features and practices. Further, some learning psychologists may focus on learning as situated and may be more likely to focus on ad hoc inventions. Thus, many definitions and elements of a college culture can be juxtaposed in conversation, particularly if the group is a multidisciplinary one. For example, as the higher education conversation increasingly turns to distance and distributed learning, the implications of new technologies for college culture can be far reaching. Questions include, "When places where faculty and students interact include a chat room or an interactive video course, what are the implications for establishing and fostering a learning community? What is an appropriate balance between Internet sources and peer experience as data for conversation for the commuter or residential, young adult or adult student?" We, along with others (Daniel, 1996; Geoghegan, 1994; Gilder, 1990; Laurillard, 1993), suggest that faculty need to make these and other changes with awareness and intent.

Identifying and Acting on Changing Perspectives and Value Priorities

The complexity of actions and the multiplicity of perspectives means that each part of an institution can experience fundamental shifts in perspective. They must *act* on value priorities as they emerge. While primary values may remain, value priorities can change, particularly when organizational paradoxes are identified and rethought for balance. For example, a shift in value priorities that can impel institutional change occurs when a campus focuses not only on developmental selection of students at entrance to college but also on student achievement of learning outcomes. Shifts may mean that faculty begin not only to focus on responsibilities to their discipline but also to include obligations for the way teaching occurs across courses and especially for how students and faculty serve their local communities (Eyler & Giles, 1999; Rothman, 1998; Zlotkowski, 1997–1999). Then the focus on how many students are passing a course is expanded to include how they are learning across courses. Appropriate levels of collaboration are seen as significant complements to autonomous, individual work.

Developing a Language for Learning That Lasts

A learning community can develop a common language (a system of terms or categories and a context of social practices in which those terms are understood) that implies a social context for learning and supports interaction among persons. Sharing this language can help individuals to relate their own experiences of learning. So it is wise for its members to stay alert to the cultural history of a college, its binding historical and value traditions, and its ongoing understanding of its cultural folklore and expectations (for example, roots in faith traditions, orientations to work as part of study, preparation for service in the military or ministry).

Language cannot be separated from culture, so a change in language can both signal and prompt a change in culture. This is one reason that the use of competing languages can become so divisive on a campus. The concern here is to examine how a college's language of learning might interact with organizing for learning that lasts. As a learning community develops its own theories of learning from experience across disciplines and roles, language concerns emerge as educators share ideas and develop designs for conversation and deliberative inquiry.

Rather than setting out to create a new language, language is likely to evolve as faculty and students wrestle with meaning. A learning community may create a shorthand language for ideas and concepts that may confuse outsiders or inadvertently fail to communicate the complexities of concepts, even as students internalize this language. For example, over the years Alverno College educators noticed that the use of terms like *coherence* and particular constructions for student learning would often be perceived by individuals outside the culture as meaning that educators at Alverno develop consensus by thinking alike. It became all the more important to communicate in the most generic terms. This has meant working at a language that would be more reflective of what Henry Louis Gates, Jr. (1996; see also 1992) calls a "politics of identification with others" rather than "identity politics." For educators at Alverno, partnerships with various consortia meant working with colleagues to be more inclusive in expressing— through language, goals, and assumptions—how they understood themselves in relationship to others.

Creating a Reflective Core

In order to take up the questions raised by members of institutions that are beginning to transform or are in continuous development, it is necessary to consider the means and structures that support reflection. These are fundamental to the overall effectiveness of a working organization and to its continuous inquiries. Creating a reflective core involves initiating and supporting structures for doing educational research and program and institutional assessment; for mastering collaborative inquiry and reflective practice; and for demonstrating organizational effectiveness. It also includes making reflection and action systemic, that is, gradually institutionalizing change through shared learning and consequent transformative acts.

Developing Shared Responsibility and Collective Accountability

The common tasks discussed in this section have a cumulative and interactive effect, and the meaning and effects of each are chronicled throughout this book. In cyclical terms, as students develop learning that is lasting, they influence the learning community and culture; faculty learn from students, systematically and at multiple levels, and integrate this learning into the ongoing development of practice. But it is equally important to see the nature of collective accountability that develops across multiple faculty and staff roles. This develops in great part out of the shared investment in understanding student learning and organizing multiple roles in relation to explicit learning outcomes.

Transformative Acts Toward Learning-Centered Education

Any common tasks or lessons learned, albeit from practice, may appear hollow or bloodless in the light of immediate experience. At the same time, studies of organizational change may yield process models that overemphasize the sequential character of change or falsely depict a component of a system, such as assessment or inquiry, as driving change by itself. So, close analyses of practice for transformative acts—critical connections that have led to change—round out the base of evidence. In this section, we examine transformative acts from both Alverno's history and the transformations identified by five consortia of institutions organized around shared program goals. These consortia have pursued transformation intentionally and collaboratively and have conducted the kind of systematic analysis of practice informed by experience, so they could discuss—through both historical narrative and lessons learned—the transforming acts that led to change.

Analyzing Practice

Systematically describing practices and their implications by individual campuses provides a critical opportunity to examine transforming effects. Alongside this approach, there are increasing efforts by funding agencies, associations, and other groups studying higher education to support undergraduate institutions that are transforming. Funded consortia of institutions can study their implementation of learning-centered education across institutional contexts of practice, increasing the depth and breadth of impact. Institutions can initiate their own changes while learning from one another and creating a broader effect. Through involvement in consortia, Alverno faculty and staff have come to identify more strongly with fellow educators—from preschool through graduate professional school—as colleagues engaged in the similar work of fostering enduring student learning. These partnerships, along with the critical appraisal of leaders from many kinds of organizations, have become a critical factor in this college's continuing transformation in the past decade (Alverno College Commission on Education in the 21st Century, 1994; Diez & Stoffels, 1992).

Each of the consortia we discuss was or is partnering with Alverno College to varying degrees. These partnerships have allowed for close analyses of consortium outcomes for transformational acts that are simultaneously being created and challenged by member institutions through deliberative, collaborative inquiry. Members of consortia have carefully documented studies and syntheses of what their institutions had learned so far about how transformation toward learning-centered education proceeds and how it influences institutional change. Their initial insights and examples provide a window on institutional transformation that can be analyzed for transforming acts, grounded in particular contexts where we have also participated as institutional representatives of a member institution.

Such data sources lead to a deeper and more durable learning about change processes than is possible from a more general survey of practice descriptions. These consortia came to consensus around a few shared purposes, some educational assumptions and questions for inquiry, and critically observed their work in progress. Member institutions were usually selected for their heterogeneity within their shared purposes. Because implementing reform is necessarily local, their institutional diversity became quickly apparent in discourse and was included as part of the analysis. Transformative acts within a consortium could be identified with some precision because the members had come together around a shared goal.

Consortium Data Sources for Learning-Centered Education

In addition to a close analysis of Alverno's practices, we gleaned observations from eleven institutions in the W.K. Kellogg Consortium for the Improvement of Teaching, Learning and Assessment (TLA) (1992). Strategies that worked to deal with constraints are extended by experiences of a like-minded consortium of seven institutions in the United Kingdom that share the goal of ability-based learning: The Ability Based Curriculum (ABC) Network (Otter, 1997). The need to generate evidence for institutional improvement is elaborated from the American Productivity & Quality Center (APQC) benchmarking study on institutional performance (1997) with twenty institutions. "What works" is extended from two studies by teacher education consortia: one four-member group of education departments where this college was an organizing force in standards-based curricula (Teaching for Tomorrow Project: Diez, 1998) and one seven-member group of education departments that participated in a study of what works in teacher education organized and conducted by the National Center for Restructuring Education, Schools, and Teaching (NCREST Study of Departments of Education: Darling-Hammond, 1997). Finally, recent observations from group meetings of six institutions that initially made up The Pew Charitable Trusts Leadership Award for the Renewal of Undergraduate Education and the nine-member Kellogg Forum on Higher Education Transformation (KFHET) served as current background for this analysis of five consortia. (See Appendix K for participating institutions in all seven consortia and their funding agencies.)

Limitations

Few, if any, consortia of partnering institutions would claim to be finished with their efforts because transformation is ongoing. The

results of analyses in this chapter are decisions, processes, principles, or structures, not specific practices. Thus, our analyses must
not be used to draw inferences about the current status of any one
member institution. Nevertheless, the following case and consortia illustrate how some institutions synthesize their experience.

Transforming Acts by Alverno College

Analyses of practice for transformative acts provide a deeper understanding of how institutions make broad initiatives into concrete decisions and activities. For example, after five years of
intensive planning and eighty-five years of history, Alverno College
implemented a major restructuring of its educational program in
1973 (Truchan & Gurria, 1997; Read & Sharkey, 1985). The transformation took place over a period of time and is ongoing; it is
based on and continues to create cooperation, self-reflection, and
self assessment throughout the institution; and it is guided by a
clearly articulated mission. Through a process of reflection, experience, and research, Alverno's faculty, administrators, and other
academic staff made decisions to strengthen the educational program toward learning outcomes and set up processes for committees and departments to spot areas of weakness. Out of this
experience of searching for meaning from experience, this college
identified a series of transformative acts—critical curriculum-related
connections and decisions that led educators to restructuring decisions—which led to institutional improvement (Alverno College
Office of Academic Affairs, 1997a; 1997b; 1997c; 1998; Alverno College Research and Evaluation Committee, 1997). A selection of
these acts and subsequent outcomes are listed in Exhibit 11.1.

As members of the college community review the past two
decades, they recognize that most of these changes could not be
anticipated. The shift in focus—requiring students to demonstrate
ability to deal effectively with information and experience as well
as to demonstrate mastery of information—was the major decision
from which all others flowed. As with most other important decisions, faculty, staff, and administrators over time perceive more
clearly the complexities and the possibilities resulting from the
original decision and the necessity to embed processes for continual evolution into the institution, so that transformation continues.
There is some risk in using transforming acts as a kind of map

**Exhibit 11.1.   Transformative Acts Toward Curriculum
and Institutional Improvement: Alverno College.**

Transformative Acts:

1. Connecting student learning outcomes across disciplines led
   to designing a parallel academic administrative structure with
   both discipline departments and interdisciplinary ability-based
   departments—each set responsible for improving the quality of
   a coherent curriculum where content and abilities are integrated.

2. Connecting emerging faculty roles and responsibilities implied
   creating periods of time for extended discussions, workshops, and
   evaluations of progress. This led to restructuring the academic
   schedule for faculty and students.

3. Defining learning outcomes as abilities that are pedagogically
   developmental and integrated in the disciplines and professions,
   integrated in student performance, and embodied in the
   development of the person led to (a) designing a student
   assessment system, establishing a council on student assessment,
   and developing an assessment center that recruited hundreds of
   external assessors from the greater metropolitan community to be
   trained by faculty and to work with them as co-assessors in specified
   areas. It also led to (b) establishing a committee on research and
   evaluation and an academic, educational research department
   that designed and conducted research on teaching/learning/
   assessment issues, including longitudinal studies on student
   learning outcomes, where shared learning led to connecting
   student, program, and institutional assessment structures. It also
   led to (c) building processes to define and develop collaborative
   inquiry and funding it with faculty fellowships.

4. Establishing experiential learning through internships on and off
   campus for all students led to structuring local and global
   partnerships that extend the college culture.

5. Expecting all students to learn and perform the required abilities
   for graduation led to structuring (a) an advising program that
   included professional academic advisors and student peer advisors,
   (b) introductory seminars and courses for first-year students and
   also for transfer students and older adults who could move more
   quickly through the beginning ability levels, and (c) a weekend time
   frame where learners could complete a degree in four years.

6. New teaching and assessment methods led to creating and staffing
   audiovisual studios for use by all faculty and students for
   preparation of teaching-learning materials and performances.

Exhibit 11.1. Transformative Acts Toward Curriculum and Institutional Improvement: Alverno College, cont'd.

7. The faculty's evolving definition of the scholarship of teaching and learning led to revised guidelines and expectations for faculty hiring, development, and criteria for promotion.

8. Developing shared learning and participative leadership led to organizational learning and continuous improvement.

9. Connecting the academic curriculum and the on- and off-campus cocurriculum led to restructuring student affairs and academic services departments to expand their involvement as "Partners in Learning" on behalf of students, with revised criteria for staff hiring, self assessment, and promotion.

10. Embedding planning within and across all the structures of the college led to ensuring that the new ability departments and the funds required for continuous educational transformation (for example, educational research and evaluation office; center for instructional communication; summer fellowships for faculty) were integrated into the budget.

11. New ways of thinking about education led to initiating and maintaining a public dialogue, through publications and on-campus workshops, with educators and other professionals throughout the country, in order to benefit from criticism and to share successes and failures through both informal and formal relationships, which then led to restructuring partnerships with professional colleagues through consortia.

12. Creating public dialogue within the college and its community stimulated and enhanced communication outside it, which led to greater trustee involvement through such structures as trustee reporting to all personnel, trustee-initiated national advisory councils, and trustee benchmarking visits with other colleges and universities.

---

through the change process, because transformation is neither linear nor two-dimensional. It is often difficult to recognize change when it is happening in a way that one can make claims for change as intentional and rational; change often is unintentional and feels irrational. We acknowledge that reasons may be falsely claimed for change post hoc, even when change led to feelings of chaos at the time it was occurring. Yet institutional change lends itself to an analysis of a series of events that later emerge as turning points in the change process (Read & Sharkey, 1985).

Experiencing a breadth of diverse perspectives is a key element of both student learning and institutional learning. While this college has gained extensive understanding of its own processes and performance, collaborative work through involvement in consortia has meant studying the implementation of learning-centered education across diverse contexts.

Consortium Across the Educational Spectrum: Transforming Acts

The Consortium for the Improvement of Teaching, Learning and Assessment (TLA) comprised eleven diverse institutions from five educational levels: secondary, community college, college, university, and graduate professional school (1992). The members identified shared purposes, goals, activities, and evaluation for their collaboration across a three-year project funded by the W.K. Kellogg Foundation. The consortium's primary purpose was to improve the education of secondary, postsecondary, and graduate professional school students through outcome-oriented, performance-based approaches to teaching, learning, and assessment. Member institutions articulated progress toward individual and interdependent member goals and recorded the strategies that worked to overcome constraints. During the partnership, they identified, created, and critiqued their goals, results, and products to provide ongoing evidence for changes toward broad curriculum and institutional progress over time.

Orientation and Process

The institutions in the TLA consortium shared a basic commitment to learning-centered education and were working on development plans to strengthen the learning orientation of their individual curricula. During the three years of the project, they met regularly in a collaborative, deliberative process to explore the implementation of their efforts and to critique and refine their approaches. The deliberative process, which shares a similar structure with the inquiries discussed throughout this book, is described in Exhibit 11.2. This framework for review, consultation, and critique played a unique function in relation to transformative change, as a means for increasing awareness of changes as they proceeded, and for consolidating learning at an organizational level.

The central conceptual effort across the participating organizations meant that each campus's faculty and staff were defining student learning outcomes. Each was dealing with various but similar directions: implications for curriculum, adjustments in the policies and procedures for assessment, the capacity to convene faculty and staff in meetings to support this level of activity, the institutional capacity to initiate and use inquiry in support of teaching and learning, and so on. The consortium activities reflected both the experiences within the participating institutions and the broad categories of action that we have seen in the development of learning: analyzing intentions and performance expectations in order

Exhibit 11.2. Deliberative Inquiry Process by the Consortium for the Improvement of Teaching, Learning and Assessment.

1. Clarified intersecting interests and commitments to create a consortium. Achieved consensus on shared purposes across heterogeneous institutions (for example, developing an outcome-oriented, performance-based curriculum; creating a vision focusing on graduates' capabilities and certifying requirements).

2. Identified individual yet interdependent goals, activities, and evaluation.

3. Generated shared educational assumptions about learning, assessment, and curriculum that reflect beliefs about education and questions for inquiry.

4. Communicated reasonable expectations for each institution, given its stage of development.

5. Documented evidence for broad curriculum and institutional changes that sustain improvement.

6. Conducted analyses of own practice for "what we learned" and goals achieved toward learning-centered education.

7. Created public dialogue at workshops and conferences as well as disseminated products.

8. Identified new challenges for the consortium.

to plan or prepare; monitoring performance at institutional and curriculum levels and studying practice in relation to student learning; and using complex analyses of student learning in a cyclical, developing construction of practice. In implementation, these resulted in transformations both direct and indirect—some to enable a stronger learning orientation, some as an effect of more sophisticated expertise in learning.

Several transformative acts describe curriculum and institutional progress during the three-year period and support the original decision to build a heterogeneous consortium with a range of experience and expertise. Institutions identified themselves as "beginning," "more experienced," and "most experienced," and so communicated reasonable expectations for institutions given their stage of development (see Exhibit 11.2, item 4). Goals, strategies that worked to deal with constraints, and evidence for change experienced across the three-year period are discussed in order from the beginning to experienced institutions (within points and across them) to probe organizational learning as developmental. Transformative acts toward broad curriculum and institutional improvement are summarized in Exhibit 11.3.

Problems and Solutions

The use of a deliberative process, which integrated and synthesized specific work across the practices of the consortium members, supported a sustained inquiry for each campus representative and for the group as a whole. In combination with more typical data on enrollment and performance, these inquiries could be directed at the contextual aspects of innovations. Consortium members reported varying types of constraints or resistance. However, they came to recognize the importance of studying these with as much attention as they gave to the strategies developed for implementation, to view constraints and barriers as legitimate responses in each context. This helped them to analyze the problems as they were experienced and explore alternative approaches to problem solving. In their sustained interaction, the consortium members identified several transformative acts that marked significant organizational shifts and developments.

Members of campus leadership groups initiated efforts to strengthen the institutional orientation to learning through a number of strategies: bringing faculty and staff together to develop

Exhibit 11.3. Transformative Acts Toward Curriculum and Institutional Improvement Across Three Years in the Consortium for the Improvement of Teaching, Learning and Assessment.

Set goals and defined outcomes

- Goal setting as identifying outcomes led to publishing outcomes required for graduation that were acceptable to students and various publics, to defining knowledge and abilities through developmental levels and developmental performance criteria, and then to defining department-specific outcomes and criteria.

- Describing broad plans led to creating action plans with specific and prioritized goals that were gradually being implemented.

- Creating a broad, strategic plan led to specifying a much more realistic and sophisticated curriculum design that targeted particular abilities to be developed and assessments to be designed, then specified the kinds of information needed for improving programs and demonstrating accountability by communicating benefits and ideas to outsiders.

Identified and dealt with constraints by creating strategies that worked

- Seeing "lack of time" as an unarticulated constraint that loomed as a major difficulty led to identifying specific resources and activities that supported institutional changes and then to gradually implementing new curricula and assessment.
- Focusing on faculty "resistance to change" led to legitimating reasons that colleagues preferred to continue what they were doing and then to creating rationales that responded to their specific concerns.
- Focusing on changing colleagues' perceptions and attitudes led to institutionalizing an ongoing, continuous process of self-education and self assessment among faculty and staff.

Generated evidence for student, program, and institutional improvement

- Documenting negative student attitudes toward a new curriculum led to realizing that students were advancing curriculum change by setting new expectations for individual courses and assessments, and then to creating ways to demonstrate that students were taking responsibility for their own learning.
- Defending curricular changes to constituencies led to identifying indicators of change and then to communicating convincing evidence of student performance to parents, community groups, or other outside constituencies.

**Exhibit 11.3. Transformative Acts Toward Curriculum
and Institutional Improvement Across Three Years
in the Consortium for the Improvement of
Teaching, Learning and Assessment, cont'd.**

- Involvement by a few interested, committed faculty in implementing change led to investment by a broad range of faculty across disciplines and departments.
- Focusing on outcomes led to including assessment of outcomes and then to including curriculum evaluation.
- Focusing on demonstrating the credibility of the curriculum and generating information that could be used to improve led to clarifying educational assumptions, assessment principles, and materials that could be used by other institutions.
- Focusing on one's own needs and seeking outside assistance led to partnering with other institutions and bringing about change from within, and then to communicating benefits and ideas to outsiders.
- Reacting or responding to external mandates led to initiating interaction with outside agencies—state departments of instruction, accrediting bodies, state boards—so that these agencies would expect information about outcomes and provide feedback from assessments that could support the emerging educational assumptions and performance assessment efforts of these institutions.

Source: Consortium for the Improvement of Teaching, Learning and Assessment (1992).

learning outcomes, analyzing underlying assumptions about learning, and discussing related concerns. A key element in each setting addressed the means for broadening involvement by diverse representatives and deepening their participation in these discussions. Different institutions used a range of approaches: faculty planning workshops, development days, retreats, and released time for working groups. In these sessions, educators brainstormed possible outcomes using student examples as a resource for refining outcomes. To engage their commitment further, campus leaders invited departments to design alternative curriculum plans. They built in clearly defined, interactive processes that engaged faculty in coming to consensus around outcomes and assessment design. They made sure that persons in attendance represented academic governance and existing curriculum committees, as well as multiple disciplines. They also readily counted on external support. They sent teams of their faculty to workshops or brought in other consultants at key times. They relied on external mandates from the larger school system, accrediting agencies, or national professional associations to stimulate the change process. High schools involved parents. Professional schools involved their graduates.

The consortium recognized that the processes of planning, program development, and critique are time-consuming and re-source intensive. Therefore, another key element in transformation was finding the time and resources for such conversations and pursuing them as a kind of self assessment among faculty and staff. Institutions were creative in solving the time and resource problems. Occasionally there was some new funding available, but not often. On their individual campuses, the consortium members and others with leadership roles brought people together for lunch, committee work, summer workshops, and seminars. Some created mini-grants for faculty to do assessment projects; these faculty discussed and shared their results. One high school provided in-service credit that counted toward license renewal for curriculum work. Another leadership group worked on becoming informed about assessment issues and practiced performance-based assessment in their own classes. Some faculty developed even more expertise and began working with others on curriculum development.

As consortium members became effective at creating discussion opportunities, they were often asked, "How did you do it?" This question reflects a pervasive idea that time for restructuring is a significant constraint (Wilger & Massy, 1993). Usually members found that they and their critics would first focus on time as both a barrier and a resource. But when time was demystified, it became an energizer for change rather than an excuse for maintaining the status quo. There was no quick fix; institutional change was labor intensive. Yet it was revitalizing. Faculty were deeply satisfied by those processes, and as they saw results from student assessments, they began to refine the learning environment. This was true, members argued, for individual faculty as well as for organized groups. Then, rather than focusing excessively on "creating time," the group focused on the combination of commitment, tasks, and resources that was needed to see some success; they chose solvable problems at first, being quick to point out benefits. Members commented that they came to see resistance to new ideas as an opportunity to probe the issues more fully, uncover flaws in their own thinking, and incorporate almost everyone's experience and concerns so that the group could maximize its chances for successes over time.

The increasing articulation of learning outcomes by faculty inevitably began to have implications for curriculum and, in each case, elicited faculty questions about the validity and coherence of the targeted changes. Initial pilot projects were immediately critiqued and challenged. Institutions were asked whether they could demonstrate that their efforts were better than what they were already doing, how what they planned was better, and which other institutions were following their lead. Thus, they had to quickly become engaged in continuous critique and improvement. They had to become adept at communicating the value and worth of the curriculum: articulating benefits to various audiences, engaging students in communicating their achievement to others, using assessment data to demonstrate student achievement, and engaging in various strategies for institutional self-evaluation.

Consortium members acknowledged the need for ongoing data on changes in student performance so they could examine whether and how outcome-oriented curricula make a difference. They were already involved to some degree in collecting such information on their own campuses. But they also hoped to use their influence to encourage groups that conduct licensing examinations to give information back to institutions so they could use it. Members wanted to influence the design of entrance examinations to college (SAT, ACT), graduate school (NTE, GRE), or professions in teaching, medicine, or pharmacy (state board examinations) toward greater use of performance assessments.

As institutions moved to refining their curriculum and institutionalizing it across departments, they tended to invest more effort in student and program assessment and to use the information from assessment to refine and improve it. These institutions with more experience in learning outcomes noted that they could now rely on established committees to engage in more in-depth work. They assumed that most academic departments had implicit expectations for student performance, which could serve as a basis for more formal development of performance-based assessment criteria. They continued to engage their colleagues at member institutions in discussions about the value and benefit of the enterprise— "faculty resistance," they noted, did not go away—and sought candid responses from faculty not invested in this approach to assessment. Campus leaders continued scheduling time to allow for full faculty involvement, engage faculty in ongoing curriculum development, and coordinate everyone's efforts in working together to draw common educational assumptions and principles from their experience.

The natural direction here was to increase procedures that would make learning outcomes more explicit and subject to review; the result was that better data on student learning outcomes could become the evidence from which to further study and improve educational practices. From the start, institutions were able to identify evidence of change that was credible to their colleagues in the consortium. These indicators included student, faculty, and administrative perspectives on and attitudes toward curriculum changes. Students, faculty, and staff had ways of telling how they were improving; faculty were public about what they expected. At the same time, a close analysis of actual practices was necessary for drawing relationships between teaching and learning. Part of a systemic culture is that faculty and staff develop and sustain changes. By describing the rationale and development of changes across time, institutions that engage in broad changes identify why and how they have progressed. Indicators of change inferred from experience soon were replaced or joined with evidence from student learning outcomes—performance examples, patterns of achievement of outcomes, number of students continuing their education— which institutions soon used to communicate progress to various groups.

The process of collaboration among campuses also pointed toward the power of these partnerships for learning at the institutional level. Within the consortium, institutions that were most experienced devoted a good deal of time and effort to assisting other institutions to develop their outcomes, assessment designs, and institutional change plans. The purpose of this consulting was to enable institutions to further their own work in ways that were appropriate and credible in their own institutional context. For example, generalizable results from one institution to another consisted of common assumptions and principles rather than common assessment instruments.

Consortium Outcomes and Experiences

The consortium members learned that a focus on student learning outcomes can yield consensus within the diversity of educational visions. This coherence clarified the direction for change and supported continuous refinements. At each institution, members noted a shift in value priorities. For example, focusing not only on student and faculty rights but also on their responsibilities meant highlighting faculty responsibility for carrying out the institution's educational mission and student responsibility for ultimately becoming their own best teachers and assessors. Both within educational level and across levels, the language of outcomes transcended existing patterns of thought and communication about student learning and assessment. "What students should learn and be able to do" replaced prior discussions that had created barriers in communication in the past (for example, focusing on content alone, belaboring the specifics of implementation, comparing student characteristics or institutional resources across institutions). Educational assumptions were articulated through principles of learning and assessment; this led to changes and benefits. For example, when educators agreed on the need to assess in ways that promote student learning, they began to look for supportive approaches, such as peer assessment and training volunteers—retired physicians, executives, teachers—to help assess. Consortium members also shared suggestions for dealing with difficulties. Members observed that peer evaluation works least well when students are dealing with new material or are unprepared.

Members noted that new kinds of relationships were created between faculty and students. In research institutions, for example, faculty began to construct roles that included coaching students in their learning; students were not as fearful of assessment. Introducing portfolios increased the contact time between faculty and students and helped overcome the negatives of testing. Self assessments that incorporated faculty criteria and judgment became a way for students to communicate to parents, who gradually came to view them as more accurate than end-of-semester grades. Students used their portfolios to communicate through new forms of assessment what they learned to outsiders: parents, employers, community members. Thus, assessment became a mechanism to convey to others a sense of a student's integrated performance. Consortium members cited this enhanced communication about student performance as an important indicator that significant change had occurred.

The TLA Consortium experience is linked to the broader themes of transformation by several observations: First, defining educational outcomes acted as a point of origin for transformations centered on student learning, and exploring educational assumptions was a significant step in this process. These assumptions, more than any particular practice or assessment approach, served as the basis for working across settings and grounding multidisciplinary conversations. Second, time and related resources that enabled faculty and staff discourse were critical concerns, but they could be dealt with creatively, and successive achievements tended to reinforce engagement. Third, transformation functioned as a learning process building on breadth and expertise. Different disciplines with multiple perspectives needed to be engaged in the work of developing and implementing a learning-centered curriculum. A deliberative inquiry program, embracing a range of evidence, judgments, and qualitative and quantitative performance measures, served as a critical element in the overall process. Inquiry efforts, by providing a recurring picture of learning in terms of student and program performance, added to the foundation for continued engagement.

Consortium Across "New Universities" in the United Kingdom

Given that learning that lasts is situated, how are strategies that worked to deal with constraints reflected by shifting the educational culture? What learning from the previous consortium is transferable? Recent experiences in the United Kingdom provide a useful comparison for extending these strategies. The Ability Based Curriculum (ABC) Network included several institutions in the United Kingdom from the "new universities" (former polytechnics that obtained university status in 1992), as well as Alverno College. Recently, the group identified accelerators and barriers to progress in developing ability-based curricula on their campuses (Otter, 1997).

Creating a vision was a key impetus. It implied focusing on graduates' capabilities, clarifying certifying requirements, and obtaining some external funding for leveraging change. Discussions toward identifying outcomes were supported by faculty networks, where key people from across the universities were brought together to discuss capability and skill development, and were hindered by faculty concerns about the movement toward national vocational quality standards, a decade-old effort in the United Kingdom. Unfamiliar terminology and language was also a barrier, but the frank reports of issues and realities that institutions faced impelled the discussion. Although some faculty were concerned that a focus on capabilities and skill development could result in "losing the context of subject matter" that would lead to a "drop" in quality, this view was overcome to a degree by locating responsibility clearly in the disciplines. A consensus formed that new teaching and learning structures were needed. Faculty enthusiasts for capability and skills development, reinforced by faculty partnering across these universities, balanced lack of faculty interest or the fact that some faculty were already demoralized by the large number of changes that were under way at their university (obstacles were often assumed that were not based in actual experience).

A tendency on the part of some senior administrators to leave resource implications to the universities rather than making an effort at resolving these issues, a lack of a senior champion for the ideas in a university, a loss of ongoing management support and continuity, or changes in senior faculty positions were also barriers to progress. Faculty fear of overcomplicated bureaucratic systems was underscored by starting with a curricular system that was initially too complicated and by the speed of other changes in their universities. These constraints were balanced by consortium development of less complex models and structures. Ultimately the consortium has accelerated because the members emphasized designing outcome-oriented curricula that were based on an established modular scheme and making sense of what it meant to design learning modules, and because the various institutions continue to articulate how they shape their individual programs (Gilbert & Reynolds, 1998; Jenkins, 1999; Page, 1998).

Consortia on Benchmarking Institutional Performance Measures

The TLA consortium's experience in generating evidence of change was recently reinforced by a benchmarking study on institutional performance measures by the American Productivity & Quality Center (1997), involving twenty institutions. The latter concluded that the best institutional performance measures communicate the institution's core values and, like the TLA consortium, found that external pressures could be a useful starting point for developing institutional performance measurement systems, particularly when they were used as problem detectors to stimulate improvement.

Similar to the TLA consortium, the American Productivity & Quality Center (APQC) group of institutions found that performance measures could emerge that were available and visible across the institutions, and that as they became so, they could become more consistent across the institution as well. They found that performance measures should be developed and used as part of a broader transformation of organizational culture. Thus, the APQC group supported the finding of the TLA consortium that there is no easy path to turning indicators inferred from experience with change into systematic evidence that is widely credible, but that such indicators do emerge and are credible to other institutions experienced in institutional transformation. A consequent benchmarking study on assessing learning outcomes was sponsored by thirty-one postsecondary educational institutions and six other corporations. They found that when indicators measure learning directly (for example, learning gains of students rather than entering qualifications used for selection; performance on student assessments rather than number of credits), then assessment of learning-centered teaching is more likely to be effective (American Productivity & Quality Center, 1998).

Consortia Across Departments of Education

Consortia of departments also collaborate on transforming activities and provide another option for observing transformation from within and across colleges. Consortia may be initiated by learned societies or professional associations. The following examples are from teacher education.

Teaching for Tomorrow Consortium

Four education departments at diverse institutions joined in shared program goals to enhance success at institutional transformation. This Teaching for Tomorrow consortium (Diez, 1998) clarified teacher candidate learning outcomes; created performance assessment processes to develop and document the development of student learning outcomes; created strategies to involve faculty across their institutions and in preschool, elementary, and secondary schools in the reform effort; and designed evaluation to guide continuous improvement. Developing a climate of trust within the group led to constructive criticism and the sharing of common problems or questions—for example, how to create experiences and assessments that develop the abilities sought in the program; how to create rubrics that support development rather than simply to sort students into achievement levels; and how to use feedback and self assessment to promote growth. By the end of a three-year grant, each of the institutions had developed clear outcomes to guide its programs, reviewed and revised curricula, developed plans for student assessment, and published handbooks for faculty and students.

The consortium made explicit four elements of the process necessary to develop a standards-based teacher education program:

- Clarity of outcomes: "What should the beginning teacher know and be able to do?"
- Coherent curriculum: "How can teacher educators design classes and field experiences so that candidates develop the intended outcomes?"
- Performance assessment: "How can teacher educators link assessment developmentally to the outcomes, embed assessment in courses as well as provide on-demand tasks, and include self assessment as integral to the process?"
- Links with K–12 schools: "How can teacher educators provide meaningful hands-on experiences; keep the outcomes, curriculum, and assessment relevant; and support similar efforts to develop curriculum and assessment at the K–12 level?"

Shifting the focus from a predominantly teacher-directed information dissemination system to a student learning-centered process of development of knowledge, abilities, and attitudes entailed changes in assumptions, relationships, and practices. Diez and Truchan (1998) note that "experiencing student criticism (verbally or in the form of transfers to other institutions), dealing with student failure to perform or to be hired, or sensing a disjuncture between the needs of the schools and the focus of a program" suggested a reexamination of assumptions underlying teacher education (p. 141). "Much of the disequilibrium related to the awareness that teacher education candidates' experiences in a set of courses did not necessarily result in their gaining the knowledge, skills, and dispositions needed to work effectively with a wide range of learner needs. Questioning the old focus of a program as a collection of courses opened the door to looking at other conceptual frameworks for programs" (p. 142). Overcoming resistance to change meant rethinking the way the departments worked rather than adding on. Change was not brought about by one person, nor did it demand that all parties move at the same rate to the same end. Rather, a core group of people interested in making improvements agreed to work toward development of a common vision. Communication and persistence emerged as important factors.

Members made an initial commitment to a collaborative enterprise, knowing that moving to a standards-based model was complex and required commitment to developing the knowledge and skills to work together effectively over a considerable period of time (Hass & Stoffels, 1998; Henn-Reinke & Kies, 1998; Mihalevich & Carr, 1998; Schnug & Shelly, 1998). Faculty in the member departments struggled to stay fresh and committed, interact effectively, and assist new faculty as they became involved in the ongoing work of the team. New participants meant new perspectives, especially when mentoring new faculty in moving toward a standards-based program became respected work and appreciated by others. Taking multiple perspectives was a way of thinking that supported change. Members began to understand the unique culture of each constituency. Allowing each culture to coexist encouraged the valuing of diverse contributions, appreciating differences, and progressing toward common goals. Accepting and appreciating the realities of restructured programs was another way of thinking: teaching as decision making and learning as interactive. Disequilibrium occurred naturally in the midst of change because new ways of thinking enabled changes in teaching methods that were neither predictable nor necessarily stable. Appreciating this disequilibrium was another way of thinking that fostered change.

Once change had been initiated, constituents needed to take responsibility for their growth and develop a process to maintain that growth pattern. Designing a continuous improvement model provided a way for faculty to routinely evaluate program progress toward specific goals. Communicating effectively, as a second way of working, challenged participants to identify issues for problem solving and for pacing the change. Creating a zone of comfort in the midst of change helped member institutions stay open to continued refinement. Faculty moved from questioning why they were engaging in the change process at all, given its real and potential frustrations, to finding ways to tolerate the ambiguity. That meant developing a willingness to postpone closure on an issue until they had experienced what it meant to change, limit the scope of the project in order to maintain faculty interest and commitment, and use frameworks as guides to the change process.

Creating new norms that affected success in an institution, such as openness for discussion, influenced the creativity of ideas. The shift to an outcomes-based learning model meant changing the culture of the campus, and probing how that was understood was critical. Developing relationships (internal and external) and designing processes (ways of thinking, working, and relating) fostered successful standards-based teacher education programs.

NCREST Study of Departments of Education

The NCREST study of seven departments of education (Darling-Hammond, 1997; Zeichner, 1997) judged as effective through a selection process supported the findings from the "Teaching for Tomorrow" consortium. Development of a clear vision that included learner-centered, constructivist, experiential, and developmental principles of learning was apparent across all seven departments. Faculty modeled effective teaching practices in coursework and field settings. They carefully constructed a knowledge base for practice, even though that knowledge base was divergent across institutions (for example, one program was more theory based; another more practice based). Each program had developed strong supports for student success and had evidence for continuity and coherence in student experience. Although there were structural differences (degree of selectivity of students, degree to which the program was field-based), there were commonalities as well (for example, program experiences were highly defined as a map for students—"here's the program; here's what we do").

Additional Consortia, New Tasks

Through the 1990s, concerns for higher education transformation have sharpened. Foundations have always supported efforts to improve practice, but some, such as The Pew Charitable Trusts and the W.K. Kellogg Foundation, have created specific initiatives to support and study transformation in groups of campuses. These consortia create opportunities to extend the common tasks with which we began this chapter. The Pew Charitable Trusts Leadership Award for Renewal of Undergraduate Education has addressed the need for change in the design and delivery of core functions in higher education. Pew asked institutions to prepare a portfolio of evidence for institutional change, visited selected institutions for confirming evidence, and recognized several institutions for distinct kinds of transformations. It asked these diverse institutions to share their different ideas and to learn from each other.

The W.K. Kellogg Foundation has sought to strengthen higher education and mobilize its resources. The Kellogg Forum on Higher Education Transformation is a consortium of five institutions: three centers for the study of higher education, a national association, and the funding foundation. The forum addresses how educational institutions become more accessible, flexible, responsive, relevant, and accountable in their services to students and society. It is beginning with questions about transformational processes: the basic elements that enable or stimulate change across an institution, the key criteria by which a range of stakeholders can recognize the progress of transformation, and the various roles of institutional leadership. Subsequent questions deal with the elements that sustain transformation and the implications that the consortium's experience may have for larger systemic change in higher education. Initial conversations among members have shown that although there are significant differences among their experiences, some kind of sustained reflection on mission, strategies, and leadership in support of broad faculty participation have been critical aspects of each institution's work.

Converging Guidelines for Institutional Transformation

Virginia Smith (1998) argues that there is no single blueprint that all of higher education should implement, nor is there just one kind of institution where change can occur. Further, not every institution that is organized for learning has identified learning that lasts as an educational goal, or learning-centered education as a primary responsibility. Nevertheless, each institution expects to be involved in organizational learning toward its own goals. So to broaden the conversation across even more diverse campuses, we turn to institutional consortia that organized around broader goals and of which Alverno is not a member. For this purpose, we have looked to consortia aimed at leadership and institutional transformation toward renewal.

Consortium Data Sources for Higher Education Renewal

Several consortia outside the partnerships of Alverno College have demonstrated that discussions about change can help focus the process at any one institution if the dialogue encourages comparisons of insights gathered—particularly when consortia clarify some common challenges, goals, or conditions for change. This was the case for the eighteen-member consortium of independent colleges and universities in the California Futures Project (Smith, 1998). The Pew Roundtables of Liberal Arts College Presidents and Deans, convened in the mid-1990s, synthesized their ideas around central themes (Pew Higher Education Roundtable, 1995a, 1995b, 1995c, 1995d; Pew Higher Education Roundtable & the American Association for Higher Education, 1996; Pew Higher Education

Roundtable & the American Council on Education's Project on Leadership and Institutional Transformation, 1996). More recently, the ACE Project on Leadership and Institutional Transformation, funded by the W.K. Kellogg Foundation, noted that consortium conversations among the twenty-six participating institutions were most effective when they explored commonalities in the light of differences, even though "no two institutions use the same itinerary, and each maps the journey as it proceeds" (Eckel et al., 1999, p. 1).

These consortia found that educators need some type of forum in which to openly discuss issues of practice, student performance, and curricular development. A faculty senate, curriculum committee, or other administrative group already in place may not necessarily serve the function of bringing faculty into adequate and dynamic interaction around issues and concerns, nor would they necessarily be sufficient to enable a broad and collective responsibility for program directions. Thus, other forums need to be developed depending on where discussion is happening and what it is about. All the consortia reviewed in this chapter worked to identify, confront, and resolve problems and barriers associated with change toward educational goals. If problems were not identified adequately or goals were not shared, efforts at change dissipated. We noted that institutions that are effective usually document evidence of changes and discuss them publicly.

Along with forums for discussion, systems are needed to recruit, select, orient, and support new administrators, faculty, and staff who are brought into the institution. Departments that successfully integrate new faculty into the institution actively clarify expectations and expect department chairs to provide direct mentoring (Perry et al., 1997; Rosch & Reich, 1996). In implementation, institutional transformation often means negotiating interests and commitments, roles and responsibilities across faculty and staff (Cranton, 1996). This includes building on or recreating interdepartmental and interdisciplinary activities, with different dynamics depending on the group. Terms and activities (for example, meetings, committees, use of faculty time) that are viewed as impediments need to be reconceptualized. Activities may differ for faculty, staff, students, trustees, and graduates. What seems clear is that communication across departments and disciplines can lead to creating new terms to facilitate communication.

Identifying Converging Guidelines for Institutional Transformation

The analyses of practice in the consortia outside the experience of this college help us explore institutional transformation further and extend the ideas in Exhibits 11.1 and 11.3. In an iterative review, we brought together the ideas from Alverno and its partnering institutions, and extended them with observations by consortia for higher education renewal, in order to infer a set of converging guidelines. Exhibit 11.4 provides guidelines synthesized from the renewal discussions as they converge with transformation focused on learning-centered education.

A common emphasis across all consortium data sources has been the importance of a central discussion around educational purposes and grounding assumptions. We also note that a central emphasis on learning in the institution's core processes must be supported by a sustained and deliberative study of teaching and learning by the educators. This has direct implications for how the campus constructs and supports scholarship. We began this chapter with a recommendation for campus conversations that integrate a dynamic institutional perspective with a focus on learning. In this discourse, it is likely to be all the more important to construct some cohering, shared frameworks for learning and performance within the diversity of the institution. Further, taking an institutional perspective requires that departments offer leadership as agents of the institution as well as agents of their disciplines. This means that departments directly grapple with the meanings of the disciplines in the context of clarifying the meaning of a degree. This is no less important for individual faculty, but in a transformative process, the departments have a distinct responsibility for participative leadership and creating a climate of trust. Examining administrative, faculty, and staff roles must be linked with reflection efforts. The importance of institutional vitality is evident across the case studies, just as is the critical role of faculty and staff discourse. An implication we draw is that the construction of academic work—as it is performed in context and through the expertise of its practitioners—needs to be expressed in the more formal statements and performance criteria used to evaluate educational effectiveness. Thinking through criteria can serve as an

Exhibit 11.4. Converging Guidelines for Institutional Transformation Toward Broad Initiatives: Higher Education Renewal and Learning-Centered Education.

- *Acknowledge the need for and direction of change* in public and private spheres.
  - Show awareness of societal changes in relation to the role and responsibilities of higher education and its current issues.
  - Articulate and make broadly known within the institution the external context in which higher education exists and the implications for any one institution that flow from these contextual shifts.
  - Foster and provide opportunities for campus members to understand, reflect on, and exchange information with others about the individual's role within the institution, the role of the institution in higher education, and the role of higher education in society.
  - Ask again who learning is for and who will benefit.
  - Take the lead in systematically reviewing the undergraduate curriculum.
  - Create critical coalitions on and off campus to spur change.
- *Pursue shared purposes within "centering" value frameworks to generate resolve* so that change is meaningful, not just manageable. Shared purposes include moving learning to the "center" of the teaching enterprise, engaging in conversation about teaching, creating a framework of shared educational values in which teaching and learning can occur, and recasting graduate education to include residencies in undergraduate institutions.
  - Create a climate and culture for communication and teamwork around teaching for learning that ensures community-wide conversations that are intellectually and emotionally engaging. Explore differences and commonalities, go beyond rational argument, and foster commitments to shared purposes.
  - Engage the participation of educators in the culture and community of the institution over the long term. Restructure interactively; identify and create visible forums for discussion; recruit, select, orient, and support administrators, faculty, and staff. Negotiate interests, commitments, roles, and responsibilities among administrators, faculty, and staff. Create critical coalitions on and off campus.

Exhibit 11.4. Converging Guidelines for Institutional Transformation Toward Broad Initiatives: Higher Education Renewal and Learning-Centered Education, cont'd.

- Expect the academic department to become an agent of the institution as well as its discipline. Foster purposeful leadership that evokes energy and commitment. Create faculty-administrative partnerships that effect institutional changes. Link proposals to pressing needs and problems rather than ready-made solutions.

- Deal with organizational paradoxes such as achieving coherence within diversity and balancing individual and interdependent responsibilities. Articulate the right and freedom to define change and to inquire within each role that serves the discipline, institution, and local community.

• *Create a climate of trust that underlies shared governance* by attributing positive motives to others rather than assigning blame. Participate in and shape communities that are both civil and affirming. Communicate that some problems will continue to be intractable, but that educators can deal with contradictory goals for collaboration and individuality, challenge and support.

• *Deal with constraints by creating strategies that build on increased participation and collaborative action.* Create economic efficiencies and active and flexible decision-making capabilities.

• *Invest in the conditions that make change possible,* that sustain innovations, and lead to serious structural changes rather than adding new procedures and programs. This "organizational capital" (Smith, 1998) is as important as physical resources and working capital.

• *Create a climate of change and experimentation* where tryouts are recognized, legitimized, and encouraged on campus. Support those who take risks to serve wide-ranging goals. Sustain change and make it systemic in a culture. Build a climate of trust to sustain involvement.

• *Demonstrate claims about education.* Open teaching to self, student, and peer evaluation and to collective inquiry.

• *Partner organizational learning,* where institutions have both distinctive and interchangeable components (for example, assess the competence of transfer students who apply to innovative programs rather than count credits, or gradually involve new leaders in consortium change processes).

extended inquiry into practice and a key investment that makes transformational change possible. Finally, we cannot emphasize enough the changes in thinking brought about by creating critical coalitions of institutions. The ideas that emerge are likely to set the tone for organizational learning in higher education.

Learning and Action Principles for Organizing for Learning That Lasts

Based on our analysis of transformative acts for institutional transformation, we find that organizational learning that lasts is integrative, experiential, transformative, purposeful, self assessed, developmental, and deeply sustained in context. For a college culture to evolve in ways that create enduring support for lasting learning, almost all of the components of an institution eventually need to become actively involved in learning. This principle becomes embedded in the collective consciousness. It does not mean, "You have to start with the whole institution." A culture is not changed deliberately in advance; each culture evolves. However, the institution eventually will have to be holistically involved. Some institutions have changed and developed their own culture, but there are pockets within them that have not changed. While every aspect of an institution need not change, those that have changed need to be visible and well known. This diversity is part of the culture, and members of institutions involved in some kind of transformation reach such a conclusion early on: "They're living in another world over there." One of the obstacles they recognize immediately is, "What if this other thing is happening over here?" Their question is not, "Who conforms?" but rather, "What kinds of processes can move changes from existing only in isolated places to becoming more organic?"

Learning that lasts is developmental and individual, transitional and transformative. The change process is a blend of alternating harmony and conflict. As individuals commit to a vision, they become interested in the ideas and start discussing them. The diversity in that conversation can lead to conflict and disharmony, making skills in creating harmony out of diversity a key institutional asset (Senge, 1990). Such a harmony of diverse ideas assists individuals in moving out from the core, and there is some rippling as well. Often individuals feel a need to be able to work together to figure out what the conflicts and contradictions are and to work through them in order to return to the ideas at a deeper level. Representing structures as more systems-like is often helpful here. Acknowledging that systems can spin out of control is often more useful to the lifeblood of what is happening than statements such as, "Here is what a good institution looks like."

In a multiuniversity, institutional change might begin in the departments most focused on undergraduate education programs, then be overwhelmed by broader institutional changes that result from multiple and often conflicting goals. Given this, it seems more effective for institutions to figure out not only how they start a chaining process—where a change in one place affects change in the next part—but also to take a cultural perspective. Rather than to start with what they think the finished product ought to look like and attempt to move toward that, it seems more helpful to support the evolution of the system for the institution gradually. Seeing organizational learning as developmental is a different perspective on the process of change than starting with the best practices that characterize a fully developed institution. This is not to say that institutions cannot depend on learning from each other, because learning that lasts, though situated, is also transferable.

Just as organizational learning may be understood as a process by which institutions change, the transformative learning cycles—connecting knowing and doing, self assessing role performance, and engaging multiple roles and activities toward integrative development—that lead to lasting learning for individuals have analogous functions in institutional processes. If that is so, then effective institutions show organizational learning that lasts. In Exhibit 11.5, we return to the principles for learning that lasts (Chapter Seven) and transform the guidelines for institutional transformation into action principles.

The critical demands for complex educational goals require that learning outcomes be connected with a coherent means for learning. The problem is how to effect these relationships across an institution. It is essential for the integrity of change that learning principles used to undergird an educational program also apply to how educators collaborate to transform an institution.

Exhibit 11.5. Principles for Learning That Lasts, with Converging Action Principles for Organizing for Learning That Lasts.

If learning that lasts is integrative and experiential, then effective institutions:

- Encourage consensus around learning goals toward curricular coherence within the diversity of ideas about what should be taught and how it should be learned; respect differences within and outside shared purposes.

- Discover where to start and what to learn and do experientially, that is, infer guidelines and action principles from direct, ongoing experience, and validate learning experientially.

- Eventually involve the institution holistically.

If learning that lasts is self-aware and reflective, self assessed and self-regarding, then effective institutions:

- Make learning that lasts visible to learners through developing individuals' awareness of learning designs, processes, and outcomes.

- Practice learning that lasts with reflection, criteria, feedback, and self assessment by documenting evidence of changes, creating a culture of evidence, clarifying institutional "developmental performance criteria," and benchmarking performance in relation to one's own ideals and the best practices of other institutions.

If learning that lasts is developmental and individual, transitional and transformative, then effective institutions:

- Respect that institutional transformation is individual: There are differences among institutions and levels of practice, and what is transformed differs at each campus.

- Acknowledge that institutional transformation is developmental in that one can decipher change over time, yet transforming activities co-occur.

- Create a culture to enhance learning; foster communication, involvement, and investment across campus toward resolving problems and removing barriers.

**Exhibit 11.5. Principles for Learning That Lasts,
with Converging Action Principles for
Organizing for Learning That Lasts, cont'd.**

If learning that lasts is active and interactive, independent and collaborative, then effective institutions:

- Build on playback between the consciousness of the student and the consciousness of faculty.
- Work toward comprehensive institutional involvement in learning across campus to indirectly influence college cultural evolution.
- Partner organizational learning in consortia toward collaborative learning communities of institutions.

If learning that lasts is situated and transferable, then effective institutions:

- Expect that sustainable changes are made in context.
- Create public dialogue to clarify transferability of assumptions, practices, and understanding about student learning outcomes.

If learning that lasts is deep and expansive, purposeful and responsible, then effective institutions:

- Expect that institutional transformation is part of the organization's learning that is lasting.
- Deliberate and clarify institutional purposes, and take responsibility for the learning of each member of the campus community.
- Seek to understand and effect institutional responsibilities, and expect to be treated individually and fairly.

Organizing for learning that lasts both contributes to and benefits from institutional transformation and indirectly influences a college culture. Our review of cases—our own institutional experiences, our studies with partnering consortia, and insights from other consortia outside our experience—provides a sense of the complex and diverse issues that campuses confront in pursuing and sustaining significant change. Some themes bind these experiences: clarifying curricular outcomes in terms of learning, working toward coherence in the curriculum, and increasing participation across administrators, faculty, and staff. At the same time, given the diverse experiences of individual campuses and program initiatives, there is no singular model for campuses. The value of analyzing institutional experience is in trying to understand one's own organizational learning dynamics and how to use such insights to effect transformative acts toward particular orientations and commitments. These dynamics and processes—some paradoxical, some very complex— may be taken up for review in consortia with both similar commitments to student learning and a broader set of responsibilities.

What we understand about learning that lasts and its relationship to teaching is what grounds curricular transformation and institutional transformation, which influence cultural transformation. The lasting learning of individuals has a homology in the organizational learning of a college. We have seen how learners become conscious of the design, process, vitality, and commonality of learning that lasts and how they can apply it. When learning is developed as a central focus at multiple academic and administrative levels, an effective institution does its own organizational learning that lasts in a way that is visible to students. In a curriculum that has learning that lasts built in and made explicit, all learners (trustees, administrators, faculty, academic and other staff) gradually construct and act out of rationales for this complex partnership, and they continue to rethink and refine them.

Chapter Twelve

Looking Ahead

At the beginning of this new millennium, we join many others who are taking stock in order to look ahead. We acknowledge that pride of place has too often been the most salient feature of graduates' reflections on their college years. Traditionally students have not been the lasting characteristic of a campus. They left; the faculty and the ivy lasted. The college became known more for who entered it, who taught there, and its physical plant rather than for those who graduated. In the next decades, the meaning of "the students," "the faculty," and "the campus" will change irrevocably for most learners and their educators as each new cohort becomes adept at shaping "the college" in a learning society. Rather than a singular focus on the constant stimulation of more and more information, easily fragmented and forgotten, the central question for higher education will be to explore new ways of organizing and educating for learning that lasts. The most visible body politic of the campus will be its students, as each generation takes its place. How well they take up their responsibilities after college will remain the question of interest.

Centering on Learning That Lasts

We have argued that learning that lasts is an essential foundation for the long-range contribution of college graduates. Students can develop it when faculty teach it as an integration of learning, development, and performance. This kind of learning during college connects to performance after college. Individuals who develop as performers contribute to the community and the workplace, and set and meet the expectations and demands of personal and family life. They move effectively among different contexts, characterized by multiple forms of collaboration, abilities, and cycles of transformative learning.

Learning that lasts is deeply embedded in the educational practices of a liberal arts degree—especially when that degree is integrated with the professions, service, and value traditions of a college. The studies in this book argue for a deeper understanding of the relationships among particular educational practices and learning that lasts rather than a comparative test of pedagogical approaches or of student learning outcomes across institutions. The result is a different kind of knowing about learning, where significance and usefulness lie in depth of understanding rather than in strict generalizability. This knowledge calls us as educators to raise significant questions about relationships among curriculum guidelines, practices, and particular learning outcomes. These insights imply rethinking and renewing our educational commitments to learners and to each other.

Learning that endures is transformative. This is the essence of the dynamism that propels healthy curricular transformation. For a curriculum to foster learning that lasts, faculty must continuously design, practice, experience, evaluate, and improve it in relation to how learners fully experience it. They ask what students bring to this experience in relation to what they know and can do across a curriculum and how graduates reach their potential beyond college. Realizing learning that lasts in a college community calls for rethinking the nature of inquiry as it contributes to that developing community. For all of its members (students, faculty, staff, administrators, trustees), transforming a curriculum and continually renegotiating the college culture entails thinking through learning and action principles for learning that lasts. It means negotiating various views of competence and meaning and exploring how members can work together to incorporate shared and individual understandings into an educational program that is coherent within its diversity, and developmental yet organized so students can meet explicit, common, and evolving expectations that maximize each student's potential. It means that educators articulate and then use their assumptions and principles to think through and assess student growth—and their own as well. Educators must reflect together to solve such problems as how to make distance learning interactive with the student growth potential of a campus.

Participating in the Conversation

Learning That Lasts best serves those who directly work across and prize the diversity in purpose, perspective, and experience that we expect will continue to characterize higher education. A common concern for improving undergraduate learning joins professional educators and other scholars, the policymaking community, and the public sector in common goals. These groups argue for a more extended conversation about how and what students should learn, how a more coherent curriculum can contribute to learning, and whether the ideals expressed by the rhetoric of educational reform are realized in the performance of graduates after college. We are impressed by the hope reflected in the interests and commitments of this expanding range of colleagues across levels of practice.

Connecting Across Levels of Practice

As the boundaries between formal divisions of schooling become more permeable, more educators recognize their common stake in the success of the individual student. Faculty are moving from a specialized focus on their discipline and classroom to also consider their department's goals in relation to those of others. Administrators and policymakers are concerned that learning be productive at the level of the classroom. Accrediting groups now require institutions to make connections between learning processes and outcomes explicit. Policymakers and legislators spur debates around undergraduate education and how it benefits the local economic community. At the national level, various groups seek to define what educational outcomes are needed. Our colleagues in other countries are coping with profound restructuring in higher education and across the full educational spectrum. They also expect to better connect education, economics, and growth of the individual by linking learning in school with performance and contribution in the workplace and civic life.

In this conversation, *Learning That Lasts* offers evidence-based perspectives on the meaning of the degree, learning outcomes, curriculum development, and institutional change. We hope to stimulate further thought within broader educational movements, to turn renewal into continuous improvement. As faculty leaders reflect on and debate the directions that they should take on behalf of students, they will want to think through the assumptions across departments about what "a good education" might come to mean in the next decades.

Using *Learning That Lasts*

As a community of educators concerned with understanding and enhancing learning, we have benefited most from works that are well grounded in both educational practice and scholarly inquiry. We designed *Learning That Lasts* to be used. It integrates the voices of teacher, researcher, administrator, professional academic staff, and policymaker because these roles need to be joined in a coherent enterprise.

Several chapters can serve as discussion points for various working groups. They can stimulate conversation about what makes a good education by inviting the participation of broad, multidisciplinary groups across and within levels of practice, from classroom to curriculum to institution. For some, the book prompts discussion through its longitudinal findings of the integration of learning, development, and performance in college and beyond; its examination of collaborative inquiry within and across consortia of institutions; and its infusion of relevant literature and practice in higher education. Groups across higher education can use evidence-based models of growth as they reflect on and examine learning-centered curriculum efforts. As they proceed, they are served by examples of how to inquire into the nature of learning in one's own contexts, test assumptions and frameworks of practice, examine student learning outcomes, and use a range of methods to infer how college culture, dedicated to learning, is transformed. Faculty, staff, and administrators will expect to create their own theory of learning with context-specific action principles for fostering learning that endures. They will also pursue the connections between educational practices and organizational structures so that inquiry, program assessment and evaluation, and a formal research program can operate effectively in service to a college's mission. Departmental and institutional representatives in consortia will expect to discuss evidence-based observations and insights grounded in public dialogue about educational practices at multiple levels and across settings.

These kinds of self-defining activities create pathways for engaging groups outside colleges and universities in educational issues and lead toward better-informed public policy.

Integrating Practice, Research, and Theory

For learning to last, educators must confront paradox, to integrate the whole yet differentiate its parts. A search for language that captures and clarifies paradoxes in constructive ways is going to be a common task for some time to come. Student learning processes and outcomes are about what transfers, is specific, and continues to change; about what is needed to focus on specialized study, to think across one's studies, and to do both in action. Learning that lasts is about integration, wholeness, integrity, coherence, and inclusion, within the individual and within programs of education. It is simultaneously about differentiation, diversity, pluralism, and individuality within a community committed to these educational ideals. To realize this kind of learning, educators need to understand deeply held perspectives and patterns of performances as well as to deal with transitory perceptions and actions, to expand access and opportunities while reaching for even higher standards, to realize ideals constrained by the practical and the possible.

How well any educator can hold on to all aspects of such paradoxes influences how well we learn what future educational efforts for learning that lasts will have to teach us. As communities of educators, we need the very skills and habits we are trying to teach—and, ironically, to build these skills for ourselves while we develop the practice of teaching for them. This means skills in interactive processes: attending to the structures, personal characteristics, and divergent perspectives that enable us to deliberate over key issues. We also need to learn new ways to use inquiry in this process.

As a college, we found that we had to redefine how disciplinary scholarship functions when faculty formulate their own educational theories and carry out their own modes of research integrated with educational practice. From this experience, we have come to understand that studies of learning within a particular educational context have direct educational significance within that context and also contribute to higher education in a more general sense. We need to continue to discipline ourselves to look within and to build meaning from diverse voices, sources of ideas and evidence, and contexts of practice. We believe that is what a college like ours needs to do: to stand in, beside, and aside simultaneously.

To do this, we must embrace paradox and bring together practical (standing in), reflective (standing beside), and theoretical (standing aside) stances to imagine education for student learning in much more powerful ways than we have so far. Connecting these should not obliterate the distinctive features of each.

The challenge of effectively describing a practically oriented theory—while also illustrating its empirical base and its derivation from reflective practice—is likely to remain part of educational research within a college. To build theory in a community has challenged us to construct and critique conventions for doing it. We have found that collaborative inquiry, as grounded in practically oriented theory, needs to weave multiple perspectives from practice—from a community that is learning by educating—into a picture of the growth of the learner in relation to what teaching and curriculum contribute. Such an empiricism can be rigorous and systematic, and also deliberative, constructive, and emergent, but it creates challenges. We found it a struggle, in our most formal inquiries, to develop a line of argument related to systematically collected and analyzed empirical observations precisely because they were in interaction with a deliberative inquiry oriented toward demands of practice. Studies in teaching, curriculum development, and institutional structure require attention to additional perspectives and paradoxical demands. But rather than limping along, an integrated inquiry of educational practice must develop still further as a cycle of learning where formal theory becomes more impressionistic and consensual and practical theory becomes more abstract and robust through reflection that includes all the voices.

In reflective practice, theoretical reflection is built into educators' conversations and deliberative inquiry. These are less driven by any overarching theory than they are by a series of practical judgments that, first and foremost, inquire into particulars. Further, we have yet to understand adequately how individual faculty and staff use their disciplinary ideas and principles to shape and analyze their own performances in class and across a department or campus. For us, the effort to better understand learning, development, and performance is worth it because we can break open what these mean for many more kinds of learners. This implies more closely studying how and why the student grows and learns in various disciplines. But it also means faculty and staff using broad, disciplinary theories that deepen, challenge, and inform reflection.

As we move to fostering learning that lasts, practical paradoxes of how to commit resources emerge. Faculty must work with more complex understandings of learning while realizing that advanced learning outcomes also require a more sophisticated analysis of their disciplines. The increasing diversity of learners' goals and their potential needs will interact with the demonstrated importance of coherence in the organization of curriculum. The institution must also become a student and researcher of its own practices, exploring forms of inquiry that allow for a useful integration of educational practice, research, and theory building. We expect that a campus organization in support of learning will require even more complex roles of educators. This development continues to present a challenge for higher education's scholarship of teaching and learning: That is, how can we pursue studies that contribute to the broad and theoretical understanding of higher education and also have meaning and consequence within teaching and learning practices? Through what criteria, as a field, can educators advance a conversation that will engage learners, colleagues, and policymakers at a variety of levels?

Taking Up the Challenge

Placing learning at the center of educational practice and its scholarship, we propose, is a critical and unifying step in dealing with some of the themes and purposes with which we began this book: maximizing individual potential in a pluralistic society; integrating learning, development, and performance; connecting work, civic, personal, and family life through education; transforming undergraduate education; and taking professional responsibility for student learning. There are daunting challenges in carrying out something as meaningful and charged with risks as transforming a college culture for learning that lasts. Transformation means not knowing how things will end. It means trusting that learning can be progressive and that one's colleagues have the community interest at heart or can be called to it. There is a great hope for revitalizing education and the spirit of our faculties. Perhaps the most often heard complaint of faculty and academic staff is that they are isolated from others. The process of renewal, if nothing else, brings a community into discourse with one another. At its best, this discourse can be reinvigorating and is the tie that binds. At its worst, it can irrevocably break it apart. The task is to see the process as part of an end that does not really end, as the community continues to build new understandings.

For students to develop lasting learning, each collegiate community must model learning in all its forms: deep and expansive, purposeful and responsible. As a language of renewal, such integrated learning is a currency for the new millennium, a medium of exchange that enables us as global citizens to cross old boundaries. Once the prerogative of a few, learning that lasts is now much more central to realizing moral imagination, human potential, meaningful achievement, and that most practical of all things in a changing world, belief in the future.

Appendix A

Alverno College Ability-Based Learning Program

Since the early 1970s, the Alverno College faculty have been developing and implementing ability-based undergraduate education. More recently, educators at every level—elementary, secondary, undergraduate, postgraduate, and professional—have become involved in an effort to redefine education in terms of abilities needed for effectiveness in the worlds of work, family, and civic community.

One of the greatest challenges to faculty in shaping an ability-based program is the tendency to think of the development of abilities in contrast to a mastery of subject matter or content, as if one precludes the other. Through our practice, we have learned that it is impossible to teach for abilities without a subject-matter context. The distinctive feature of an ability-based approach is that we make explicit the expectation that *students should be able to do something with what they know.*

Few educators would argue with the proposition that a close reading of a philosophic text should have an impact on the thinking of students beyond merely grasping the meaning. The encounter with complex ideas should help develop the students' ability to reason and question and help them one day to think and act effectively in contexts removed from the original concern of the text. By making such expectations explicit and by clarifying steps one can take to develop cognitive and affective habits, we assist students in learning how to learn.

Ability-Based Learning Outcomes

The specific abilities identified by our faculty as central to our approach to liberal arts and professional education are:

- Communication
- Analysis
- Problem Solving
- Valuing in Decision-Making
- Social Interaction
- Global Perspectives
- Effective Citizenship
- Aesthetic Responsiveness

These are the most visible features of our learning program. However, it would be a fundamental misperception to see students' development and demonstration of these eight abilities as the primary outcome or end of an Alverno education. Our ultimate goal is the development of each student as an educated, mature adult with such personal characteristics as:

- A sense of responsibility for her own learning and the ability and desire to continue learning independently
- Self-knowledge and the ability to assess her own performance critically and accurately
- An understanding of how to apply her knowledge and abilities in many different contexts

Essentially, our goal for students is independent lifelong learning, and the development and demonstration of specific abilities in disciplinary and inter-disciplinary contexts are a means to that end. For example, our formal requirement that students develop specific abilities in one course context and then apply them to the subject matter of other courses encourages *every* student in the college to transfer learning independently because the explicit expectation makes *every* student aware of the possibility.

Individual Abilities as Frameworks for Learning

In the educational program described above, individual abilities cannot be separated from each other or from the individual who performs them. There can be no effective social interaction, for example, without the ability to speak clearly and persuasively; one cannot respond aesthetically without a sensitivity to the values that underlie judgment.

But we make conceptual distinctions among the abilities in order to teach for them. Each ability provides a framework or a plan for students to work effectively with the subject matter of their courses. As students gain experience, they begin to draw upon various abilities they have learned and combine them in more complex ways.

Teaching and Assessing Student Abilities

In order to make these complex abilities teachable, we have articulated each one as a series of developmental levels corresponding to student progress across her college career, from general education (levels one through four) to specialized work in the majors and supporting areas of study (levels five and six). For each level of ability we have devised criteria for the ability being performed.

These criteria serve two purposes. They provide a student with a tangible goal for her learning, and they give the faculty a standard for judging and certifying that she has demonstrated the ability. These college-wide criteria are generic in the sense that they are not tied to specific courses. Each faculty member writes specific performance criteria in language appropriate to the context of specific courses. But the common understanding on the part of faculty helps to ensure that the student recognizes that the same basic ability has relevance in multiple course contexts and that she is refining her ability through multiple applications.

As a context for evaluating student demonstration of abilities, we have developed the concept of student assessment as a multidimensional process of judging the individual in action. Assessment is multidimensional, both in the sense that students have multiple opportunities to demonstrate specific abilities, and that individual assessments engage students in multiple ways—as writers, as speakers, as creators of artifacts.

In both course-based assessments and integrative assessments that focus student learning from several courses, we elicit samples of performance representing the expected learning outcomes of a course or program. Faculty and other trained assessors observe and judge a student's performance based on explicit criteria. Their diagnostic feedback, as well as the reflective practice of self assessment by each student, helps to create a continuous process that improves learning and integrates it with assessment.

General Education

Each department emphasizes the abilities most closely related to its studies and is responsible for providing learning and assessment opportunities for those abilities. In beginning courses, students develop and demonstrate levels one and two of the abilities. They continue to advance through the levels within a coherent arrangement of courses. The distribution of learning and assessment opportunities among all general education courses in the humanities, fine arts, natural and behavioral sciences as well as the introductory courses in majors and supporting areas of study, assures students of multiple opportunities to demonstrate all eight abilities through level four. And since each course beyond the introductory level carries ability prerequisites as well as course prerequisites, students are assured of taking each course when they are ready to develop the levels of abilities emphasized there.

Specialization

Each department has specified the integrated knowledge/performance expectations of advance level undergraduate specialization in its major and has related those to the appropriate general abilities of the entire college curriculum. For example, English faculty have determined that one of the outcomes they expect for their majors is to "communicate an understanding of literary criticism, question its assumptions, and use its frameworks to analyze and evaluate works." The department has made explicit connections between this outcome and communication, analysis, valuing, and aesthetic response abilities at the advanced levels.

For a major in chemistry, students must "use different models of chemistry to analyze and synthesize chemical data and to critique the data, strategies, and models of chemistry." The primary focus of these outcomes is level six of analysis—independent application of theory. But a student must also draw upon her valuing ability to critique the underlying assumptions of the theoretical models, and she must be able to communicate her analysis and criticism effectively in different modes. In essence, students at the advanced level must be able to engage all of their abilities to be effective.

This brief overview represents a curriculum in the process of ongoing development. Over the years we continue to revise our sense of the meaning of the abilities. Our insights grow from our experience of teaching them and studying how our students develop them. We expect that our ability-based curriculum will always be a "work in progress" and that we will be able to serve as models of lifelong learners for our students.

Abilities and Developmental Levels*

1. Develop communication abilities by connecting with everything involved in communication: people, ideas, texts, media, and technology

   Level 1—Identify own strengths and weaknesses as communicator

   Level 2—Demonstrate the interactive nature of communication in a variety of situations that involve combinations of speaking, writing, listening, reading, quantitative literacy, and computer literacy

---

*Alverno faculty are constantly engaged in refining and extending their understanding of the abilities and their developmental levels. If you are interested in further refinements, please contact the Alverno College Institute.

Level 3—Effectively and purposefully make meaning using a variety of communication modes (speaking, writing, listening, reading, quantitative literacy, media literacy, and computer literacy) in a given communication situation

Level 4—Communicate creatively in ways that demonstrate integration using disciplinary frameworks

In majors and areas of specialization:

Level 5—Communicate with habitual effectiveness in relation to disciplinary/professional positions or theories

Level 6—Communicate with creativity and habitual effectiveness using strategies, theories, and technology that reflect engagement in a discipline or profession

2. Develop analytical abilities

Level 1—Show observational skills

Level 2—Draw reasonable inferences from observations

Level 3—Perceive and make relationships

Level 4—Analyze structure and organization

In majors and areas of specialization:

Level 5—Establish ability to employ frameworks from area of concentration or support area discipline in order to analyze

Level 6—Master ability to employ independently the frameworks from area of concentration or support area discipline in order to analyze

3. Develop facility in using problem solving processes

Level 1—Articulate own problem solving process, making explicit the steps taken to approach the problem(s)

Level 2—Analyze the structure of discipline- or profession-based problem solving frameworks

Level 3—Use discipline- or profession-based problem solving frameworks and strategies

Level 4—Independently examine, select, use, and evaluate various approaches to develop solutions

In majors and areas of specialization:

Level 5—Collaborate in designing and implementing a problem solving process

Level 6—Solve problems in a variety of professional settings and advanced disciplinary applications

At each level, using any or all parts of a problem solving process means:

- Define the problem
- Analyze/brainstorm
- Select a strategy
- Implement a strategy
- Evaluate

4. Develop facility in making value judgments and independent decisions

Level 1—Identify own values

Level 2—Infer and analyze values in artistic and humanistic works

Level 3—Relate values to scientific and technological developments

Level 4—Engage in valuing in decision-making in multiple contexts

In majors and areas of specialization:

Level 5—Analyze and formulate the value foundation/framework of a specific area of knowledge, in its theory and practice

Level 6—Apply own theory of value and the value foundation of an area of knowledge in a professional context

5. Develop facility for social interaction

Level 1—Identify own interaction behaviors utilized in a group problem solving situation

Level 2—Analyze behavior of others within two theoretical frameworks

Level 3—Evaluate behavior of self within two theoretical frameworks

Level 4—Demonstrate effective social interaction behavior in a variety of situations and circumstances

In majors and areas of specialization:

Level 5—Demonstrate effective interpersonal and intergroup behaviors in cross-cultural interactions

Level 6—Facilitate effective interpersonal and intergroup relationships in one's professional situation

6. Develop global perspectives

Level 1—Assess own knowledge and skills to think about and act on global concerns

Level 2—Analyze global issues from multiple perspectives

Level 3—Articulate understanding of interconnected local and global issues

Level 4—Apply frameworks in formulating a response to global concerns and local issues

In majors and areas of specialization:

Level 5—Generate theoretical and pragmatic approaches to global problems, within a disciplinary or professional context

Level 6—Develop responsibility toward the global environment in others

7. Develop effective citizenship

Level 1—Assess own knowledge and skills in thinking about and acting on local issues

Level 2—Analyze community issues and develop strategies for informed response

Level 3—Evaluate personal and organizational characteristics, skills and strategies that facilitate accomplishment of mutual goals

Level 4—Apply own developing citizenship skills in a community setting

In majors and areas of specialization:

Level 5—Show ability to plan for effective change in social or professional areas

Level 6—Exercise leadership in addressing social or professional issues

8. Develop aesthetic responsiveness: involvement with the arts

Level 1—Articulate a personal response to various works of art

Level 2—Explain how personal and formal factors shape own responses to works of art

Level 3—Connect art and own responses to art to broader contexts

Level 4—Take a position on the merits of specific artistic works and reconsider own judgments about specific works as knowledge and experience change

In majors and areas of specialization:

Level 5—Choose and discuss artistic works which reflect personal vision of what it means to be human

Level 6—Demonstrate the impact of the arts on own life to this point and project their role in personal future

Materials are available for further reading on teaching for outcomes across the curriculum, on student assessment, and on ability-based curricula in major fields. Institutional and program assessment and research and evaluation studies of the value, worth, and effectiveness of the curriculum are also available from:

Alverno College Institute

3400 South 43rd Street

P.O. Box 343922

Milwaukee, WI 53234–3922

Telephone: (414) 382–6087

Fax: (414) 382-6354

E-mail: institute@alverno.edu

Webpage: www.alverno.edu

Studies of Longitudinal Perspectives Interviews with Students and Alumnae

| | Perspectives Interview Report[a] | Longitudinal Cohort and Interview Occasions | Sample | | Age |
			Persons	Interviews[b]	
1982	Much, N., & Mentkowski, M. Student perspectives on liberal learning at Alverno College: Justifying learning as relevant to performance in personal and professional roles.	Entered 1976 (weekday); students at third year (students at each year in college)[c]	13(37)[c]	13(100)[c]	17–18 at entrance (n = 13)
1983	Mentkowski, M., Much, N., & Giencke-Holl, L. Careering after college: Perspectives on lifelong learning and career development.	1978 graduating class (weekday); graduating students and as two-year alumnae	32	64	21–22 at graduation (n = 25) 23–50 at graduation (n = 7)
1983	Mentkowski, M. Career and family: Perspectives and strategies for relating personal and professional roles.	1978 graduating class (weekday); graduating students and as two-year alumnae	32	64	21–22 at graduation (n = 25) 23–50 at graduation (n = 7)
1984	Much, N., & Mentkowski, M. Student perspectives on learning and development in college.	Entered 1976/1977 (weekday); students at each year in college	47	178	17–18 at entrance (n = 47)

1985	Giencke-Holl, L., Mentkowski, M. Much, N., Mertens, S., & Rogers, G. *Evaluating college outcomes through alumnae studies: Measuring postcollege learning and abilities.*	1978 graduating class (weekday); graduating students and as two-year alumnae	32	64	21–22 at graduation ($n = 25$) 23–50 at graduation ($n = 7$)
1993	Deemer, D., *Perspectives and outcomes of five-year alumnae: Making causal links to the Alverno culture and curriculum[d]*	Entered 1976/1977 (weekday and weekend); five-year alumnae	25	25	17–18 at entrance ($n = 17$) 25–43 at entrance ($n = 8$)
1998	Mentkowski, M., Much, N., Kleinman, L., & Reisetter Hart, J. *Student and alumna learning in college and beyond: Perspectives from longitudinal interviews.*	Meta-analysis of all of the above studies plus an additional sample weekend[e]	100[f]	25	17–18 at entrance ($n = 72$) 19–46 at entrance ($n = 28$)

[a]Each report is available from Alverno College Institute.

[b]A total of 479 Perspectives Interviews were collected longitudinally over the ten-year time frame; 308 were analyzed across these studies.

[c]The number in parentheses represents the number of students contributing interviews (or the number of interviews) that were read at least twice to identify themes prior to the extensive thematic analysis. "Reading" the interview text is a complex reiterative process of documenting, revising, and verifying emerging themes. The third year was selected as the focal point for the report because it encapsulated the most intense involvement with the educational system.

[d]Deemer, D., in collaboration with the Alverno College Office of Research and Evaluation (1993, November). *Analyzing and exploring alumna perspectives in higher education assessment and evaluation* is the version of this report that includes a process and example of faculty interpretation and use of the findings.

[e]The meta-analysis includes an additional sample of thirteen selected older adults from the weekend college time frame. Analysis of the additional sample focused on forty-one interviews, including thirteen five-year alumna interviews and twenty-eight student interviews stratified across each year in college.

[f]The numbers do not add up to 100 because samples overlap.

Human Potential Measures Through Time: Means and Standard Deviations for Fully Longitudinal Data

| | | Time of Assessment | | | | | | | |
| | | Time 1 | | Time 2 | | Time 3 | | Time 4 | |
Human Potential Measure	N	Mean	S.D.	Mean	S.D.	Mean	S.D.	Mean	S.D.
Measure of Intellectual Development[a]									
Essay A: Best Class	141	3.2	(1.0)	3.5	(1.2)	3.7	(1.3)	4.3	(1.6)
Essay B: Recent Decision	140	3.5	(1.0)	3.7	(1.1)	3.8	(1.3)	4.4	(1.3)
Essay C: Career Choice	126	3.1	(1.2)	3.3	(1.1)	3.5	(1.1)	4.4	(1.5)
Sentence Completion Test[b]	153	5.4	(0.8)	5.3	(1.0)	5.3	(1.0)	5.7	(1.0)
Moral Judgment Interview[c]	32	345.9	(34.5)	347.0	(31.2)	355.3	(25.7)	359.9	(27.2)
Stages of Adaptation (Integrative)	100	51.5	(8.6)	49.5	(10.3)	47.9	(9.4)	49.6	(9.9)
Defining Issues Test[d]	91	38.8	(13.8)	46.3	(15.0)	49.9	(14.2)	50.4	(15.5)
Test of Cognitive Development	38	11.1	(4.1)	12.6	(4.2)	12.6	(4.9)	12.9	(4.6)
Critical Thinking Appraisal									
Inference	135	9.6	(3.0)	10.2	(3.0)	10.4	(3.2)	10.9	(3.0)
Recognition of Assumptions	135	11.2	(2.3)	11.1	(2.5)	11.6	(2.8)	11.8	(2.5)
Deduction	135	16.2	(3.0)	16.5	(3.4)	17.1	(3.1)	17.6	(3.2)
Test of Thematic Analysis (DAC)[e]	133	1.0	(0.9)	1.0	(0.9)	0.9	(0.8)	0.7	(0.8)
Learning Style Inventory									
ACCE[f]	168	-0.7	(5.0)	1.8	(5.8)	2.4	(5.9)	3.2	(5.4)
AERO[g]	168	0.7	(5.2)	2.5	(6.2)	2.8	(6.0)	4.1	(6.0)

Note: Reported means include only data from participants who completed the instrument on each of four occasions of assessment.
[a]Separate means for population group main effects are not shown.
[b]Total protocol rating.
[c]Written form of interview. Weighted average moral maturity score.
[d]P percent score. Excludes protocols with "meaningless and inconsistent" responses.
[e]Develop and Articulate Categories.
[f]Abstract Conceptualization minus Concrete Experience. Separate means for Population Group × Time interaction are not shown.
[g]Active Experimentation minus Reflective Observation. Separate means for population group main effect are not shown.

Appendix D

Causal Modeling and Measurement Specifications

This appendix addresses issues of measurement reliability, measurement model specifications, and sensitivity analyses in the causal modeling of change across the human potential measures.

Measurement Reliability for Longitudinal Indicators

In the context of statistical analyses, reliability is one key component to validity in measurement. Evaluation of reliability findings from other research has the advantage of giving independent evidence for what are probable estimates of measurement error. Measurement error, the opposite of reliability, may have many sources. Although the LISREL models reported in Chapter Four statistically account for error, the plausibility of these LISREL estimates of reliability for multiple indicators and of our judgments that specify error for single indicators can be evaluated in relation to other evidence for measurement reliability. (For the reliability indices we are reporting here, the scale values theoretically range between 0 and 1—that is, no reliability and perfect reliability.)

Estimates of reliability based on our own sample have the virtue of establishing the evidence base for the quality of measurement achieved in our formal research effort. Of particular interest are the estimates of reliability for open-ended measures, because reliability is often harder to achieve for these kinds of measures. For open-ended measures, two kinds of reliability accounting for two distinct potential sources of error in measurement are of special concern: alpha, which examines consistency of responses across test items, and inter-rater reliability, which examines the degree to which judges agree on the coding of responses for measures with open-ended responses.

With the fourth wave of longitudinal data collection, we rescored the open-ended data, interleaving data from each of the four times of data collection to prevent rater drift. The SCT, however, was rescored only for a random subsample of the first three waves of assessment ($n = 75$), which demonstrated no measurable rater drift (Reisetter Hart & Mentkowski, 1994). With rescoring of the SCT, MID (Reisetter Hart, Rickards, & Mentkowski, 1993), and TCD, we are able to report inter-rater reliability *between* the consensus judgments of two independent scoring teams. Although the TTA also used multiple scorers within and across time, scorers did not systematically engage in a face-to-face consensus process, and so we can report inter-rater reliability only between independent individual scorers.

Estimates of inter-rater reliability (Pearson r) summarized across the three times of assessment that were rescored varied considerably by instrument: SCT (.94), TCD (.84), MID "best class" essay A (.82), MID "career" essay (.78), MID "recent decision" essay (.75), TTA egocentric affect (.72), MJI weighted average score (.69), TTA clear direct contrasts (.56), and TTA develop and articulate categories (.51). Although the estimate of inter-rater reliability for the SCT appears to exceed those for the MID essays (cf. Mentkowski, Miller, Davies, Monroe, & Popovic, 1981; Mentkowski, Moeser, & Strait, 1983) and the SCT internal consistency is quite high (average =.89), LISREL estimated more error in the SCT than in the MID essays. Nonetheless, this seems plausible given the relatively low one-year test-retest reliability estimates reported by other researchers (Gfellner, 1986; Loevinger et al., 1985). In general, reliability estimates for the TTA subscales are low enough to be of concern (see Rogers & Schwan Minik, 1994), and so we have relatively less confidence in the TTA as a precise measure of critical thinking abilities. The MJI inter-rater reliability was lower than other published research; one possible reason is that in rescoring all of the data from the first three waves of data collection, we chose to use the latest version of the scoring manual (Colby et al., 1987).

Although we have multi-indicators that make up Critical Thinking and Integration of Self in Context, the DIT serves as a single indicator for the Moral Reasoning construct across the four waves of data collection. Thus, it is of particular importance to estimate the reliability of the DIT in relation to estimates from prior research. Estimates of test-retest reliability are especially desirable because they provide information on how sensitive test scores are to contaminating influences such as participant mood or administration conditions (McAdams, 1986). Rest (1979a, 1979b) provides estimates of both inter-item consistency (.77) and test-retest reliability (.82) for samples somewhat similar to our own. We set a fixed error at about .21 in our causal models, implying a reliability of .79. Other single indicators in the model rely on measures constructed specifically in the context of this study. Therefore, we tested the sensitivity of the final student and alumna models in relation to alternative plausible estimates of error.

Technical Specifications of the LISREL Measurement Model

All statistical analyses assume a statistical model. Structural equation modeling enables the researcher to set and test these for plausibility and to examine the overall fit of the model.

Specification of Correlated Error and Equal Measurement

Modeling involves making several decisions based on knowledge of the data and the performance of the model. For constructs modeled in both the student and alumna models, we made identical assumptions. In both models, we asked LISREL to estimate the error in the SCT, TCD, and the three CTA scales and the relationship of these indicators to their latent constructs. For each of these indicators, we set an equal measurement model across time, which enabled us to estimate correlated error in the indicators across time. Seven of these ten estimates of correlated error in the two models were statistically significant, suggesting the need to model them as we did. Initially we also similarly modeled correlated error across time for the three MID essays. None of these approached statistical significance, however, and we became concerned about potential correlated error within time of assessment for the MID. In particular, we noted that LISREL estimated the SCT to be less reliable than the MID, and this ran counter to some of our own estimates of reliability (see above). The three MID essays share a similar format distinct from the SCT, and we reasoned that they might therefore also share method-specific measurement error. In order to enable LISREL to estimate correlated error for three MID essays within time of assessment, we set them as equal indicators within time of assessment. This seemed reasonable given the overlap in scoring criteria, the similar length of the essays, and the similar LISREL estimates of their value when each was separately estimated. Although the results did not support our suspicion of correlated error due to common format, we retained this approach to correlated error, since cross-time correlated error was equally a nonfactor.

Although we were able to use a common approach to specifying estimates in the student and alumna models where they overlapped, the alumna model added multiple indicator measures of breadth of preparation and breadth of learning goals five years later. We set an equal measurement model for interpersonal ability and civic and cultural appreciation, as two indicators of preparation and as two separately measured indicators of learning goals of five-year alumna. In other words, they were set equal within time and across the two latent constructs. We did this because they seemed similar in reliability and content, and model estimation is generally improved if some reasonable constraints can be placed on the model. Cross-time tests of correlated error for the indicators of breadth of preparation did not approach statistical significance (t values < 1).

Sensitivity Analyses

For single-indicator constructs, we had to specify measurement error, and in some cases, reliability information was not available from prior research. We conducted sensitivity analyses aimed at determining whether the estimations in the model were stable across differing assumptions of reliability by rerunning the model with a range of plausible error specifications. For the student model, we estimated error in progress in the curriculum at 17 percent as well as at 35 percent, and replicated all of the findings in the model. For the alumna model, we found some minor differences in the model with differing specifications of error in the single indicators. When we specified 25 percent error, instead of 50 percent, in the indicator for breadth of activities, we found that the path from Integration of Self to breadth of activities dropped from .40 to .31, falling just below statistical significance, $t = 1.95$. At the same time, the stability coefficient for Integration of Self increased to .67 from .61, and, as would be expected, breadth of activities was estimated to have a smaller (though still significant) effect on breadth of learning goals (from .52 to .40) and on Integration of Self (from .38 to .26). Those interested in more details may contact the Office of Educational Research and Evaluation at Alverno College.

Model Fit

Measurement specialists have created a range of indices that attempt to scale descriptively how well the overall model mathematically fits the data, recognizing that it will not completely fit. Two widely used indices are goodness of fit (GFI) and adjusted goodness of fit (AGFI). A value of 0 on these means the model does not at all fit the data, and a value of 1 indicates it completely fits the data. For the student causal model, GFI was .92 and AGFI was .89, and for the alumna model GFI was .85 and AGFI was .82.

Loadings on Ability Factors from Behavioral Event Interviews in Paid Employment Settings

438

| | Ability Factor | | | |
Ability	I *Collaborative Organizational Thinking and Action*	II *Balanced Self Assessment and Acting from Values*	III *Developing Others and Perspective Taking*	IV *Analytic Thinking and Action*
Developing organizational influence	.64	.06	-.21	.31
Achievement action	.62	.15	.11	.09
Conceptualization	.61	.09	-.10	.29
Diagnostic pattern recognition	.54	.17	.12	.32
Systematic planning	.52	-.12	-.17	.15
Social process conceptualization	.49	-.14	.17	.15
Initiative	.48	.08	.12	.11
Concern with achievement	.47	.37	.15	.00
Collaborative organizational action	.42	-.06	.18	.14
Considering alternatives	.39	.10	.11	.08
Formal communication	.37	.21	.10	-.14
Ego strength	.36	.14	.08	.05
Commitment to improve	-.07	.60	.04	.18
Reflective thinking	-.03	.58	.07	.12
Self assessment of abilities	.21	.49	.21	.22
Developing self	.08	.46	-.12	.02
Reflective valuing	.21	.40	.16	.02

Correlations of Ability Factors with Human Potential Measures: Five-Year Alumnae

Human Potential Measure	N	Ability Factor			
		I Collaborative Organizational Thinking and Action	II Balanced Self Assessment and Acting from Values	III Developing Others and Perspective Taking	IV Analytic Thinking and Action
Measure of Intellectual Development	142				
Best Class (A)		.16	.04	.04	.11
Recent Decision (B)		.29**	.07	.04	.11
Career Choice (C)		.26**	.20*	.17*	.19*
Sentence Completion Test[a]	144	.10	.15	.07	.12
Moral Judgment Interview[b]	50	.33*	.09	-.02	.09
Defining Issues Test[c]	123	.27**	-.06	-.02	.09
Test of Cognitive Development	142	.08	-.06	.07	-.01
Critical Thinking Appraisal[d]	144	.29***	.04	-.04	.05
Test of Thematic Analysis	137				
Develop and Articulate Categories		.16	.15	-.10	.12
Clear and Direct Contrasts		.09	.03	.14	-.04
Egocentric Affect		.01	-.02	.16	-.06
Stages of Adaptation	139				
Receptive		-.13	-.05	.07	-.07
Autonomous		.10	.08	.01	.08
Assertive		.00	-.07	-.04	.03
Integrative		.17	.17*	-.03	.06
Learning Style Inventory	148				
ACCE[e]		.11	.04	.05	.07
AERO[f]		.15	.10	.12	.12

Note: Correlations are for alumnae who reported paid employment as their primary activity. Factor informed ability scales weight developmentally advanced abilities more than abilities that are necessary but less advanced.
[a]Total protocol rating.
[b]Weighted average moral maturity score.
[c]P percent score. Excludes protocols with "meaningless and inconsistent" responses.
[d]Total score for three subscales.
[e]Abstract Conceptualization minus Concrete Experience.
[f]Active Experimentation minus Reflective Observation.
*$p < .05$; **$p < .01$; ***$p < .001$.

Deliberative Inquiry Process for Thinking Through Principles for Learning That Lasts

Learning and action principles are one part of Alverno's educational theory of learning that lasts. The deliberative inquiry process that undergirds the learning and action principles in Chapter Seven is a sustained activity with structured conversations at key points. It is designed to articulate learning principles that are comprehensive and transferable and examples of action principles that are situated in practice yet transportable.

Criteria for the Conversation

A deliberative process involves an evidence-based discourse based on analyses of literature, findings on student learning outcomes, faculty and staff publications and documents, and transcribed conversations. It is connected to practical questions and common tasks, iterative and feasible within and across roles, and inclusive of faculty and staff at various levels of expertise, experience, and practice. For example, the participants in the conversation in Chapter Seven had various levels of experience at Alverno College in the following tasks: determining learning outcomes and developmental performance criteria; designing curriculum elements across a college and within disciplines and professions; creating and using assessment theory, process, plans, instruments, and validation strategies; and collaborating with faculty and staff at other institutions.

The Deliberative Process

To pursue such an evidence-based inquiry collaboratively, we brought together nine sources of evidence in a semester-long inquiry of Alverno's and other learning principles and incorporated more recent ideas into the principles. We then used *thinking through learning principles* and *generating action principles,* a portion of the design in Figure 7.1, to facilitate a two-hour conversation about learning that bears on teaching by faculty and academic personnel from across this college.

1. We began with the faculty's published learning principles (Alverno College Faculty, 1979/1994).
2. We began a revision of the learning principles by excerpting and then analyzing previous faculty and staff publications at this college over the past ten years, to create a broad synthesis of these educators' emerging thinking about learning. Thus, this process made explicit the current thinking that was grounded in prior faculty inquiry and teaching practices. This review of prior writing, and tacit and expressed understanding of current student learning drawn from reports of seven standing and ad hoc committees, stimulated us to think about more recent ideas in relation to prior faculty and staff work (just as an educator expects learners to do as they build on their prior learning).
3. Concurrently, we identified and reviewed other principles about learning from outside groups, other writings about learning that faculty and staff had already encountered in their inquiry and practice, and the most recent literature. Many of these sources are cited in this book.
4. Working in dyads, we began to integrate the above first, second, and third sources with emerging understanding gained from Alverno's formal research, collaborative inquiry, and literature review on student and alumna learning, as reflected in Chapters Three through Five, including Alverno's emerging educational theory of integrated learning and domains of growth (Chapter Six). Of the theory's four pathways for growth, we particularly focused on transformative cycles of learning.

5. We deliberated as an author group, debating key observations each dyad offered and audiotaping, transcribing, and analyzing these conversations for common themes, patterns, and unique insights. The result was seven expanded and refined principles for learning that lasts that extend the faculty's previously published learning principles.

6. Faculty and staff tested these extended learning principles through a two-hour "conversation about learning as it bears on teaching" (Alverno Institute, May 21, 1998) and a similar three-hour session for professional staff advisors (Alverno College Advising Department, June 12, 1998). The purpose of each conversation was to incorporate faculty and staff *learning by educating* as a fourth way of knowing (see Chapter Two) by critiquing the principles and generating and recording action principles. To ensure cross-disciplinary debates, each conversation was framed by an activity in which 110 faculty and academic staff members participated in twenty-one multidisciplinary teams of 4 to 7 persons each. Each team deliberated on one of the expanded learning principles. To deliberate, each team reviewed a prepared synthesis of the most recent faculty writing relevant to that principle, evidence from our semester-long inquiry, and findings from the formal research program (with emphasis on conclusions from Chapter Six). Each team then generated its own related action principles, explicitly drawing on additional evidence from their practice and other sources. Each team also recorded specific connections to or differences from the evidence in the prepared synthesis—to distinguish cited evidence from expressed, tacit, or conflicting knowledge about current students and teaching practice. The learning principles in Chapter Seven incorporate these critiques and so extended the principles from six to seven.

7. Following the team discussions in the two-hour conversation using a portion of the design in Figure 7.1, the action principles were assembled, coded for blind review, entered into a master list, and analyzed to estimate the general character and variability of the responses. For each learning principle, five to ten distinct action principles were developed that represent the range of responses, to serve as a sample for Chapter Seven. To

reflect individual faculty and staff voices in conversation, action principles were elaborated with direct quotations.

8. In order to illustrate one learning principle in depth—*learning that lasts is developmental and individual, transitional and transformative*—and to show how one department might generate action principles for a particular role and context (advising beginning students), seven professional staff advisors used the design during their year-end retreat. Their three-hour conversation was recorded, transcribed, analyzed, edited, and excerpted with the further involvement of the advisors (see Exhibit 7.1) as an example of a language of learning in use, showing how advising and teaching are linked in experience and context (Alverno College Advising Department, 1998).

9. To extend the work to the level of collaborative authorship, selected members of the all-faculty group, for example, the seven-member learning-in-context committee, and others reviewed sequential drafts of Chapter Seven. Written feedback was elaborated orally, and feedback sessions were taped and transcribed. We revised and edited the chapter for clarity over several months. The advising department also met to judge the adequacy and accuracy of the edited conversation and to review and shape the edited transcript for clarification.

Developing Perspectives of Students on Self Assessment, Using Feedback, Commitment to Improvement, and Role of Criteria

Developing Perspectives Leading to Taking Responsibility for Learning and Using Different Ways of Learning.

Self Assessment	Using Feedback	Commitment to Improvement
Beginning Student		
• Makes judgments on her own behavior when someone else points out concrete evidence to her	• At this point, experiences evaluation of her performance as general affirmation or rejection of herself	• Knows she should improve, wants to improve, tries to improve in quality ways
• Recognizes that her attitudes affect her work	• Her emotional response to evaluation, as of yet, interferes with insight into her performance	• Recognizes negative attitudes; expresses willingness to change
• Recognizes contradictory evaluations of her work	• Can connect feedback received to subsequent classroom experience	
• Expects the teacher to take the initiative in recognizing her problems and approaching her about them		
• Responds to divergent values with self assessment insights		
Developing Student		
• Senses when her own performance in a given situation is essentially competent or incompetent	• Sees the value in separating emotional response to feedback from more objective stance	• Thinks about how to improve
• Aware that the learning process requires a change in approach to learning	• Sees that feedback on strengths and weaknesses provides explicit information on progress and success	• Builds on her strengths
• Knows her strengths	• Accepts criticism and suggestions and follows through	• Sees that criteria given ahead of time tell you what to learn and what to do
• Reflects on a given performance as representative of a pattern in her own behavior		• Motivated to achieve by explicit criteria
• Sees criteria as a framework for feedback and self assessment		• Performs well in structured situations; follows through if there are external demands
• Sees criteria as providing a picture of the ability to perform		• Completes assignments in weak areas; is becoming aware of her weaknesses

- Compares self to self, rather than just self to others
- Achieves sufficient awareness of self to assess her own abilities and how they contribute to a situation (rather than an undifferentiated sense of how "she" contributed)

- Sees own abilities apart from a given situation
- Sees abilities as frameworks for performing and criteria as a picture of the ability for performing and self assessment
- Emphasizes reliance on self-evaluation and self assessment
- Consistently applies self-awareness of self (therefore has more knowledge of her abilities and acts accordingly)
- Shapes her aspirations realistically, commensurate with her abilities
- Gives evidence of internalizing standards of self assessment
- Sets personal standards out of her expectations of her professional needs
- Shows interest in her ability relative to other professionals

Advanced Student

- Seeks out formative evaluation of her work (doesn't just wait for someone else's summative evaluation)
- Self-applies formative evaluations of her work
- Acts on feedback
- Expects feedback that helps her take charge
- Expects feedback that helps her see patterns and relationships to her performance in other ability areas

- Knows what she needs to do to improve
- Consistently makes an effort to improve processes
- Uses resources to help her improve processes
- Takes initiative to improve her work, finds help when she needs it

Source: Adapted from Alverno College Faculty (1979/1994). The Alverno College council for student assessment drew this framework from research on Alverno students completed by the college's office of educational research and evaluation (Much & Mentkowski, 1984) and the department of business and management.

Developing Perspectives for Student Understanding of Independent Learning and Self Assessment.

Criteria Make Independent Learning Possible	Criteria Make Self Assessment Possible
from content to abilities	from grades to criteria
from vague to explicit to flexible interpretation	from quantity to quality
from external to internal self assessment	from opinion to evidence

Beginning Student

Criteria Make Independent Learning Possible	Criteria Make Self Assessment Possible
• Sees learning objectives as vague directions for what to learn • Finds explicit directions too picky	• Sees assessor judgments as arbitrary and vague and dependent on factors beyond own and assessor's control • Finds explicit assessment criteria too picky
• Sees learning objectives as directions for how much content to learn	• Sees assessor judgments as based on standards for how much to learn • Sees number or letter grades as the standards for how close you are to learning enough of the right answers
• Sees competencies or abilities as directions for what to do • Asks for explicit directions for what to do to perform, to get validated, or to "pass"	• Sees criteria as feedback on strengths and weaknesses but as vague with little meaning for "passing"
	• Sees that assessor judgments are based on criteria, but finds interpretation of criteria arbitrary and vague and dependent on personal opinion of the assessor and self • Often doesn't understand why validated or not
	• Sees criteria expressed as percentage of correct response • Worries about motivation to achieve where can pass by just getting by

Developing Student

- Sees that criteria given ahead of time tell you what to learn and what to do
- Asks for explicit learning objectives and criteria
- Sees abilities as steps in a process that you use in school and personal life

- Sees learning as a process (you learn how to learn and it does not disappear afterward)

- Sees criteria as providing a picture of the ability to perform

- Sees that feedback on strengths and weaknesses provides explicit information on progress and success
- Sees criteria as a framework for feedback and self assessment

- Asks for explicit criteria
- Motivated to achieve by explicit criteria
- Rejects grades as a source of information on progress and success

- Sees criteria for assessment as more flexible and ambiguous, as more open to interpretation

Advanced Student

- Sees criteria as one part of a process for learning and assessment
- Sees abilities as frameworks for performing and criteria as a picture of the ability for performing and for self assessment
- Sees criteria as a cognitive framework for learning that enables transfer of learning
- Sees criteria as being met in more ways than one, and uses in a flexible way to guide independent learning
- Sees criteria as internalized and uses for self assessment
- Creates own criteria

Source: Adapted from Alverno College Faculty (1979/1994). The Alverno College council for student assessment drew the framework from research on Alverno College students completed by the college's office of educational research and evaluation (Much & Mentkowski, 1984). A slide-tape of student examples illustrates this framework of student perspectives.

Student and Two-Year Alumna Perspectives on Learning Outcomes and Causal Attributions to Alverno Curriculum

Student Perspectives on Learning	Two-Year Alumna Perspectives on Learning	Student Learning Outcomes and Their Causal Attributions
Self-sustained learning is a process of: • Experiencing • Reflecting • Forming new concepts • Testing one's judgment and abilities in action	Self-sustained learning is a process of: • Experiencing learning as a continuous process • Tying knowledge, theory, and experience to productive action • Applying abilities in action, getting a response, and adjusting accordingly • Accurately self assessing • Integrating and adapting abilities • Thinking and performing in context	• Students attributed instructor attention and empathy, feedback, and self assessment as causes for their taking responsibility for their own learning. • Similarly, students found that experiential validation and instructor coaching as well as emphases on professional applications and the integration of abilities were instrumental in their making relationships between abilities and their use in a range of contexts. • To the extent that the curriculum provided them with practice opportunities, experience in working with feedback, modeling, and peer learning, students developed the capacity to use different ways of learning. • Students found the learning experiences in the curriculum overall to be particularly helpful in assisting their development of abilities integrated with content; the development of skills, capacities, and strategies for self assessment; the capacity to think analytically; and to think and act independently.

Sources: Giencke-Holl, Mentkowski, Much, Mertens, & Rogers (1985); Mentkowski, Much, & Giencke-Holl (1983); Much & Mentkowski (1982, 1984).

Five-Year Alumna Perspectives on Learning Outcomes and Causal Attributions to Alverno Curriculum and Culture

Alumna-Attributed Causes in the Curriculum →	Alumna Perspectives on Learning Outcomes	Alumna-Attributed Causes in the College Culture →	Alumna Perspectives on Learning Outcomes
• Experiential, individualized, sequential, active learning processes • Teaching as coaching, individualized attention, modeling, and positive regard • Performance assessment with criteria, feedback, self assessment • Off-campus experiential learning with internships, placements • Learning structured around collaborative activities and reasoning about small group process • Processes for developing willingness and ability for independent learning; expectation of responsibility for own learning and press for efficacy and efficiency • Organization toward the development of abilities integrated with content: Communication, Analysis, Problem Solving, Valuing in	• Internalized performance assessment toward self-awareness, goal setting, continuous improvement, self-confidence • Internalized abilities toward lifelong, independent learning such as: – Effective social interaction and communication – Internalized small group processes – Communicating effectively in various media and contexts – Problem solving, analysis: looking at the whole, not just the parts in isolation; learning to look at something from different angles, analyze it, take action – Valuing: being aware of values for oneself and others, thinking through and weighing values and value frameworks in making decisions and	• An environment organized toward excellence with high expectations and efficacy messages • Climate that encourages voice • Collaborative orientation of the college with positive regard, collaborative thinking and learning, and shared responsibility with faculty and staff, external assessors and mentors, and peers • Climate that encourages trust • Atmosphere of acceptance, support, respect • Personal attention, individualized learning, and variable learning pace	• Self-expression, exploration, risk taking • Experience of personal growth toward self-awareness, self-respect, efficacy, risk taking, emotional stamina • Internalized value of collaboration • Concern for others • Leadership • Integrated multiple involvements in academic, personal, work, and civic roles

Decision-Making; Social Interaction
- Broad areas of liberal arts contents
- Speaking and writing instruction and practice

- solving problems
- Decision making; setting priorities, goals
- Understanding the liberal arts toward broadened perspectives
- Perspective taking: understanding differing points of view on issues or problems while interacting around course content
- Self-awareness, self-expression, self assessment
- Reflecting, self-reflection, questioning the self regarding goals and direction, using a self-analysis process, reflecting on events
- Strategies for study and memory organizing techniques (for example, outlining, diagraming, mapping); planning, organizing, gathering, and using information; constructing one's own understanding of information; asking questions when needed

Source: Based on Deemer (1993) and Mentkowski, Much, Kleinman, and Reisetter Hart (1998).

Appendix K

Participating Institutions in Selected Consortia

Network for Innovation in Critical Thinking: Psychology Network (Halonen, 1986), funded by a grant to Alverno College from the Fund for the Improvement of Post Secondary Education, U.S. Department of Education (1983–1985)

Participating Institutions

Alverno College, Milwaukee, Wisconsin

Doane College, Crete, Nebraska

Illinois College, Jacksonville, Illinois

Kamehameha Secondary School, Honolulu, Hawaii

McKendree College, Lebanon, Illinois

Our Lady of the Lake University, San Antonio, Texas

University of Houston, Houston, Texas

University of Wisconsin–Green Bay, Green Bay, Wisconsin

Western Carolina University, Cullowhee, North Carolina

Network for Innovation in Critical Thinking: Arts and Humanities Network (Cromwell, 1986), funded by a grant to Alverno College from the Fund for the Improvement of Post Secondary Education, U.S. Department of Education (1983–1985)

Participating Institutions

Alverno College, Milwaukee, Wisconsin

Clayton College and State University, Morrow, Georgia

College of St. Catherine, St. Paul, Minnesota

Doane College, Crete, Nebraska

East Texas State University, Marshall, Texas

Northland Community College, Thief River Falls, Minnesota

University of Louisville, Louisville, Kentucky

University of Puerto Rico, Rio Piedras, Puerto Rico

Ursuline College, Cleveland, Ohio

Faculty Consortium for Assessment Design (Schulte & Loacker, 1994), funded by a grant to Alverno College from the Fund for the Improvement of Post Secondary Education, U.S. Department of Education

Participating Institutions

Alverno College, Milwaukee, Wisconsin

Bethany College, Lindsborg, Kansas

Brenau University, Gainesville, Georgia

Brigham Young University, Provo, Utah

Capital University, Columbus, Ohio

Clayton College and State University, Morrow, Georgia

Gallaudet University, Washington, D.C.

Glassboro State College, Glassboro, New Jersey

Holyoke Community College, Holyoke, Massachusetts

Kean College of New Jersey, Union, New Jersey

Macomb Community College, Warren, Michigan

Manchester Community Technical College, Manchester, Connecticut

Marshalltown Community College, Marshalltown, Iowa

Mercy College of Detroit, Detroit, Michigan

Millsaps College, Jackson, Mississippi

Mohawk College, Hamilton, Ontario, Canada

Mount St. Clare College, Clinton, Iowa

Pennsylvania College of Technology, Williamsport, Pennsylvania

Purdue University School of Pharmacy and Pharmacal Sciences, West Lafayette, Indiana

St. John Fisher University, Rochester, New York

Selma University, Selma, Alabama

Spalding University, Louisville, Kentucky

University of Cincinnati, Cincinnati, Ohio

University of Montevallo, Montevallo, Alabama

Consortium for the Improvement of Teaching, Learning and Assessment (1992), funded by a grant to Alverno College from the W.K. Kellogg Foundation (1989–1992)

Participating Institutions

Alverno College, Milwaukee, Wisconsin

Bloomfield Hills Model High School, Bloomfield Hills, Michigan

Central Missouri State University, Warrensburg, Missouri

Clayton College and State University, Morrow, Georgia

Gallaudet University, Washington, D.C.

Macomb Community College, Warren, Michigan

Purdue University School of Pharmacy and Pharmacal Sciences, West Lafayette, Indiana

South Division High School, Milwaukee, Wisconsin

Township High School District 214, Arlington Heights, Illinois

University of New Mexico School of Medicine, Albuquerque, New Mexico

University of Wisconsin Medical School, Madison, Wisconsin

Teaching for Tomorrow Project (Diez, 1998), funded by grants to Alverno College from the Philip Morris Companies, Inc.

Participating Institutions

Alverno College, Milwaukee, Wisconsin

Clayton College and State University, Morrow, Georgia

University of Northern Colorado, Greeley, Colorado

Winston-Salem State University, Winston-Salem, North Carolina

National Center for Restructuring Education, School, and Teaching (NCREST) Study of Departments of Education (Darling-Hammond, 1997), sponsored by the National Commission on Teaching and America's Future

Participating Institutions

Alverno College, Milwaukee, Wisconsin

Bank Street College, New York, New York

Trinity University, San Antonio, Texas

University of California at Berkeley, Berkeley, California

University of Southern Maine, Portland, Maine

University of Virginia, Charlottesville, Virginia

Wheelock College, Boston, Massachusetts

American Productivity & Quality Center (APQC): Benchmarking Study on Institutional Performance (1997), funded by Study Sponsors

Study Sponsors

California State University System

Cornell University, Ithaca, New York

Fashion Institute of Technology, New York, New York

Florida Board of Regents

Hunter College, City University of New York, New York, New York

Mississippi State University, Mississippi State, Mississippi

North Carolina State University, Raleigh, North Carolina

SCT (Systems & Computer Technology)

State University of New York at Cortland, Cortland, New York

University of Missouri–Columbia, Columbia, Missouri

University of Missouri–Rolla, Rolla, Missouri

Virginia Polytechnic Institute and University, Polacksburg, Virginia

Westark Community College, Arkansas, Fort Smith, Arkansas

Winona State University, Winona, Minnesota

Best Practice Partner Organizations

Alverno College, Milwaukee, Wisconsin

Indiana University–Purdue University Indianapolis (IUPUI), Indianapolis, Indiana

Raytheon T. I. Systems (RTIS), Lewisville, Texas

Truman State University, Kirksville, Missouri

University of Central England (UCE), Birmingham, England

University of Phoenix, Phoenix, Arizona

Pew Leadership Award for the Renewal of Undergraduate Education, funded by The Pew Charitable Trusts (1997)

Participating Institutions

Alverno College, Milwaukee, Wisconsin

Babson College, Babson Park, Massachusetts

Eastern New Mexico University, Portales, New Mexico

Mount St. Mary's College, Los Angeles, California

Portland State University, Portland, Oregon

Rensselaer Polytechnic Institute, Troy, New York

W.K. Kellogg Forum on Higher Education Transformation, funded by the W.K. Kellogg Foundation (1996–1999)

Participating Institutions

Alverno College, Milwaukee, Wisconsin

Minnesota State Colleges and Universities

Olivet College, Olivet, Michigan

Portland State University, Portland, Oregon

University of Arizona, Tucson, Arizona

Additional Participants

American Council on Education, Washington, D.C.

New England Resource Center for Higher Education, University of Massachusetts, Boston, Massachusetts

University of California at Los Angeles: Higher Education Research Institute, Los Angeles, California

University of Michigan: Center for the Study of Postsecondary and Higher Education, Ann Arbor, Michigan

W.K. Kellogg Foundation, Battle Creek, Michigan

Ability Based Curriculum (ABC) Network (Otter, 1997), one of the thirty-four discipline networks set up by the United Kingdom Department for Education and Employment in 1986, for people with a common interest in developing key capabilities—key skills—in higher education

Participating Institutions

Alverno College, Milwaukee, Wisconsin

Brunel University, Uxbridge, England

De Montfort University, Leicester, England

Napier University, Edinburgh, Scotland

Northumbria University, Newcastle Upon Tyne, England

Open University, Milton Keynes, England

Oxford Brookes University, Oxford, England

Surrey University, Surrey, England

University of North London, London, England

Wolverhampton University, Wolverhampton, England

References

Adorno, T. W., Frenkel-Brunswik, E., Levinson, D. J., & Sanford, R. N. (1950). *The authoritarian personality*. New York: HarperCollins.

Albanese, M. A., & Mitchell, S. (1993). Problem-based learning: A review of literature on its outcomes and implementation issues. *Academic Medicine, 68*(1), 52–81.

Alexander, P. A. (1992). Domain knowledge: Evolving themes and emerging concerns. *Educational Psychologist, 27*(1), 33–51.

Alverno College. (1997). *The Alverno educator's handbook*. Milwaukee, WI: Alverno College Institute.

Alverno College Advising Department. (1998). *Generating learning and action principles in role and context: A discussion by professional staff advisors*. Milwaukee, WI: Alverno College Institute.

Alverno College Assessment Committee/Office of Research and Evaluation. (1983). *Validating assessment techniques in an outcome-centered liberal arts curriculum: Six performance characteristics ratings*. Milwaukee, WI: Alverno Productions. (ERIC Document Reproduction Service No. ED 239 562)

Alverno College Commission on Education in the 21st Century. (1994). *Report of the Alverno College Commission on Education in the 21st Century*. Milwaukee, WI: Author.

Alverno College Curriculum Committee. (1998). *Taking a curriculum perspective: A faculty conversation*. Milwaukee, WI: Alverno College Institute.

Alverno College Education Faculty. (1996). *Ability-based learning program: Teacher education* [brochure]. Milwaukee, WI: Alverno College Institute.

Alverno College Educators. (1977/1998). *Faculty handbook on learning and assessment*. Milwaukee, WI: Alverno College Institute. (Original work published 1977, revised 1986, 1991, 1992, 1996, 1997, and 1998)

Alverno College Faculty. (1973/1996). *Ability-based learning program* [brochure]. Milwaukee, WI: Alverno College Institute. (Original work published 1973, revised 1980, 1983, 1985, 1988, 1991, 1992, 1993, 1994, and 1996)

Alverno College Faculty. (1976/1992). *Liberal learning at Alverno College.* Milwaukee, WI: Alverno College Institute. (Original work published 1976, revised 1981, 1985, 1989, and 1992)

Alverno College Faculty. (1979/1994). *Student assessment-as-learning at Alverno College.* Milwaukee, WI: Alverno College Institute. (Original work published 1979, revised 1985 and 1994)

Alverno College Faculty. (1992). *Valuing in decision-making: Theory and practice at Alverno College.* Milwaukee, WI: Alverno College Institute.

Alverno College Faculty. (2000). *Student self assessment at Alverno College.* Milwaukee, WI: Alverno College Institute.

Alverno College History Faculty. (1994). *Ability-based learning program: The history major* [brochure]. Milwaukee, WI: Alverno College Institute.

Alverno College Intermediate Student Study Committee. (1994). *Improving the efficiency and effectiveness of teaching and learning of struggling intermediate students at Alverno College: A pilot project.* Milwaukee, WI: Alverno College Institute.

Alverno College Mathematics Faculty. (1999). *Ability-based learning program: The mathematics major* [brochure]. Milwaukee, WI: Alverno College Institute.

Alverno College Nursing Faculty. (1999). *Ability-based learning program: Nursing education* [brochure]. Milwaukee, WI: Alverno College Institute.

Alverno College Office of Academic Affairs. (1997a). *An institution in process.* Unpublished manuscript available from Alverno College, 3400 South 43rd Street, Milwaukee, WI 53234–3922.

Alverno College Office of Academic Affairs. (1997b). *Partners in learning: Staff collaboration in promoting student learning across the college.* Unpublished manuscript available from Alverno College, 3400 South 43rd Street, Milwaukee, WI 53234–3922.

Alverno College Office of Academic Affairs. (1997c). *Institutional transformation.* Unpublished manuscript available from Alverno College, 3400 South 43rd Street, Milwaukee, WI 53234–3922.

Alverno College Office of Academic Affairs. (1998). *How institutional transformation works and becomes visible.* Milwaukee, WI: Alverno College Institute.

Alverno College Office of Research and Evaluation. (1985). *Reflecting on then . . . and now: An Alverno College questionnaire.* Milwaukee, WI: Alverno Productions.

Alverno College Office of Research and Evaluation. (1993). *Criteria for Educational Research Positions.* Milwaukee, WI: Alverno College Institute.

Alverno College Professional Communication Faculty. (1999). *Ability-based learning program: The professional communication major* [brochure]. Milwaukee, WI: Alverno College Institute.

Alverno College Psychology Faculty. (1995). *Ability-based learning program: The psychology major* [brochure]. Milwaukee, WI: Alverno College Institute.

Alverno College Religious Studies Faculty. (1997). *Ability-based learning program: The religious studies major* [brochure]. Milwaukee, WI: Alverno College Institute.

Alverno College Research and Evaluation Committee. (1997). Cassette recordings of three meetings: Sept. 30, Oct. 7, and Oct. 30, 1997.

Alverno College Research and Evaluation Committee. (1998). *Transcripts of thirty-eight meetings of the Research and Evaluation Committee: November 1995 to May 1998.* Unpublished manuscript, Alverno College, 3400 South 43rd Street, Milwaukee, WI 53234-3922.

Alverno College Research and Evaluation Committee, Office of Research and Evaluation, and Additional Faculty and Staff. (1993, Apr.). Reflecting on our practice: Practitioner-based inquiry to understand and improve teaching and learning across the curriculum. In W. Rickards (Chair), *Practitioner research as an evaluation strategy in higher education.* Paper presented at a symposium at the annual meeting of the American Educational Research Association, Atlanta. Milwaukee, WI: Alverno Productions.

Alverno College Social Interaction Department. (1994). *Teaching social interaction at Alverno College.* Milwaukee, WI: Alverno College Institute.

Alverno College Social Science Faculty. (1998). *Ability-based learning program: The social science major* [brochure]. Milwaukee, WI: Alverno College Institute.

Alverno College Research and Evaluation Committee, Office of Research and Evaluation, and Additional Faculty and Staff. (1993, Apr. 12). *Reflecting on our practice: Practitioner-based inquiry to understand and improve teaching and learning across the curriculum.* Paper distributed and discussed at the annual meeting of the American Educational Research Association, Atlanta, GA.

American Association for Higher Education, American College Personnel Association, & National Association of Student Personnel Administrators. (1998, June). *Powerful partnerships: A shared responsibility for learning* [on-line]. Available: http://www.aahe.org/assessment/joint.htm

American Association for Higher Education Research Forum. (1999, Mar.). *Organizing for learning: A research agenda.* Document created at the annual meeting of the American Association for Higher Education, Washington, DC. Available: http://www.aahe.org/99research_agenda.htm

American Association of University Professors. (1995). The work of faculty: Expectations, priorities, and rewards. In *Policy documents and reports*, pp. 129–132. Washington, DC: Author.

American Council on Education. (1997). *Defining transformation: A working paper for the Forum of Change Projects*. Washington, DC: Author.

American Productivity & Quality Center. (1997). *Measuring institutional performance outcomes*. Houston: Author.

American Productivity & Quality Center. (1998). *Assessing learning outcomes*. Houston: Author.

American Psychological Association Presidential Task Force on Psychology in Education. (1993, Jan.). *Learner-centered psychological principles: Guidelines for school redesign and reform*. Boulder, CO: American Psychological Association and the Mid-Continent Regional Educational Laboratory.

Anastasi, A. (1980). Abilities and the measurement of achievement. In W. B. Schrader (Ed.), *Measuring achievement: Progress over a decade* (pp. 1–10). San Francisco: Jossey-Bass.

Anastasi, A. (1983). Evolving trait concepts. *American Psychologist, 38*(2), 175–184.

Anderson, J. R. (1982). Acquisition of cognitive skill. *Psychological Review, 89*(4), 369–406.

Angelo, T. A. (Ed.). (1991). *Classroom research: Early lessons from success.* New Directions for Teaching and Learning, no. 46. San Francisco: Jossey-Bass.

Angelo, T. A., & Cross, K. P. (1993). *Classroom assessment techniques: A handbook for college teachers* (2nd ed.). San Francisco: Jossey-Bass.

Applebee, A. N. (1996). *Curriculum as conversation: Transforming traditions of teaching and learning*. Chicago: University of Chicago Press.

Arendt, H. (1958). *The human condition*. Chicago: University of Chicago Press.

Arendt, H. (1978). *The life of the mind*. Orlando, FL: Harcourt Brace Jovanovich.

Arlin, P. K. (1975). Cognitive development in adulthood: A fifth stage? *Developmental Psychology, 11*(5), 602–606.

Arlin, P. K. (1984). Adolescent and adult thought: A structural interpretation. In M. L. Commons, F. A. Richards, & C. Armon (Eds.), *Beyond formal operations: Late adolescent and adult cognitive development* (pp. 258–271). New York: Praeger.

Armour, R. A., & Fuhrmann, B. S. (1993). Confirming the centrality of liberal learning. In L. Curry, J. F. Wergin, & Associates, *Educating professionals: Responding to new expectations for competence and accountability* (pp. 126–147). San Francisco: Jossey-Bass.

Association of American Colleges (AAC). (1985). *Integrity in the college curriculum: A report to the academic community.* Washington, DC: Author.

Astin, A. W. (1977). *Four critical years.* San Francisco: Jossey-Bass.

Astin, A. W. (1991). *Assessment for excellence: The philosophy and practice of assessment and evaluation in higher education.* New York: Macmillan.

Astin, A. W. (1993). *What matters in college? Four critical years revisited.* San Francisco: Jossey-Bass.

Astin, A. W., Banta, T. W., Cross, K. P., El-Khawas, E., Ewell, P. T., Hutchings, P., Marchese, T. J., McClenney, K. M., Mentkowski, M., Miller, M. A., Moran, E. T., & Wright, B. D. (1992). Principles of good practice for assessing student learning. *AAHE Bulletin, 45*(4).

Atkinson, J. W. (1958). Thematic apperceptive measurement of motives within the context of a theory of motivation. In J. W. Atkinson (Ed.), *Motives in fantasy, action, and society: A method of assessment and study* (pp. 596–616). Princeton, NJ: Van Nostrand.

Bakan, D. (1966). *The duality of human existence: Isolation and communion in Western man.* Boston: Beacon Press.

Bandura, A. (1997). *Self-efficacy: The exercise of control.* New York: Freeman.

Banta, T. W., & Associates. (1993). *Making a difference: Outcomes of a decade of assessment in higher education.* San Francisco: Jossey-Bass.

Banta, T. W., Lund, J. P., Black, K. E., & Oblander, F. W. (1996). *Assessment in practice: Putting principles to work on college campuses.* San Francisco: Jossey-Bass.

Barr, R. B., & Tagg, J. (1995). From teaching to learning: A new paradigm for undergraduate education. *Change, 27*(6), 12–25.

Barrick, M. R., & Mount, M. K. (1993). Autonomy as a moderator of the relationships between the big five personality dimensions and job performance. *Journal of Applied Psychology, 78*(1), 111–118.

Barrowman, C. E. (1996). Improving teaching and learning effectiveness by defining expectations. In E. A. Jones (Ed.), *Preparing competent college graduates: Setting new and higher expectations for student learning.* New Directions for Higher Education, no. 96, 103–114. San Francisco: Jossey-Bass.

Barrows, H. S. (1994). *Practice-based learning: Problem-based learning applied to medical education.* Springfield: Southern Illinois University School of Medicine.

Barrows, H. S., & Tamblyn, R. M. (1980). *Problem-based learning: An approach to medical education.* New York: Springer.

Basseches, M. (1984). *Dialectical thinking and adult development.* Norwood, NJ: Ablex.

Bateman, W. (1990). *Open to question: The art of teaching and learning by inquiry.* San Francisco: Jossey-Bass.

Bateson, M. C. (1989). *Composing a life.* New York: Atlantic Monthly Press.

Baxter Magolda, M. B. (1992). *Knowing and reasoning in college: Gender-related patterns in students' intellectual development.* San Francisco: Jossey-Bass.

Bebeau, M. J., Rest, J. R., & Narvaez, D. F. (1999). Beyond the promise: A perspective on research in moral education. *Educational Researcher, 28*(4), 18–26.

Becher, T. (1984). The cultural view. In B. R. Clark (Ed.), *Perspectives on higher education* (pp. 165–198). Berkeley: University of California Press.

Belenky, M. F., Clinchy, B. M., Goldberger, N. R., & Tarule, J. M. (1986). *Women's ways of knowing: The development of self, voice, and mind.* New York: Basic Books.

Bellah, R. N., Madsen, R., Sullivan, W. M., Swidler, A., & Tipton, S. M. (1985). *Habits of the heart: Individualism and commitment in American life.* New York: HarperCollins.

Ben-Ur, T. (1986, Oct.). *Longitudinal research data bank management: Design and procedures.* Paper presented at the annual meeting of the Mid-Western Educational Research Association, Chicago. Milwaukee, WI: Alverno Productions.

Ben-Ur, T., & Rogers, G. (1994, June). *Measuring alumna career advancement: An approach based on educational expectations.* Paper presented at the annual meeting of the Association for Institutional Research, New Orleans. Milwaukee, WI: Alverno College Institute.

Ben-Ur, T., Rogers, G., Deemer, D., & Mentkowski, M. (1989). *Can past student performance inform current practice? Issues of generalizability in a longitudinal study of college outcomes.* Milwaukee, WI: Alverno Productions. (ERIC Document Reproduction Service No. ED 378 855)

Ben-Ur, T., Rogers, G., Reisetter, J., & Mentkowski, M. (1987). *Changes in learning style preference across undergraduate education and professional experience: A longitudinal study of nurse and business professionals.* Milwaukee, WI: Alverno Productions.

Berberet, J., & Wong, F. F. (1995). The new American college: A model for liberal learning. *Liberal Education, 81*(1), 48–52.

Berkowitz, M. (1996). Integrating structure and content in moral education. In L. Nucci (Chair), *Developmental structures and approaches to moral education.* Symposium at the annual meeting of the American Educational Research Association, Chicago.

Berryman, S. E. (1993). Learning for the workplace. In L. Darling-Hammond (Ed.), *Review of research in education* (pp. 343–401). Washington, DC: American Educational Research Association.

Berryman, S. E., & Bailey, T. R. (1992). *The double helix of education and the economy.* New York: Institute on Education and the Economy, Teachers College, Columbia University.

Birnbaum, R. (1988). *How colleges work: The cybernetics of academic organization and leadership.* San Francisco: Jossey-Bass.

Birnbaum, R. (1992). *How academic leadership works.* San Francisco: Jossey-Bass.

Blalock, H. M. (1982). *Conceptualization and measurement in the social sciences.* Thousand Oaks, CA: Sage.

Bloland, H. G. (1995). Postmodernism and higher education. *Journal of Higher Education, 66*(5), 521–559.

Bloom, A. (1987). *The closing of the American mind.* New York: Simon & Schuster.

Bloor, D. (1983). *Wittgenstein: A social theory of knowledge.* New York: Macmillan.

Boud, D., Keogh, R., & Walker, D. (Eds.). (1985). *Reflection: Turning experience into learning.* London: Kogan Page.

Boyatzis, R. E. (1982). *The competent manager: A model for effective performance.* New York: Wiley.

Boyatzis, R. E. (1993). Beyond competence: The choice to be a leader. *Human Resource Management Review, 3*(1), 1–14.

Boyatzis, R. E., Cowen, S. S., Kolb, D. A., & Associates. (1995). *Innovation in professional education: Steps on a journey from teaching to learning.* San Francisco: Jossey-Bass.

Boyer, E. L. (1987). *College: The undergraduate experience in America.* New York: HarperCollins.

Boyer, E. L. (1990). *Scholarship reconsidered: Priorities of the professoriate.* Special report of the Carnegie Foundation for the Advancement of Teaching. Princeton, NJ: Princeton University Press.

Brabeck, M. B. (1983). Critical thinking skills and reflective judgment development: Redefining the aims of higher education. *Journal of Applied Developmental Psychology, 4*(1), 23–34.

Bray, D. W., Campbell, R. J., & Grant, D. L. (1974). *Formative years in business: A long-term AT&T study of managerial lives.* New York: Wiley.

Brookfield, S. D. (1991). The development of critical reflection in adulthood: Foundations of a theory of adult learning. *New Education, 13*(1), 39–48.

Brookfield, S. D. (1995). *Becoming a critically reflective teacher.* San Francisco: Jossey-Bass.

Brown, A. L., Bransford, J. D., Ferrara, R. A., & Campione, J. C. (1983). Learning, remembering, and understanding. In P. H. Mussen (Series Ed.), & J. H. Flavell & E. M. Markman (Vol. Eds.), *Handbook of child psychology: Vol. 3. Cognitive development* (4th ed., pp. 77–166). New York: Wiley.

Brown, J. S., Collins, A., & Duguid, P. (1989). Situated cognition and the culture of learning. *Educational Researcher, 18*(1), 32–42.

Bruffee, K. A. (1995). A nonfoundational curriculum. In J. G. Haworth & C. F. Conrad (Eds.), *Revisioning curriculum in higher education* (pp. 26–34). (ASHE Reader Series). New York: Simon & Schuster.

Bruner, J. S. (1986). *Actual minds, possible worlds.* Cambridge, MA: Harvard University Press.

Bruner, J. S. (1990). *Acts of meaning.* Cambridge, MA: Harvard University Press.

Buchmann, M., & Floden, R. E. (1992). Coherence, the rebel angel. *Educational Researcher, 21*(9), 5–9.

Burke, K. (1969). *A grammar of motives.* Berkeley: University of California Press.

Cameron, K. S. (1985). Institutional effectiveness in higher education: An introduction. *Review of Higher Education, 9,* 1–4.

Cameron, K. S. (1986a). Effectiveness as paradox: Consensus and conflict in perceptions of organizational effectiveness. *Management Science, 32,* 539–553.

Cameron, K. S. (1986b). A study of organizational effectiveness and its predictors. *Management Science, 32,* 87–112.

Cameron, K. S., & Smart, J. (1998). Maintaining effectiveness amid downsizing and decline in institutions of higher education. *Research in Higher Education, 39*(1), 65–86.

Campbell, D. T., & Stanley, J. C. (1963). Experimental and quasi-experimental designs for research on teaching. In N. L. Gage (Ed.), *Handbook of research on teaching* (pp. 171–246). Chicago: Rand McNally.

Campion, M. A., Campion, J. E., & Hudson, J. P., Jr. (1994). Structured interviewing: A note on incremental validity and alternative question types. *Journal of Applied Psychology, 79*(6), 998–1002.

Campione, J. C., & Brown, A. L. (1979). Toward a theory of intelligence: Contributions from research with retarded children. In R. J. Sternberg & D. K. Detterman (Eds.), *Human intelligence: Perspectives on its theory and measurement* (pp. 139–164). Norwood, NJ: Ablex.

Candy, P. C. (1991). *Self-direction for lifelong learning: A comprehensive guide to theory and practice.* San Francisco: Jossey-Bass.

Carnevale, A. P., Gainer, L. J., & Meltzer, A. S. (1990). *Workplace basics: The essential skills employers want.* San Francisco: Jossey-Bass.

Chaffee, E. E. (1984). *After decline, what? Survival strategies at eight private colleges.* Boulder, CO: National Center for Higher Education Management Systems.

Chickering, A. W. (1972). *Education and identity.* San Francisco: Jossey-Bass.

Chickering, A. W., & Associates. (1981). *The modern American college.* San Francisco: Jossey-Bass.

Chickering, A. W., & Gamson, Z. F. (1987). Seven principles for good practice in undergraduate education. *AAHE Bulletin, 40*(3), 3–7.

Chickering, A. W., & Reisser, L. (1993). *Education and identity* (2nd ed.). San Francisco: Jossey-Bass.

Chodorow, N. (1978). *The reproduction of mothering*. Berkeley: University of California Press.

Cochran-Smith, M., & Lytle, S. L. (Eds.). (1993). *Inside/outside: Teacher research and knowledge*. New York: Teachers College Press.

Cochran-Smith, M., & Lytle, S. L. (1999). The teacher research movement: A decade later. *Educational Researcher, 28*(7), 15–25.

Cohn, L. D. (1998). Age trends in personality development: A quantitative review. In P. M. Westenberg, A. Blasi, & L. D. Cohn (Eds.), *Personality development* (pp. 133–143). Hillsdale, NJ: Erlbaum.

Colby, A., & Damon, W. (1992). *Some do care: Contemporary lives of moral commitment*. New York: Free Press.

Colby, A., Kohlberg, L., Speicher, B., Hewer, A., Candee, D., Gibbs, J., & Power, C. (1987). *The measurement of moral judgment: Standard issue scoring manual* (Vol. 2). New York: Cambridge University Press.

Cole, M. (1977). An ethnographic psychology of cognition. In P. N. Johnson-Laird & P. C. Wason (Eds.), *Thinking: Readings in cognitive science* (pp. 468–482). New York: Cambridge University Press.

Cole, M. (1996). *Cultural psychology: A once and future discipline*. Cambridge, MA: Belknap Press.

Commons, M. L., Armon, C., Richards, F. A., Schrader, D. E. (with Farrell, E. W., Tappan, M. B., & Bauer, N. F. (1989). A multidomain study of adult development. In M. L. Commons, J. D. Sinnott, F. A. Richards, & C. Armon (Eds.), *Adult development* (Vol. 1, pp. 33–56). New York: Praeger.

Commons, M. L., Richards, F. A., & Armon, C. (Eds.). (1984). *Beyond formal operations: Late adolescent and adult cognitive development*. New York: Praeger.

Consortium for the Improvement of Teaching, Learning and Assessment. (1992). *High school to college to professional school: Achieving educational coherence through outcome-oriented, performance-based curricula*. Final Report to the W.K. Kellogg Foundation. Milwaukee, WI: Alverno Productions.

Cook, T. D., & Campbell, D. T. (1979). *Quasi-experimentation: Design and analysis issues for field settings*. Boston: Houghton Mifflin.

Cowan, J. (1998). *On becoming an innovative university teacher*. Philadelphia: Open University Press.

Cranton, P. (1996). *Professional development as transformative learning: New perspectives for teachers of adults*. San Francisco: Jossey-Bass.

Cromwell, L. (Ed.). (1986). *Teaching critical thinking in the arts and humanities*. Milwaukee, WI: Alverno Productions.

Cromwell, L. (1993, May–June). Active learning in the classroom: Putting theory into practice. *Experiential Learning Quarterly, 18*(3), 1, 18–23.

Cromwell, L., & Sharkey, S. (1994, April). *The making of educators.* Unpublished manuscript, Alverno College, 3400 South 43rd Street, Milwaukee, WI 53234-3922.

Cronbach, L. J., & Associates. (1980). *Toward reform of program evaluation.* San Francisco: Jossey-Bass.

Cross, K. P. (1971). *Beyond the open door: New students to higher education.* San Francisco: Jossey-Bass.

Cross, K. P. (1981). *Adults as learners.* San Francisco: Jossey-Bass.

Cross, K. P. (1993). Improving the quality of instruction. In A. Levine (Ed.), *Higher learning in America, 1980–2000* (pp. 287–308). Baltimore, MD: Johns Hopkins University Press.

Cross, K. P., & Steadman, M. H. (1996). *Classroom research: Implementing the scholarship of teaching.* San Francisco: Jossey-Bass.

Curry, L., Wergin, J., & Associates. (1993). *Educating professionals: Responding to new expectations for competence and accountability.* San Francisco: Jossey-Bass.

Daedalus. (1999, Winter). Distinctively American: The residential liberal arts colleges. *Daedalus: Journal of the American Academy of Arts and Sciences, 128*(1).

Daloz, L. A. P., Keen, C. H., Keen, J. P., & Parks, S. D. (1996). *Common fire: Lives of commitment in a complex world.* Boston: Beacon Press.

D'Andrade, R. G. (1981). The cultural part of cognition. *Cognitive Science, 5,* 179–195.

D'Andrade, R. G. (1984). Cultural meaning systems. In R. A. Shweder & R. A. LeVine (Eds.), *Culture theory: Essays on mind, self and emotion* (pp. 88–119). New York: Cambridge University Press.

D'Andrade, R. G. (1990). Some propositions about the relation between culture and human cognition. In J. W. Stigler, R. A. Shweder, & G. Herdt (Eds.), *Cultural psychology: Essays on comparative human development* (pp. 65–129). New York: Cambridge University Press.

Daniel, J. S. (1996). *Mega-universities and knowledge media.* London: Kogan Page.

Darling-Hammond, L. (Chair). (1997, Mar.). *Issues of learner- and learning-centered teacher education: Development and dilemmas.* Interactive symposium conducted at the annual meeting of the American Educational Research Association, Chicago.

Dave, R. H. (1973). *Lifelong education and school curriculum.* Hamburg: UNESCO Institute for Education.

Davis, W. E., & Chandler, T. J. L. (1998). Beyond Boyer's *Scholarship Reconsidered:* Fundamental change in the university and the socioeconomic systems. *Journal of Higher Education, 69*(1), 23–64.

DeBack, V., & Mentkowski, M. (1986). Does the baccalaureate make a difference? Differentiating nurse performance by education and experience. *Journal of Nursing Education, 25*(7), 275–285.

De Corte, E. (1995). Learning theory and instructional science. In P. Reimann & H. Spada (Eds.), *Learning in humans and machines: Towards an interdisciplinary learning science* (pp. 97–108). Tarrytown, NY: Elsevier Science Inc.

Deemer, D. (1993). *Perspectives and outcomes of five-year alumnae: Making causal links to the Alverno culture and curriculum.* Milwaukee, WI: Alverno College Institute.

Deemer, D. (in collaboration with Alverno College Office of Research and Evaluation). (1993, Nov.). Analyzing and exploring alumna perspectives in higher education assessment and evaluation. In R. L. Durham (Chair), *Student perspectives in higher education assessment and evaluation.* Paper presented at a panel at the annual meeting of the American Evaluation Association, Dallas. Milwaukee, WI: Alverno College Institute.

Deemer, D., & Mentkowski, M. (1990). *Studying the outcomes of college from the perspective of the student: A rationale and method for the student/alumna perspectives interview approach.* Milwaukee, WI: Alverno Productions.

Denison, D., & Mishra, A. K. (1995). Toward a theory of organizational culture and effectiveness. *Organization Science, 6*(2), 204–223.

Deutsch, B., Rogers, G., Schall, C., Ben-Ur, T., Chomicka, D., & Frederick, J. R. (1995, May). *Integrating teaching, advising, and research tools: The Student as Learner Inventory as retention and learning intervention.* Paper presented at the annual meeting of the Association for Institutional Research, Boston. Milwaukee, WI: Alverno College Institute. (ERIC Document Reproduction Service No. ED 386 997)

Dewey, J. (1916). *Democracy and education.* New York: Free Press.

Dewey, J. (1938). *Experience and education.* New York: Macmillan.

Diamond, R. M. (1998). *Designing and assessing courses and curricula: A practical guide* (rev. ed.). San Francisco: Jossey-Bass.

Diez, M. E. (1990). A thrust from within: Reconceptualizing teacher education at Alverno College. *Peabody Journal of Education, 65*(2), 4–18.

Diez, M. E. (Ed.). (1998). *Changing the practice of teacher education: Standards and assessment as a lever for change.* Washington, DC: American Association of Colleges for Teacher Education.

Diez, M., & Stoffels, J. (1992, Fall). Promoting conditions for school change through instructional leadership. In R. J. Krajewski & L. Cozad (Eds.), *Fast forward 1: Transforming leadership in Wisconsin schools* (pp. 86–92). Madison, WI: A-R Editions.

Diez, M. E., & Truchan, L. C. (1998). Creating the climate for change. In M. E. Diez (Ed.), *Changing the practice of teacher education: Standards and assessment as a lever for change* (pp. 139–144). Washington, DC: American Association of Colleges for Teacher Education.

Doherty, A., Chenevert, J., Miller, R. R., Roth, J. L., & Truchan, L. C. (1997). Developing intellectual skills. In J. G. Gaff, J. L. Ratcliff, & Associates, *Handbook of the undergraduate curriculum: A comprehensive guide to purposes, structures, practices, and change* (pp. 170–189). San Francisco: Jossey-Bass.

Doherty, A., Mentkowski, M., & Conrad, K. (1978). Toward a theory of undergraduate experiential learning. In M. T. Keeton & P. J. Tate (Eds.), *Learning by experience—what, why, how.* New Directions for Experiential Learning, no. 1 (pp. 23–36). San Francisco: Jossey-Bass.

Donaldson, T. (1996). Values in tension: Ethics away from home. *Harvard Business Review, 74*(5), 48–62.

Duval, S., & Wicklund, R. A. (1972). *A theory of objective self-awareness.* New York: Academic Press.

Earley, M., Mentkowski, M., & Schafer, J. (1980). *Valuing at Alverno: The valuing process in liberal education.* Milwaukee, WI: Alverno Productions.

Eckel, P., Green, M., & Hill, B. (1997). *Transformational change: Defining a journey.* Washington, DC: American Council on Education.

Eckel, P., Hill, B., Green, M., & Mallon, B. (1999). *Reports from the road: Insights on institutional change.* Washington, DC: American Council on Education.

Edgerton, R. (1997). *Summing things up* (cassette recording No. 97 AAHE-87). Final plenary at the annual meeting of the American Association for Higher Education, Washington, DC.

Edgerton, R., Hutchings, P., & Quinlan, K. (1991). *The teaching portfolio: Capturing the scholarship in teaching.* Washington, DC: American Association for Higher Education.

Elbow, P. (1986). *Embracing contraries: Explorations in learning and teaching.* New York: Oxford University Press.

Engelkemeyer, S. W., & Brown, S. C. (1998). Powerful partnerships: A shared responsibility for learning. *AAHE Bulletin, 51*(2), 10–12.

Eraut, M. (1994). *Developing professional knowledge and competence.* Bristol, PA: Falmer Press.

Erwin, T. D. (1991). *Assessing student learning and development.* San Francisco: Jossey-Bass.

Evers, F. T., Rush, J. C., & Berdrow, I. (1998). *The bases of competence: Skills for lifelong learning and employability.* San Francisco: Jossey-Bass.

Ewell, P. T. (Ed.). (1985). *Assessing educational outcomes.* New Directions for Institutional Research, no. 47. San Francisco: Jossey-Bass.

Ewell, P. T. (1991). To capture the ineffable: New forms of assessment in higher education. In G. Grant (Ed.), *Review of research in education* (pp. 75–125). Washington, DC: American Educational Research Association.

Eyler, J., & Giles, D. E., Jr. (1999). *Where's the learning in service-learning?* San Francisco: Jossey-Bass.

Falbe, C. M., & Yukl, G. (1992). Consequences for managers of using single influence tactics and combinations of tactics. *Academy of Management Journal, 35*(3), 638–652.

Feldman, A., & Atkin, J. M. (1995). Embedding action research in professional practice. In S. E. Noffke and R. B. Stevenson (Eds.), *Educational action research: Becoming practically critical.* New York: Teachers College Press.

Feldman, K. A. (1989). The association between student ratings of specific instructional dimensions and student achievement: Refining and extending the synthesis of data from multisection validity studies. *Research in Higher Education, 30*(6), 583–645.

Feldman, K. A., & Newcomb, T. M. (1969). *The impact of college on students.* San Francisco: Jossey-Bass.

Feltovich, P. J., Ford, K. M., & Hoffman, R. R. (Eds.). (1997). *Expertise in context: Human and machine.* Menlo Park, CA: AAAI Press.

Feynman, R. P. (1995). *Six easy pieces: Essentials of physics explained by its most brilliant teacher.* Reading, MA: Addison-Wesley.

Fiddler, M., McGury, S., Marienau, C., Rogers, R. R., & Scheideman, W. (1996). Broadening the scope of scholarship: A suggested framework. *Innovative Higher Education, 21*(2), 127–139.

Fivars, G., & Gosnell, D. (1966). *Nursing evaluation: The problem and the process.* New York: Macmillan.

Flavel, J. H. (1963). *The developmental psychology of Jean Piaget.* New York: Van Nostrand Reinhold.

Fleishman, E. A., & Quaintance, M. K. (1984). *Taxonomies of human performance: The description of human tasks.* Orlando, FL: Academic Press.

Ford, M. E. (1986). For all practical purposes: Criteria for defining and evaluating practical intelligence. In R. J. Sternberg & R. K. Wagner (Eds.), *Practical intelligence: Nature and origins of competence in the everyday world* (pp. 183–202). New York: Cambridge University Press.

Frederiksen, N. (1986). Toward a broader conception of human intelligence. In R. J. Sternberg & R. K. Wagner (Eds.), *Practical intelligence: Nature and origins of competence in the everyday world* (pp. 84–116). New York: Cambridge University Press.

French, J. R. P., Jr., & Raven, B. H. (1959). The bases of social power. In D. Cartwright (Ed.), *Studies in social power* (pp. 150–167). Ann Arbor: University of Michigan.

Fromm, E. (1947). *Man for himself: An inquiry into the psychology of ethics.* New York: Fawcett.

Gabelnick, F. (1997). Educating a committed citizenry. *Change, 29*(1), 30–35.

Gabelnick, F., MacGregor, J., Matthews, R. S., & Smith, B. L. (Eds.). (1990). *Learning communities: Creating connections among students, faculty, and disciplines.* New Directions for Teaching and Learning, no. 41. San Francisco: Jossey-Bass.

Gaff, J. G. (1997). Tensions between tradition and innovation. In J. G. Gaff, J. L. Ratcliff, & Associates, *Handbook of the undergraduate curriculum: A comprehensive guide to purposes, structures, practices, and change* (pp. 684–705). San Francisco: Jossey-Bass.

Gaff, J. G., Ratcliff, J. L., & Associates. (1997). *Handbook of the undergraduate curriculum: A comprehensive guide to purposes, structures, practices, and change.* San Francisco: Jossey-Bass.

Gardner, H. (1983). *Frames of mind: The theory of multiple intelligences.* New York: Basic Books.

Gates, H. L., Jr. (1992). *Loose canons: Notes on the culture wars.* New York: Oxford University Press.

Gates, H. L., Jr. (1996, Mar.). *Crossing boundaries.* Opening keynote at the annual meeting of the American Association for Higher Education, Chicago.

Geoghegan, W. (1994). Stuck at the barricades: Can information technology really enter the mainstream of teaching and learning? *AAHE Bulletin, 47*(1), 13–16.

Gfellner, B. M. (1986). Changes in ego and moral development in adolescents: A longitudinal study. *Journal of Adolescence, 9*(4), 281–302.

Gibbs, G. (Ed.). (1996). *Improving student learning: Using research to improve student learning.* Oxford, UK: Oxford Centre for Staff Development.

Giencke-Holl, L., Mentkowski, M., Much, N., Mertens, S., & Rogers, G. (1985, Apr.). *Evaluating college outcomes through alumnae studies: Measuring postcollege learning and abilities.* Paper presented at the annual meeting of the American Educational Research Association, Chicago. Milwaukee, WI: Alverno Productions.

Gilbert, J., & Reynolds, S. (1998). An institutional strategy for transferable skills and employability. In J. Stephenson & M. Yorke (Eds.), *Capability and quality in higher education.* London: Kogan Page.

Gilder, G. (1990). *Life after television.* Knoxville, TN: Whittle Direct Books.

Gilligan, C. (1982). *In a different voice: Psychological theory and women's development.* Cambridge, MA: Harvard University Press.

Glaser, R. (1991). The maturing of the relationship between the science of learning and cognition and educational practice. *Learning and Instruction, 1*(2), 129–144.

Glassick, C. E., Huber, M. T., & Maeroff, G. I. (1997). *Scholarship assessed: Evaluation of the professoriate.* San Francisco: Jossey-Bass.

Gleick, J. (1987). *Chaos: Making a new science.* New York: Penguin.

Goffin, R. D., Rothstein, M. G., & Johnston, N. G. (1996). Personality testing and the assessment center: Incremental validity for managerial selection. *Journal of Applied Psychology, 81*(6), 746–756.

Goldberger, N., Tarule, J., Clinchy, B., & Belenky, M. (Eds.). (1996). *Knowledge, difference, and power: Essays inspired by* Women's Ways of Knowing. New York: Basic Books.

Goldstein, I. L. (1993). *Training in organizations: Needs assessment, development, and evaluation.* Pacific Grove, CA: Brooks/Cole.

Goleman, D. (1995). *Emotional intelligence: Why it can matter more than IQ.* New York: Bantam Books.

Goleman, D. (1998). *Working with emotional intelligence.* New York: Bantam Books.

Graham, S. E. (1998). Developing student outcomes for the psychology major: An assessment-as-learning framework. *Current Directions in Psychological Science, 7*(6), 165–170.

Grant, G., & Associates. (1979). *On competence: A critical analysis of competence-based reforms in higher education.* San Francisco: Jossey-Bass.

Grantz, R., & Thanos, M. (1996). Internships: Academic learning outcomes. *NSEE Quarterly, 21*(1), 10–27.

Gray, P. J. (Ed.). (1989). *Achieving assessment goals using evaluation techniques.* New Directions for Higher Education, no. 67. San Francisco: Jossey-Bass.

Green, M. F. (Ed.). (1997). *Transforming higher education: Views from leaders around the world.* Phoenix, AZ: Oryx Press.

Greenleaf, R. K. (1976). *The institution as servant.* Indianapolis: Robert K. Greenleaf Center for Servant-Leadership.

Greenleaf, R. K. (1991). *The servant as leader.* Indianapolis: Robert K. Greenleaf Center for Servant-Leadership. (Original work published 1970)

Greeno, J. G., & the Middle School Mathematics Through Applications Project Group. (1998). The situativity of knowing, learning, and research. *American Psychologist, 53*(1), 5–26.

Hakel, M. D., Sorcher, M., Beer, M., & Moses, J. L. (1982). *Making it happen: Designing research with implementation in mind.* Thousand Oaks, CA: Sage.

Halonen, J. S. (Ed.). (1986). *Teaching critical thinking in psychology.* Milwaukee, WI: Alverno Productions.

Halpern, D. F., & Associates. (1994). *Changing college classrooms: New teaching and learning strategies for an increasingly complex world.* San Francisco: Jossey-Bass.

Harré, R. (1995). Discursive psychology. In J. A. Smith, R. Harré, & L. Van Langenhove (Eds.), *Rethinking psychology* (pp. 143–159). Thousand Oaks, CA: Sage.

Harris, I. B. (1985). An exploration of the role of theories in communication for guiding practitioners. *Journal of Curriculum and Supervision, 1*(1), 27–55.

Harris, I. B. (1991a). Deliberative inquiry: The arts of planning. In E. C. Short (Ed.), *Forms of curriculum inquiry* (pp. 285–308). Albany: State University of New York Press.

Harris, I. B. (1991b, Sept.). Contributions to professional education from the field of curriculum studies: Research and practice with new traditions of investigation. *Professions Education Researcher Quarterly,* pp. 3–13.

Harris, I. B. (1993). New expectations for professional competence. In L. Curry, J. F. Wergin, & Associates, *Educating professionals: Responding to new expectations for competence and accountability* (pp. 17–52). San Francisco: Jossey-Bass.

Harvey, L., & Knight, P. (1996). *Transforming higher education.* Bristol, UK: Open University Press.

Hass, J. M., & Stoffels, J. A. (1998). Supporting change in teacher education institutions. In M. E. Diez (Ed.), *Changing the practice of teacher education: Standards and assessment as a lever for change* (pp. 145–155). Washington, DC: American Association of Colleges for Teacher Education.

Hativa, N. (1995). The department-wide approach to improving faculty instruction in higher education: A qualitative evaluation. *Research in Higher Education, 36*(4), 377–413.

Haworth, J. G., & Conrad, C. F. (Eds.). (1995). *Revisioning curriculum in higher education* (ASHE Reader Series). New York: Simon & Schuster.

Haworth, J. G., & Conrad, C. F. (1997). *Emblems of quality in higher education: Developing and sustaining high-quality programs.* Needham Heights, MA: Allyn & Bacon.

Hayduk, L. A. (1987). *Structural equation modeling with LISREL: Essentials and advances.* Baltimore, MD: Johns Hopkins University Press.

Heath, D. H. (1977). *Maturity and competence: A transcultural view.* New York: Gardner Press.

Heath, D. H. (with the assistance of Heath, H. E.). (1991). *Fulfilling lives: Paths to maturity and success.* San Francisco: Jossey-Bass.

Heath, D. H. (1994). *Schools of hope: Developing mind and character in today's youth.* San Francisco: Jossey-Bass.

Helmreich, R. L., Wiener, E. L., & Kanki, B. G. (1993). The future of CRM training in the cockpit and elsewhere. In E. L. Wiener, B. G. Kanki, &

R. L. Helmreich (Eds.), *Cockpit resource management* (pp. 3–45). Orlando, FL: Academic Press.

Helson, R., Mitchell, V., & Hart, B. (1985). Lives of women who became autonomous. *Journal of Personality, 53*(2), 257–285.

Henn-Reinke, K., & Kies, K. M. (1998). Institutionalizing a standards-based approach to teaching, learning, and assessment. In M. E. Diez (Ed.), *Changing the practice of teacher education: Standards and assessment as a lever for change* (pp. 157–167). Washington, DC: American Association of Colleges for Teacher Education.

Heyns, R. W., Veroff, J., & Atkinson, J. W. (1958). A scoring manual for the affiliation motive. In J. W. Atkinson (Ed.), *Motives in fantasy, action, and society: A method of assessment and study* (pp. 205–218). Princeton, NJ: Van Nostrand.

Heywood, J. (1989). *Assessment in higher education* (2nd ed.). New York: Wiley.

Hill, P. J. (1982). Communities of learners: Curriculum as the infrastructure of academic communities. In J. W. Hall (with B. L. Kevles) (Eds.), *In opposition to core curriculum: Alternative models for undergraduate education* (pp. 107–134). Westport, CT: Greenwood Press.

Hirsch, E. D., Jr. (1988). *Cultural literacy: What every American needs to know.* New York: Random House.

Holland, D. C., & Eisenhart, M. A. (1990). *Educated in romance: Women, achievement, and college culture.* Chicago: University of Chicago Press.

Howard, A., & Bray, D. W. (1988). *Managerial lives in transition: Advancing age and changing times.* New York: Guilford Press.

Huck, J. R., & Bray, D. W. (1976). Management assessment center evaluations and subsequent job performance of white and black females. *Personnel Psychology, 29,* 13–30.

Huffcutt, A. I., Roth, P. L., & McDaniel, M. A. (1996). A meta-analytic investigation of cognitive ability in employment interview evaluations: Moderating characteristics and implications for incremental validity. *Journal of Applied Psychology, 81*(5), 459–473.

Hulbert, K. D., & Schuster, D. T. (Eds.). (1993). *Women's lives through time: Educated American women of the twentieth century.* San Francisco: Jossey-Bass.

Hunt, E. (1995). *Will we be smart enough? A cognitive analysis of the coming workforce.* New York: Russell Sage Foundation.

Hutchings, P., & Shulman, L. S. (1999). The scholarship of teaching: New elaborations, new developments. *Change, 31*(5), 11–15.

Hutchings, P., & Wutzdorff, A. (Eds.). (1988). *Knowing and doing: Learning through experience.* New Directions for Teaching and Learning, no. 35. San Francisco: Jossey-Bass.

Hy, L. X., & Loevinger, J. (1996). *Measuring ego development* (2nd ed.). Hillsdale, NJ: Erlbaum.

Inhelder, B., & Piaget, J. (1958). *The growth of logical thinking from childhood to adolescence.* New York: Basic Books.

Jacob, P. (1957). *Changing values in college.* New York: Harper & Row.

Jaques, E. (1989). *Requisite organization: The CEO's guide to creative structure and leadership.* Arlington, VA: Cason Hall and Co.

Jarvis, P. (1992). *Paradoxes of learning: On becoming an individual in society.* San Francisco: Jossey-Bass.

Jenkins, A. (1999, January). Institution-wide staff development events: Oxford Brookes' IT term. *Journal of the National Association for Staff Development, 40,* 17–25.

Johnstone, D. B. (1993). Enhancing the productivity of learning. *AAHE Bulletin, 46*(4), 3–8.

Jöreskog, K. G., & Sörbom, D. (1989). *LISREL 7: A guide to the program and applications* (2nd ed.). Chicago: Authors/SPSS.

Josselson, R. (1987). *Finding herself: Pathways to identity development in women.* San Francisco: Jossey-Bass.

Josselson, R. (1996). *Revising herself: The story of women's identity from college to midlife.* New York: Oxford University Press.

Katz, J., & Henry, M. (1988). *Turning professors into teachers: A new approach to faculty development and student learning.* New York: American Council on Education, Macmillan.

Kegan, R. (1982). *The evolving self: Problem and process in human development.* Cambridge, MA: Harvard University Press.

Kegan, R. (1994). *In over our heads: The mental demands of modern life.* Cambridge, MA: Harvard University Press.

Kim, P. H. (1997). When what you know *can* hurt you: A study of experiential effects on group discussion and performance. *Organizational Behavior and Human Decision Processes, 69*(2), 165–177.

King, P. M., & Kitchener, K. S. (1994). *Developing reflective judgment: Understanding and promoting intellectual growth and critical thinking in adolescents and adults.* San Francisco: Jossey-Bass.

King, P. M., Kitchener, K. S., Wood, P. K., & Davison, M. L. (1989). Relationships across developmental domains: A longitudinal study of intellectual, moral, and ego development. In M. L. Commons, J. D. Sinnott, F. A. Richards, & C. Armon (Eds.), *Adult development: Vol. 1. Comparisons and applications of developmental models* (pp. 57–72). New York: Praeger.

Klemp, G. O., Jr. (circa 1977). *Test of Cognitive Development scoring key.* Unpublished manuscript, McBer & Company, Boston.

Klemp, G. O., Jr. (1991, Jan.). *Cognitive strategies and practical intelligence.* Paper presented at the 77th annual meeting of the Association of American Colleges. Boston: Cambria Consulting.

Klemp, G. O., Jr., & McClelland, D. C. (1986). What characterizes intelligent functioning among senior managers? In R. J. Sternberg &

R. K. Wagner (Eds.), *Practical intelligence: Nature and origins of competence in the everyday world* (pp. 31–50). New York: Cambridge University Press.

Knefelkamp, L. (1974). *Developmental instruction: Fostering intellectual and personal growth in college students.* Unpublished doctoral dissertation, University of Minnesota.

Knefelkamp, L. (1978). *Training manual for Perry raters and rater training cue sheets.* Unpublished mimeograph, University of Maryland, College Park.

Knefelkamp, L., & Slepitza, R. (1976). A cognitive-developmental model of career development: An adaptation of the Perry Scheme. *Counseling Psychologist, 6*(3), 53–58.

Kohlberg, L. (1969). Stage and sequence: The cognitive-developmental approach to socialization. In D. Goslin (Ed.), *Handbook of socialization theory and research* (pp. 347–480). Skokie, IL: Rand McNally.

Kohlberg, L. (1976). Moral stages and moralization: The cognitive-developmental approach. In T. Lickona (Ed.), *Moral development and behavior: Theory, research, and social issues* (pp. 31–53). Austin, TX: Holt, Rinehart & Winston.

Kohlberg, L. (1981a). *Essays on moral development: The philosophy of moral development* (Vol. 1). San Francisco: HarperCollins.

Kohlberg, L. (1981b). *The meaning and measurement of moral development.* Worcester, MA: Clark University Press.

Kohlberg, L., Colby, A., Gibbs, J., & Speicher-Dubin, B. (1978). *Standard form scoring manual.* Cambridge, MA: Center for Moral Education, Harvard University.

Kohn, M. L., & Schooler, C. (1978). The reciprocal effects of the substantive complexity of work and intellectual flexibility: A longitudinal assessment. *American Journal of Sociology, 84*(1), 24–52.

Kolb, D. A. (1976). *The Learning Style Inventory: Technical manual.* Boston: McBer and Company.

Kolb, D. A. (1984). *Experiential learning: Experience as the source of learning and development.* Englewood Cliffs, NJ: Prentice Hall.

Kuh, G. D., & Whitt, E. J. (1988). *The invisible tapestry: Culture in American colleges and universities.* ASHE-ERIC Higher Education Report No. 1. Washington, DC: Association for the Study of Higher Education.

Kuhmerker, L., Mentkowski, M., & Erickson, V. L. (Eds.). (1980). *Evaluating moral development and evaluating educational programs that have a value dimension.* Schenectady, NY: Character Research Press.

Kuhn, D. (1997). The view from giants' shoulders. In L. Smith, J. Dockrell, & P. Tomlinson (Eds.), *Piaget, Vygotsky, and beyond* (pp. 246–259). New York: Routledge.

Kuhn, T. S. (1962). *The structure of scientific revolutions.* Chicago: University of Chicago Press.

Kurfiss, J. G. (1988). *Critical thinking: Theory, research, practice, and possibilities* (ASHE-ERIC Higher Education Report No. 2). Washington, DC: Association for the Study of Higher Education.

Labouvie-Vief, G. (1992). A neo-Piagetian perspective on adult cognitive development. In R. J. Sternberg & C. A. Berg (Eds.), *Intellectual development* (pp. 197–228). Cambridge: Cambridge University Press.

Lambert, N. M., & McCombs, B. L. (Eds.). (1998). *How students learn: Reforming schools through learner-centered education.* Washington, DC: American Psychological Association.

Langenberg, D. N. (1997, Sept. 12). Diplomas and degrees are obsolescent. *Chronicle of Higher Education,* p. A64.

Laurillard, D. (1993). *Rethinking university teaching: A framework for the effective use of educational technology.* New York: Routledge.

Lave, J., & Wenger, E. (1991). *Situated learning: Legitimate peripheral participation.* New York: Cambridge University Press.

Lee, L., & Snarey, J. (1988). The relationship between ego and moral development: A theoretical review and empirical analysis. In D. K. Lapsley & F. C. Power (Eds.), *Self, ego, and identity: Integrative approaches* (pp. 151–178). New York: Springer-Verlag.

Levine, A. (1997, Fall). How the academic profession is changing. *Daedalus: Journal of the American Academy of Arts and Sciences, 126*(4), 1–20.

Lincoln, Y. (1995). Emerging criteria for quality in qualitative and interpretive research. *Qualitative Inquiry, 1*(3), 275–289.

Loacker, G. (1988). Faculty as a force to improve instruction through assessment. In J. H. McMillan (Ed.), *Assessing students' learning.* New Directions for Teaching and Learning, no. 34, 19–32. San Francisco: Jossey-Bass.

Loacker, G. (1991). *Designing a national assessment system: Alverno's institutional perspective.* Paper commissioned by the U.S. Department of Education, National Center for Education Statistics, in response to the National Education Goals Panel: *America 2000: An Education Strategy.* Milwaukee, WI: Alverno College Institute. (ERIC Reproduction Service No. 340 758)

Loacker, G., Cromwell, L., Fey, J., & Rutherford, D. (1984). *Analysis and communication at Alverno: An approach to critical thinking.* Milwaukee, WI: Alverno Productions.

Loacker, G., Cromwell, L., & O'Brien, K. (1986). Assessment in higher education: To serve the learner. In C. Adelman (Ed.), *Assessment in higher education: Issues and contexts* (Report No. OR 86–301, pp. 47–62). Washington, DC: U.S. Department of Education.

Loacker, G., & Jensen, P. (1988). The power of performance in developing problem solving and self assessment abilities. *Assessment and Evaluation in Higher Education, 13*(2), 128–150.

Loacker, G., & Mentkowski, M. (1993). Creating a culture where assessment improves learning. In T. W. Banta & Associates (Eds.), *Making a difference: Outcomes of a decade of assessment in higher education* (pp. 5–24). San Francisco: Jossey-Bass.

Loacker, G., & Palola, E. G. (Eds). (1981). *Clarifying learning outcomes in the liberal arts.* New Directions for Experiential Learning, no. 12. San Francisco: Jossey-Bass.

Loevinger, J. (1976). *Ego development: Conceptions and theories.* San Francisco: Jossey-Bass.

Loevinger, J. (1979). Construct validity of the Sentence Completion Test of ego development. *Applied Psychological Measurement, 3*(3), 281–311.

Loevinger, J., Cohn, L. D., Bonneville, L. P., Redmore, C. D., Streich, D. D., & Sargent, M. (1985). Ego development in college. *Journal of Personality and Social Psychology, 48,* 947–962.

Loevinger, J., & Wessler, R. (1970). *Measuring ego development: Construction and use of a sentence completion test* (Vol. 1). San Francisco: Jossey-Bass.

Loevinger, J., Wessler, R., & Redmore, C. (1970). *Measuring ego development: Scoring manual for women and girls* (Vol. 2). San Francisco: Jossey-Bass.

Lourenco, O., & Machado, A. (1996). In defense of Piaget's theory: A reply to 10 common criticisms. *Psychological Review, 103*(1), 143–164.

Loxley, J. C., & Whiteley, J. M. (1986). *Character development in college students* (Vol. 2). Schenectady, NY: Character Research Press.

Lundy, A. (1988). Instructional set and Thematic Apperception Test validity. *Journal of Personality Assessment, 52*(2), 309–320.

MacCorquodale, P., & Lensink, J. (1995). Integrating women into the curriculum: Multiple motives and mixed emotions. In J. G. Haworth & C. F. Conrad (Eds.), *Revisioning curriculum in higher education* (pp. 491–503). (ASHE Reader Series). New York: Simon & Schuster.

MacIntyre, A. (1981). *After virtue: A study in moral theory.* Notre Dame, IN: University of Notre Dame Press.

Marchese, T. (1998). Not-so-distant competitors: How new providers are remaking the postsecondary marketplace. *AAHE Bulletin, 50*(9), 3–7.

Marienau, C. (1999). Self-assessment at work: Outcomes of adult learners' reflections on practice. *Adult Education Quarterly, 49*(3), 135–146.

Markus, H. (1977). Self-schemata and processing information about the self. *Journal of Personality and Social Psychology, 35*(2), 63–78.

Marton, F., Hounsell, D., & Entwistle, N. (Eds). (1984). *The experience of learning.* Edinburgh: Scottish Academic Press.

Mason, M. G., & Gibbs, J. C. (1993). Social perspective taking and moral judgment among college students. *Journal of Adolescent Research, 8*(1), 109–123.

Matthews, R., Smith, B. L., MacGregor, J., & Gabelnick, F. (1996). Learning communities: A structure for educational coherence. *Liberal Education, 82*(3), 4–9.

McAdams, D. P. (1992). The intimacy motive. In C. P. Smith (in association with J. W. Atkinson, D. C. McClelland, & J. Veroff) (Eds.), *Motivation and personality: Handbook of thematic content analysis* (pp. 224–228). New York: Cambridge University Press.

McAdams, J. (1986). Alternatives for dealing with errors in the variables: An example using panel data. *American Journal of Political Science, 30*(1), 256–278.

McBer & Company. (1978). *Coding manual for clusters and skill level competencies.* Boston: Author.

McClelland, D. C. (1971). *Assessing human motivation.* New York: General Learning Press.

McClelland, D. C. (1975). *Power: The inner experience.* New York: Irvington.

McClelland, D. C. (1976). *A guide to job competency assessment.* Boston: McBer & Company.

McClelland, D. C. (1978). *Guide to behavioral event interviewing.* Boston: McBer & Company.

McClelland, D. C. (1987). *Human motivation.* New York: Cambridge University Press.

McClelland, D. C., Atkinson, J. W., Clark, R. A., & Lowell, E. L. (1953). *The achievement motive.* Englewood Cliffs, NJ: Appleton-Century-Crofts.

McDaniel, M. A., Whetzel, D. L., Schmidt, F. L, & Maurer, S. D. (1994). The validity of employment interviews: A comprehensive review and meta-analysis. *Journal of Applied Psychology, 79*(4), 599–616.

McEachern, W., & O'Brien, K. (1993). Constancy of purpose: Ability-based education and assessment-as-learning. In D. L. Hubbard (Ed.), *Continuous quality improvement: Making the transition to education* (pp. 454–473). Maryville, MO: Prescott Publishing.

McGovern, T. V. (Ed.). (1993). *Handbook for enhancing undergraduate education in psychology.* Washington, DC: American Psychological Association.

McGregor, I., & Little, B. R. (1998). Personal projects, happiness, and meaning: On doing well and being yourself. *Journal of Personality and Social Psychology, 74*(2), 494–512.

McLeod, D. B. (1990). Information-processing theories and mathematics learning: The role of affect. *International Journal of Educational Research, 14,* 13–29.

McNeel, S. P. (1994). College teaching and student moral development. In J. R. Rest & D. F. Narvaez (Eds.), *Moral development in the professions: Psychology and applied ethics* (pp. 27–49). Hillsdale, NJ: Erlbaum.

Meiklejohn, A. (1942). *Education between two worlds.* New York: Harper-Collins.

Menges, R. J., Weimer, M., & Associates. (1996). *Teaching on solid ground: Using scholarship to improve practice.* San Francisco: Jossey-Bass.

Mentkowski, M. (1983). *Career and family: Perspectives and strategies for relating personal and professional roles.* Milwaukee, WI: Alverno Productions.

Mentkowski, M. (1988). Paths to integrity: Educating for personal growth and professional performance. In S. Srivastva & Associates (Eds.), *Executive integrity: The search for high human values in organizational life* (pp. 89–121). San Francisco: Jossey-Bass.

Mentkowski, M. (1991a). Creating a context where institutional assessment yields educational improvement. *Journal of General Education, 40,* 255–283.

Mentkowski, M. (1991b). *Designing a national assessment system: Assessing abilities that connect education and work.* Paper commissioned by the U.S. Department of Education, National Center for Education Statistics, in response to the National Education Goals Panel: *America 2000: An Education Strategy.* Milwaukee, WI: Alverno Productions. (ERIC Reproduction Service No. ED 340 759)

Mentkowski, M. (1996). Reflecting on our practice: Research to understand and improve student learning across the curriculum. In G. Gibbs (Ed.), *Improving student learning: Using research to improve student learning* (pp. 12–32). Oxford, UK: Oxford Centre for Staff Development.

Mentkowski, M. (1998). Higher education assessment and national goals for education: Issues, assumptions, and principles. In N. M. Lambert & B. L. McCombs (Eds.), *How students learn: Reforming schools through learner-centered education* (pp. 269–310). Washington, DC: American Psychological Association.

Mentkowski, M., & Bishop, J. (1981). *Alverno College Student Careering Questionnaire.* Milwaukee, WI: Alverno Productions.

Mentkowski, M., & Doherty, A. (1983). *Careering after college: Establishing the validity of abilities learned in college for later careering and professional performance* (Final Report to the National Institute of Education). Milwaukee, WI: Alverno Productions. (ERIC Document Reproduction Service No. ED 239 556 to ED 239 566)

Mentkowski, M., & Doherty, A. (1984a). Abilities that last a lifetime: Outcomes of the Alverno experience. *AAHE Bulletin, 36*(6), 5–6, 11–14.

Mentkowski, M., & Doherty, A. (1984b). *Careering after college: Establishing the validity of abilities learned in college for later careering and professional performance* (Final report to the National Institute of Education: Overview and Summary). Milwaukee, WI: Alverno Productions. (ERIC Document Reproduction Service No. ED 239 556). (Original work published 1983)

Mentkowski, M., & Giencke-Holl, L. (1982). *Changes in student profiles on the Learning Style Inventory: Report to participants in a second longitudinal study of learning style preferences during the college years (1978–1982)*. Milwaukee, WI: Alverno Productions.

Mentkowski, M., & Loacker, G. (1985). Assessing and validating the outcomes of college. In P. T. Ewell (Ed.), *Assessing educational outcomes*. New Directions for Institutional Research, no. 47, 47–64. San Francisco: Jossey-Bass.

Mentkowski, M., Loacker, G., & O'Brien, K. (1998). *Ability-based learning and judicial education: An approach to ongoing professional development* (JERITT Monograph No. 8). East Lansing, MI: Judicial Education Reference, Information and Technical Transfer Project [sponsored by the State Justice Institute].

Mentkowski, M., Miller, N., Davies, E., Monroe, E., & Popovic, Z. (1981). *Using the Sentence Completion Test measuring Loevinger's stages of ego development as a college outcomes measure: Rating large numbers of protocols and maintaining validity*. Milwaukee, WI: Alverno Productions.

Mentkowski, M., Moeser, M., & Strait, M. (1983). *Using the Perry Scheme of Intellectual and Ethical Development as a college outcomes measure: A process and criteria for judging student performance* (Vols. 1 and 2). Milwaukee, WI: Alverno Productions.

Mentkowski, M., & Much, N. (1980). *Alverno College Student Perspectives Interview*. Milwaukee, WI: Alverno Productions.

Mentkowski, M., & Much, N. (1980/1985). *Alverno College Alumna Perspectives Interview*. Milwaukee, WI: Alverno Productions. (Original work published 1980)

Mentkowski, M., Much, N., & Giencke-Holl, L. (1983). *Careering after college: Perspectives on lifelong learning and career development*. (Final Report to the National Institute of Education). Milwaukee, WI: Alverno Productions. (ERIC Document Reproduction Service No. ED 239 563)

Mentkowski, M., Much, N., Kleinman, L., & Reisetter Hart, J. (1998). *Student and alumna learning in college and beyond: Perspectives from longitudinal interviews*. Milwaukee, WI: Alverno College Institute.

Mentkowski, M., O'Brien, K., McEachern, W., & Fowler, D. (1982). *Developing a professional competence model for management education* (Final Report to the National Institute of Education: Research Report No. 10). Milwaukee, WI: Alverno Productions. (ERIC Document Reproduction Service No. ED 239 566)

Mentkowski, M., & Rogers, G. (1993). Connecting education, work, and citizenship: How assessment can help. *Metropolitan Universities: An International Forum, 4*(1), 34–46.

Mentkowski, M., Rogers, G., Deemer, D., Ben-Ur, T., Reisetter, J., Rickards, W., & Talbott, M. (1991, April). *Understanding abilities, learning and development through college outcomes studies: What can we expect from higher education assessment?* Symposium conducted at the annual meeting of the American Educational Research Association, Chicago. Milwaukee, WI: Alverno Productions. (ERIC Reproduction Service No. ED 342 296)

Mentkowski, M., & Strait, M. (1983). *A longitudinal study of student change in cognitive development, learning styles, and generic abilities in an outcome-centered liberal arts curriculum* (Final Report to the National Institute of Education: Research Report No. 6). Milwaukee, WI: Alverno Productions. (ERIC Document Reproduction Service No. ED 239 562)

Mertens, S., & Rogers, G. (1986). *Personnel issues in maintaining longitudinal designs.* Paper presented at the annual meeting of the American Educational Research Association, San Francisco. Milwaukee, WI: Alverno Productions. (ERIC Document Reproduction Service No. ED 282 896)

Metcalfe, J., & Shimamura, A. P. (Eds.). (1994). Metacognition: Knowing about knowing. Cambridge, MA: MIT Press.

Mezirow, J. (1991). *Transformative dimensions of adult learning.* San Francisco: Jossey-Bass.

Mihalevich, C. D., & Carr, K. S. (1998). Central Missouri State University: One university's journey toward teacher education restructuring. In M. E. Diez (Ed.), *Changing the practice of teacher education: Standards and assessment as a lever for change* (pp. 71–79). Washington, DC: American Association of Colleges for Teacher Education.

Mines, R. (1982). Student development assessment techniques. In D. Hanson (Ed.), *Measuring student development.* New Directions for Student Services, no. 20, 65–91. San Francisco: Jossey-Bass.

Minnich, E. K. (1990). *Transforming knowledge.* Philadelphia: Temple University Press.

Mishler, E. G. (1979). Meaning in context: Is there any other kind? *Harvard Educational Review, 49*(1), 1–19.

Mohrman, K. (1983). *Building bridges between business and campus.* Washington, DC: Association of American Colleges.

Moore, W. (1983). *The Measure of Intellectual Development: A brief review.* Unpublished manuscript, Center for Applications of Developmental Instruction, University of Maryland at College Park.

Morgan, C., & Murray, H. (1935). A method for examining fantasies: The Thematic Apperception Test. *Archives of Neurology and Psychiatry, 34,* 289–306.

Morgan, G. (1986). *Images of organization.* Thousand Oaks, CA: Sage.

Morgan, G. (1997). *Images of organization* (2nd ed.). Thousand Oaks, CA: Sage.

Morrow, I. J., & Stern, M. (1990). Stars, adversaries, producers, and phantoms at work: A new leadership typology. In K. E. Clark & M. B. Clark

(Eds.), *Measures of leadership* (pp. 419–439). West Orange, NJ: Leadership Library of America.

Much, N. (1995). Cultural psychology. In J. A. Smith, R. Harré, & L. Van Langenhove (Eds.), *Rethinking psychology* (pp. 97–121). Thousand Oaks, CA: Sage.

Much, N., & Mentkowski, M. (1982). *Student perspectives on liberal learning at Alverno College: Justifying learning as relevant to performance in personal and professional roles* (Final Report to the National Institute of Education: Research Report No. 7). Milwaukee, WI: Alverno Productions. (ERIC Document Reproduction Service No. ED 239 563)

Much, N., & Mentkowski, M. (1984). *Student perspectives on learning and development in college.* Milwaukee, WI: Alverno Productions.

National Center for Education Statistics. (1996). *Integrating research on faculty: Seeking new ways to communicate about the academic life of faculty* (NCES 96–849). Washington, DC: U.S. Department of Education.

National Society for Internships and Experiential Education. (1990). *Combining service and learning: A resource book for community and public service.* Raleigh, NC: Author.

Neisser, U., Boodoo, G., Bouchard, T. J., Jr., Boykin, A. W., Brody, N., Ceci, S. J., Halpern, D. F., Loehlin, J. C., Perloff, R., Sternberg, R. J., & Urbina, S. (1996). Intelligence: Knowns and unknowns. *American Psychologist, 51*(2), 77–101.

Noddings, N. (1984). *Caring: A feminine approach to ethics and moral education.* Berkeley: University of California Press.

Noffke, S. E., & Stevenson, R. B. (Eds.). (1995). *Educational action research: Becoming practically critical.* New York: Teachers College Press.

Nussbaum, M. C. (1997). *Cultivating humanity: A classical defense of reform in liberal education.* Cambridge, MA: Harvard University Press.

O'Brien, K. (1990). *Portfolio assessment at Alverno College.* Milwaukee, WI: Alverno Productions.

O'Brien, K., Matlock, M. G., Loacker, G., & Wutzdorff, A. (1991). Learning from the assessment of problem solving. In D. Boud & G. Feletti (Eds.), *The challenge of problem based learning* (pp. 274–284). New York: St. Martin's Press.

O'Connell Killen, P., & de Beer, J. (1994). *The art of theological reflection.* New York: Crossroad.

Ohlsson, S. (1995). Learning to do and learning to understand: A lesson and a challenge for cognitive modeling. In P. Reimann & H. Spada (Eds.), *Learning in humans and machines: Towards an interdisciplinary learning science* (pp. 37–62). New York: Elsevier.

Olguin, E., & Schmitz, B. (1997). Transforming the curriculum through diversity. In J. G. Gaff, J. L. Ratcliff, & Associates, *Handbook of the undergraduate curriculum* (pp. 436–456). San Francisco: Jossey-Bass.

Otter, S. (1997, June). *The ability based curriculum: Some snapshots of progress in key skills in higher education.* (Available from Alan Jenkins, ABC Network, Oxford Brookes University, Oxford, United Kingdom).

Otter, S. (1999). The Dearing report: A year later. *Assessment Update, (11)*1, 5–7.

Pace, C. R. (1979). *Measuring outcomes of college: Fifty years of findings and recommendations for the future.* San Francisco: Jossey-Bass.

Page, B. (1998). The new capability curriculum at the University of North London. In J. Stephenson & M. Yorke (Eds.), *Capability and quality in higher education.* London: Kogan Page.

Palmer, P. J. (1983). *To know as we are known: A spirituality of education.* San Francisco: HarperCollins.

Palmer, P. J. (1997). *The courage to teach: Exploring the inner landscape of a teacher's life.* San Francisco: Jossey-Bass.

Parker, S. K., Wall, T. D., & Jackson, P. R. (1997). "That's not my job": Developing flexible employee work orientations. *Academy of Management Journal, 40*(4), 899–929.

Pascarella, E. T., Edison, M., Nora, A., Serra Hagedorn, L., & Terenzini, P. T. (1996). Influences on students' openness to diversity and challenge in the first year of college. *Journal of Higher Education, 67*(2), 174–195.

Pascarella, E. T., & Terenzini, P. T. (1991). *How college affects students: Findings and insights from twenty years of research.* San Francisco: Jossey-Bass.

Patton, M. Q. (1990). *Qualitative evaluation and research methods* (2nd ed.). Thousand Oaks, CA: Sage.

Perkins, D. (1995). *Outsmarting IQ: The emerging science of learnable intelligence.* New York: Free Press.

Perry, R., Menec, V., Struthers, C., Hechter, F., Schonwatter, D., & Menges, R. (1997). Faculty in transition: A longitudinal analysis of the role of perceived control and type of institution in adjustment to postsecondary institutions. *Research in Higher Education, 38*(5), 519–555.

Perry, W. G., Jr. (1970). *Forms of intellectual and ethical development in the college years: A scheme.* Austin, TX: Holt, Rinehart & Winston.

Perry, W. G., Jr. (1981). Cognitive and ethical growth: The making of meaning. In A. W. Chickering & Associates, *The modern American college* (pp. 76–116). San Francisco: Jossey-Bass.

Perry, W. G., Jr. (1998). *Forms of intellectual and ethical development in the college years: A scheme.* San Francisco: Jossey-Bass. (Original work published 1970)

Pew Higher Education Roundtable. (1995a, Jan.). Cross currents. *Policy Perspectives, 5*(4), sec. A.

Pew Higher Education Roundtable. (1995b, Jan.). Voices. *Policy Perspectives, 5*(4), sec. B.

Pew Higher Education Roundtable. (1995c, Apr.). Cases. *Policy Perspectives, 6*(1), sec. B.

Pew Higher Education Roundtable. (1995d, Apr.). Twice imagined. *Policy Perspectives, 6*(1), sec. A.

Pew Higher Education Roundtable and the American Association for Higher Education. (1996, Feb.). Double agent. *Policy Perspectives, 6*(3).

Pew Higher Education Roundtable and the American Council on Education's Project on Leadership and Institutional Transformation. (1996, Apr.). Shared purposes. *Policy Perspectives, 6*(4), 1–10.

Piaget, J., & Voyat, G. (1979). The possible, the impossible, and the necessary. In F. B. Murray (Ed.), *The impact of Piagetian theory on education, philosophy, and psychology* (pp. 65–85). Baltimore: University Park Press.

Pinar, W. F. (1999). Response: Gracious submission. *Educational Researcher, 28*(1), 14–15.

Pintrich, P. R., & Garcia, T. (1994). Self-regulated learning in college students: Knowledge, strategies, and motivation. In P. R. Pintrich, D. R. Brown, & C. E. Weinstein (Eds.), *Student motivation, cognition, and learning: Essays in honor of Wilbert J. McKeachie* (pp. 113–134). Hillsdale, NJ: Erlbaum.

Popkewitz, T. S. (1998). The culture of redemption and the administration of freedom as research. *Review of Educational Research, 68*(1), 1–34.

Pressley, M., Borkowski, J. G., & Schneider, W. (1987). Cognitive strategies: Good strategy users coordinate metacognition and knowledge. In R. Vasta (Ed.), *Annals of child development* (Vol. 4, pp. 89–129). Greenwich, CT: JAI.

Pring, R. A. (1995). *Closing the gap: Liberal education and vocational preparation*. London: Hodder and Stoughton.

Putnam, R. (1995). Bowling alone: America's declining social capital. *Journal of Democracy, 6*(1), 65–78.

Quinn, R. E. (1988). *Beyond rational management: Mastering the paradoxes and competing demands of high performance*. San Francisco: Jossey-Bass.

Quinn, R. E., & Cameron, K. S. (1988a). Paradox and transformation: A framework for viewing organization and management. In R. E. Quinn & K. S. Cameron (Eds.), *Paradox and transformation: Toward a theory of change in organization and management* (pp. 289–308). New York: Ballinger.

Quinn, R. E., & Cameron, K. S. (Eds.). (1988b). *Paradox and transformation: Toward a theory of change in organization and management*. New York: Ballinger.

Ratcliff, J. L. (1997). What is a curriculum and what should it be? In J. G. Gaff, J. L. Ratcliff, & Associates, *Handbook of the undergraduate curriculum: A comprehensive guide to purposes, structures, practices, and change* (pp. 5–29). San Francisco: Jossey-Bass.

Ravitch, M. (Chair). (1997, Mar.). *What do we mean by problem-based learning? Toward a terminology to better classify and describe some approaches to learning.* Interactive symposium conducted at the annual meeting of the American Educational Research Association, Chicago.

Read, J., & Sharkey, S. R. (1985). Alverno College: Toward a community of learning. In J. S. Green & A. Levine (Eds.), *Opportunity in adversity* (pp. 195–214). San Francisco: Jossey-Bass.

Reisetter, J., & Sandoval, P. (1987, Oct.). *Flexible procedures for efficiently maximizing participation in a longitudinal study.* Paper presented at the annual meeting of the Midwest Educational Research Association, Chicago. Milwaukee, WI: Alverno Productions.

Reisetter Hart, J., & Mentkowski, M. (1994, April). *The development of the whole person: Women's ego development from entrance to five years after college.* Paper presented at the annual meeting of the American Educational Research Association, New Orleans. Milwaukee, WI: Alverno College Institute.

Reisetter Hart, J., Rickards, W., & Mentkowski, M. (1993, October). *Best class, decision-making, and career choice essays: Results and applications for the Perry Scheme from the Alverno Longitudinal Study.* Paper presented at Perry Network Meeting, North Bend, WA. Milwaukee, WI: Alverno College Institute.

Reisetter Hart, J., Rickards, W. H., & Mentkowski, M. (1995, Apr.). *Epistemological development during and after college: Longitudinal growth on the Perry Scheme.* Paper presented at the annual meeting of the American Educational Research Association, San Francisco. Milwaukee, WI: Alverno College Institute.

Renner, J., Fuller, R., Lochhead, J., John, J., Tomlinson-Keasey, G., & Campbell, T. (1976). *Test of Cognitive Development.* Norman: University of Oklahoma.

Rest, J. R. (1979a). *Development in judging moral issues.* Minneapolis: University of Minnesota Press.

Rest, J. R. (1979b). *Revised manual for the Defining Issues Test: An objective test of moral judgment development.* Minneapolis: Minnesota Moral Research Projects.

Rest, J. R. (1986). *Moral development: Advances in research and theory.* New York: Praeger.

Rest, J. R., & Deemer, D. (1986). Life experiences and developmental pathways. In J. R. Rest, *Moral development: Advances in research and theory* (pp. 28–58). New York: Praeger.

Rest, J. R., & Narvaez, D. F. (1994). *Moral development in the professions: Psychology and applied ethics.* Hillsdale, NJ: Erlbaum.

Rest, J. R., Narvaez, D. F., Bebeau, M. J., & Thoma, S. J. (1999). *Postconventional moral thinking: A neo-Kohlbergian approach.* Hillsdale, NJ: Erlbaum.

Rest, J. R., Thoma, S., & Edwards, L. (1997). Designing and validating a measure of moral judgment: Stage preference and stage consistency approaches. *Journal of Educational Psychology, 89*(1), 5–28.

Rice, R. E. (1996). *Making a place for the new American scholar.* Washington, DC: American Association for Higher Education.

Richardson, J. T. E., & King, E. (1998). Adult students in higher education: Burden or boon? *Journal of Higher Education, 69*(1), 65–88.

Riordan, T. (1993). *Beyond the debate: The nature of teaching.* Milwaukee, WI: Alverno College Institute.

Rogers, G. (1994). Measurement and judgment in curriculum assessment systems. *Assessment Update, 6*(1), 6–7.

Rogers, G. (1999a). *Ability factors for five-year alumnae: Defining criteria and illustrating outcomes.* Milwaukee, WI: Alverno College Institute.

Rogers, G. (1999b, April). Learning through curriculum abilities: College learning at work. In M. Eraut (Chair), *Professional learning in the workplace.* Paper presented in a symposium at the annual meeting of the American Educational Research Association, Montreal. Milwaukee, WI: Alverno College Institute.

Rogers, G. (in collaboration with Kleinman, L., Wagner, K., & Schwan Minik, K.). (1994, Apr.). Envisioning alumnae abilities. In M. Mentkowski (Chair), *Is higher education adequately meeting its responsibility to its alumni and to society?* Interactive paper presented as part of an interactive symposium conducted at the annual meeting of the American Educational Research Association, New Orleans.

Rogers, G., & Mentkowski, M. (1994). *Alverno faculty validation of abilities scored in five-year alumna performance.* Milwaukee, WI: Alverno College Institute.

Rogers, G., & Reisetter, J. (1989). *Flexible strategies for behavioral event interviewing: Exploring events and situations.* Milwaukee, WI: Alverno College Institute.

Rogers, G., & Schwan Minik, K. (1994). *Scoring procedures and reliability for the Test of Thematic Analysis in the Alverno Longitudinal Study.* Milwaukee, WI: Alverno College Institute.

Rosch, T., & Reich, J. (1996). The enculturation of new faculty in higher education: A comparative investigation of three academic departments. *Research in Higher Education, 37*(1), 115–131.

Rothman, M. (Ed.). (1998). *Service matters: Engaging higher education in the renewal of America's communities and American democracy.* Providence, RI: Campus Compact.

Salomon, G. (Ed.). (1993). *Distributed cognitions: Psychological and educational considerations.* New York: Cambridge University Press.

Schall, C., Guinn, K., Qualich, R., Kramp, M. K., Schmitz, J., & Stewart, K. (1984). *Competence and careers: A study relating competences acquired in college to career options for the liberal arts graduate.* Milwaukee, WI: Alverno Productions.

Schein, E. H. (1990). Organizational culture. *American Psychologist, 45*(2), 109–119.

Schlossberg, N. K., Lynch, A. Q., & Chickering, A. W. (1989). *Improving higher education environments for adults: Responsive programs and services from entry to departure.* San Francisco: Jossey-Bass.

Schneider, C. G., & Shoenberg, R. (1998). *The academy in transition: Contemporary understandings of liberal education.* Washington, DC: American Association of Colleges and Universities.

Schnug, J., & Shelly, A. C. (1998). Mission: Possible. In M. E. Diez (Ed.), *Changing the practice of teacher education: Standards and assessment as a lever for change* (pp. 61–69). Washington, DC: American Association of Colleges for Teacher Education.

Schoenfeld, A. H. (1992). Learning to think mathematically: Problem solving, metacognition, and sense-making in mathematics. In D. A. Grouws (Ed.), *Handbook of research on mathematics teaching and learning* (pp. 334–370). New York: Macmillan.

Schön, D. A. (1983). *The reflective practitioner.* New York: Basic Books.

Schön, D. A. (1987). *Educating the reflective practitioner: Toward a new design for teaching and learning in the professions.* San Francisco: Jossey-Bass.

Schön, D. A. (1995). The new scholarship requires a new epistemology. *Change, 27*(6), 26–34.

Schratz, M. (1992, April). Researching while teaching: Promoting reflective professionality in higher education. Paper presented at the annual meeting of the American Educational Research Association, San Francisco.

Schulte, J., & Loacker, G. (1994). *Assessing general education outcomes for the individual student: Performance assessment-as-learning.* Milwaukee, WI: Alverno College Institute.

Schwan Minik, K., & Rogers, G. (1994). *Test of Thematic Analysis supplemental scoring materials.* Milwaukee, WI: Alverno College Institute.

Schwan Minik, K., Rogers, G., & Ben-Ur, T. (1994). *Test of Cognitive Development revised scoring manual.* Milwaukee, WI: Alverno College Institute.

Secretary's Commission on Achieving Necessary Skills (SCANS). (1991, June). *What work requires of schools: A SCANS report for America 2000.* Washington, DC: U.S. Department of Labor.

Selden, A., & Selden, J. (1993). Collegiate mathematics education research: What would that be like? *College Mathematics Journal, 24*(5), 431–445.

Senge, P. M. (1990). *The fifth discipline: The art and practice of the learning organization.* New York: Currency Doubleday.

Senge, P. M., Kleiner, A., Roberts, C., Ross, R. B., & Smith, B. J. (1994). *The fifth discipline fieldbook: Strategies and tools for building a learning organization.* New York: Doubleday.

Sessa, V. I. (1996). Using perspective taking to manage conflict and affect in teams. *Journal of Applied Behavioral Science, 32*(1), 101–115.

Sheckley, B. G., Lamdin, L., & Keeton, M. T. (1993). *Employability in a high performance economy.* Chicago: Council for Adult and Experiential Learning (CAEL).

Shore, P. (1992). *The myth of the university: Ideal and reality in higher education.* Lanham, MD: University Press of America.

Shulman, L. S. (1989). Toward a pedagogy of substance. *AAHE Bulletin, 41*(10), 8–13.

Shweder, R. A. (1990). Cultural psychology: What is it? In J. W. Stigler, R. A. Shweder, & G. Herdt (Eds.), *Cultural psychology: Essays on comparative human development* (pp. 1–43). New York: Cambridge University Press.

Smith, B. L. (1991). Taking structure seriously. *Liberal Education, 77*(2), 42–48.

Smith, B. L. (1993). Creating learning communities. *Liberal Education, 79*(4), 32–39.

Smith, J. W. (1983). *A search for the liberal college: The beginning of the St. John's Program.* Annapolis, MD: St. John's Press.

Smith, V. (1998). *The futures project: Final report.* Unpublished manuscript.

Snyder, B. R. (1971). *The hidden curriculum.* New York: Knopf.

Spangler, W. D. (1992). Validity of questionnaire and TAT measures of need for achievement: Two meta-analyses. *Psychological Bulletin, 112*(1), 140–154.

Spencer, L. M. (1983). *Soft skill competencies: Their identification, measurement, and development for professional, managerial, and human services jobs.* Edinburgh: Lindsay.

Spencer, L. M., & Spencer, S. M. (1986). *Revised generic competency dictionary.* Unpublished manuscript.

Spencer, L. M., & Spencer, S. M. (1993). *Competence at work: Models for superior performance.* New York: Wiley.

Sprinthall, N. A. (1994). Counseling and social role taking: Promoting moral and ego development. In J. R. Rest & D. F. Narvaez, *Moral development in the professions: Psychology and applied ethics* (pp. 85–99). Hillsdale, NJ: Erlbaum.

Stake, R. E. (1995). *The art of case study research.* Thousand Oaks, CA: Sage.

Stark, J. S., & Lattuca, L. R. (1997). *Shaping the college curriculum: Academic plans in action.* Needham Heights, MA: Allyn & Bacon.

Stark, J. S., & Lowther, M. A. (1988). *Strengthening the ties that bind: Integrating undergraduate liberal and professional study.* Ann Arbor, MI: Regents of the University of Michigan.

Stark, J. S., & Thomas, A. (Eds.). (1994). *Assessment and program evaluation*. (ASHE Reader Series). New York: Simon & Schuster.

Stephenson, J., & Yorke, M. (Eds.). (1998). *Capability and quality in higher education*. London: Kogan Page.

Sternberg, R. J. (1986). *Beyond IQ: A triarchic theory of human intelligence*. New York: Cambridge University Press.

Sternberg, R. J. (1996). Myths, countermyths, and truths about intelligence. *Educational Researcher, 25*(2), 11–16.

Sternberg, R. J. (1998). Abilities are forms of developing expertise. *Educational Researcher, 27*(3), 11–19.

Sternberg, R. J., & Horvath, J. A. (Eds.). (1999). *Tacit knowledge in professional practice*. Hillsdale, NJ: Erlbaum.

Sternberg, R. J., Wagner, R. K., Williams, W. M., & Horvath, J. A. (1995). Testing common sense. *American Psychologist, 50*(11), 912–926.

Stewart, A. (1977). *Scoring manual for stages of psychological adaptation to the environment*. Unpublished manuscript, Boston University.

Stewart, A. (1978). *Revised scoring manual for self-definition and social definition*. Unpublished manuscript, Boston University.

Stewart, A. (1982). The course of individual adaptation to life changes. *Journal of Personality and Social Psychology, 42*(6), 1100–1113.

Taylor, K., & Marienau, C. (1997). Constructive-development theory as a framework for assessment in higher education. *Assessment and Evaluation in Higher Education, 22*(2), 233–243.

Tennant, M., & Pogson, P. (1995). *Learning and change in the adult years: A developmental perspective*. San Francisco: Jossey-Bass.

Thoma, S. J. (1986). Estimating gender differences in the comprehension and preference of moral issues. *Developmental Review, 6*, 165–180.

Thornton, G. C., III. (1992). *Assessment centers in human resource management*. Reading, MA: Addison-Wesley.

Thornton, G. C., III, & Byham, W. C. (1982). *Assessment centers and managerial performance*. Orlando, FL: Academic Press.

Tierney, W. G. (1988). Organizational culture in higher education: Defining the essentials. *Journal of Higher Education, 59*(1), 2–21.

Tierney, W. G. (1995). Cultural politics and the curriculum in postsecondary education. In J. G. Haworth & C. F. Conrad (Eds.), *Revisioning curriculum in higher education* (pp. 35–47). (ASHE Reader Series). New York: Simon & Schuster.

Tierney, W. G. (1997). Organizational socialization in higher education. *Journal of Higher Education, 68*(1), 1–16.

Tomlinson-Keasey, C., & Eisert, D. (1978). Second year evaluation of the ADAPT program. In R. Fuller (Ed.), *Multidisciplinary Piagetian-based programs for college freshmen: ADAPT*. Lincoln: University of Nebraska.

Trosset, C. (1998). Obstacles to open discussion and critical thinking: The Grinnell College Study. *Change 30*(5), 44–49.

Truchan, L. C., & Gurria, G. (1997). Thriving with change at an institution of higher education. In M. W. Caprio (Ed.), *From traditional approaches toward innovation* (pp. 87–93) [Monograph]. Gallatin, TN: Society for College Science Teachers.

Vaill, P. B. (1996). *Learning as a way of being: Strategies for survival in a world of permanent white water.* San Francisco: Jossey-Bass.

Vaillant, G. E. (1977). *Adaptation to life.* Boston: Little, Brown.

Vallacher, R. R., & Wegner, D. M. (1989). Levels of personal agency: Individual variation in action identification. *Journal of Personality and Social Psychology, 57*(4), 660–671.

Van Scotter, J. R., & Motowidlo, S. J. (1996). Interpersonal facilitation and job dedication as separate facets of contextual performance. *Journal of Applied Psychology, 81*(5), 525–531.

Wagner, J. (1997). Discourse innovations in a restructuring elementary school: Alternative perspectives on linking research and practice. *Elementary School Journal, 97*(3), 271–292.

Walker, L. J. (1984). Sex differences in the development of moral reasoning: A critical review. *Child Development, 55,* 677–91.

Watson, G., & Glaser, E. M. (1964). *Critical Thinking Appraisal* (Manual for Forms YM and ZM). Orlando, FL: Harcourt Brace.

Westenberg, P. M., Blasi, A., & Cohn, L. D. (Eds.) (1998). *Personality development.* Hillsdale, NJ: Erlbaum.

Weston, C., & McAlpine, L. (1996, Apr.). How outstanding professors view teaching and learning. In A. Saroyan (Chair), *Professors' and students' perceptions of teaching and learning.* Paper presented at a symposium at the annual meeting of the American Educational Research Association, New York.

White, E. (1994). *Teaching and assessing writing* (2nd ed.). San Francisco: Jossey-Bass.

Widick, C. (1975). *An evaluation of developmental instruction in a university setting.* Unpublished doctoral dissertation, University of Minnesota.

Wilger, A. K., & Massy, W. F. (1993). Prospects for restructuring: A sampling of the faculty climate. *Policy Perspectives, 5*(2), 1B–4B.

Winter, D. G. (1973). *The power motive.* New York: Free Press.

Winter, D. G. (1984). *Scoring manual for Test of Thematic Analysis.* Middletown, CT: Wesleyan University.

Winter, D. G. (1988). The power motive in women—and men. *Journal of Personality and Social Psychology, 54*(3), 510–519.

Winter, D. G., McClelland, D. C., & Stewart, A. J. (1981). *A new case for the liberal arts: Assessing institutional goals and student development.* San Francisco: Jossey-Bass.

Wraga, W. G. (1999). "Extracting sun-beams out of cucumbers": The retreat from practice in reconceptualized curriculum studies. *Educational Researcher, 28*(1), 4–13.

Wyer, R. S., Jr., & Srull, T. K. (Eds.) (1989). *Advances in social cognition* (Vol. 2). Hillsdale, NJ: Erlbaum.

Youtz, B. (1984). The Evergreen State College: An experiment maturing. In R. M. Jones & B. L. Smith (Eds.), *Against the current: Reform and experimentation in higher education* (pp. 93–118). Cambridge, MA: Schenkman.

Yukl, G. (1989). Managerial leadership: A review of theory and research. *Journal of Management, 15*(2), 251–289.

Yukl, G., & Tracey, J. B. (1992). Consequences of influence tactics used with subordinates, peers, and the boss. *Journal of Applied Psychology, 77*(4), 525–535.

Zeichner, K. M. (1987). Preparing reflective teachers: An overview of instructional strategies which have been employed in preservice teacher education. *International Journal of Educational Research, 11*(5), 565–575.

Zeichner, K. M. (1997, Aug.). *Ability-based teacher education: Elementary teacher education at Alverno College.* New York: National Center for Restructuring Education, Schools, and Teaching (NCREST), Teachers College, Columbia University.

Zemsky, R., & Cappelli, P. (Eds.). (1998). *Annals of the American Academy of Political and Social Science: Vol. 559. The changing educational quality of the workforce.* Thousand Oaks, CA: Sage.

Zemsky, R., & Massy, W. F. (1995). Toward an understanding of our current predicaments: Expanding perimeters, melting cores, and sticky functions. *Change, 27*(6), 40–49.

Zerubavel, E. (1995). The rigid, the fuzzy, and the flexible: Notes on the mental sculpting of academic identity. *Social Research: An International Quarterly of the Social Sciences, 62,* 1093–1106.

Zlotkowski, E. (Ed.). (1997–1999). AAHE series on service-learning in the disciplines [monograph series]. Washington, DC: American Association for Higher Education.

Name Index

Subject Index

A

Abilities: alumna, 74–75, 151–176; Alverno College curriculum, 63; complex, social learning and, 70–71; conceptual, 75–79; defined, 10; depth model of, 149–150, 164–165; developed, 9, 10–11; for future workforce, 144–146; identification of, 58; integrated, 57, 63–64, 75, 78–79, 161–166, 175–176; integrated with content, 318–321; integrated with disciplines, 57, 63–64, 313, 317–318; interpersonal, 78–82; metacognitive, 9, 75, 147–148; multidimensional, 10–11, 145, 147–176; for professional performance, 147; related to self-directed learning, 132–133; for research associates, 357–358; as theory of knowledge and performance, 75–77; validation of, 82–88. *See also* Conceptual abilities; Critical Thinking; Interpersonal abilities

Ability Based Curriculum (ABC) Network, 376, 389–390

Ability factors. *See* Alumna ability factors

Ability-based curriculum, 63–64; alumna performance related to, 167–170; elements of Alverno College's, 63–64; engagement with diversity and, 200–204; experiential validation of, 82–88; growth in relation to, 121–142, 194–195; identity growth and, 92–102; independent and social

learning in, 88–92; for learning that lasts, 103–104; metacognitive strategy use and, 194–196; self assessment of role performance and, 196–200; student and alumna perspectives on, 74–103; student understanding of, 75–77, 84–85, 89, 103; transformative cycles of learning and, 189–205. *See also* Curriculum

Ability-based learning, 63–64, 304, 309

Abstract thinking, 88, 184, 211, 232

Academic dean's perspective, 292

Academic planning, 326

Academic position level criteria for effective teaching, 262–263, 267, 286–287

Accountability for transformation, 374

Accrediting agencies, 366, 408

Accurate empathy, 152, 173–174

Achievement action, 163

Acquisition of skill, 10. *See also* Abilities

Action in context, 37, 82–83, 85. *See also* Experiential learning; Experiential validation

Action principles, 60–61, 216, 217, 218, 225–248; based on principle of experiential learning, 231–232; based on principle of integrative learning, 228–230; based on principle of learning as active and interactive, independent and collaborative, 241–242; based on principle of learning as deep and expansive, purposeful and